The Non-Professional Actor

The Non-Professional Actor

Italian Neorealist Cinema and Beyond

Catherine O'Rawe

BLOOMSBURY ACADEMIC
LONDON · NEW YORK · OXFORD · NEW DELHI · SYDNEY

BLOOMSBURY ACADEMIC
Bloomsbury Publishing Inc, 1385 Broadway, New York, NY 10018, USA
Bloomsbury Publishing Plc, 50 Bedford Square, London, WC1B 3DP, UK
Bloomsbury Publishing Ireland, 29 Earlsfort Terrace, Dublin 2, D02 AY28, Ireland

BLOOMSBURY, BLOOMSBURY ACADEMIC and the Diana logo are trademarks of
Bloomsbury Publishing Plc

First published in the United States of America 2024
Paperback edition published 2025

Copyright © Catherine O'Rawe, 2024

For legal purposes the Acknowledgements on pp. ix–x constitute an extension
of this copyright page.

Cover design: Eleanor Rose
Cover photograph: Enzo Staiola, on-set of the Italian film, *Bicycle Thieves* (aka *Ladri Di Biciclette*), 1948 © Glasshouse Images / Alamy Stock Photo

All rights reserved. No part of this publication may be: i) reproduced or transmitted in any form, electronic or mechanical, including photocopying, recording or by means of any information storage or retrieval system without prior permission in writing from the publishers; or ii) used or reproduced in any way for the training, development or operation of artificial intelligence (AI) technologies, including generative AI technologies. The rights holders expressly reserve this publication from the text and data mining exception as per Article 4(3) of the Digital Single Market Directive (EU) 2019/790.

Bloomsbury Publishing Inc does not have any control over, or responsibility for, any third-party websites referred to or in this book. All internet addresses given in this book were correct at the time of going to press. The author and publisher regret any inconvenience caused if addresses have changed or sites have ceased to exist, but can accept no responsibility for any such changes.

A catalog record for this book is available from the Library of Congress.

Library of Congress Cataloging-in-Publication Data

Names: O'Rawe, Catherine, author.
Title: The non-professional actor : Italian neorealist cinema and beyond / Catherine O'Rawe.
Description: New York : Bloomsbury Academic, 2024. | Includes bibliographical references and index.
Identifiers: LCCN 2023019825 (print) | LCCN 2023019826 (ebook) | ISBN 9781501394355 (hardback) | ISBN 9781501394393 (paperback) | ISBN 9781501394362 (epub) | ISBN 9781501394379 (pdf) | ISBN 9781501394386 (ebook other)
Subjects: LCSH: Motion pictures–Italy–History. | Realism in motion pictures. | Motion picture acting.
Classification: LCC PN1993.5.I88 O73 2024 (print) | LCC PN1993.5.I88 (ebook) | DDC 791.430945–dc23/eng/20230727
LC record available at https://lccn.loc.gov/2023019825
LC ebook record available at https://lccn.loc.gov/2023019826

ISBN: HB: 978-1-5013-9435-5
PB: 978-1-5013-9439-3
ePDF: 978-1-5013-9437-9
eBook: 978-1-5013-9436-2

Typeset by Newgen KnowledgeWorks Pvt. Ltd., Chennai, India

For product safety related questions contact productsafety@bloomsbury.com.

To find out more about our authors and books visit www.bloomsbury.com
and sign up for our newsletters.

For Enzo, Lamberto, Maria, Antonio, Carmela, Tina, Renato, Pierino, Nella, Agnese, Alfonso, Gabriella, Giorgio, Vito, and all the others …

CONTENTS

List of figures viii
Acknowledgements ix

Introduction – The non-professional actor: Histories, theories, performances 1

1 Acting, stardom, and the non-professional in Italy from fascism to the post-war 25

2 Bodies, voices, afterlives: Case studies of *Bicycle Thieves'* Lamberto Maggiorani and the cast of *La Terra Trema* 53

3 Girls, stardom, and the danger of cinema 85

4 The non-professional child actor: Beyond *Bicycle Thieves* 127

5 The non-professional in contemporary global cinema 173

Conclusion 203

Works cited 209
Index 243

FIGURES

1. Yalitza Aparicio improvises in a key scene from Cuarón's *Roma* 9
2. Vittorio De Sica inspects an aspiring actress at auditions for *The Roof* 45
3. Antonio (Lamberto Maggiorani) puts up the poster of Rita Hayworth in *Gilda* 58
4. Enzo Staiola magically produces tears as Bruno in *Bicycle Thieves* 63
5. *La terra trema*: The Sicilian actresses merge into the rocks of Aci Trezza 81
6. A mother faints on hearing her daughter has not been given a part in *The Roof*, from *Cinema Nuovo*, 1955 86
7. Lucia Bosè's character is stared at by girls entering Cinecittà in *The Lady Without Camelias* 89
8. *We, the Women*: The visual threat represented by the mass of girls hoping for a film role in the episode 'Four Actresses, One Hope' 89
9. Federico Patellani's photo of Lucia Bosè in her first evening gown, published in *Tempo*, 1947 99
10. Rossellini's *Paisan*: Carmela Sazio as Carmela, in a long shot highlighting her 'unruly' body 112
11. Maria Fiore in a customary dynamic moment of performance in *Two Cents of Hope* 120
12. The undifferentiated and uncredited group of 'scugnizzi' in *Hey Boy* 144
13. Little Alfonso Bovino, wearing his own military-style jacket in *Paisan* 146
14. Vito Annicchiarico as Tranquillo outfoxes Vittorio De Sica in *Peddlin' in Society!* 150
15. *The Gold of Naples*: Pierino Bilancione as Gennarino boredly displays his card-playing skills 161
16. Angelo Maggio on the set of *Strange Witness* (De Mitri, 1950) 166
17. Alessandra di Sanzo (Mery) and Michele Placido (Marco) face off in *Forever Mery* 179
18. Pio Amato, star of *A Ciambra*, looks uncomfortable on stage at the Cannes Film Festival, 2017 194

ACKNOWLEDGEMENTS

This book is the product of a British Academy Mid-Career Fellowship, and I would like to thank them, and the research office staff at Bristol, for the grant which made it all possible.

During the research for the book, I benefitted hugely from a period as a visiting scholar at Fordham University, at the kind invitation of Jackie Reich, who has been a stalwart supporter and interlocutor. I also presented research from the book at a number of conferences and invited seminars: many thanks to hosts and audiences at Birmingham, Leicester, Leeds, Warwick, Bowdoin, New Hampshire, Bari, Bologna, Milan, Turin, and at AAIS, FAScinA, and BAFTSS.

I am grateful to the editors at Bloomsbury with whom I have worked: Katie Gallof, Stephanie Grace-Petinos, and Alyssa Jordan, as well as copy-editing and typesetting staff.

In finishing the book, I was also lucky to have a period in Rome as a visiting professor at Sapienza University: sincere thanks to Valerio Coladonato for organizing this and for discussing Enzo with me. I'm grateful to the other colleagues there who have been very generous with me over the years: Francesca Cantore, Damiano Garofalo, and Andrea Minuz.

At Turin University, Giulia Carluccio, Mariapaola Pierini, and Giulia Muggeo kindly co-organized a conference with me in 2018, and I'm grateful to everyone who took part in that event.

I started writing the book properly at the start of lockdown, and the many challenges that suddenly appeared were mitigated by the help of people who kindly sent me copies of their work. I am sure I have forgotten many people as time has become a flat circle, but thanks to J. D. Rhodes, Tom Whittaker, Elena Alampi, Louis Bayman, Stephen Gundle, Charles Leavitt, Fabien Landron, Federico Vitella, Luca Barra, Valentina Re, and Chiara Tognolotti. A special word of thanks also for Dan Finch-Race, who stepped in when I had COVID in Bologna.

I am also grateful to Mattia Boccuti and Valentina Geri for allowing me to collaborate with them on their interview with Alfonso Bovino.

At Bristol, I have benefitted from the support of academics and professional services staff in the School of Modern Languages and Arts Faculty, and in the library. In particular, I'd like to thank my colleagues in Italian for their interest in my research, particularly John Foot, Tristan Kay, Rhiannon Daniels, and Ruth Glynn. Jo Crow read and commented on part of the book, and also offered crucial tapas-related support at crucial moments. Carla Mereu Keating has also been a great sounding board and has offered valuable archival snippets. Conversations on the non-professional actor with Miguel Gaggiotti have helped direct and clarify my thinking, and I am excited for his own book to come out so our perspectives can be in dialogue, and we can officially announce the Era of the Non-professional.

I am endlessly grateful to those who have read parts of my work and given their advice. Paolo Noto and Francesco Pitassio, in particular, have been invaluable sources of guidance on the intellectual and historical substance of my arguments, and I have truly appreciated their expertise and friendship. Giorgio Bertellini and Sue Harris have also given supportive feedback, and Derek Duncan and Alan O'Leary remain great sources of encouragement. Robert Gordon has helped me both by reading work and giving advice, but also by being probably the only person as invested in Lamberto Maggiorani as I am (#Justice4Lamberto).

Sincere thanks to my writing group who have read and commented on work, and given general advice in the last few years: Elena Past, Monica Seger, Allison Cooper, Amy Boylan, Dana Renga, and Danielle Hipkins. A special word for Dana and Danielle, who have read practically all the book, given positive feedback in times of near-despair, and practical suggestions when (often) requested. Thanks to them for lockdown yoga, aperitivi in sunny places, Borghi studies, and much more.

I would be remiss not to thank the CCs (Tristan and James) for their endless hilarity, voice notes, and dubious impressions. These helped keep me sane in difficult times and I promise not to go rogue and release the archive. Thanks also to James for French lessons and for listening patiently to tales of (near)-collapse. I'd also like to thank Andrea and Carmel for moral support and wine.

Thanks to my family for all their support (especially my brother Philip for endless printing during the first lockdown!) to my auntie Joan for moral support, and to my mum, who was always there for me. Although she did not live to see this book come out, she and I would both like to thank Jürgen and the boys for the last few years. YNWA.

This book is dedicated to all those who 'lent their face' to Italian cinema, particularly in the 1940s and early 1950s. They're 'still there, immortal'.

Introduction

The non-professional actor: Histories, theories, performances

In the summer of 2020, eighty-year-old Enzo Staiola, former child star of Vittorio De Sica's 1948 *Ladri di biciclette/Bicycle Thieves*, was approached by a journalist while on the balcony of his apartment in Rome. In a clip that circulated online, the journalist shouted questions up to the former actor about his experience working with De Sica, to which Staiola replied with shrugs, grunts and sighs, presumably not helped by the Roman heat and the pandemic lockdown.[1] Staiola has given countless interviews over the years on the same subject, to the extent that he once remarked ambiguously (Anon. 2013) that 'per me il neorealismo non finisce mai'/'for me neorealism never ends'. Still, this journalist sought him out to repeat those questions, highlighting the 'auratic presence' (Upton 2011: 215) of the star, even (or especially?) an unconventional one like Staiola, who retired from acting as a teenager having aged out of his childish appeal and whose other films never came close to the cinephile pull of *Bicycle Thieves*.

The amazed statements of the interviewer – 'you have the same face! The same expression! The same colour eyes!' – show that the encounter is charged with the awareness of Staiola as a bodily memory or instantiation of post-war Italian neorealism, Italian cinema's high point, within which are embedded both historicity (he is a testimonial relic of a glorious bygone age) and change (a time that is irrevocably past, with the young child of De Sica's film now an old man in a vest on a balcony). He also embodies the 'authentic iconicity' (Watson 1999: 139) of the non-professional actor typical of that cinema, whose fascination has endured well into the twenty-first century.

The films of Rossellini, De Sica, Visconti, and others circulated widely internationally and drew attention to the 'rebirth of Italian film identity'

---

[1] https://www.youtube.com/watch?v=RQ9F3i8IhcA&feature=youtu.be. Accessed 24 May 2023.

(Marcus 1987: xv) following twenty years of fascism. The closure of the main film studios upon German occupation of Italy in September 1943 encouraged a greater use of location shooting, one of the supposed tenets of post-war filmmaking, even though classics such as *Bicycle Thieves*, *Roma città aperta/Rome Open City* (Rossellini 1945), and *Sciuscià/Shoeshine* (De Sica 1946) were all partially studio-shot. Accounts of neorealism have emphasized its rediscovery of the Italian natural landscape and cityscape, which required an equivalent rediscovery of ordinary Italian people as cinematic protagonists. As Marxist critics Mario Alicata and Giuseppe De Santis wrote in a famous 1941 essay,

> vogliamo portare la nostra macchina da presa nelle strade, nei campi, nei porti, nelle fabbriche del nostro paese: anche noi siamo convinti che un giorno creeremo il nostro film più bello seguendo il passo lento e stanco dell'operaio che torna alla sua casa, narrando l'essenziale poesia d'una vita nuova e pura. (1941b: 315)[2]

The class-based nature of neorealism's investigation of the everyday still resonates in its status as a counter-cinema.

Over the years neorealism became the centrepiece of Italian cinema history and part of its 'masterpiece tradition'. Its global influence, its vernacular style, and ethical commitment to representation of the lives of the underprivileged have been widely celebrated and emulated. The 'scriptural idea of neorealism's ethical or aesthetic superiority' (O'Leary and O'Rawe 2011: 125) has given rise to endless myths and has obscured the heterogeneous nature of film production in the years following the war.[3] Not only was there no 'neorealist orthodoxy' (Leavitt 2020: 15), but one of the most attentive contemporary thinkers on neorealism, André Bazin, went so far as to write in 1955 that 'neorealism as such does not exist' (Bazin 1971: 99). While it has become more common now to recognize that 'neorealism is a flexible container for a range of non-classical variations found in many Italian films of the day' (Hallam and Marshment 2000: 41), the discursive centrality of certain films inevitably endures, particularly through constant references back to the period as soon as a film shot on location featuring non-professional actors comes out. So when, for example, Italian director Roberto De Paolis's drama about Nigerian sex workers in Rome, *Princess*, premiered at the Venice

---

[2]'We want to take the camera into the streets, the fields, the docks, the factories of this country. We are convinced that our most beautiful film will follow the slow and exhausted walk home of the worker, narrating the essential poetry of a new and pure life.' (All translations are mine, unless otherwise stated.)

[3]See Farassino (1988) on this diversity of modes of production of films that might be considered 'neorealist'.

Film Festival in 2022, it was instantly hailed as 'un nuovo Neorealismo'/'a new neorealism' (Panattoni 2022) for its use of real sex workers alongside established actors.

Given the centrality of the non-professional actor to the definitions and redefinitions of neorealism over many years, and the ongoing prevalence of this figure in global arthouse cinema, it was stunning to me when I began to research this area that, despite the huge number of books on neorealism, there was very little written on the non-professional.[4] Indeed, in this cinema of 'brutal humanism' (Schoonover 2012a: xiv), the human element has often been strikingly ignored. It seems that the contribution of the non-professional actor has been taken for granted, or considered merely as an element in the mise-en-scène, part of the ideological weaponry of neorealism in its rebellion against the star system.

Even in scholarship on contemporary global arthouse cinema, there has been only sporadic engagement with the deployment of non-professionals, their ideological significance, their experiences on set, and their performance styles. The sudden ascent of Indigenous Mexican non-actor Yalitza Aparicio to stardom in Alfonso Cuarón's *Roma*, via a surprise Best Actress nomination at the 2019 Oscars, raised important questions about the possible professional futurity of the non-actor, especially for those from racially minoritized backgrounds, something I will explore in the book's final chapter. However, mainstream film reviews preferred to focus on the film's presumed debt to neorealism (Andrews 2018), and the simple bodily authenticity Aparicio was felt to bring to her casting as a domestic servant.

If non-professionals generate an 'authenticity-effect' through their 'untrained phenomenological bodies' (Katuszewsk and Donath 2020: 74, 73), it remains then to be seen what the effects of that 'effect' are. In examining films produced in Italy between 1945 and 1955 I will investigate precisely what the non-professional brings to the screen, how they are recruited and directed, and what might be useful approaches to analysing their performance styles. My interest is not just in the performative effects generated by the non-professional, however, but in their profilmic existence, which is, after all, the thing that made them valuable to the directors and producers of post-war Italy.

Re-examining this period through the lens of the non-professional can also assist us in understanding what it means to perform the self, especially in an age when individuals had very limited media exposure. It can allow us to reflect upon what we understand to be 'good acting' and

---

[4]Naremore (1988: 273) mentions 'amateur actors' as being intrinsically connected to neorealist cinema. He goes on to list as other examples of their use 'local color' films and Brechtian experimentation.

how contingent that concept is. And perhaps we might begin to rethink the commonplace notion of 'authenticity' that has often lazily enveloped the non-professional. Jacqueline Nacache (2005: 129) evocatively dubbed the non-professional 'un des grands fantasmes du cinéma'. 'Fantasme' in this context can be translated as 'dream' or 'fantasy', suggesting that the non-professional is both a longed-for (and illusory?) promise of authentic life and a ghostly presence that haunts both the cinema and the professional actor.

Even the terminology used to describe the non-professional is complicated and fuzzy and leads us to consider different aspects of their being (see Scandola 2020: 48; Gaggiotti 2021: 243). 'Non-actor' suggests someone who does not act at all; 'amateur', someone who acts only for pleasure and is unpaid; the Soviet concepts of 'type' or 'naturshchik' have quite specific connotations, as we will see in Chapter 1, as does the Bressonian 'model' (Bresson 1991; Nacache 2005: 76). Bertolt Brecht's concept of the non-actor, meanwhile, is resolutely class-bound: his 'proletarian actor' (1964) is a theatre actor who performs in the evening, after working in a factory all day. Interestingly, Sean Baker, director of *Tangerine* (2015) and *The Florida Project* (2017), 'started using the term *first-timer* after finding that *nonprofessional* tended to make people in the industry write performers off' (Willmore 2021). Baker's implicit challenge to the ontological status of the non-actor (*first-time* versus *non*) will be explored further in this book.

The Italian terms are equally variegated: 'attore occasionale'/'casual actor' emphasizes the randomness of the non-actor's employment, while the 'attore improvvisato'/'improvised actor', a term much used in the 1940s and 1950s in Italy, puts the focus on the makeshift or unpredictable nature of their performance. Its etymology also points to the problems the non-professional will face on set: the *attore improvvisato* is someone who is unprepared, without resources, someone for whom no provision (*provisus*) has been made, as is frequently the case for non-professionals. One of the most frequently used terms in Italy in the post-war period, alongside the purely descriptive 'attore non-professionista', is the resonant 'attore preso dalla strada', literally 'taken from the street'. This was used much more widely than the fairly equivalent 'presi dalla vita'/'taken from life', and the emphasis placed on the street refers both to casting processes, with many of these individuals spotted in public places, and to the vital link between performer and material place, outside the studio walls, wished for and foretold by Luchino Visconti in his important 1943 essay 'Il cinema antropomorfico'/'Anthropomorphic Cinema'. All of these terms, however, operate in relation to the master term: professional. The non-professional is always, in an apophatic sense, defined by the fact they are *not* a professional (but also what a professional is not). But what is a professional (actor)?

What is a (non-)professional?

The 1996 Venice Film Festival awarded its prestigious Coppa Volpi for Best Actress to four-year-old Victoire Thivisol, the star of Jacques Doillon's *Ponette*. This award was greeted by boos from some critics during the ceremony, driven by the idea that little Victoire could not possibly be acting in a meaningful sense of the term (see Paternò 1996). The outrage was matched by what later happened in 1999 at the Cannes Film Festival: the Best Actress prize was shared by non-professionals Séverine Caneele (for Dumont's *L'humanité/Humanity*) and Émilie Dequenne (for the Dardennes' *Rosetta*), while Caneele's co-star Emmanuel Schotté took home the Best Actor prize. Austin (2004: 252) records the boos that greeted these awards, amid accusations that French cinema was being 'murdered' and that these 'performances' could not possibly be compared to those of seasoned professionals such as Gérard Depardieu or Daniel Auteil.[5]

These examples showcase the ambivalent status of non-professionals; they not only attract attention and admiration but can also trigger anger when they are seen to encroach too much on the hard-won status of professionals. Doillon also defended his use of such a young child, saying that the playful experience of shooting had been therapeutic for Victoire (M.S.P. 1996), but he did not allow her to pick up the prize, in order to protect her from publicity and media frenzy. As we will see later in this book, the non-professional actor is thus an ambiguous object of curiosity, especially on the festival circuit, as their very existence calls into question the legitimacy of their counterpart, the professional.

André Bazin, the French critic whose essays on post-war Italian film were 'responsible for the simultaneous appreciation and misunderstanding of the history of Italian cinema' (Fabbri 2015: 182), singled out the contribution of the non-professional actor in his 1948 essay 'An Aesthetic of Reality: Cinematic Realism and the Italian School of the Liberation'. His declaration (or prescription?) regarding non-actors attributes to them a peculiar ontological status: 'indispensable as are the factors of inexperience and naïveté, obviously they cannot survive repetition' (1971: 24). They can exist successfully only in the (singular) time of their performance, as we will see.

This difference of the non-professional is inherent in much criticism that involves them, and speaks to the profession of acting itself: as McDonald (2021: 268) points out, 'acting requires no formally regulated and certificated routes to employment'. While formal training is valued, and while unions gatekeep membership of the profession and define

---

[5]Dequenne and Caneele have continued to act, with Dequenne in particular building a substantial career in television and film.

professional norms (Fortmueller 2021: 12), these norms and, indeed, actors' unions themselves, are of course historically contingent, with post-war Italian cinema operating very differently in this regard to the Hollywood studio system. Fortmueller (ibid.) quotes Vicki Mayer on the difficulty of defining 'professionalism': 'unmoored from any objective criteria, the word professional ... has rather served as a historical articulation of status and privilege in relation to changing labor markets and their organizing hierarchies'. Thinking about the non-professional actor therefore throws into relief ideologies of professionalism. It also intersects with recent emphases on labour histories of film production.

David Vasse, in his work on the non-professional actor in Doillon's films (2018: 121), lists four arguments in favour of their use: economic, ethical, experimental, and anthropological. Of these, the first is generally the most overlooked, but yet the most salient in terms of film production. Regardless of the desire for authenticity or the ethnographic urge to document a given community, the question of recompense bubbles under the surface of the non-professional's employment, as we will see throughout this book. Michael Kennedy (2005) has been particularly vehement in this regard, seeing exploitation as inherent in the use of the non-professional by bourgeois cinema: 'in choosing to extract its non-actors from the poorest classes in the material sense neorealism provides these individual non-actors with a temporary source of food, drink and money; a brief respite from unrelenting poverty', yet he notes that their status remains subaltern and precarious. One critique of this 'underdog mythology' (Celli cited in Gaggiotti 2019: 96) is that not all non-professionals are poor or marginalized (although those type of performing subjects are often targeted by filmmakers). Vittorio De Sica, for example, recruited impoverished children and factory workers for his post-war films, as well as a highly educated university professor (Carlo Battisti, the eponymous *Umberto D.*). Nevertheless, it is true that non-professionals are often not in a position to demand a good salary, nor will they generally have a union to advocate for their financial retribution.

The non-professional makes visible the material conditions of film casting and acting, precisely according to the logic that 'craft, skill, training, and professionalism – in a conventional understanding of screen acting – necessitate a dematerialization of the conditions and techniques of work in the interest of diegetic illusion' (Gorfinkel 2012: 181). Because the non-professional operates at the interstices of work and play, or work and 'being oneself', they can offer an 'alternative figure for artistic labour' (Kear 2005: 36). Yet the 'spectrality of labour' (Schoonover 2012b: 77 n. 16) and its conditions hover over these seemingly authentic representations. The non-professional as ideal embodiment of resistance to the commodification of labour demanded by capitalist productivity contains its own impediment, in the prevalent failure of the arthouse cinema system to accommodate or recognize these people as 'real actors'. The manifestation of this is often in film credits, where traditionally non-actors might not even be mentioned, or may be given a collective credit, in the same vein as extras (see Didi-Huberman 2009).

However, the economic argument for the use of non-professionals does not exhaust their relevance, far from it. 'In addition to the surplus of material value extracted from non-actors there is a less tangible surplus to be harvested, in political, ethical and spiritual terms' (Kennedy 2005), and the non-professional is called upon to represent values far beyond what their individual bodily presence connotes. In this sense, the distinction between professional and non-professional goes beyond payment. Bazin's words on the non-professional's essential 'naïveté' elaborate this distinction as one connected to temporality: the non-professional is significant precisely because they have *not yet* acted and lost their lustre. Indeed, in post-war Italy, director Renato Castellani, who used them extensively, declared that after ten minutes in front of the camera they became professionals (cited in Pitassio 2007: 163). Jean-Luc Godard (in Godard and Delahaye 1967: 16) was even more playfully specific, alleging that a non-actor is transformed as soon as they have filmed for 'one twenty-fourth of a second', and comparing them to a non-Christian who becomes Christian the instant they are plunged into the baptismal waters. The threshold of professionalism, once crossed, can never be uncrossed in this reading, even if the non-actor still does not enjoy the recognition of the professional. As we will see, this movement from *non-* to professional is figured by some as from lack to plenitude (acquiring acting skills), while for others the plenitude of the non-actor (their truth or authenticity) is irrevocably lost once they 'act properly'.

The identity of the professional actor can also be understood in multiple ways, when seen through the lens of the non-professional: the professional is, etymologically, someone who publicly professes, avows or declares their commitment to a particular status or role. Those entering a religious order formally professed their faith, something that still occurs in the rite of Catholic baptism and in the Mass. The difference between amateur and professional therefore is not just a financial one: the professional is a trusted figure, usually with the requisite training and qualifications, or with an acknowledged and stable reputation.[6]

The question of training also invokes time: the non-actor is brought over time to a new state of expertise and competence, through mastery of the requisite skills. Actorly training, or its absence, was a topic of much debate in post-war Italy, as we will see in Chapter 1, but it has continued to be one of the benchmarks of the professional, as the ongoing deep interest in

---

[6]Christine Geraghty's category of the 'star-as-professional' (2000: 191), as opposed to the star-as-celebrity or star-as-performer, is notably characterized by stability, repetition, and consistency.

the Method shows (see Butler 2022). Lury (2010: 156) points out how the Method, understood as a system of training to allow actors to 'produce a conscious recollection of their unconscious actions in response to particular emotional states', is problematic when it comes to child performers, for whom professional training is often seen to be 'bad'. Children, and non-professionals more broadly, are useful in films precisely because they are not trained, and they bring an appealing 'lack of self-consciousness' (ibid.) to their roles.

This of course ignores the fact that training programmes such as the Method can allow actors to draw upon difficult past memories in order to offer a more emotionally naturalistic performance. While the Method in particular has become subject to many inaccurate clichés about its self-indulgence or its propensity to bring about emotional breakdowns through an identification of actor and part (Walsh 2021: 34), its practical techniques were designed to both allow for the accessing of emotions and the management of these by actor and director (Carnicke 1999: 86). This is particularly important when it comes to the performance or re-enactment of trauma: a non-professional actor instructed by a director to respond to an event in a script, or to re-enact their own difficult experiences, may lack the protection offered by technique. For example, during the filming of Cuarón's Oscar-winning *Roma*, in shooting a central, very traumatic scene for her character Cleo, Cuarón admitted that he deliberately withheld from non-professional Yalitza Aparicio what would happen. Her anguished reaction was thus genuine – and presumably she could not be trusted to generate that response otherwise (see O'Rawe 2019) (Figure 1).

Many productions in Italy now employ acting coaches to work with young non-professionals on set (see Pierini 2015), in order to avoid these kinds of issues. However, any avowal of training for the non-professional risks damaging the mythical status they possess, that of 'pure, non-acting, mysterious presence' (Ramos-Martinez 2016: 96). Likewise, as Baron and Carnicke note (2008: 18), Hollywood and mainstream cinema often suppressed publicity about actors' training in order to foster the myth of the 'born performer'. A somewhat paradoxical situation therefore emerges whereby the 'invisibility' of actorly craft allows for discourses of natural performance to prevail – the highly trained but spontaneous-seeming Marlon Brando is a prime example of this – but a focus on training in discussions of acting stops us from seeing acting as work. As McDonald suggests (2021: 268): 'By privileging understanding of acting labour as skills development, training discourse frames acting-as-craft, with the actor presented as a performing artist. Absent from this is an account of acting-as-employment, the conditions of getting and having work.' These conditions, as many of the case studies in this book will analyse, are vital to understanding the precarious figure of the non-professional.

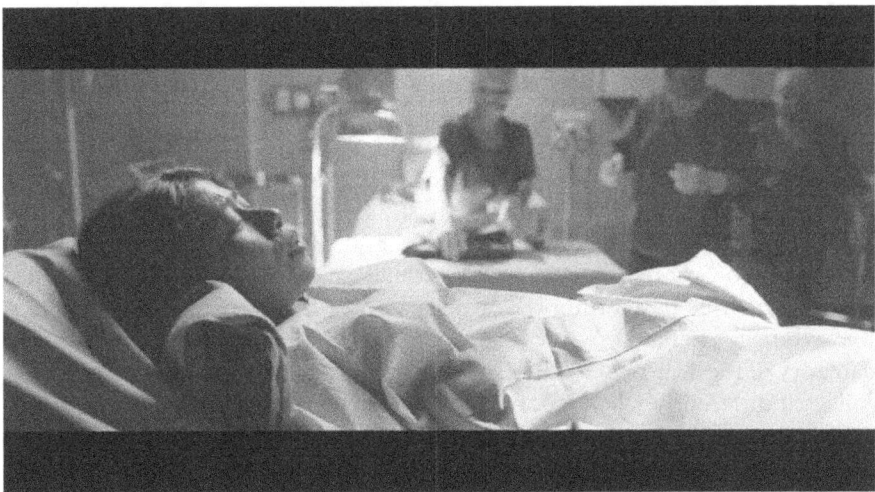

FIGURE 1 *Yalitza Aparicio improvises in a key scene from Cuarón's* Roma.

While the question of training is important to discussions of the non-professional, it is not definitive – many professional actors have no formal training, after all. Thus 'it is not so much the question of acting training or experience that is important but simply the fact that, once the nonprofessional has acted in several films, it becomes more and more possible to recognize the performances as part of a body of work' (Gaggiotti 2019: 103). This aligns with the view of the great screenwriter and theoretician of neorealism, Cesare Zavattini, when he wrote in 1953 in favour of the use of non-actor: 'lo spettatore … dovrebbe sorvegliarsi nei confronti del complesso di inferiorità che ha per il mito-attore'/'the audience should be in a position to become aware of its own inferiority complex in respect of the actor-myth' (2002: 749).[7] What Gaggiotti (2021: 248) terms the 'non-professional effect' means that knowledge of the performer's biography seeps into our understanding of their performance and removes the hieratic distance between spectator and actor/star. This knowledge of the real conditions of the non-professional's life is often key to the promotion of films they appear in, functioning as a kind of 'extra-cinematic folklore' (Gleghorn 2017: 2015) that can produce a voyeuristic thrill in the spectator.

Just as a trained actor can still be a 'bad' actor, a professional actor can still be deemed 'unprofessional'. See, for example, the 2022 statement by Johnny Depp's former agent that he lost roles due to 'unprofessional behaviour', including lateness, drug and alcohol abuse, and not knowing lines (Durney

---

[7]The translation here is by Brancaleone in Zavattini (2021: 139).

2022). Such tales are commonplace in the film and entertainment industries. The terms 'professional' and 'unprofessional' are of course constructs that speak to and enforce particular norms operating in culture, and may be specific to particular professions (a successful actor may turn up late and drunk to set and continue to be employed, a labourer is unlikely to enjoy the same privilege). Professionalism as a construct operates to discipline and regulate labour (Carpenter et al. 2021: 48); it is also, as many have acknowledged, deeply gendered, classed, and racialized. In analysing how the term 'professional' operates within the legal field, Goodridge (2022: 41) argues that it is 'based on a set of beliefs grounded in racial subordination and white supremacy'. We will see at various points in this book how the category of the non-professional, already a precarious and ambivalent one, is inflected differently when it comes to minoritized and marginalized subjects.

The prevailing scholarly and mainstream view of the non-professional as a 'disruptive presence' (Brody 2021) in the economy of cinema sets up an opposition between professional and non-professional, whereby the non-professional always represents a challenge to the hegemonic norms of filmmaking, or even to the apparatus itself (Campbell 2017: 70). And the term 'professional' can often carry vaguely pejorative connotations: doing a 'professional job' of painting a bedroom is praised, while 'a professional performance' on stage or screen may seem boring or lacking in inspiration or flair. This opposition, however, which positions non-actors outside of the norms of professional employment practices and performance standards, leaves them always destined to remain experimental, one-off figures. Exploring different types of non-professional usage can allow us a more nuanced take on the figure. It can also encourage us to go beyond an evaluation of them as symptomatic or symbolic figures and look closely at the variegated nature of what they *do* on screen. Ramos-Martinez's statement (2016: 93) that the non-professional actor 'challenges prevailing protocols in Western culture based on professional, gender, and economic identities that determine who acts and who does not act, and that validate what is to act in the social, cultural, political fields' brings us to the fundamental question: what does it mean to act on screen? Or as Alberto Scandola asks (2012: 32), 'Di fronte a un attore non educato, possiamo parlare ancora di interprete o semplicemente di corpo?'/'when faced with an untrained actor, can we still call them a performer, or are they simply a body?'

Performing the self on film

For a long time the study of acting was neglected within film studies.[8] In the period I am addressing, post-war Italy, film critics routinely ignored performance and would typically end a long review of a film with a few

---

[8]Taylor (2012: 1) discusses this 'topos of neglect'.

sentences on the actors (see Aristarco 1983: 5). The films of neorealism, while analysed and debated for their ideological charge, to a large extent saw the work of their actors and non-actors ignored (Scandola 2020: 18), and even until recently acting was treated in 'parenthesis' (Nacache 2005: 142), a legacy of the dominant screen theory in the 1970s. More recently, this neglect of the mechanics of screen performance has been blamed on the focus on the construction of the star image that arose with star studies (see Yu 2017: 8). This is despite the fact that the foundational text of star studies, Richard Dyer's *Stars* (first published in 1979), actually included a chapter on 'Stars and Performance'. Dyer called out the lack of precision in discussions of acting (1998: 133) and argued that performance is not merely created through editing, and that performance elements should be understood as on a par with all other cinematic elements, a view that has now become conventional among theorists of film acting.[9]

However, Dyer mainly approached performance as a tool for the construction of character, a view typical of much scholarship; the privileging of realism in Western film acting has contributed to an idealization of the unity of actor and image, and actor and character (Clark 1995: 25). If acting is widely believed to 'sustain the illusion of a unified self' (Naremore 1988: 5), through techniques that discipline the voice and body, then what the non-actor does inevitably problematizes this. It is also necessary to try to distinguish acting from performance, and Drake's definition (2006: 85) is useful here: he considers acting as a

> subset of 'performance', as describing a dramatic mode of performance that highlights the presence of character. Other kinds of performance – song and dance routines, action and stunts, physical comedy – are often less committed to character and instead focus upon the display of skills (comic timing, for instance).

Acting, that is, creating a character or impersonating a type of person, has traditionally been considered somewhat ethically suspect.[10] As Lowe (2016: 200) states, 'acting is an ethical issue. In a fundamental sense to act is to deceive; the word actor itself comes from the Greek word for "hypocrite"'. The actor was described as a counterfeiter of emotion by Rousseau, feigning emotions and taking the place of another.[11] This aligns

---

[9]See Baron (2007).
[10]See Schechner: 'To act means to feign, to simulate, to represent, to impersonate. ... [N]ot all performing is acting' (2002: 40). Kirby's definition of non-acting or 'non-matrixed acting' (1972: 6) also involves the absence of simulation: he places non-acting at one end of a continuum on which 'the amount of simulation, representation, impersonation and so forth increase[s] as we move along the scale'.
[11]See Colless (2009: 241).

broadly with Coquelin's theorization of the actor's two selves, the first of which conceives the performance and the second is its instrument (in Maltby 2003: 383).

The non-professional, even if performing as a fictional character, putatively abolishes this 'evil distance, the distance of representation' (Ramos-Martinez 2016: 9). Widely viewed as 'extemporaneous bodies' (ibid.), non-actors are felt to be themselves and not act. Indeed, they are often cast because their physical presence refers back directly to their sociological origin, and they operate primarily as a 'socio-historical body' (Graver 1997: 229). The non-professional performance on screen often thus involves the kind of 'everyday performance' theorized by Erving Goffman, in which communicative social activity is given 'particular semiotic intensity' (Marquis 2013: 48) by the cinematic apparatus. This aligns with Naremore's concept of ostensiveness, which distinguishes 'quotidian behaviour' from 'theatrical performance' through the imposition of a 'theatrical frame' (1988: 17, 23).

As we will investigate in a later chapter of this book, there is often a presumed overlap between non-professional performance in fiction films and documentary performance. Both documentary and fiction films with non-actors offer examples of 'capturing natural behaviour' rather than 'crafted' performances (Czach 2012: 154). Czach goes on to argue that this binary opposition between 'acting naturally' and 'behaving naturally' is inadequate, a view that will be supported by our examination of a wide range of performances and directing techniques.

If acting is linked to simulation, it is also of course a *doing* – it derives from the Latin 'agere', meaning 'bringing something into being'. In the same way, to 'perform' is to carry out or execute an action. So despite quite widespread views of the non-actor as merely demonstrating their 'real self', that self is brought into being through the performative act: 'performance is constitutive of the reality of the performer' (Upton 2011: 213). Performance thus produces presence – as Drake (2006: 86) notes, 'presence ... is a discourse produced by performance during its reception; it does not precede it' – so the socio-historical weight of the body of the non-professional is also a complex product of their on-screen performances.

Re-enactment and performance

This question of presence, performance, and time is made most salient in cases of re-enactment. Non-professionals are often deployed to portray events they themselves have lived through. An example will suffice: in *The Rider* (2017), director Chloé Zhao cast former rodeo rider Brady Jandreau to play a version of himself. Jandreau is a Lakota horse trainer, and the film shows his and his family's existence on their South Dakota reservation after

Brady's debilitating brain injury.[12] The praise for the film, and for Jandreau's performance which shows off his professional skill with horses, shows the importance of 'authentic' casting, especially given the long tradition of non-Indigenous actors playing Indigenous roles (see Schweninger 2013: 7).

Yet using the authentic body that has lived through the experiences now re-presented on screen, while making clear the 'material stakes of the cinematic image' (Schoonover 2012a: xxvii), opens up the potential for trauma or distress provoked by re-enactment. In many films, non-actors are recruited to relive their own difficult experiences, or those of their group or community. While Cambodian doctor Haing S. Ngor, Best Actor winner at the Academy Awards for *The Killing Fields* (Joffe, 1984), was acting out horrific experiences based on the life of Cambodian journalist Dith Pran, Ngor was also a survivor of the Cambodian genocide. Ngor's comment (in Donahue 1985) that 'I spent four years in the Khmer Rouge school of acting' aligns his past with that of Pran and all other victims of Pol Pot. It also speaks to the prevalent view of the non-actor as one who 'already carries within themself the environment in which the narrative is located' (Vasse 2018: 121).

Upton (2011: 216) notes that asking people to revisit their former suffering risks fetishizing these experiences for a 'voyeuristic' audience. Especially knowing that these performers are untrained and thus possibly unable to control their emotional responses, she asks (ibid.) whether 'participants or audience [can] have ethical investment in the public ritual re-enactment of their personal distress'. In fact, not only victims but perpetrators may also be invited to re-enact their own actions in a complex revisiting of the traumatic past. Paul Greengrass's 2002 docudrama *Bloody Sunday* returns to the day in 1972 when British Army soldiers murdered fourteen unarmed civilians in Derry, Northern Ireland. Alongside established actors Greengrass cast ordinary people, many of whom had been present on the day in question, but he also cast former British paratroopers who had served in Northern Ireland (but who had not been directly involved in Bloody Sunday). The director is quoted as saying (in Lavery 2002) that the 'aggression, anguish and terror' the film was depicting found its way into the real-life filming experiences, as the past was re-activated in its representation.[13]

The practice of re-enactment again directs our attention to the non-actor's peculiar relation to temporality: for Ivone Margulies (2019: 5) the 'belatedness' of re-enactment makes of the non-actor a 'disturbing revenant',

---

[12]Zhao also used non-professionals both in her debut, *Songs My Brothers Taught Me* (2015), also set on the Pine Ridge reservation in South Dakota, and her acclaimed 2020 *Nomadland*, for which Frances McDormand won the Best Actress Oscar. McDormand was flanked by non-professional 'nomads' playing themselves, as they journey across the United States.

[13]In this vein, we can also think of the complex and genre-crossing re-enactments by Indonesian perpetrators of massacres in *The Act of Killing* (Oppenheimer, 2012).

whose phantasmatic power is drawn from its ability to highlight the gap between an unrepresentable past and a current approximation, 'between past reference and present actualization'. Re-enactment is ontologically ambivalent (Carrigy 2021: 18) as it troubles the borders of fact and fiction, past and present, and actor and 'social actor' (ibid.: 33). In *performing* something one *did* before, we see that re-enactment is its own contradiction, just as Margulies (2019: 63) argues that 'acting constitutes the aporia of re-enactment', drawing attention to its status as a 'copy' of an unseen original.

For Cesare Zavattini, the great advocate of the use of non-professionals in post-war Italian cinema, it was important not just to employ them, but that they be used to (re)enact their own experiences. He professed (Zavattini 2002: 139) that filmmakers should observe and follow ordinary individuals, in what he termed a 'pedinamento', that is, shadowing or stalking. In having them recreate their experiences as 'actors of themselves' (ibid.: 731), Zavattini attaches a sacred importance to their on-screen repetition of their actions, calling it a kind of religious rite (ibid.: 708). However, he also acknowledged the psychologically scarring potential of re-enactment, when he reflected on his own short film, *Storia di Caterina/Story of Caterina*, included in the portmanteau film *L'amore in città/Love in the City* (1953).[14]

The eponymous protagonist, Caterina Rigoglioso, was a Sicilian domestic servant who had been prosecuted for abandoning her infant due to poverty. Zavattini had attended her trial, and decided she must be the one to interpret her tragic story, in order to engage viewer sympathy (Zavattini 2006: 164).[15] The short film follows Caterina as she tries to find work, makes us witness her decision to leave the boy in a public park, and concludes with newspaper headlines of her trial. While the film offers Caterina the possibility of a 'penitential path' (Margulies 2019: 48), or a do-over, a 'second chance' (Kahana 2009: 47) that can only be actualized by having the real person retrace her painful steps, this obviously raises ethical questions regarding the vulnerable protagonist. Zavattini (2002: 749) acknowledges that some thought it 'monstrous' to make Caterina repeat her actions, and that she wept with remorse at points during the filming (ibid.: 149).[16] But he pushes back on this criticism as a bourgeois fear of facing hard truths.[17] Nevertheless, as

---

[14]The film was directed by Francesco Maselli, with Zavattini as writer and co-director.

[15]Producers apparently wanted glamorous star Silvana Pampanini to play the role as Caterina was deemed too ugly, but Zavattini fiercely resisted (Dentice 1953: 75).

[16]Caterina was dubbed for the film by actress and author Goliarda Sapienza, who helped Caterina overcome her anxieties about filming, speaking to her in Sicilian dialect to reassure her (Gobbato 2011: 109).

[17]It is interesting that when the film had a special screening in Milan in February 1954, with spectators invited to write down their reactions, several mentioned the unease the re-enactment caused them, with one calling it 'cruel' (G. D. 1954).

we will see at various points in this book, the filmmaker generally assumes the right to impose distress on the non-professional, with the broader aim of presenting an exemplary story that will awaken the spectator's pity or political consciousness.

Caterina disappeared after the film, and we do not know the impact it had on her. Although Zavattini later muttered (2006: 165) that he had learned that she was not as innocent as he had made out in the film, her story was never revisited. Caterina had no aspirations at all to be an actor, and was employed for the sole task of re-enacting her trauma, but her story nonetheless speaks to the impossible futurity of the non-actor. Just as Bazin (1971: 24) said that the use of non-professionals 'contains within itself the seeds of its own destruction' as they can only be used once before losing their authentic appeal, it's accepted that they should have no professional future, except on rare occasions (some of which we will encounter later).[18] Schoonover (2012b: 76) identifies two temporalities of the 'ideal neorealist body', which are the past experiences that have left an indelible mark on the individual and the present labour of performance. These necessarily exclude a third temporal dimension: the future. Thus when a former non-professional 'taken from the streets' achieves enduring success, like Scottish teenager Martin Compson who won a role in Ken Loach's *Sweet Sixteen* (2002), now well known in the UK for his starring role in the BBC series *Line of Duty* (2012–21), this brings about a category shift, not just from non-actor to professional actor but from eternal present to ongoing, future-projected career. And when this happens, it is normally through the more or less benevolent operations of the auteur.

Auteurs and power relations

Loach, like other directors who regularly use non-professionals, is famous for 'discovering' them, despite the contemporary prominence of the casting director (see Shields 2017). If star studies emerged in the academy in the late 1970s as a partial response to auteur theory, the history of non-professionals, whether in mainstream or independent cinema, has generally been auteur-focused. There is a long list of well-known international directors who are frequently cited when non-professionals are mentioned: these range from Sergei Eisenstein and Robert Flaherty to Jean Rouch, Abbas Kiarostami, Satyajit Ray, Ousmane Sembène, Mohsen and Samira Makhmalbaf, Jafar Panahi, Tsai Ming-liang, Hector Babenco, Pedro Costa, Jia Zhangke, the

---

[18]In this vein, Kennedy (2005) confirms that 'non-actors are able to live only in the present tense, any sense of future is either pragmatically resisted or cast in the immaterial terms of fantasy/spirituality'.

Dardennes, Jean-Marie Straub and Danièle Huillet, Djibril Diop Mambéty, and Apichatpong Weerasethakul. The films these directors made are part of the canon of global art cinema, and often explicitly invoke Italian post-war practices.[19] These directors approached working with non-professionals in a variety of ways, although they often treated them as, in Vittorio De Sica's words, 'raw material that can be moulded at will' (in Gaggiotti 2019: 132). I will briefly discuss here two of the most famous examples from European arthouse cinema, Pier Paolo Pasolini and Robert Bresson.

Pasolini used non-actors consistently from *Accattone* (1961) to his last film, *Salò: o le 120 giornate di Sodoma/Salò, or the 120 Days of Sodom* (1975). They were often drawn from the proletariat and sub-proletariat, cast for their unconventional or 'deformed' faces which resisted the visual homogeneity of mainstream stardom (Viano 1993: 37).[20] While several of Pasolini's collaborators – most notably Franco Citti and Ninetto Davoli – went on to work with him multiple times, Pasolini's directorial techniques were designed to work against any seamless integration of the actor into the apparatus of cinema. Pasolini's professed antipathy to naturalistic acting performance was allied to an attachment to non-professionals as 'shreds of reality ... like a landscape, a sky, the sun, a donkey passing along the road' (quoted in Schwartz 1995: 351). In order to get what he wanted from them, he used short takes, and often dubbed actors' voices with different dialogue to achieve an 'unreal "polyvalent speech"', which prevented any development of a 'personal acting style' (Greene 2017: 42).

This desire to block any performing idiolect from emerging was shared by Robert Bresson, albeit via different techniques. Bresson's non-professionals, or 'models', repeated the scenes over and over to become like automatons (Reader 2000: 129). In a fascinating documentary, *The Models of Pickpocket* (Mangolte, 2003), Pierre Leymarie, who appeared in Bresson's 1959 *Pickpocket*, recounts having done up to thirty-six takes of a scene to achieve the mechanical line readings desired, saying it had a 'brainwashing' effect. Bresson was determined to erase any attempts at 'acting' or self-projection from the non-professionals and wanted to avoid audience identification with the performance. His view of the ontological hiatus between professional and non-professional actor informed all of his work with the latter: he said (in Godard and Delahaye 1967: 16):

> There is an uncrossable gulf between an actor, even trying to forget himself ... and a person, virgin of cinema, virgin of theatre, considered as crude matter that does not know what it is and that surrenders to you what it did not intend to surrender to anyone.

---

[19]This influence will be explored further in Chapter 5.
[20]Both Rhodes (2012) and Gaggiotti (2022) discuss Pasolini's use of non-professionals in *Salò*.

The 'virginity' of the non-actor (echoing Bazin's thoughts on the actors of De Sica's *Bicycle Thieves* when he mentions their 'cinematic virginity') codes the director–actor relationship as one of power and domination.[21] Bresson adds to that in the same interview, comparing himself as a director of actors to a surgeon extracting something from a patient, who must therefore remain absolutely still. While in the Mangolte documentary the three people who appeared in *Pickpocket* have positive recollections of the film and their role in creating an artwork, the question of unequal power relations lingers.[22] Godard, in typically provocative fashion, asked Bresson whether the director cannot destroy a professional actor's acquired habits, rather than having to use non-professionals, with all the difficulty that involves. When Bresson demurred, Godard (who himself predominantly used professional actors) insisted: 'one can destroy him, the same way that the Germans destroyed the Jews in the concentration camps' (ibid.). Bresson placidly objected that this was impossible. The violent and grotesque nature of Godard's analogy hyperbolizes the often coercive relationship between director and actor, heightened in the case of the non-actor by their lack of protection in the industry. The book written by Anne Wiazemsky (2007), cast at seventeen by Bresson in *Au hazard Balthazar/Balthazar* (1966), makes uncomfortable reading for its account of sexagenarian Bresson's repeated advances towards her, his sadistic treatment on set, and her inexperience and awe of him as a director.

Bresson's 'sadistic urges towards his models' (Reader 2000: 130) might be merely the more radical end of a directorial spectrum in which, as we will see, non-professionals are often stripped of agency, 'caught in the maze of the plot like laboratory rats being sent through a labyrinth' (Bazin 1971: 66). We will encounter in this book examples of problematic treatment and exploitation of non-professionals, as well as extremely positive experiences. I don't quite share Kennedy's rather essentializing view (2005) that the non-professional is 'the perfection of capitalist downsizing in that they freely consent to work for nothing', not least because most are paid something, even though it is often hard to find out how much. Nonetheless, the risk to the non-actor, who may be uprooted from their environment and then discarded, is clear. Likewise the potential for violence or sexual exploitation: Pasolini frequently sought out his sub-proletarian cast members in the same way he sought out his sexual partners, and so we can say that his casting and cruising practices were almost indistinguishable (Ninetto Davoli is an example). Tom Whittaker's account of the Spanish *quinqui* or 'delinquent' films of the late 1970s and early 1980s, which

---

[21]Bazin writes 'virginité cinématographique' (Bazin 1975: 304). The English translation renders this as 'purity' (1971: 55).
[22]The three are Pierre Leymarie (who became a professor), and Martin LaSalle and Marika Green, both of whom, interestingly, went on to forge acting careers.

starred real-life juvenile delinquents, also tells us about directors having sex with the vulnerable boys they were casting.[23]

The widespread view of the non-professional as a disruptive figure, whose very being offers 'an opportunity for thinking outside the limits of the existing relations and forces of production' (Kear 2005: 36) thus requires nuance. The non-professional seems to exist on what Fred Zinneman (1950: 87), who directed non-actors in *The Men* and *The Search*, called 'the razor-sharp edge between truth and amateurishness'. Their innate challenge to the logic of stardom can indeed offer a rethinking of stardom itself as 'the putrefaction of culture as commodity' (Schoonover 2010: 175). And it is important to note that sometimes the non-actor can literally strike back: Mario Vitale, the fisherman cast to play Ingrid Bergman's husband in *Stromboli* (1950), recounted (in Iaccio 2006: 94) that he was supposed to strike Bergman in one scene when her character had betrayed him. Director Roberto Rossellini taunted him about his virility in order to extract 'real' violence from him until Vitale, enraged, hit her for real and would have killed her, he said, had he not been pulled away.[24]

This political charge of the non-actor has obviously been harnessed many times in cinema that is socially engaged or radical. In important anti-colonial films like Gillo Pontecorvo's *La battaglia di Algeri/The Battle of Algiers* (1966) or Sarah Maldoror's *Sambizanga* (1972), former militants are among those who re-enact the violent struggles for decolonization. But there are also many examples of 'colonial casting', such as in Italian film of the 1930s, where colonial subjects in Ethiopia and Eritrea were used in the fascist regime's empire-building films. The ambivalent nature of the non-professional requires consideration of the context in which they are used and the aim of that use, and their use must not automatically be considered progressive. A final example here might illustrate this: the film *También la lluvia/Even the Rain* (Bollaín, 2010) is set in Bolivia and depicts the making of a film about Columbus's conquest of the New World. The director, played by Mexican and global star Gael García Bernal, is shown looking for Indigenous people to play the cast, some of whom refuse to take part in the traumatizing and dangerous stunts involved. The film's critique of colonialism and of the exploitative aspects of colonial casting, as the fictional crew underpay the Indigenous actors and are careless of their actual provenance, invites the spectator to reflect upon the treatment of the real Indigenous non-actors used

---

[23]Whittaker (2020: 108) discusses how director Eloy de la Iglesia cast in his films teenage boys who sold him drugs and sex.
[24]On the 'radical incommensurability' between a star like Bergman and the non-professionals she acted with, see Gelley (2012: 93) and passim.

by Spanish director Bollaín to make this critique (Martínez-Expósito 2018: 33).[25]

Rather than essentializing the non-professional, we will try in this book to locate them in their specific industrial and cultural context, and analyse their variegated qualities and use. Where possible, we will examine any details available of employment conditions, pay, and contracts, 'the material and discursive sites where actors become wedged between forces of production (labor) and forces of exchange' (Clark 1995: xiii). These are difficult to ascertain in post-war Italy. While accounting for the cultural weight of the director and their role in disciplining and/or nurturing the non-professional (especially given that neorealism has been commonly thought of as an authorial cinema), as far as possible I have tried to privilege the point of view of the non-professional actor, even where evidence of their experience or opinion is lacking.

Post-war Italy and this book

Post-war Italian cinema tends to be read exclusively through the lens of neorealism, with new books emerging all the time on the period. The scholarly emphasis has often been on the elements of the period that represent a break with or reaction against the cinema of fascism, such as the turning away from studio shooting and bourgeois settings, and the rejection of the American and Italian stars who were popular in the 1930s and early 1940s.[26] While these features were certainly not as new as has sometimes been supposed – non-professionals and location shooting had been used in Italian cinema at various points in the twentieth century – the rhetoric of neorealism was potent. Bazin's essay on post-war Italian cinema contained the dramatic sub-heading 'Rupture and Renaissance', while Millicent Marcus in her widely cited account of neorealism (1987: 33) referred to *Rome Open City* as 'the founding'.

Much work has been done by scholars within Italy and outside it to problematize easy periodization and reveal continuities between pre- and post-war Italian cinematic practices, as well as to enlarge the post-war canon and pay attention to other vital filmic modes.[27] The group of films termed 'neorealist' was only ever a very small part of the Italian film industry's

---

[25]To further complicate the film's use of Indigenous non-professionals, the role of the lead Bolivian actor who leads the cast in rebellion against their treatment (and against the corporate privatization of their water supply) was taken by Juan Carlos Aduviri, a non-actor, yes, but a local professor of cinema. See Cabitza (2011).
[26]The Hollywood majors withdrew in 1938 from the Italian market, triggering an increase in Italian production and the formation of an Italian national star system (Gundle 2013: 54).
[27]See, for example, Bayman (2014a) and Marmo (2018).

output in the period 1945–55 (Noto and Pitassio 2010: viii), declining in number and cultural status as the 1940s ended, but also influencing more commercial filmmaking in a number of ways (ibid.: 18–19). Rather than thinking of 'neorealism' as a concrete and discrete phenomenon, I prefer to adopt the term 'neorealist galaxy', which suggests a cinematic universe in constant expansion, with objects of different types and sizes orbiting in loose association.[28] Tracing relations and influences between canonical films and lesser-known ones, and situating them in relation to the complex galaxy or ecology of post-war Italian cultural production, through the *fil rouge* of the non-professional actor, allows us to find new meanings and associations in this period.

However, much as we can explode some of the myths of neorealism, the shadow cast by these myths has been long, especially in terms of the (non) actor. An important tradition of *antidivismo* or anti-stardom still holds sway in Italy, as we will see later in the book, often explicitly linked to neorealism (see Carluccio and Minuz 2015). What Deleuze termed the 'professional non-actor' (1989: 19–20) who gained visibility in this period has obscured the processes by which Italian stars still continued to emerge. As Mariapaola Pierini has argued (2017: 148), the complex relations between stardom and acting or performance in neorealism have been obscured because of its presumed rejection of stardom. Yet to establish a binary of stardom and its antithesis would also be problematic, as it fails to account for the vast body of actors, jobbing actors, and even extras (those individuals who are 'faceless, bodiless, and without any personal gestures' (Didi-Huberman 2009: 20)) who populated post-war screens.[29] We will be examining the ways that the recruitment of non-professionals actually created new stars, whether that be beauty contest winners Sophia Loren and Gina Lollobrigida, or Franco Interlenghi, who achieved Italian and European fame after appearing in De Sica's *Shoeshine* as a boy.

Outline and method

Chapter 1 examines the multifarious influences, histories, practices, and debates that circulated around the non-professional actor in the post-war period. It traces the genealogy of the non-professional, through the impact of Soviet theory and practice on Italian film culture of the late 1930s, and discusses significant earlier uses of the figure, including in Italian colonial

---

[28]This term is used by Stefano Pisu (2016: 142) and Francesco Pitassio (2019: 271). We might also bear in mind Antonio Pietrangeli's 1948 description of neorealism as a 'common climate' (cited in Leavitt 2020: 5).

[29]Even extra roles were sought after in a time of economic precarity. Valerio Zurlini's 1952 documentary, *Il mercato delle facce/The Market of Faces*, poignantly depicted the melancholy quest for extra roles of a variety of individuals.

cinema under fascism. The chapter maps out the principal ways in which non-professionals were recruited, from organized searches and competitions to random encounters, identifying a key tension between intention and chance in the selection of non-actors, and the creation of a new, low-fi, star system. By the 1950s, the chapter argues, the non-professional had become a divisive presence, seen by many in a changing film industry as a threat to their livelihood, and I look at the debates that arose around this troublesome figure.

Chapter 2 scrutinizes two non-professional case studies: *Bicycle Thieves*' Lamberto Maggiorani, and the cast of Visconti's *La terra trema/The Earth Trembles*, both produced in 1948, the high-water mark of neorealism. While I examine the directorial choices that shaped the different performance styles of each film, I also excavate some of the biographical surround of the performances: Maggiorani famously lost his job after appearing in the film, and the chapter explores his difficult afterlife, including the screenplay for the unmade film about his experience. Some of the Sicilians likewise recounted their experience with Visconti as a kind of traumatic exploitation, redolent of colonialism. The chapter thus considers the ethical and performance issues that arise from considering humans as 'raw material' in an artistic process, even one that produces masterpieces.

In Chapter 3, we see how the use of non-professionals 'taken from the streets' had a particular resonance for girls: this chapter examines the phenomenon of girls who gained fame via cinema in this period, and how they were frequently seen in press and popular discourses, from both left and right, as simultaneously 'dangerous and pathetic' (Pullen 2005: 5). They were represented as both threatened by the immorality of the cinema industry and a threat to it via their lack of professional training. As well as globally celebrated examples such as Sophia Loren and Gina Lollobrigida who were catapulted to sudden stardom via beauty contests, I consider forgotten cases such as Carmela Sazio, the peasant girl discovered by Roberto Rossellini for *Paisà/Paisan* (1946), who was then discarded by him despite her pleas and who met a tragic end. A less tragic example is Maria Fiore, a Roman teenager chosen by Renato Castellani for his hit film *Due soldi di speranza/Two Cents of Hope* (1952). However, while Fiore went on to a career in film, it was irrevocably overshadowed by her teenage success.

We have seen that the emblematic face of neorealism is probably Enzo Staiola, who played little Bruno in De Sica's *Bicycle Thieves*. But Chapter 4 restores the broader and more complex picture of children working in the film industry after the war, using contemporary evidence to document their contributions. The chapter asks to what extent children – who are often considered non-professionals par excellence – can understand and consent to what happens, and documents the sometimes harsh treatment they received from directors. It also analyses their work as a form of labour, in a national context where children frequently entered the labour market at the age of ten or so, and where employment rights and protections were generally slim or non-existent.

Chapter 5 moves to the present and addresses the non-professional in contemporary global cinema. It examines the legacy of neorealism in recent Italian cinema, thinking about the use of the non-professional as a totemic embodiment or memory of the glorious past of Italian cinema. I show how the non-professional is still used, both in Italian and global arthouse cinema, to generate an 'effect of quality' and to address difficult social realities that their own marginalization is thought to embody. Meanwhile, analysing appearances at film festivals by non-professionals demonstrates their centrality to the intangible mechanisms of the 'prestige economy' and their value to the global arthouse circuit.

In writing this book, I have encountered a number of challenges: the lack of reliable sources about the non-professional actors who appeared in films in the 1940s and 1950s is the primary one. Few contracts or official documents related to their employment can be found. I tracked down interviews and newspaper articles that have relevant information, but many individuals were never interviewed and left no material trace (apart from their film performance), and we have few reliable written production histories. Reconstructing their lives or their acting choices from the testimonies of the male auteurs who chose them is inevitably highly problematic. The reliance on anecdote that we encounter in many of the chapters also highlights the precarious status of knowledge about the non-professional, and you will note the number of times I have written 'apparently' or 'allegedly' when reconstructing film productions. Working with 'scraps of the archive' (Hartman 2018) inevitably directs our attention to what we do not know as well as what we have managed to find out.

Filling in these lacunae is impossible. As Dever et al. (2010: 100) point out, as researchers

> we often harbour an insistent (deeply suppressed and often denied) desire to find in our archival sources a whole where there can only ever be random parts, to perform acts of reconstitution in the service of producing a coherent and seamless account of our subject.

We might speculate about what happened to some of these performers or whether a particular director's account of working with them is accurate, and I am sad that so many of these people did not get to tell their own stories. I have attempted to restore some of these stories, in a very partial and imperfect fashion here. I am also aware of the dangers of focusing on the already-documented, where it is easier to locate information. I have tried to range as widely as possible across the period, accounting for, but not centring, the great auteurs and the canonical films of post-war Italy, and writing about comedies and melodramas, to give a sense of the richly variegated panorama of the time.

Throughout the book I have paid attention to the details of performance in order to grasp the 'micromeanings' of voice and body (McDonald 2004: 32), bearing in mind that most of these non-actors were dubbed by others in the final cut. I try to understand how the mechanics of on-screen performance are shaped by the relationship between director and actor, and how the (non)actor's work is also part of the performance of an identity, in a moment in which the ordinary Italian person was being made visible on the big screen.[30] If the non-actor was chosen for their proximity to the everyday, what did their on-screen presence communicate about what it meant to be an Italian man, woman, or child in the difficult post-war reconstruction period? To what extent were non-professionals performing the self, and to what extent did they consider themselves to be actors?

Most importantly, the non-professional remains a totemic figure in arthouse cinema, with their uniqueness both their calling card and their perceived weakness. Yet in many ways they are aligned with their seeming antithesis, the star: as Siegfried Kracauer wrote (2004: 24), 'the typical Hollywood star resembles the non-actor in that he acts out a standing character identical with his own'. The star, who is felt to personify themselves on screen, to 'be themselves' at all times, and often to be a prisoner of their star image, is coterminous with the non-professional in many ways, even as their economic and cultural value is incomparable. Richard Dyer (1987: 17) argued that 'being interested in stars is being interested in how we are human now', because of their ability to embody and negotiate ideological beliefs about identity; the non-actor, whose ordinariness bypasses the charisma and awe emanating from the star, nonetheless raises the question of *how* we are human, standing as they do at the cusp of being and seeming, and pointing back always towards their own presence beyond the film text.

---

[30]See Albritton et al. (2016: 5–7).

1

Acting, stardom, and the non-professional in Italy from fascism to the post-war

Introduction

A 1952 headline in the *New York Times* (*NYT*) magazine announced that 'In Rome the People are Movie Stars': with a sub-heading of 'Casting – al fresco', the article featured photos from the street casting of children for Roberto Rossellini's *Dov'è la libertà...?/Where Is Freedom?* and stills from his *Francesco, giullare di Dio/Flowers of St. Francis* (1950), Vittorio De Sica's *Umberto D.* (1950), and Renato Castellani's 'pink neorealist' *Due soldi di speranza/Two Cents of Hope* (1952). While praising the non-professionals who bring 'vitality' to the Italian film industry, the article (Hawkins 1952) also includes, slightly incongruously, a large image of the shooting of *Roman Holiday* (Wyler, 1952), then filming in Rome, and a small picture of child actor Vittorio Manunta. While Manunta might seem to be emblematic of the children familiar from neorealist films, the film he was shooting was actually Joseph Losey's thriller *Imbarco a mezzanotte/Stranger on the Prowl* (1952), starring Hollywood actor Paul Muni and co-produced by US and Italian companies. The *NYT* piece is testament to how the use of non-professionals had permeated the international consciousness, in tandem with Academy Awards for *Shoeshine* and *Bicycle Thieves* in 1948 and 1950, respectively, but this assortment of films highlights the extent to which the Italian film industry had already changed by 1952.[1]

The prestige of the 'neorealist brand' (Pisu 2016: 142), of which non-professionals were a key part, was in competition with the popularity of Italy as a host for Hollywood's 'runaway productions': with the success of *Quo Vadis?* (LeRoy, 1951), produced in Rome by MGM, the city became known as 'Hollywood on the Tiber', attracting producers, directors, and

---

[1]On the success of neorealist films in the United States, and particularly in New York, see Balio (2010: 40–61); Brennan (2012); Schoonover (2009).

stars for the next decade or so (see Corsi 2001: 66–70; Steinhart 2019). Changing public tastes following post-war reconstruction, alongside government opposition to the critical narratives of neorealist films, created a complex ecosystem, in which, as we will see, new Italian stars emerged, many of them from the non-professional world.

The narrative of a sudden emergence in Italy after the war of 'volti e corpi inediti, reclutati "per strada"'/'unfamiliar faces and bodies, recruited "on the streets"' (Parigi 2014: 73) has had a powerful resonance, especially as the link between post-fascist Italy and the new performers seemed so tight: as Carlo Lizzani wrote in his review of Rossellini's *Rome Open City* in November 1945, 'il mondo oggi non vuole dei divi, cerca degli uomini, gente della strada'/'the world today doesn't want stars, it is looking for men, people taken from the street' (Lizzani 1945). But the attention given to the 'antidivi' or *anti-stars* (Masi 2003: 337) who emerged in the immediate post-war period in films by Rossellini and De Sica has somewhat obscured two key factors: firstly, that the use of non-professionals in Italian cinema was not new and in fact emerged out of debates and practices that happened during the 1930s. And secondly, that the use of the non-professional was not confined to the small group of films canonically thought of as 'neorealist', but rather that a culture of 'attori improvvisati' or impromptu actors worked its way through mainstream Italian film genres.

The transition from the heavily centralized industry of the late fascist period to the post-war saw the earlier 'divismo domestico'/'domestic stardom' (Castello 1957: 407) or 'paradivismo provinciale'/'provincial para-stardom' (Pistagnesi 2010: 248) reconfigured; many stars fell out of favour, due to their association with the regime (most prominently Luisa Ferida and Osvaldo Valenti, executed by partisans for collaboration at the end of the war), while others had their image transformed: 'dalle macerie del cinema autarchico non nasce solo l'attore nuovo ma riprende vita anche l'attore vecchio'/'from the ruins of fascist cinema, not only does the new actor emerge but the old actor takes on a new life' (Brunetta 1982: 250). So as Lizzani commented in the review of *Roma città aperta*, comic stars like Anna Magnani and Aldo Fabrizi were 'made new' by neorealism's reworking of their persona. Likewise, one of Italy's most popular pre-war stars, Amedeo Nazzari, known as 'una sorta di Clark Gable delle zone depresse'/'the Clark Gable of Italy's poor regions' (Castello 1957: 408), became a tortured antihero of post-war cinema in films like Lattuada's '*noir* neorealist' *Il bandito/The Bandit* (1946).[2]

Film critics in the transition to democracy decried the style of theatrical acting often associated with the artifice of the 'white telephone' films of fascism, 'quel genere bastardo e vacuo'/'that bastard and vacuous genre'

---

[2] See Gundle (2019: 19–33) for more on this transition.

(ibid.: 401). While a dedicated film training school had been set up in 1935, the Centro Sperimentale per la Cinematografia, its students were not necessarily highly rated: a 1944 piece in the magazine *Star* notes irascibly the American influence on acting styles observed during a visit to the Centro, the artifice and lack of authenticity of performances, as well as the 'effeminacy' of the male acting students (Baldini 1944). Overall, the combination of inauthenticity and amateurishness in comparison to the Hollywood stars well known to Italian spectators resonated with a broader desire for a renewal of Italian screen acting. While Antonio Pietrangeli's vicious criticism (1944: 3) of the current crop of Italian film actors as a 'massa gesticolante e urlante di tante larve inespressive'/'gesticulating and yelling mass of inexpressive spectres' seems somewhat harsh, it builds upon Luchino Visconti's rallying cry in his 1943 essay 'Il cinema antropomorfico '/'Anthropomorphic Cinema' to strip away actorly training to arrive at the authentic core of each performer, restoring them as a human presence.

While the non-actor may be the extreme end of the desire for a more authentic, ethically informed, and stripped-down form of acting, to match the antirhetorical nature of a cinema emerging from twenty years of dictatorship, the landscape of Italian screen acting remained a complicated one in the immediate post-war years. New faces were called upon to represent the new type of characters that post-war Italy needed and produced: an emblematic example might be the little-seen and now lost 1945 Resistance film *Cuore di partigiano/A Partisan's Heart* which starred ex-partisans (see Ambrosino 1989: 65), and American G.I.s stationed in Italy like John Kitzmiller were also recruited.[3] However, theatrical actors continued to be used, alongside former film stars. Cesare Zavattini's position, expressed in the 1952 essay 'Alcune idee sul cinema'/'Some Ideas on Cinema', that neorealist cinema was anti-American and anti-star was merely one view in a chorus of overlapping voices, and neorealism itself was a subject of endless and unresolved debate. By the early 1950s, not only was the promise of neorealism as a new way of seeing the world felt to be exhausted and in crisis, the non-professional actor had become the target of polemic and opprobrium.

In order to unravel the knotted threads of this period, I will try to investigate the influences, histories, practices, and debates that run through it. I will first examine how debates in the 1930s on the non-actor, derived from the dissemination of Soviet film theory in the period, prepared the terrain for the eruption of the non-actor onto the post-war film scene, as well as earlier uses of the figure, including in 1930s Italian colonial cinema. The practices of recruitment of non-professionals were also more varied and complex than has been assumed: alongside reader competitions and beauty

---

[3] Kitzmiller's career, which started in *Vivere in pace/To Live in Peace* (Zampa, 1947) and continued into the 1960s, is discussed in Giovacchini (2012, 2015).

contests, potential actors were spotted on the street or drawn from sport, in a sustained tension between chance and design. The creation of what turned out to be a new system of 'low-definition stardom' (Grignaffini 1989: 44) was hotly debated, and the final part of the chapter examines some of those debates, seeking to understand how and why non-professionals became considered a threat to the film industry itself. By the early 1950s, although non-professionals like Sophia Loren were staples of the cinema industry, their status was still contested. These debates reveal a deep discomfort with the untrained actor, even as they continued, and still continue, to occupy an important cultural space in Italy. While the non-professional gained international visibility post-war, they did not appear ex nihilo and had a complicated history in Italian cinema, both in terms of theory and of practical use.

Soviet theory and the actor

Italy's modern film culture and its institutions developed and were consolidated in the late 1920s and 1930s, in transnational dialogue with other cinemas, particularly that of the Soviet Union, as well as Hollywood.[4] As Salazkina (2014: 182) notes, 'Italian institutional and cultural discourses and practices relied heavily on Soviet examples, creating a rich site for transmission and translation of Soviet cinema and theory in Italy during the first phase of the fascist regime.' The Soviet influence on key early Italian sound films such as *Acciaio/Steel* (Ruttmann, 1933), *Rotaie/Rails* (Camerini, 1931), and *Terra madre/Mother Earth* (Blasetti, 1931) – the first two employing non-professional actors – has been well documented (see Garofalo 2002: 223).

This national film culture was strongly marked by debates on the actor and non-actor: as Pitassio notes (2010: 45), 'il tema dell'attore'/'the theme of the actor' was a 'snodo cruciale nella edificazione di una cinematografia nazionale'/'crucial issue in the construction of a national cinema'. A key vector for the institutionalization and promotion of Italian films in the 1930s was the translation by critic Umberto Barbaro of works by Pudovkin, Eisenstein, and others, including Balázs and Arnheim.[5] Barbaro was, with Luigi Chiarini, co-founder of the Centro Sperimentale di Cinematografia and co-director of the prestigious film journal *Bianco e Nero*, which began publication in 1937 under the auspices of the Centro. Barbaro argued in 1953 that Soviet realism had prepared the ground for neorealism, and that

---

[4] On the influence of American realism, see Prezzolini (1937).
[5] On this translation and dissemination, see Garofalo (2002); Salazkina (2014); Lento (2017: 7–8).

the study of Soviet theoretical texts and showing of films at the Centro had created a direct line to neorealist films (see Barbaro 1975).

Barbaro translated Pudovkin's work as the volume *Film e fonofilm* in 1935.[6] He also included excerpts from Pudovkin's essay ('Tipi e non-attori'/'Types Instead of Actors') in the first volume of the anthology he and Chiarini curated in 1938 on the role of the actor).[7] In 1939, Barbaro also translated, as *L'attore nel film*, Pudovkin's reflections on film acting, first published in English in 1933. It was in *Bianco e Nero* that Barbaro reflected extensively on the question of the actor, drawing upon Soviet theory, and giving particular emphasis to the figure of the non-actor. Eisenstein and Pudovkin were the first directors to cast non-professionals recurrently in fiction films and had been among the first to develop a theoretical apparatus around them, although they were mainly used in secondary roles in Soviet films (see Gaggiotti 2021: 246).

Barbaro drew upon this theory and practice for his reflection on the cinematic 'types' represented by the non-actor. As Pitassio (2019: 275) notes, 'the "type" was crucial to an aesthetic tradition striving to achieve a Marxist representation, as the theory of the Soviet "typazh" demonstrates. According to Soviet theoreticians, human types, when carefully selected, acted as social masks and enabled filmmakers to visually represent class warfare.' Eisenstein's use of the type saw it as a kind of 'gestic summation of ideological traits' (Higson 1986: 126), and thus the type and the non-actor exist in perfect synchrony or even tautology. The actor chosen as a 'type' can stand synecdochally and deterministically for a class or group.[8] As would become visible in certain post-war Italian films, rather than relating to individual psychology, 'typage relates the character's individual personality and problems to larger social forces, such as poverty, and uses non-actors to represent [in Eisenstein's terms] "ideas, elements in an intellectual argument"' (Wojcik 2003: 232). While praising the type, in terms inherited from Eisenstein and Pudovkin, Barbaro (1937: 9) was critical of any attempt to draw on the actor's psychology, deploring, for example, Stanislavsky's 'interior work'.

Pudovkin moved away from the somewhat limited formulation of Eisensteinian typage to an understanding of the actor as 'centre of creative expressivity in the film' (Wright-Wexman 2004: 130). Pudovkin's argument

---

[6]These essays had been published in 1929 in English as *Film Technique*.
[7]The volume is *L'attore: saggio di antologia critica*, in *Bianco e Nero*, 2(2–3), February–March 1938. See 'Tipi e non-attori', pp. 192–8. On the importance of Barbaro's encounter with Pudovkin's texts in particular, see Brunetta (1969: 9) and Pitassio and Venturini (2014: 265, n. 32).
[8]Purificato (1942: 645) longed for 'tipi per un cinema nostro'/'types for an Italian cinema', listing as potential 'types': 'operai, contadini, benestanti, uomini e donne, vecchi e ragazzi/'workers, peasants, the well-off, men and women, old people and children'.

in 1933 that even the non-actor was 'not out of place in film and indeed can serve as an example to the trained actor' (see Pudovkin 1954: 118) was eagerly taken up by Barbaro who (in 1937: 20) wrote that the theory of 'cinema senza attori'/'cinema without actors' was important in the development of film aesthetics, citing Eisenstein, Murnau's *Tabu: A Story of the South Seas* (1931), and Blasetti's *1860* (1934). While Pudovkin ultimately regarded the non-actor as 'human material' and subject to the control of the director, his thoughts on what Barbaro termed the 'montaggio della recitazione' (literally 'the montage of acting' or the techniques through which a performance can be created through judicious use of editing), and his reflections on the cunningness needed by a director to elicit the effect of acting from a non-professional, would resonate through later Italian cinema. Barbaro (1937: 19) agreed on the necessary limits to the role of the non-professional, referring to 'l'attore non professionista, del film di cui sia unico autore il regista'/'the non-professional actor, the sole author of whose film is the director'.[9]

For Barbaro, the non-actor functioned partially as a useful tool in order to demonstrate, by implied antithesis, the mastery of technique and understanding of the cinematic apparatus required from professional film actors, and the vital role of the director. It is clear that the transmission of Soviet thought on the topic had a long Italian legacy: Barbaro argued (1937: 21) that the Soviet 'cinema without actors' worked to emphasize fundamental concepts for actors and directors: 'contrapponendo il tipo all'attore si è intesa e dimostrata la grandissima importanza dello studio, attualissimo nella psicologia e nella medicina, del comportamento psicologico dei vari biotipi'/'contrasting the type with the actor we can understand the importance of studying the psychological behaviour of the various biotypes, which is very prevalent now in Italy'. Here he was referring to contemporary scientific debates led in Italy by Nicola Pende on the 'science of the somatic and psychic individual biotypes' (Beccalossi 2017). The study of biotypology aimed to classify morphological and functional characteristics of a given ethnic group: while the scientific racism and proximity to eugenics of Pende was not embraced by Barbaro or later thinkers on cinema in Italy, it is hard to ignore the biological and physiognomic underpinning of the selection of the 'type'.[10] In later Italian cinema we will often see a preoccupation with

---

[9]See Gaggiotti (2019: 57–63) on Pudovkin's manipulation of the non-professional performer in *The Deserter* (1933). Chiarini and Barbaro also state that the director must necessarily resort to manipulation of non-professionals in order to obtain 'reazioni espressive utilizzabili'/'usable expressive reactions' (1941: 142).

[10]At the same time, Raffaello Maggi (1939) argued along the lines of Pende for casting processes focused on biological, aesthetic, and clinical traits. On this debate, see Brunetta (1969: 104); Eugeni (2006: 525–6); Pitassio (2010: 51, n. 32).

casting according to biological or physical type, especially when it comes to southern Italians.

Likewise, the importance devoted to casting according to physiognomic traits by Vittorio De Sica and others can, to some extent, be traced back to the debates of the 1930s. Balázs's work on 'microphysiognomy', for example, was translated in the first part of the anthology on the actor in *Bianco e Nero* in 1938: for the Hungarian theorist, the face of the non-professional (in this case a non-actor from Eisenstein's 1929 *The Old and the New*) functions as a document to be read by the camera (in Chiarini 1938: 204). As we will see in Chapter 2, the neorealist focus on the face as avatar of a new realist attention to physiognomy, announced by De Sica in his 1942 article 'Volti nuovi per un cinema nuovo'/'New Faces for a New Cinema', therefore has a rich pre-history in the debates of the 1930s.

While Barbaro and others recognized the important contribution of the non-professional actor, ultimately they valorized professional training and actorly preparation for the film actor, who was counterposed to the theatre actor, seen as a mere 'translator' of a theatrical text. Some of this training would of course be entrusted to the Centro Sperimentale, which when it began in 1935 offered courses only in acting and directing. In fact, Chiarini, co-founder of the Centro Sperimentale and its first director, went further when he wrote in 1938 that the period of the non-actor was now a remnant of the past: 'caduto il mito del film senza attori'/'the myth of the film without actors having collapsed', he announces (1938: 5), it was clear that film actors needed schools and education. Chiarini's focus on the need for the actor to educate himself and develop good taste (1938: 23) demonstrates, if demonstration were needed, that the debates framing the actor and the non-actor in this period and later are imbricated in ideas of class and cultural capital. Indeed, when Barbaro writes (1937: 20) that non-professionals are indispensable for particular cases such as 'documentari romanzati'/'dramatized documentaries', or settings which need 'authentic actors', for example, 'film di ambienti tropicali o polari, film di particolari classi lavoratrici, pescatori ad esempio'/'films with tropical or arctic settings, films about the working classes or fishermen, for example', we see a clear association of the non-actor with the primitive, the exotic, and the proletarian. Here Barbaro was likely influenced by Pudovkin, who discussed in *Film Technique* how he had worked with Mongols, who were uncultured but good actors (1954: 143). Similarly, in 1930 Balázs (2011: 108) had reflected on the 'primitive physiognomies' of 'exotic races' as excellent cinematic raw material in the films of Flaherty. The connection here to the 'almost colonial attitude' (Pitassio 2019: 276) shown by Italian filmmakers to the casting of southerners is striking, and is something we will encounter at later points in the book.

The legacy of the 1930s, in which Soviet and European theory was filtered through discussions in *Bianco e Nero*, saw the non-professional as both crucial to the development of a new poetics of cinema and as a mere tool in the hands of the director. Both of these views would prove prescient. However, while it has been important for Italian film criticism to understand post-war cinema not as a radical break with the fascist past but as an evolution (see Ricci 2008), it is equally important to understand that the non-professional existed and was used well before the 'new beginning' represented by neorealism.

Earlier uses of the non-professional actor

The 1930s debates referenced here show a widespread attention to the non-professional in the theory of acting, heavily influenced by the Soviets, although neorealist cinema moved beyond mere typage and gave space (within limits) to the expressive and creative potential of the non-actor. And while the non-professional became an 'emblem' of neorealism after the war (Pitassio 2007: 147), a significant earlier tradition of their employment in Italy has been identified by critics (see Noto and Pitassio 2010: 31). Going back to the silent period, Campanella (1956: 127) notes that non-professionals are 'as old as cinema itself', pointing to an example like Lucio D'Ambra's 1916 film *Il re, le torri e gli Alfieri/The King, the Rook, the Bishop*, which he argues is the first Italian film to feature non-professionals, although these were mainly aristocrats rather than the proletarians normally associated with the category. Camerini (1983) even identifies a polemic from 1908 on the use of non-professional actors in films – including dancers, waiters, circus performers, and lion tamers – which risked, it was feared, creating a group of 'spostati'/'misfits' who would never find long-term film employment. This polemic has a strong resonance in the post-war anxieties about the fate of the non-actor, which I will discuss later in the chapter and book, but it suffices to say that the recruitment of non-professionals with no training was common, such as the discovery of Bartolomeo Pagano, a stevedore from Genoa who went on to play the heroic slave Maciste in over two dozen films between 1914 and 1926, becoming an international star (see Reich 2015).

It is the use of the non-professional actor by certain Italian directors of the 1930s, however, which is thought to presage neorealism, as seen in Alessandro Blasetti's films *Sole/Sun* (1929) and *1860* (1934). Pitassio (2019: 285), for example, notes the importance of Blasetti for 'tracing a lineage between inter-war and post-war filmmaking', and Blasetti was cited approving by Barbaro (1937), Chiarini and Barbaro (1941), Renzi (1948), and Rossellini (in Rossellini and Verdone 1952) for his realist use of 'types'. Other directors of the fascist period adopted similar practices, such as Gioacchino Forzano for his propaganda film *Camicia nera/Black Shirt* (1933). While Forzano erroneously claimed this was the first Italian film to use ordinary people instead of professional actors (Griffith 1995: 300), in private he lamented that several of the protagonists he had recruited from the countryside near Rome ran away during filming in protest at the low pay, and he had to involve police to retrieve them (ibid.: 301). Forzano's view of the non-professional, then, was surely motivated by economic advantages, as well as by artistic ones, and he further claimed that avoiding professionals was helpful as you avoided the petty creative rivalries that marred other films (Vitti 2019: 73).[11]

Other Italian directors such as Giorgio Ferroni (in *L'ebbrezza del cielo/The Thrill of the Skies*, 1940) and Francesco De Robertis (*Uomini sul fondo/Men on the Sea Floor*, 1941) used non-professionals in their war films, and in fact Commander Nicola Morabito who played himself in the latter film went on to become a good character actor in post-war cinema (Campanella 1956). The use of non-professionals in 'documentari narrativi'/'*narrative documentaries*' (Caminati 2011: 62) which mixed fact and fiction means they are regarded as some of the numerous 'precursors' to neorealism; this teleological account of neorealism (Leavitt 2020: 175) positions *Uomini sul fondo* (a film on which Rossellini collaborated with De Robertis) alongside Rossellini's 'war trilogy' of narrative documentaries, particularly the first instalment, *La nave bianca/The White Ship* (1941), as the key link to the post-war.[12] In 1950, critic Franco Venturini in his essay exploring the origins of neorealism highlighted the importance of these films' use of types in opening a 'nuova via al cinema italiano'/'new direction for Italian cinema' (Venturini 1950: 44). While I do not have the space here to engage in detailed discussion of documentary, it is clear that the non-professional actor of documentary (who is juxtaposed with the professional actor in the other films of Rossellini's 'war trilogy', *Un pilota ritorna/A Pilot Returns* (1942) and *L'uomo della croce/The Man with the Cross* (1943)) is a key figure who has been neglected by critics and who should be studied as a performer rather than just a type.[13] I will return to this figure in Chapter 5.

Another film of fascist propaganda, Goffredo Alessandrini's well-known *Luciano Serra, pilota/Luciano Serra, Pilot* (1938), which brought Amedeo Nazzari to stardom, employed a different type of non-professional: shot

---

[11]A film like *La fossa degli angeli/Tomb of the Angels* (Bragaglia, 1937), filmed on location in the Apuan Alps in Tuscany, was also praised at the time for its use of real quarrymen alongside stars. See Bragaglia (1937) for discussion of this. Actress Elsa De' Giorgi recalls how Mario Camerini cast 'real working-class women' as patients in the hospital scene in *T'amerò sempre/I'll Always Love You* (1933) which made it difficult for her to weep in front of them (in Comand 2022: 25).

[12]See O'Leary (2008: 284) on the 'paradoxical effect' generated by teleological discourses on neorealism, 'of asserting that anything of quality, including that which comes before, centrifugally derives from it'.

[13]See Caminati (2011) for further details on debates on documentary in the 1930s, and Pitassio (2019: 141–202) for a slightly contrasting take.

partly on location in colonial Eritrea, the film used Eritreans in order to recreate the Italian invasion of Ethiopia. Alessandrini recalled (in Savio 1979a: 33) that these *askaris* or local soldiers had just finished fighting for Italy so they were trained to obey Italians and were grateful to be ordered! He went on to discuss (ibid.: 38) how in his 1939 *Abuna Messias*, also shot in Eritrea, the indigenous locals recruited to play themselves didn't understand what they needed to do and had to be kicked and whipped to perform.

These problematic casting practices were seen in other colonial films such as Romolo Marcellini's *Sentinelle di bronzo/Sentinels of Bronze* (1937), set in Somalia, and the Libya-shot *Lo squadrone bianco/The White Squadron* (Genina, 1936). Ben-Ghiat (2015: 158) points out how indigenous participation in these films 'relied on and furthered a system of colonial labor'. The non-actors, recruited by a variety of methods including jungle drums, were ultimately 'subject to the same practices of surveillance and exploitation that marked Fascism's African occupations in general' (ibid.: 7), and recruitment of film extras in the colonies replicates other labour practices in the imperial 'contact zone' (see Fortmueller 2016). While these coercive directorial techniques anticipate some of the practices we will see used on Italian non-actors in the post-war period, Ben-Ghiat (2015: 110) notes the specificity of the colonial power relation here in 'taming' the actors, saying accurately that 'the submission of the indigenous to the will of the director and the camera stand[s] in for obedience to Fascist political authority'. It is also intriguing to reflect upon the way that Italian productions descending upon colonial villages disrupted local relationships and 'exacerbated bad feelings' (ibid.: 8), making participants re-enact recent deadly battles without any attention to local tensions and loyalties.

While the use of African non-professionals in Italian colonial film deserves further study, with Ben-Ghiat thus far the only scholar to address it, even in passing, it points to a more capacious understanding of the non-professional in this period than has been generally alluded to, as well as alluding to the power dynamics and problematic exploitation commonly found in their recruitment and use. It is clear, though, that beyond the canonical examples of realist films by Blasetti and De Robertis and a few others, there were, in fact, myriad examples of untrained individuals, 'found' in different ways, being placed in front of a camera.

Modes of recruitment: Sports, beauty contests, competitions

By the 1940s there was much criticism of the established theatrical tradition and the way that theatre actors were being used in cinema: attacks on their rhetorical acting style were commonplace (see Paolucci 1939; Pietrangeli 1944; Marinese 1946; Bolchi 1951; Jandelli 2013). While debates raged about the distinctions between theatre and cinema actors, as Pitassio (2010: 45) points out, the first acting teachers at the Centro Sperimentale were in fact principally drawn from the stage. And there was simultaneously appreciation for the numerous actors from the popular stage and *rivista* who appeared on film, who brought a freshness and dialectal style to film. This 'nuova massiccia operazione di innesto di elementi teatrali nel cinema'/'massive new infusion of theatrical performers into the cinema' (Brunetta 1995: 206) went beyond those actors who became internationally known through neorealism, such as Aldo Fabrizi and Anna Magnani, and included comics such as Totò, Macario, Eduardo De Filippo, Angelo Musco, and Dina Galli (see Gundle 2013: 48–9).

The perceived weakness of the Centro Sperimentale as a training operation remained a concern, as it was deemed incapable of producing the new faces required to revive cinema.[14] In the absence of a robust training school, actors were often produced in other sectors. One of these under-examined areas of recruitment was from sport: in numerous films of the 1930s sportsmen made appearances as actors. By 1944, in fact, journalist and screenwriter Antonio Pietrangeli, in lambasting the entire cohort of Italian screen actors since 1930, reserved special ire for sportsmen and singers, whom he alleged were only favoured by producers to increase revenue, decrying their 'incapacità a qualsiasi forma di espressione'/'inability to express themselves in any way' (1944: 4).[15] Pietrangeli named three former professional boxers, Enzo Fiermonte, Erminio Spalla, and Primo Carnera, all of whom appeared in numerous Italian films from the late 1930s onwards. Fiermonte recounted how he was approached on Via Veneto in Rome: he initially thought he was being sexually importuned, so his story mirrors those of dozens of girls who ended up working in cinema, as we'll see in Chapter 3. He was cast in *L'ultimo combattimento/The Last Fight* (Ballerini, 1940) as a boxer, but later went on to do a wide variety of roles, and notched up over 100 film appearances. When interviewed about his career in the 1970s, Fiermonte was keen to distinguish himself from both Spalla and Carnera, dubbing the latter 'immobile', and 'un bonaccione, che prima di fargli dire una battuta ci volevano due anni'/'a gentle giant, who took two years to say a single line of dialogue' (in Savio 1979b: 540).[16]

---

[14]On the Centro Sperimentale, see Mida (1943); Ferreri (1944); Chiarini (1951c); Barbaro (1951); Brunetta (1982: 249).
[15]Pietrangeli also names the opera stars Beniamino Gigli, Tito Schipa, Alberto Rabagliati, and Ferruccio Tagliavini, all of whom moved into cinema in the 1930s and 1940s. See Pescatore (2001) on the opera film and its stars.
[16]Martera (2021: 116–17) discusses the interesting case of Ludovico Longo, a mixed-race Italian boxer (and later maths professor) cast in Gallone's *Harlem* (1943). Longo appeared alongside hundreds of Black South Africans taken from the prisoner of war camp in Cinecittà.

While in the early 1930s there was an occasional use of sportsmen such as former Serie A striker Pietro Pastore, cast as a steelworker in Ruttman's Soviet-influenced *Acciaio*, among other films, and rugby players used in Campogalliani's 1934 *Stadio/Stadium* (see Campanella 1956: 127–8), it was in the late 1930s that a more widespread attempt was made to introduce variegated 'new faces' to the budding Italian star system (see Brunetta 1995: 242). Certain production companies such as Scalera were particularly known for employing sportsmen and entertainers in an effort to dominate the box office in the late 1930s and early 1940s (Farassino 2003: 221). In the midst of now-forgotten appearances by fencer Ciro Verratti in adventure film *Il corsaro nero/The Black Corsair* (Palermi, 1937) and tennis player Renato Bossi who appeared in several films in the early 1940s, several new stars emerged from the preference for athletic types. Guido Celano was, by his own account, a gymnast who moved into stunt work and then into speaking parts throughout the 1930s and 1940s (in Savio 1979a: 298). Massimo Serato, an expert javelin thrower, was spotted in a search for extras with an athletic physique and later went on to study acting and to a lengthy career (Savio 1979c: 997).

Water polo champion Massimo Girotti also got his break in cinema because his trainer was set designer Fulvio Jacchia, who recommended him to Mario Soldati as a 'new face' for his film *Dora Nelson* (1939) (see Savio 1979b: 603). Girotti broke out as a star firstly in *La corona di ferro/The Iron Crown* (Blasetti, 1941) and then with Visconti's *Ossessione/Obsession* (1943), partly due to his physique and his 'untheatrical' performance style. Gundle notes (2019: 98), interestingly, that 'his athleticism was of a type taken for granted in Hollywood where it had been turned explicitly into a trope by Douglas Fairbanks and the swimming champion-turned-actor Johnny Weissmuller (the first cinematic Tarzan)'.[17] For male sports stars, crossing over to cinema due to particular physical attributes did not necessarily cause them issues, as the huge success of post-war star Raf Vallone, who successfully turned to film after a career in top-flight football, demonstrated (see O'Rawe 2020a). For women, though, it was often a different matter.

Competitions

The girls who emerged as stars in the post-war period via beauty contests, such as Sophia Loren, Gina Lollobrigida, and Silvana Mangano, among others, have been much discussed and celebrated, and will be addressed in

---

[17]In fact, Pietrangeli (1944: 4) criticized Girotti's 'intepretazioni "tarzanesche"'/'"Tarzan-esque" roles' – apart from in *Ossessione*.

detail in Chapter 4. Yet the post-war pipeline from magazine competitions and contests to the film industry was not a new one, as Saponari (2017) shows: magazines in the 1930s such as *Stelle* held competitions to find new faces for the film industry and girls were encouraged to send in their photographs.[18] The most celebrated star search was undoubtedly producer and publisher Angelo Rizzoli's competition to find the heroine of his new film, *La signora di tutti/Everybody's Woman* (Öphuls, 1934). The film launched Isa Miranda who became one of Italy's biggest stars.[19] Parigi (2008: 255) discusses a 1938 competition launched by the magazine *Le Grandi Firme* to find *La Signorina Grandi Firme*, from which 'La vincitrice verrà lanciata nel cinema dalla casa di produzione di Giuseppe Amato'/'the winning girl will be launched in the cinema by the production company of Giuseppe Amato'.[20] Dina Sassoli also famously won a 1939 competition run by the magazine *Film* and the production company Scalera, and went on to a long career (see Lancia and Poppi 2003a: 326). Other female stars of the 1930s who became stars through competitions of various kinds were Orietta Fiume, Laura Solari, and Elsa de' Giorgi. Furthermore, in the late 1930s, the magazine *Tempo* launched the wildly successful national competition '5000 lire per un sorriso'/'5000 lire for a smile', led by Dino Villani (again in collaboration with Zavattini);[21] Villani would go on in 1946 to launch the Miss Italia contest, to be discussed in a later section.

The acute economic pressures of the post-war period, the changing media landscape, including the rise of illustrated *fotoromanzi*, and the growth and diversification of film publications and the popular press (De Berti 2000: 111; Vitella 2015: 53) combined to drive the increased proximity of film fans to the industry and encourage their 'produttività spettatoriale'/'spectatorial productivity' as active fans (Vitella 2016: 154).[22] The partnerships between magazines and production companies that helped stimulate the growth of the Italian film industry in the late 1940s, and the transformation of popular culture also opened up a bigger aspirational space for girls in particular. As Gundle notes, 'the spread of the medium [of cinema] was accompanied,

---

[18] See Calvino (1940) on the search for the child star of Soldati's *Piccolo mondo antico/The Little World of the Past*. See also the search for new faces for the cinema industry launched in the pages of *Cinema* on 10 April 1937.
[19] See Gundle (2013: 126–7).
[20] The proposed film ended up being *Bionda sotto chiave/Blonde Under Lock and Key* (Mastrocinque, 1939), written by Zavattini and starring established actress Vivi Gioi.
[21] The winner of the 1941 version of the contest, Adriana Serra, was offered film contracts and appeared in a number of pre- and post-war films, starting with *La prigione/The Prison* (Cerio, 1943). See Lancia and Poppi (2003a: 336). The film *Due milioni per un sorriso/Two Million for a Smile* (Borghesio and Soldati, 1939), whose plot features a search for a girl star, includes a moralistic message about the virtues of *not* being an actress.
[22] See also Comand (2020).

driven even, by the numerous competitions, beauty contests and searches for "new faces", which proliferated in the 1940s' (2019: 74–5).

Some examples of the post-war competitions run by magazines can help demonstrate this: the magazine *Star* ran several searches for new talent, including a competition in August 1945 in partnership with Ambrosia Film to find the star of the film *L'angelo e il diavolo*/*The Angel and the Devil* (Camerini, 1946), written by Zavattini. The magazine called upon female readers who had a 'simple and lively beauty' and dreams of cinema fame, counselling them that 'non tutti i sogni sono ingannevoli e non tutte le ambizioni sono sbagliate'/'not all dreams are deceptive and not all ambitions are mistaken' (Anon. 1945: 3), thus hitting a note of concern about female ambition which, as we will see in Chapter 3, was to become more and more pronounced as the 1940s went on. The eventual star of the film was actually an established face of pre-war Italian cinema, Carla del Poggio, illustrating the extent to which many of these searches were mere marketing ploys (see Pierini 2016–17: 38). However, the magazine's comment in September (Borselli 1945) that they had been overwhelmed with letters, many of them written under false names as the girls' mothers, boyfriends, and husbands were suspiciously checking their mail, speaks to the still widespread suspicion of film acting for girls, in tandem with its growing appeal.

One of the key players in the popular press-to-cinema pipeline was the magazine *Hollywood*, launched in 1945. Sarah Culhane's detailed work (2017a) on the magazine's relationship with its readers via competitions and letters pages shows *Hollywood*'s role in the unearthing of new faces for the film industry. In 1950, for example, the magazine launched a competition in conjunction with the production company Taurus Film. As with the competition in *Star*, the pictures submitted by aspiring actresses were published in the magazine, alongside those of American and Italian stars. This fits into a broader pattern by which ordinary Italian girls achieved a level of visibility, even if not of actual stardom, through the widespread reproduction of their image in the popular press.[23]

In another example, Gundle (1999: 366) notes that *La Domenica degli Italiani* (the illustrated weekly supplement to the Milanese newspaper the *Corriere d'Informazione*) between 1945 and 1946 would publish photos of anonymous young female readers.[24] Another newspaper, the *Corriere*

---

[23] These developments went hand in hand with the growth of photography as a mass activity: see Grespi (2015: 184) on this. Zavattini's original 1938 treatment for *Signorina Grandi Firme* (Zavattini 2021: 40–9) dwelled on girls constantly being photographed on the street.

[24] According to Cicognetti and Servetti (1996: 558), the magazine *Tempo* printed mostly women on its covers (29 out of 50 in 1946), with unknowns and stars alternating. This phenomenon is referred to ironically by Marcello Mastroianni's photographer character in *La fortuna di essere donna*/*What a Woman!* (Blasetti, 1956) who says he spotted a half-starving girl at Ostia, took

Lombardo, in December 1945 published a picture of a pretty girl taken on the street and asked readers to identify her. They went on to publish photographs of 'authentic' Italian girls on the streets, calling it a 'respectful persecution' (ibid.). This kind of 'stalking' of Italian girls, which has resonances with the theory developed by Cesare Zavattini of *pedinamento* or 'shadowing' the potential cinematic character as a neorealist practice (see Margulies 2019: 56), establishes a dynamic between the press and these young female subjects that sees them as prey, but also as themselves predatory.

The winners of these competitions were almost never heard from again, although Berti (1953) points to both Luciana Vedovelli and Liliana Bonfatti as girls who had won magazine competitions and had then been offered film parts: Bonfatti's friend apparently sent in her picture to director Luciano Emmer who then cast her in his *Le ragazze di Piazza di Spagna/ The Girls of Piazza di Spagna* (1952). Yet, what is key here is the visibility of young attractive women and the opening up of this media space in a kind of democratizing impulse, or what Masi (2003: 343) calls 'una sorta di immensa lotteria popolare'/'a sort of immense popular lottery', albeit one that by definition excluded girls who were not considered conventionally attractive.

By the early 1950s, Loren, Lollobrigida, Silvana Mangano, Silvana Pampanini, Lucia Bosè, and others were starring in some of the most popular Italian films. Most of them emerged via beauty contests, as well as, in some cases, modelling for *fotoromanzi*. This 'accidental' stardom often turned out to be a product of the synergy of the press and the film industry. As Pitassio (2019: 293) notes:

> This new female stardom was not a spontaneous phenomenon. It was, rather, part of the national film industry's strategies. A key player in fostering post-war original stardom was Lux Film, where then world-renowned producers Dino De Laurentiis and Carlo Ponti put their hands to the plough.

Ponti and De Laurentiis were regular figures on the juries for beauty contests, along with writers and directors such as Zavattini, De Sica, and Visconti, and actors like Gino Cervi and Totò.[25] The synergies between neorealist production and casting methods and beauty contests are obvious, and as Parigi (2008: 252) comments:

---

her photos, and got them published in *Tempo*. Now, he says, she is married to a producer and owns a villa.

[25] As is well known, Ponti married Sophia Loren, and De Laurentiis Silvana Mangano, and both men had a strong controlling interest in their wives' careers.

> Nel dopoguerra, Zavattini è contemporaneamente l'ispiratore del concorso Miss Italia e di *Ladri di biciclette*. A prima vista sembrano due eventi inconciliabili. Nonostante appaia paradossale, essi nascono dallo stesso principio etico ed estetico: distruggere le strutture tradizionali della finzione, curvare il cinema verso l'orizzonte della vissuto, innalzare la vita quotidiana al rango dello spettacolo.[26]

The beauty contest as institution was transversal: the left promoted more wholesome versions of Miss Italia such as *Stellina dell'Unità* and *Miss Vie Nuove* in the same period, to find 'ragazze comuni'/'ordinary girls' (Zilioli 2019: 16).[27] Again, figures such as Zavattini, De Sica, and Visconti were judges; Ponti and De Laurentiis were also fixtures on the left-wing jury circuit, demonstrating a continuum between 'neorealist' practice and a more institutionalized mode of finding new faces (and bodies).[28] These supposedly more progressive beauty contests[29] resulted in some small film parts for the winners, but showed on all sides of the political and aesthetic spectrum, 'the unquestioned right for men to judge women' (Hipkins 2016: 147), although some on the left decried the practice as degrading, or as a commodification of female beauty (see Zilioli 2019: 14). In addition, when we come to examine further the self-narratives of some of the beauty queens in Chapter 4, we will see how, as Hipkins (2016: 148) notes, 'the beauty cult and anxiety about controlling female consumption and ambition collided'.

Chance and design

While chance prevailed heavily in narratives of accidental stardom or discovery in the post-war period, there was in fact a structuring tension between chance and design in the recruitment of new faces. As Gundle writes (2019: 306), 'there were three main ways in which people without

---

[26]'In the post-war period, Zavattini is simultaneously the brains behind the Miss Italia pageant and *Bicycle Thieves*. These seem at first sight irreconcilable. Although it appears paradoxical, they both spring from the same ethical and aesthetic principle: the destruction of the traditional structures of fiction, bending cinema towards lived live, and elevating daily life to the level of spectacle.'

[27]See also Gundle (1999) and (2000: 67–9) on these phenomena.

[28]See Leprini (2018: 183–9).

[29]A 1950 piece in the Communist Party-affiliated *L'Unità* asked the readers, 'sapete che differenza passa fra l'elezione della stellina dell'Unità e quelle elezioni che i giornali a rotocalco lanciano ogni giorno per distribuire titoli di miss a destra e a sinistra? Semplicissimo. Alle elezioni dell'«Unità» la stellina si veste …. Alle altre elezioni la miss … si sveste'/'do you know what the difference is between the Stellina dell'Unità competition and those that popular magazines launch every day to give out "Miss" titles left, right, and centre? It's very simple. In the *Unità* contest the girls are dressed, in the others they undress.' Quoted in Zilioli (2019: 14).

previous experience were cast in postwar films: through being spotted on the street, through open auditions and by means of competitions of one sort or another'. I have already mentioned competitions and will discuss these further in Chapter 3, but will now turn to the other two modes of recruitment.

Chance discovery is a core narrative of Hollywood stardom, as McNally argues (2021: 25). She quotes David Thomson on how Hollywood 'stardom films' like *What Price Hollywood?* (Cukor, 1932 – later remade as *A Star Is Born*) show 'the chanciness of elevation, the way any pretty face could be the right one given the right circumstances'. I have shown how this spotting of potential stars on the street has a particular focus on girls, and indeed Edgar Morin in his classic study of stardom (2005: 40) associates it with a presumptively male gaze: 'every pretty girl can say "why not me?"', noting how Silvana Mangano was accosted on the street to be invited for the screen test that brought her fame. There are dozens of examples of this type of 'serendipity' even before the war, many of them girls, including stars Marina Berti, Maria Denis, Assia Noris, and Laura Nucci, all stopped on the street by producers or directors (see Gundle 2013: 111).

However, the power of contingency extended to both genders: many male actors were also found in this accidental way. One example here will suffice: Carlo Battisti, the university professor selected to play the protagonist of De Sica's classic *Umberto D.* (1952), wrote a book about his experience. He confirmed (Battisti 1955: 10) that he was walking down the street in Rome when he was approached by people who transpired to be the film's producers. They shouted, 'è lui, è Umberto D.!'/'It's him, it's Umberto D.!' and invited the confused man, who thought they were perhaps police officers, to come for an audition.

Unlike some other adventitious protagonists we will hear from, Battisti was highly educated, a full professor of glottology at Florence University, and reflected extensively on his experience of surprise recruitment and semi-stardom. He realized that he had been chosen by De Sica purely for his 'abito somatico'/'somatic features' (ibid.: 19) rather than for his character or potential acting ability. This was a defining characteristic of De Sica's casting practice, as we will see in the next chapter, when we encounter young Enzo Staiola, recruited near the set of *Bicycle Thieves* due to his amazing face. De Sica's close collaborator Zavattini was a huge influence on this practice, with his obsessive desire for a 'materialità autentica'/'authentic materiality' of the non-actor, and the 'massima coincidenza tra personaggio e attore, tra persona e personaggio, tra essenza e apparenza, tra sostanza e forma'/'maximum coincidence between character and actor, between person and character, between essence and appearance, between substance and form' (Parigi 2014: 73–4).

The third modality of recruitment mentioned by Gundle is the open audition: this can be conflated more broadly with the 'star search' typical of Hollywood and also used in earlier Italian cinema. This more systematic approach to rooting out new faces was adopted by many directors of the period, including Vittorio De Sica, who put out radio adverts looking for the stars of *Bicycle Thieves* (Bruni 2022: 14–15): I will look briefly at two examples of searches for protagonists which have been, luckily, well documented: Castellani's *Two Cents of Hope* (1952) and De Sica's *Il tetto/The Roof* (1955).

In 1951 Renato Castellani began to recruit for his third film using non-professionals, after *Sotto il sole di Roma/Under the Roman Sun* (1948) and *È primavera…/It's Forever Springtime* (1950). *Two Cents of Hope* was to be shot in southern Italy, near Naples, but evidence we have of Castellani's search for protagonists suggests it was focused on Rome. Castellani had carried out a similar search in Rome for his first film, during which the production team went round peripheral areas of Rome with loudspeakers announcing the details, looking for male and female working-class youth, who were then auditioned in local gyms (I.A.M. 1948). When that failed, as was the case with the search for *Sotto il sole di Roma*'s female lead, he apparently was persuaded to consult a soothsayer, who dangled a pendulum over a map of Rome and announced that their star was in Trastevere. This was indeed where they came across Liliana Mancini (see Trasatti 1984: 46).

For *Two Cents of Hope*, Castellani and his team went about recruitment more systematically. They eventually found the female star, Maria Fiore, in Quarticciolo, a fascist-era working-class district to the south-east of Rome. Fiore has talked about her experience of the casting process, which I will detail further in Chapter 3. Her account of being approached while she was playing in the street with local boys (in Cavicchioli 1961a: 9) leans heavily on the narrative of chance and a characteristic denial of ambition for girls, as she rudely told the production team to clear off. However, documents in the archive of the Museo del Cinema in Turin show us that the production company Universalcine were scouting quite systematically in poor areas of Rome (confirmed in Solleville 1952b).[30] This evidence, and Fiore's testimony, contradicts the fabricated account published in the trade press at the time (L.U. 1951), presumably supplied by the production, of Castellani 'discovering' Maria in a picturesque village near Naples, and spotting her as she stood on her simple geranium-filled balcony. The production files have typed lists of girls' names and addresses, occasionally with ages scribbled alongside and, even more rarely, telephone numbers. In a couple of instances there is a brief description: one girl is marked as 'brunetta in nero'/'brunette

---

[30]In fact, in a 1952 interview Castellani said that he liked to 'divide Rome into quarters – like the Germans used to do to round up suspects'. He continues his problematic analogy by saying that he would line up potential actors in the street and start 'eliminating' them (Mitgang 1952).

in black', while another is designated simply 'pacioccona'/'plump and jolly'! Yet another is 'naso lungo ma spiritosa'/'long nose but funny'.

Many are from Quarticciolo, but there are also girls from other working-class areas such as Tiburtino, San Lorenzo, and Trastevere. Interestingly, a number of girls' addresses are listed as 'Campo Profughi Centocelle' – this was one of the Displaced Persons camps operating in Italy until the 1960s, hosting refugees from Istria-Dalmatia after Yugoslavia took possession of the territories after the war, as well as other displaced groups. The lists, from March 1951, indicate that these girls have been selected for invitation to an audition (presumably at a film studio) that week. One list is headed 'girls photographed' and a handwritten note reads 'annuncio sui quotidiani'/'notice in the papers', suggesting that this might be a story placed in the press to generate more publicity for the film, consistent with the promotional use of non-professionals as part of the branding of neorealism (see Pitassio 2015).

One of the names listed is Iolanda di Fiore, later renamed Maria when she was cast in the film. While the search, from Fiore's testimony, seemed to involve visiting the relevant locations and looking around for suitable girls of the right age, a note beside another girl's name indicates that she is the daughter of the 'macchinista' or technician of the same name, presumably a reference to a studio worker. This suggests that the Italian system of *raccomandazione* might still be working, and widespread poverty often led people to beg for chances to audition for films. Fiore's photographs, taken in the studio, are included in the file, and they show a diffident young girl in a polka-dot sweater, looking uncertainly at the camera. She later recalled being overwhelmed and tearful at the audition experience (Anon. 1951a), and in only one of her pictures does she break out the smile that became famous when she played Carmela in the film. The other girls' photographs, all professionally lit and shot, show them with a range of expressions, from thoughtful to lively. They are mostly dressed plainly, in blouses and cardigans, perhaps trying to match the character of Carmela the *popolana*. As Barthes notes, the effect of the photograph is 'not to restore what has been abolished (by time, by distance) but to attest that what I see has indeed existed' (1981: 82), and while these girls, apart from Fiore, disappeared into the black hole of history, the photos remain to tell us that they once dreamed, briefly, of cinema.[31]

Il tetto was De Sica's supposed 'return' to neorealism after his ill-fated collaboration with producer David O. Selznick on *Stazione Termini* (1953). His recourse to the non-professional actor after working with stars like Jennifer Jones and Montgomery Clift (and with Totò, Sophia Loren, and Silvana Mangano on his 1954 *L'oro di Napoli/The Gold of Naples*) was seen, at this stage, as 'anachronistic' (Aristarco 1956) and out of step with

---

[31] Sadly I am unable to reproduce the photographs here due to copyright restrictions.

contemporary production practices in Italy, in the era of 'Hollywood on the Tiber'. Rather than relying on some of the new Italian stars, De Sica launched an intense and almost obsessive search for the two non-actors to star in *Il tetto* as a young working-class Roman couple desperate for housing, declaring that he wanted spectators to feel as if the strangers they saw on screen could be themselves (Birri 1999: 25). The costly search lasted six months and saw thousands of ordinary people photographed and auditioned (Cristofani and Manetti 1956: 180; Birri 1999). De Sica travelled across Italy north and south, visiting factories, army barracks, naval yards, and schools. He placed adverts in newspapers and on the walls of Terracina, a coastal town south of Rome, inviting girls aged between sixteen and twenty-one to come for auditions at the Titanus studios in Rome. The two successful protagonists were Giorgio Listuzzi, a football goalkeeper who played for Serie C. team Ponziana in Trieste, and Gabriella Pallotta, a secretary from Rome. Listuzzi was stopped on the street in Trieste, while Pallotta saw the advert and turned up at the studio. The documentation of this search – published in a contemporaneous *inchiesta* in *Cinema Nuovo* (Martini 1955) and then in a 1956 book edited by Michele Gandin – enables us to draw some conclusions. The desperation, whether for fame, money, or escape from a humdrum background, comes across in interviews and in photos, and the material stakes were clearly high, judging by the thousands who turned up to the open-call auditions.

Although De Sica was on record (quoted in Birri 1999: 25) as saying that he needed an actor with the hands of a builder to be convincing (in line with Zavattini's strict line on casting non-professionals in accordance with their own social type), Listuzzi, as noted, was a footballer and not a builder. He was cast because of his physique and appearance, in line with De Sica's 'somatic casting'.[32] Listuzzi admitted (in De Santi and De Sica 1999: 23) that during the audition he blushed when told his character's wife was pregnant, and he thinks this genuine reaction secured him the role. The focus on physiognomy for which De Sica had become notorious in casting *Bicycle Thieves* and *Umberto D.* can also be seen clearly in the many photographs reproduced in the book about the film. As well as images of people queuing in the studios for the auditions and De Sica inspecting them, there is a series of photos of individual would-be actors: these are head-and-shoulders or full-length shots, and what is striking about them is that each person looking at the camera is holding a card with their name on it.

The viewer is immediately struck by the resemblance of these images to criminal mugshots: while the divergence from professional headshots, the lack of glamour, and poor lighting all testify to these individuals'

---

[32] De Sica (in Gandin 1956: 240) said he looked at the 'fisico'/'physical appearance' first and afterwards ascertained if they might be able to act.

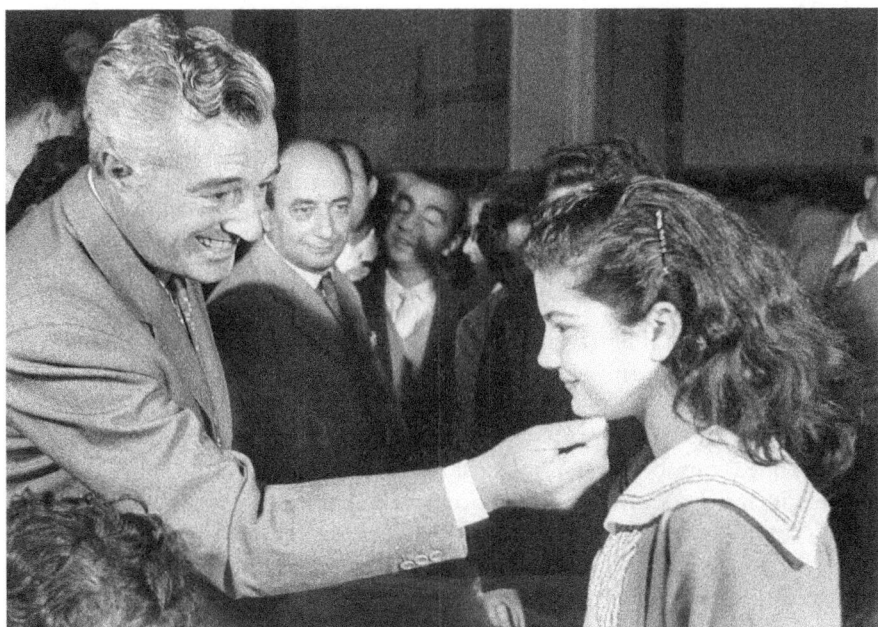

FIGURE 2 *Vittorio De Sica inspects an aspiring actress at auditions for* The Roof. *Photo Credit: © SZ Photo/Max Scheler/Bridgeman Images.*

position as non-actors, the combination of the pose and the labelling of them edges them towards another type of classification. While clearly the archive of photos was designed to remind the director and producers of all the faces they had seen in the six-month search, the camera gaze on the faces, some eager, some diffident, speaks to the function of the mugshot, when it was created in the late nineteenth century, in othering potential criminals or subaltern people: 'mugshots played a part in the construction of subjective notions of "the other", "the lesser" or "sub-human" on the grounds of class, race and religion' (Lashmar 2014: 68–9). There is, in the classificatory gaze of De Sica and his team, an echo of this use of the mugshot as a tool of power: in this case, of course, it is the power to select the lucky individuals from their background and offer them a chance to earn money and distinguish themselves, rather than anything more punitive.[33] Yet the focus on the 'type' which we have seen working its way through discussion of the non-professional in Italy has the corollary

---

[33]Pitassio (2002: 253) notes that Eisenstein had already made this connection between casting the type and criminal anthropology, writing in the 1930s that the director could learn from the police how to examine faces.

of legitimating and normalizing this typologizing gaze, with all its inherent limitations, producing a 'generalizzazione del singolare'/'generalization of the singular' (Pitassio 2002: 22). As Pitassio says (2019: 287), 'in the postwar era, non-professional performers often worked as types, bringing to films their complexion, face, and behaviour according to a limited typology, either geographical (the Southerner, the Roman) or social (the worker, the fisherman, the policeman, the rice picker)'. Alongside this typological instinct, the inclusion of a photo of famous boxer Tiberio Mitri, who had already begun acting in films, auditioning at Titanus alongside Pallotta, returns us to the use of the 'athletic type' that began in the late 1930s, as well as alluding to the presence in films in the early 1950s of former boxers such as Renato Tontini and, of course, generating valuable publicity for the film.

De Sica protested that the search for non-professionals was not a money-saving endeavour, because it had cost him more than 10 million lire. Yet this, as we will see, is a frequent accusation levelled at the use of the non-actor. In fact, *Il tetto* was the object of complaints from the actors' union, which called out (in Anon. 1955) 'l'imperversare in tutti i settori dello spettacolo italiano di attori e di elementi improvvisati, l'inesistenza di una qualsiasi tutela della nostra nobilissima professione'/'the damage inflicted on all sectors of Italian entertainment by unqualified actors, the non-existence of any care for our noble professions' as 'mali che affliggono la nostra categoria'/'evils afflicting our category', specifically in relation to this film.[34] In calling for a register of professional actors to distinguish them from 'aspiranti', the union is weighing in on the economic and artistic danger represented by the non-professional. However, as we will see, this debate had been raging for quite some time.

Debates on the non-professional

The initial excitement at the use of non-professionals was very quickly coloured with scepticism and doubt. While the impact of *Rome Open City* and *Shoeshine*, especially internationally, seemed to respond to the earlier cries by Pietrangeli and others for a revitalization of Italian cinema through its acting corps, unqualified praise did not last long. Pitassio (2019: 277) observes that 'from the late 1940s, a series of patronising articles and commentaries appeared discussing the perils that non-professional performers underwent, having been deceived in their naivete by cinema and show business'. By early 1948, debates on the dangers of the non-professional had begun, and by the early 1950s these became 'systematic' (Pitassio 2007: 149). There are

---

[34]See also Russo (1955).

three broad and interlinked tendencies in these debates: firstly, they focus on the economic risk non-professionals represent to the Italian film industry; secondly, the artistic danger they incarnate; and thirdly, a specifically gendered take on the problem, which considered the 'risk' posed by the girls who won beauty contests and arrived in the industry through a range of routes that eschewed conventional training.

By 1948, as Pitassio notes (ibid.), a critique of the non-professional based on their potential or real threat to the economic success of the film industry had emerged. By then the type of film seen as canonically neorealist was in decline (Visconti's 1948 *La terra trema*, as we will see in the next chapter, is widely thought to be the beginning of the end for this type of production), so the debate, like the broader debate on neorealism, is almost retrospective, 'una sistemazione après coup'/'a settling of accounts after the fact' (ibid.).[35] By August 1948 screenwriter Steno was able to include among his satirical list of 'inevitable characters of the neorealist film' 'pescatori siculi, contadini di una cooperativa, reduci, camionisti, e rurali a scelta'/'Sicilian fishermen, peasants from a co-operative, ex-soldiers, lorry drivers, and various rural types' (Steno 1989). By 1950 an editorial in *Araldo dello Spettacolo* (Anon. 1950a) declared the use of non-professionals a 'ciclo utile esaurito'/'useful but now exhausted cycle' that the public had had enough of. This awareness of casting clichés predates what we now think of as some of the key theorizing of the non-professional and neorealism, in essays by Cesare Zavattini, that didn't appear until 1952–3.[36] What we can see is an attempt by critics and industry figures to come to terms with the redefinition of the actor in Italian cinema, which would have far-reaching consequences. Pistorio's point (1949) that the romantic idea of the actor as artist was being challenged by the non-professional, as the actor became mere raw material for the director, is accurate.[37]

By 1948 articles were appearing that pointed to unforeseen repercussions of a widespread use of the non-professional: Ilario Fiore in *Rivista del Cinematografo* argued that the low pay accepted by non-professionals was a threat not only to the star system but also to the structure of the film industry full stop. He worried that 'al posto di Amedeo Nazzari, lavora Oscar Blando, Massimo Girotti viene sostituito da un fattorino in servizio sulla camionale Genova-Serravale Scrivia,

---

[35] See also Dagrada (2017: 211) on the lateness of the debates.
[36] Zavattini's essays 'Alcune idee sul cinema'/'Some Ideas on Cinema' and 'Tesi sul neorealismo'/'Theses on Neorealism' appeared in 1952 and 1953, respectively. By 1953, Leavitt argues (2020: 174), neorealism had become a 'national mythology', partly through Zavattini's essays.
[37] This is analogous to Zavattini's opposition (in 'Theses on Neorealism') to the concept of the 'attore-sacerdote'/'actor-as-high-priest' (Zavattini 2002: 749).

Maria Denis e Mariella Lotti, dall'operaia del reparto 13 della Fiat-Lingotto'.[38] While Fiore was one of the few to worry about the fate of these 'spostati' or misfits who will be abandoned once they have served their purpose, he targets blame at the producers who have jumped on the neorealist bandwagon and churned out films using non-actors, saving money and acquiring prestige.

Other critics in a variety of film journals were of the same opinion: Luigi Chiarini (1948) reproved Italian directors' 'corsa disperata verso il mito dell'autentico'/'desperate pursuit of the myth of authenticity' and targeted non-professional casting by sniffing that he had never seen a truer railwayman than Jean Gabin in Renoir's *La bête humaine*. Nediani (1948) talked of a state of alarm in the industry, where established actors were unable to get work due to the preference for 'authentic' types. Di Giammatteo agreed (1949), saying that actors are worried because 'una schiera sempre più folta di uomini comuni, di gente completamente digiuna di preparazione artistica, gli sta sottraendo le possibilità di lavoro'/'an ever-increasing band of ordinary men, completely devoid of artistic training, is taking work away from them'.[39] He went on to ask why the state should continue to fund actors' training at the Centro Sperimentale if its best pupils were doomed to lose parts to those new to cinema, touching again on the hot topic of actorly training.

The ease with which a critic like Di Giammatteo slips from an economic argument about the damage caused to professional ranks by non-actors grateful to accept poor pay, to a moral one about the outrageous waste of valuable acting training, shows how the issue strikes at the heart of questions of dignity and professionalism. Why, he asks rhetorically, should actors be sacrificed for 'ignari nati per tutt'altro mestiere, senza preparazione, senza mestiere'/'ignorant people who were destined for totally different careers, without training and without knowledge of the job' (ibid.)? His conclusion that the use of non-actors is 'immoralissimo'/'totally immoral' hits a note of broader ethical affront that is supported by other critics. Castello (1949: 54) lists the 'effetti perniciosi'/'pernicious effects' and 'malcostume industriale'/'industrial malpractice' wrought by the non-professional, and Dentice (1953: 75) fumes about the 'lancio di speculativi di sprovveduti e pseudofotogenici'/'risky launch of ill-equipped and pseudo-photogenic folk' which was undermining the industry and leading to the humiliation of professional actors. This was exacerbated by the widespread practice

---

[38]'In place of Amedeo Nazzari, we have Oscar Blando [star of two Castellani films], Massimo Girotti is being replaced by a messenger boy working the Genoa-Serravale Scrivia highway, and Maria Denis and Mariella Lotti by a girl working in the Fiat factory' (Fiore 1948: 14).

[39]See Kezich (2006: 401) on the use of non-professionals in the period as a cynical 'strumento di speculazione da parte dei produttori'/'commercial gamble by producers'.

of post-synchronization, meaning that actors did not even have to master dialogue effectively.[40]

Industry workers also expressed their disapproval: in 1951 Umberto Sacripanti, secretary of the actors' union Sindacato Nazionale Attori Cinematografici, attacked the phenomenon violently in the trade press (Sacripanti 1951), and later film producer Gastone Ferranti (in Agnoletti 1952b) insisted on the need for technique and training which allowed for actors to deliver varied performances and distinguish themselves from non-professionals. Producer Alfredo Guarini, at the Parma conference on neorealism in 1953, accused directors of not valuing actors enough, and of not training non-actors effectively either, and thus failing to produce a new acting corps (Guarini 1953). Veteran stage and screen actor Eduardo De Filippo also argued (in Agnoletti 1952a) that only the professional was capable of doing more than just representing a particular type, and that the distance between the non-actor and the actor should be maintained. Screenwriter Ettore Margadonna (1950: 1) lamented the 'autocastrazione'/'auto-castration' inflicted on the industry by the lack of trained actors. Zavattini, meanwhile, publicly and somewhat vainly hoped that Italian actors would not be threatened by the use of non-professionals, or indeed, by the idea of a world in which 'we will all be actors' (2002: 735). By 1956, however, Hank Kaufman of the Kaufman Lerner talent agency in Italy was warning that one of the biggest threats to actors was the non-professional, and for this reason a proper union was urgently needed (see Lalonde 1983).

It is no exaggeration to say that a moral panic develops over the non-professional, held responsible by some for the decline of the industry; this is sometimes framed as faux-concern for the 'misfits' who cannot find a place in the industry, exemplified by one of the figures studied in Chapter 2, Lamberto Maggiorani of *Bicycle Thieves* (who is directly invoked by both Fiore and Cristofani in their articles). However, we can understand it as more broadly reflecting anxieties about a period of transition in Italian film production, when the prestige of neorealism gave way to more commercial productions, many of which, nonetheless, starred new homegrown, sometimes untrained stars. As Pitassio (2019: 293) observes: 'Much post-war film stardom in its early days was associated with non-professional performers', listing films such as *Riso amaro/Bitter Rice* (De Santis, 1949), *Non c'è pace tra gli ulivi/No Peace Under the Olive Tree* (Germi, 1950), and *Campane a Martello/Alarm Bells* (Zampa, 1949), starring former beauty queens Silvana Mangano, Lucia Bosè, and Gina Lollobrigida respectively (the first two also featuring Raf Vallone, himself a former non-professional).

---

[40] See veteran director Mario Soldati's 1953 condemnation of Renato Castellani's dubbing of non-professionals (in Pitassio 2007: 162).

The fear that Italian cinema was not producing its own fully trained stars placed it at an international disadvantage: as Alberto Moravia sniffed in 1953, complaining about the lack of 'real actors', 'altrove gli attori del cinema vengono dal teatro, da noi vengono dalla strada oppure dai concorsi di bellezza'/'elsewhere cinema actors come from theatre, but here they come from the streets, or else from beauty contests'. Nediani had made the same point back in 1948, that the 'dignity' of the industry was threatened by these casting practices, saying that Jean Gabin acts opposite Michèle Morgan, not 'Miss Paris'! Partly as a response to these anxieties, in 1957 producer Franco Cristaldi introduced an acting school within his production company Vides, providing training to stars like Claudia Cardinale (see Masi 1987).

The seeming discursive contradiction whereby Italian cinema lacked both good, trained actors and stars, partly because of the use of non-professionals, *and* neorealism, its anti-star, anti-actor genre was agreed to be in crisis (see De Santis 1951; Chiarini 1951b), is not fully resolvable. The 'crisis' of neorealism was aided by the Andreotti Law of 1949, introduced by then-undersecretary in charge of entertainment Giulio Andreotti with the aim of boosting more commercial Italian production: one of its provisions, that in order to be considered Italian and avail of state subsidy, films had to be shot with direct sound and with 70 per cent of interior shots carried out in fully equipped studios, directly targeted a certain kind of production that featured non-professionals and location shooting. The lengthy dispute which ran for months in 1952 between the government's Direzione Generale per la Cinematografia and the producers of Castellani's *Two Cents of Hope* over the latter's insistence that it was useless and expensive for them to shoot with direct sound (as the Neapolitan non-actors they were using were unable to perform and absolutely required to be dubbed) is testament to the increasing difficulty of getting funding for these films featuring what the producers condescendingly termed 'elementi indigeni'/'indigenous individuals'.[41] It also underlies the widespread denigration of the acting skills of non-professionals, whose voices would most likely not even be used.

Conclusion

Theatrically trained film star Vittorio Gassman was definitely being hyperbolic when he announced in 1968 that neorealism had killed stars (quoted in Minuz 2017: 39). They continued to exist, and many of them came from the ranks of the beauty contest winners. There were also plenty

---

[41]See correspondence in the Archivio Centrale dello Stato, Direzione Generale dello Spettacolo Files, CF1107. See also the piece by 'Q' on the Andreotti law which expressed the hope that the need to record with direct sound might force producers to actually hire actors who could act, or train those already hired ('Q' 1950).

of more measured or positive critical takes on the non-professional in the period (see e.g. Mida 1946; Renzi 1949; Auriol 1949; *Bianco e Nero* editors 1949; Viazzi 1951; Calendoli 1952), including arguments that the presence of non-professionals should stimulate professional actors to do better and master their craft (Maggiore 1952; Mida 1952). Yet the warning issued by Diego Fabbri in 1949 that use of the non-professional now risked accusations of 'maniera'/'modishness' or 'retoric'/'rhetoric', by the early 1950s seemed to be proven: in 1951 Luigi Chiarini was criticizing Genina's 1949 film about Saint Maria Goretti, *Cielo sulla palude*/*Heaven over the Marshes*, shot on location using rural protagonists, for its 'mannered' use of non-professionals, a fault that was deemed squarely part of what Chiarini labelled the 'involution' of neorealism as a movement (Chiarini 1951a).[42]

The repetitive nature of these debates means that, as we have seen, and will see in more detail in the following chapters, certain tropes emerge and become resistant: one of these is a slight fixation on the question of when the non-professional becomes a professional: Bosco (1949) argues that it's when they shoot their second scene, as from that moment they have already gained experience and learned something: 'l'attore veramente vergine non esiste in realtà'/'the truly virginal actor doesn't really exist'. Director Castellani (in Cristofani and Manetti 1956: 174) argues similarly that anyone who has been in front of a camera for even a few minutes can be considered a professional actor.

The fixation on when the non-professional loses that status correlates with a recurrent idea that they must only be used once: 'egli è l'uomo di un solo film'/'he is the man of just one film' (Di Giammatteo 1949). Both he and Castello agree that the non-actor can be allowed to appear as a one-off, but that he must have the tact to retire from the film industry afterwards. We will see in the next chapter what happens when the non-actor refuses to take this paternalistic advice to remain 'l'interprete singolare, perfetto, unico'/'the perfect, singular, one-off actor' (Pitassio 2007: 152) and tenaciously aspires to create a professional career.

---

[42]See also Baracco (1950) on the 'retorica del neorealismo'/'rhetoric of neorealism', as well as Casetti and Malavasi (2003).

2

Bodies, voices, afterlives: Case studies of *Bicycle Thieves*' Lamberto Maggiorani and the cast of *La Terra Trema*

The Cuban director and intellectual Julio García Espinosa recounted his experience of meeting Lamberto Maggiorani, the former star of Vittorio De Sica's *Bicycle Thieves* (1948) at a Communist rally in Rome. García Espinosa had studied at the Centro Sperimentale di Cinematografia in Rome and had been influenced heavily by neorealism. As Michael Chanan reports it, '[García Espinosa] learned what a miserable life this man now led, and how he had felt frustration and indignity when he was approached to figure in an advertising campaign for a bicycle firm! People talk about the aesthetics of non-professional screen acting, said García Espinosa, but no one ever asks what happens to these people in their real lives afterwards' (Chanan 2004: 109).[1]

Former factory worker Maggiorani, who emerged as probably the most visible face of Italian neorealism internationally, thanks to the Oscar won by *Bicycle Thieves* and the film's international circulation, became a haunting presence in Italian cinema after his one starring role. Maggiorani's story has a 'before' and an 'after', with the high profile of *Bicycle Thieves* marking a radical change in his circumstances. After his performance as unemployed father Antonio, whose quest to find his stolen bicycle indexes the economic precarity of Italy's post-war period for the working classes, Maggiorani's fleeting appearances in later films, and his struggles to construct a career for himself, became a kind of cautionary tale of neorealism and its failure, as we will see.

---

[1]This anecdote is undated, but García Espinosa studied in Rome in the early 1950s, so it is probable that the encounter occurred then.

In this chapter, Maggiorani's extremely precarious 'stardom' will be interrogated in relation both to the production of *Bicycle Thieves* and the persona of the (non)-actor. It will then be placed in dialogue with that of the non-professional Sicilian cast of Luchino Visconti's *La terra trema/The Earth Trembles*. The films, both released in 1948, for some critics the last year of true neorealist filmmaking (Chiarini 1951a), although filmed in very different ways, raise important issues around the casting and use of their non-professional actors. Questions of their agency and exploitation will be addressed in the chapter, along with the ethical and performance issues triggered when non-actors are used as raw material. The chapter suggests that ultimately, the presence and afterlife of non-professionals might signal 'the limits of the neorealist aesthetic' (Schoonover 2012a: 227) and the unrepeatable nature of the experiment.

Bicycle Thieves: Casting the body

Bicycle Thieves was financed from multiple sources and produced by De Sica's own production company on a much bigger budget than his previous film, 1946's *Shoeshine* (Grignaffini 1989: 42; Gordon 2008: 26). The writing team who adapted it from Luigi Bartolini's 1946 novel was led by Zavattini and included Suso Cecchi D'Amico and Sergio Amidei, who had worked with De Sica and Zavattini on *Shoeshine* and with Roberto Rossellini on his post-war films. As we will see, however, the influence of Zavattini went beyond the screenplay, and his theories of the importance of the non-professional actor left their imprint beyond the film, especially in the unmade screenplay he later wrote about Maggiorani. As with other films discussed in this book, it is the deployment of non-professional actors in the lead roles that has driven a lot of the attention on *Bicycle Thieves*, even if the dynamics of casting and performance have never been fully explored.

De Sica cast professional actors in many of the film's smaller roles (see Wagstaff 2007: 316); however, it is the two non-professional leads who grabbed the headlines. The process of casting Lamberto Maggiorani and Enzo Staiola, who played his little son, Bruno, has been the subject of extensive anecdote and myth. Gordon refers to 'oft-repeated casting anecdotes' (2008: 27), and without a properly documented history of the film's production we have had to rely on a piecemeal collage of stories, interview fragments, and autobiographical snippets, many of them retrospectively embellished through endless retelling both by the protagonists and by third parties. What is important to note from analysing these multiple and conflicting accounts is not whether they are accurate or not, but the kind of discursive power they have, and the ways in which they might seek to render intelligible some complex ideological positions around the poetics of the non-professional.

Various versions of the casting stories have been told and retold over the years: in most accounts, Maggiorani accompanied his son to a casting session, having heard about it on the radio, and De Sica was immediately struck by his face (see De Sica 2004: 102), an aspect I will go on to consider in more detail. In another telling, Maggiorani's wife sent in a picture of her son which included her husband, and which attracted De Sica's interest (see Cristofani and Manetti 1956: 178). Despite the supposed commitment to a non-professional lead, De Sica actually screen-tested professional actor (and later film star) Gabriele Ferzetti for the role but rejected him because he was too similar to Laurence Olivier (Caldiron 2002: 88). This near miss resonates with the famous stories of De Sica's involvement with David O. Selznick for a planned English-language version of the film, which might star such Hollywood luminaries as Cary Grant, Danny Kaye, or Henry Fonda (Eaton 2019), stories which function to emphasize the unique power of De Sica's film by contrasting it with what it is not, or what it so easily might have been.[2]

Meanwhile, accounts of the casting of Enzo Staiola to play little Bruno generally assert that he was spotted by De Sica while hanging around the production but even here there is contradiction: Staiola and others claim that De Sica had already cast another boy, Enzo Cerusico, who had already appeared with De Sica in Coletti's popular film *Cuore*/*Heart and Soul*, released earlier in 1948 (see Gordon 2008: 27). Staiola, in fact, recalled that he and Cerusico, who went on to be a well-known actor and singer, worked together on several scenes, with each filming before De Sica decided on his favourite (Criterion Collection interview, 2016). This would mirror De Sica's practice on *Shoeshine*, where he started filming with both Franco Interlenghi and another boy, before deciding on Interlenghi. Zavattini (2002: 156) backs up Staiola and interestingly claims that it was he who selected Staiola, and that De Sica 'aveva scelto un bambino bello ma privo di umanità'/'had chosen a kid who was attractive but lacking human appeal' (presumably Cerusico).

However, De Sica (2004: 102) says that he began filming *Bicycle Thieves* without a boy at all, and that noting Staiola on the street where they were filming was a kind of 'miracle': 'Questo me l'ha mandato San Gennaro'/'This

---

[2]Most histories have understood Selznick as wanting to make *Bicycle Thieves* himself with one of these big stars (see Wagstaff 2007: 32; Gordon 2008: 26). However, Steve Eaton's work, using the Selznick archive at the Harry Ransom Center, University of Texas at Austin, has recently shown that

> Selznick's intention was to fund half of the 100 million lire cost (as estimated by De Sica) for the Italian version of *Bicycle Thieves* that De Sica planned to direct, plus some extra amount for De Sica to direct, simultaneously or subsequently, a second, English-language version. The film was not to be dubbed, but filmed with an English-speaking star substituting for whoever played the lead role of Antonio in the 'Italian' version. (Eaton 2019: 223)

boy was sent to me by St. Gennaro' (De Sica 1975d: 281).[3] This nod to his popular Neapolitan roots by De Sica also encourages readers to understand the entire casting process in a melodramatic register of both chance and fate, and speaks to the 'almost mystical encounter between character and actor' (Nacache 2005: 38) that we hear so much about in casting stories.[4] For example, when De Sica tells the story of the casting of journalist Lianella Carell in the role of Antonio's wife, Maria, it is also presented in this register. Carell was a journalist who had come to interview him, and De Sica's account of their accidental meeting and his sudden epiphany that she was perfect for the part is glossed by Caldiron (2002: 93) thus: 'sembra un'*agnition* da *feuilleton* o una rivelazione da racconto confessionale'/'it resembles the moment of agnition in a *feuilleton* or a revelation from a confessional tale'.[5] These narratives of chance and providence seem somewhat at odds with the laborious casting process – as De Sica noted (2004: 102), he saw hundreds of children for the part of Bruno, as he would later do in casting *Il tetto*. Yet according to André Bazin in his seminal 1948 essay on the film, 'De Sica hesitated for months between this person and that, took a hundred tests only to decide finally, in a flash and by intuition on the basis of a silhouette suddenly come upon at the bend of a road' (Bazin 1971: 56). Bazin resolves this supposed tension between the labour of a long casting search and the sudden revelation offered by the 'right' face or body or silhouette by showing that De Sica was equipped with an extraordinary ability to divine the tangible and intangible qualities needed at first sight, an ability that will extend to extracting performances from sometimes refractory non-actors.[6]

The intangible qualities offered by Lamberto Maggiorani were read by De Sica firstly in his face: De Sica's memory (2004: 102) that Maggiorani 'aveva un volto che mi interessò per la sua forza emotiva, degli occhi pieni di spavento e buoni'/'had a face that interested me for its emotive power, and eyes that were frightened but good' shows the perceived capacity of the face to act as a transparent window to the soul.[7] Here Maggiorani's face, on its

---

[3]Suso Cecchi D'Amico, co-writer of the film, meanwhile asserted that Staiola was found in a school (in E. Cost. 2001).
[4]Staiola (Criterion Collection interview 2016), meanwhile, asserts that De Sica had already seen him coming out of school the day before and followed him home in his car. His account also alludes to the dangers that children faced in Rome from paedophiles, and references the infamous case of the 'Monster of Rome', a child rapist and killer in Rome in the 1920s.
[5]Carell's recollection of the moment is that 'lui mi ha guardata e mi ha detto: "Ma questa è Maria!"'/'he looked at me and said: "She's Maria!"' (Caldiron and De Sica 1997: 18).
[6]In Zavattini's account of the casting in his treatment for the unmade film *Tu, Maggiorani/You, Maggiorani*, De Sica points his finger at Maggiorani when he sees him and simply says 'Tu'/'You'. Thus De Sica both acknowledges the indexical link between Antonio and Maggiorani, and brings 'Maggiorani-as-Antonio' into being. See Zavattini (2006: 138).
[7]Enzo Staiola was also cast for his (unconventional) face: 'aveva un volto buffo, un naso all'insù e degli occhi tondi, grigio gialli'/'he had a funny face, a turned-up nose, and big, greeny-yellow

first sight, shows its potential to display and express the suffering that his character will endure. This face, which Franco Fortini in his 1949 review of the film (1973: 155) called 'il viso del reduce di tutte le guerre'/'the face of a veteran of all the wars', has a universal valence, as well as an epic one (Fortini also calls him the 'Noè di un'Europa sommersa'/'Noah of an underwater Europe' (ibid.)). In this sense, the value of Maggiorani's face, which is both intimately individual *and* universal, can be connected to De Sica's own use of the face as a synecdoche of a new type of screen character, expressed in his 1942 article 'Volti nuovi per un cinema nuovo'/'New Faces for a New Cinema'. The director's statement that 'mi piacciono soprattutto i volti, a dir così inediti, gli attori che non sono attori, quelli non ancora corrotti dal mestiere e dalla pratica e nei quali tutto è genuino e schietto' (1975a: 253) refers to the 'authentic' and unglamorous quality of the face as it might represent the reality of suffering Italy.[8] The 'anonymity' of Maggiorani's face, his 'faccia anonima scelta attraverso un lungo e spesso disperante scrutinio di volti e di gesti'/'anonymous face, chosen by means of a long and often desperate scrutiny of faces and gestures' (Caldiron 1975: 5) gives a face to the faceless crowd of working-class Italians.[9] This 'uncorrupted' face and person is of course highlighted in the film by the famous juxtaposition of Maggiorani with Rita Hayworth, as he attempts to affix the poster of *Gilda* (Vidor, 1946) in an early scene (Figure 3).[10]

The second element of this 'divismo della fisionomia'/'physiognomic stardom' (Grande 1992: 33) that leaps out in accounts of the casting process is Maggiorani's hands.[11] De Sica recalls being struck by 'come muoveva le mani, piene di calli, mani di operaio, non di attore'/'how he moved his hands, covered in callouses, the hands of a manual worker, not an actor' (1975d: 281). Maggiorani's hands were thus a somatic marker of manual labour, an index of his job at the arms factory where he worked. Indeed, De Sica (2004: 103) recounted that when Maggiorani went back to work after the shoot his hands were painful, as he had lost the callouses during filming. Manual labour is proof of both Maggiorani's class identity and of his status as a non-actor, and as we will see, what is foregrounded here is the question of acting as labour, mystified in most accounts of the film.

---

eyes' (De Sica 2004: 102). De Sica also referred to his 'visino clownesco'/'clown-like little face' (in Bruni 2022: 90).
[8]'Above all, I like faces that have never been seen before, actors who aren't actors, who aren't corrupted by the profession and by the job, and in whom everything is genuine and pure'.
[9]Again we see the Eisensteinian idea of Antonio as a 'type' representing an entire working class through a widely recognized 'codice fisiognomico'/'physiognomic code' (Pitassio 2002: 251).
[10]Waller (1997: 256) writes of this scene's 'decolonization of the Italian screen' and its 'ironic perversion of Hollywood's visual and narrative seductions'.
[11]Gordon (2008: 27) comments on De Sica's casting 'of people as raw material, as faces, looks, walks, which he as a director (and as seasoned actor) could mould to his needs', and compares his casting practice to those of Fellini and Pasolini.

FIGURE 3 *Antonio (Lamberto Maggiorani) puts up the poster of Rita Hayworth in* Gilda.

The third casting element is that of movement: 'come si muoveva, come si sedeva ... tutto in lui era perfetto'/'how he moved, how he sat ... everything was perfect in him' (De Sica 1975d: 281). The quality of how Maggiorani (and Staiola) occupied space gave rise to Bazin's famous statement (1971: 55) that 'it would be no exaggeration to say that *Ladri di biciclette* is the story of a walk through Rome by a father and his son'; the idea of the narrative of the film *being* the physical movement of its characters has been explored with regard to the materiality of the city spaces.[12] However, it is the idea of walking itself as performance that interests me, that Maggiorani's 'natural' walk is the inimitable performance element that every other candidate for the role lacked. 'Before choosing this particular child, De Sica did not ask him to perform, just to walk', Bazin (ibid.: 54) argues of Staiola, and this real body in space was, as we saw in this book's introduction, a crucial cornerstone of Zavattini's neorealist theory of *pedinamento*, the laborious process of following individuals in order to represent their daily experiences

---

[12]Gordon (2008: 107) describes the relation of the two bodies in space as a 'pas de deux' and a 'situational ballet'.

as if they were being caught unawares. The fact that De Sica shot without sound and the actors were dubbed by professional actors, something to which we will return, renders the body more acutely important as an expressive tool: we can consider the walking of Maggiorani and Staiola as 'pedestrian speech acts' (De Certeau 1988: 97). The premium placed on their natural or authentic bodies, their unrehearsed way of walking that could not be taught, helps produce a sense of this as a physiognomic performance that has tended to efface the effortful nature of their performances.

The 'natural' labour of performance

One of the enduring tropes about performance by non-professional actors is the frequent failure to recognize or conceptualize it as performance. The rhetoric of Bazin in particular, when he characterized *Bicycle Thieves* as showing 'the disappearance of the concept of the actor into a transparency seemingly as natural as life itself' (1971: 57), was especially influential in this regard.[13] Bazin, of course, did not argue for an uncomplicated photographic representation of reality, as his view of *Bicycle Thieves* as the result of 'an ever-present although invisible system of aesthetics' (ibid.: 58) makes clear. However, he did not account for the construction, effect, and meanings of non-professional performance in the film, and neither have other scholars.

On the one hand, it is possible to isolate the technical means that contribute to the effects of performance in the film: these include the use of the follow shot, where the camera is 'pulled' by the character movement (Wagstaff 2007: 323); conventional shallow-focus medium close-ups, bespeaking the 'language of emotional engagement' (ibid.: 347); and the relative absence of long takes (an average shot length of 6.7 seconds according to Wagstaff). The 'slick and conventional' aspects of *Bicycle Thieves*' style (Thompson 1988: 215), including the 'over-sentimental score' by Alessandro Cicognini (Gordon 2008: 29), challenge certain assumptions derived from Bazin about the connection between the long take and the 'spatial unity made visible through the body' (Schoonover 2012a: 31). The idea of the non-professional 'filmed body' as a bare element of the mise-en-scène, often read as a mere effect of slow tempo and long takes, is thus absent from *Bicycle Thieves*, yet some critics still record an impression of 'non-recitazione'/'non-acting' (Torri 1992: 43), which elides the labour that went into the performances.[14]

The bodies of both Magggiorani and Staiola might be said to be overdetermined partly because their vocal performance was irrelevant: in

---

[13]See Ricciardi (2006) on the importance of Bazin in the idealization of neorealism.
[14]Minghelli's (2013: 112) assertion that 'the most telling features for understanding Antonio's story are the formal values of his physiognomy, the spatial relations that it entertains with the world' also ascribes to Maggiorani's body a self-evident and self-limiting quality.

accordance with most Italian practice since fascism, the actors' voices were dubbed in post-production 'into heavily Romanised Italian' (Gordon 2008: 29).[15] The lack of attention to this aspect of performance in the film highlights the extent to which voice acting is generally overlooked when analysing performance.[16] But the ultimate effect of the dubbing (unlike *La terra trema*, which, as we will see, used direct sound recording) is to make the actors' bodies bear the principal interpretive weight of the film.

Maggiorani's body is thus both self-explanatory 'guarantor of the image's realism' (Schoonover 2012a: 4) and also a working body whose labour is effaced and mystified. Schoonover astutely observes the 'two temporalities of labour' in the neorealist body:

> (1) a *present* labor that requires no effort, demanding only that bodies go through the motions rather than commanding a performance that requires the display of intention, skill, and virtuosity; and (2) a *past* labor that has left indelible physical markers. (Schoonover 2012b: 76, n. 12)

As Maggiorani exemplifies it, the effect of non-acting, or what Gaggiotti terms the 'non-professional effect' (2019: 106), effaces any performative effort, while his past biography and his physical appearance validate him in the present for viewers.

This 'unbelabored labor' (Schoonover 2012b: 69) takes further Clark's view of the failure of studies of stardom to fully address the work of acting and performance. If, as Clark (1995: 25) argued, actors are often 'sutured into a discourse that naturalised their labor as performance and linked performances to narrative identity', the non-professional actor is doubly naturalized. Non-actors are a being, or body, who are not thought of as producing acting in the sense of 'discernible human actions infused with connotations conveyed by the quality of actors' gestures and expressions' (Baron and Carnicke 2008: 79). The idea that for a director like De Sica, skilled at working with non-professionals, they were merely 'cera molle'/'soft wax' (Pintus 1975: 159) in his hands or a kind of 'raw material' (Gordon 2008: 27) works to negate any skill or agency they might have. De Sica himself referred to non-actors in 1942 as 'docili educande'/'docile schoolgirls' that he needed to 'plasmare'/'shape' (1975a: 254), which matches Caldiron's view of the 'disponibile argilla dei volti anonimi'/'anonymous faces that are clay for the use of [the director]' (in Caldiron and De Sica 1997: 33).

It is thus important to look to the directorial techniques that De Sica used to extract performance from non-professionals. He was renowned as

---

[15]As Gaggiotti (2019: 96) notes, however, De Sica later claimed that the actors dubbed themselves (in his 1965 interview with James Blue), but there is no evidence for this. Gaggiotti considers this claim to be part of the 'branding' of neorealism.
[16]See Wojcik (2006).

a magisterial director of non-actors: as fellow director Luigi Comencini wrote 'riusciva a far recitare i sassi'/'he could get a performance from a stone' (1975: 123).[17] Caldiron's analogous view that 'sa fare recitare anche le sedie'/'he can get a performance from a chair' (Caldiron 2002: 94) highlights the critical view of non-actors as inanimate objects – or 'biological symptoms' (Naremore 1988: 65) – who might briefly come to life in the master's hands.

One of De Sica's principal techniques appears to have been acting out scenes and getting performers to imitate him closely. De Sica himself of course was a renowned and accomplished stage and screen actor, and this view of acting as a kind of imitation is important; what Pintus terms this 'mostruouso mimetismo animale'/'monstrous animalesque mimicry' (1975: 159) suggests the director's belief in the capabilities of his non-actors to take on De Sica' actorly qualities.[18] Maggiorani (in Hochkofler 1975: 209), however, offered the more nuanced view that after a couple of rehearsals of a scene

> entravo nel personaggio e lavoravo. Le parole venivano fuori da sé, non quelle del copione. E lui con due, tre ciak tirava fuori la scena. Un po' l'impressione l'ho imparata da lui, certamente; non ero un attore professionista, però veniva spontanea.[19]

Maggiorani's struggle to carve out a contribution for himself, which he significantly names as work ('lavoravo'/'I began working'), tries to counter the narrative of either simple aping of the director's movements or of De Sica as having a singular ability to elicit performance from his 'inert' cast.[20] While not having any vocabulary that could speak of performance on a technical level, his emotional investment in the part is clear: he said that in the final scene where he was set upon after stealing a bike, 'allora stavo veramente nel personaggio, e sentivo la scena'/'I was really in the character, and I was feeling the scene' (ibid.), to the extent that he was really beaten

---

[17] Sergio Leone, who made a brief appearance in the film as a priest, declared De Sica a 'mago'/'wizard' in getting non-professionals to perform (Caldiron and De Sica 1997: 22). Chiaromonte (1949: 623) likewise argued that De Sica could lure a sack of potatoes into acting!

[18] Gaggiotti (2019: 101) points out that there are examples of De Sica using his 'mimetic directing' method with professional actors such as Marcello Mastroianni too.

[19] 'I became one with the character and began working. The words came out on their own, they weren't the ones in the script. And in two or three takes he would get the scene. I learned the reactions a bit from him, of course; I wasn't a professional actor, but it all came spontaneously to me.' Maggiorani's 'two or three takes' are contradicted by Zavattini in the treatment for *Tu, Maggiorani*, where it is suggested that the number might be eight (2006: 139).

[20] See Pintus's view (1975: 159) that once De Sica was done with the likes of Maggiorani, 'abbandonati da lui, sottratti al sortilegio, ritornavano materiale qualunque, inerte, inespressivo'/'abandoned by him, removed from his spell, they went back to being just inert and inexpressive raw material'.

up, mirroring De Sica's desire to install a kind of 'osmosis' in Maggiorani between himself and Antonio (Nuzzi and Iemma 1997: 106).

A potentially more sinister side of De Sica's directorial techniques needs to be addressed also: as with other films discussed in this book, and as will be the case with *La terra trema*, reports of sadistic treatment of non-actors have circulated very widely. One famous anecdote concerns De Sica's attempts to make Staiola cry at the end of the film, when his father has been publicly humiliated. De Sica recounted that he had tried pinching and slapping Staiola to no avail: eventually he placed cigarette butts in his pocket and De Sica pretended to discover them and shouted out that Staiola was a 'ciccarolo' (someone who collected butts to sell them). 'Si mise istintivamente le mani nelle tasche e quando si accorse che erano piene di cicche scoppiò a piangere'/'He instinctively put his hands in his pockets and when he realised they were full of cigarette butts he burst into tears' (Nuzzi and Iemma 1997: 106). The public shaming of Staiola, who was then eight years old, was, as De Sica's assistant Luisa Alessandri cheerfully admits, 'sadico'/'sadistic' (ibid.: 108). But it was deemed effective and therefore worth it: 'tentò di difendersi, ma la sua voce era rotta dai singhiozzi. E pronunciò un'ingiuria. Fu così che girai una delle scene-chiavi del film'/'he tried to defend himself, but his voice was full of sobs. He swore. That was how I filmed one of the key scenes of the film' (De Sica, quoted in ibid.).[21]

Staiola has generally denied this version of what happened, saying that De Sica instead used the traditional expedient of glycerine to produce tears (TV2000it interview, no date).[22] Yet the anecdote has had enduring power: in Ettore Scola's celebrated 1974 film *C'eravamo tanto amati/We All Loved Each Other So Much*, one of the protagonists loses his winnings on the TV quiz show *Lascia o raddoppia?/Double or Quits?* because he insists that the answer to the question of why Staiola cried at the end of the film is because of the cigarette butts. The 'correct' answer is 'because his father was caught stealing a bike'. As Wagstaff (2007: 33) points out, the scene is 'satirizing the mystifications of the media', but it is also, I argue, speaking to the pervasive appeal of Staiola's 'real' suffering, and responds to our cultural sense that 'manipulative trickery is often used to elicit tears because the child is not trusted to be able to simply "act" them. If the child effects what seems like real grief, the adult must be "really" cruel' (Williams 2012: 460). Staiola's inability to produce tears on command, which would make him seem a 'freak' (Lury 2010: 10), reassures us that he is not a precocious child

---

[21] In his 1965 interview with James Blue, De Sica explained that he made fun of Staiola in front of the crew for sleeping in a bedroom with six other brothers and sisters (in Gaggiotti 2019). According to some contemporary reports, Staiola's family lived in a kind of cave, having lost their home in the war (see Bruni 2022: 53).

[22] Though, confusingly, in another interview (Marucci 2018) he says it is true. In yet another interview (Anon. 2018), he says instead that smoke was blown into his eyes to make him cry.

FIGURE 4 *Enzo Staiola magically produces tears as Bruno in* Bicycle Thieves.

actor, validates his untrained nature, and aligns the spectator with him in sympathy (Figure 4).[23]

De Sica was also psychologically sadistic to both Carell and Maggiorani,[24] but he mentioned that he felt particularly bad for shaming Staiola.[25] As

---

[23]De Sica himself complicated things further with his contribution to the 1950 collective documentary project *Documento mensile, n.1*. De Sica's short film, entitled *Ambienti e personaggi/Settings and Characters*, featured a simulation of the making of some scenes from *Bicycle Thieves* (see Castelli 2018). In the fragment available on the extras of the Arrow DVD (2017) we see De Sica recreate precisely this scene: he shakes Staiola and lightly slaps him, crying out 'Piangi! Piangi!'/'Cry! Cry!' Staiola obligingly turns to the camera and smiles 'va bene cosi'?'/'is this ok?' De Sica: 'Benone! Bravo!/'Great! Well done!'. De Sica then gives him sweets. The *mise-en-abyme* effect of this extract illustrates the extent to which the episode is part of De Sica's, and the film's, mythology and, to some extent, neutralizes its sadistic overtones.

[24]He encouraged Carell to imagine her husband had run off with another woman in order to get her to cry (Nuzzi and Iemma 1997: 108), while he tormented Maggiorani by making him think of his son, who had polio (Caldiron 2002: 94).

[25]Pillon (2018) reads the 'ciccarolo' story interestingly as part of a broader cultural idea: 'A dispetto del suo valore di verità, la storia del ciccarolo ci piace; ci piace così tanto che continuiamo a raccontarcela ... ogni volta che celebriamo il film, come se quell'episodio – inventato dal regista "per fare teatro" – fosse diventato parte integrante del fascino immortale della sua opera cinematografica. Il mito del genio maschile e abusante ... è così pervasivo da avere comunque la meglio nell'immaginario collettivo.'/'Regardless of its truth value, the ciccarolo story appeals to us; it appeals to us so much that we continue to recount it ... every time we celebrate the

Ahmed (2013: 103) notes, part of shame's intensity is that it 'works on and through bodies'; in this case, it immediately caused Staiola to cry. This negative affect connects the bodily response to the exposure of a 'failure to live up to a social ideal' (ibid.: 106). Here we can suggest that the social ideal might be also that of the professional actor, or the person able to produce the appropriate reactions on command. For all the rhetoric that De Sica elicited performances of a quasi-professional level,[26] these anecdotes and their persistence reinforce a sense of the *shortfall* felt by the non-actor, or the difficulty of this work for them, which may be felt as shame. As Zavattini wrote (2002: 857), Maggiorani and film star Vittorio Gassman are 'due cose imparagonabili'/'two incomparable things', and Maggiorani's post-film trajectory confirms this disparity.

Before and after

The shortfall between the non-professional actor and the ability to produce a convincing performance naturally when required was made apparent in the aftermath of *Bicycle Thieves*. Maggiorani became the international face of neorealism along with Staiola, featuring heavily in US press coverage, to the extent that De Sica claimed in 1952 that Americans kept sending him dollar bills to pass on to the pair (1975b: 270).[27] De Sica, by 1954, admitted that for non-professionals, 'esiste sempre il problema di ciò che saranno "dopo" questi ragazzi; questi uomini o donne che io traggo dalla vita reale'/'there is the perennial problem of what these kids will be "afterwards"; these men and women that I take from real life' (1975c: 281). De Sica was already well aware of the 'problema del dopo'/'problem of "afterwards"' because he had been so closely exposed to what had happened to Maggiorani after the film came out in late 1948. Maggiorani's story became a cautionary tale of the consequences of taking

---

film, as if that episode – invented by the director as a "moment of theatre" – had become an integral part of the enduring fascination of his film. The myth of the abusive male genius ... is so pervasive that it will always win out in the collective imaginary'.

[26]'De Sica, imponendo agli attori improvvisati, in virtù di una magistrale sapienza direttiva, le forme e i modi di una recitazione qualificata al livello professionale'/'De Sica imposed on the non-professional actors, by dint of a magisterial directing ability, the forms and modes of professional-level acting' (Bettetini 1975: 112). See Varese's view also (1950: 14) that Maggiorani and Carell are 'attori che recitano come attori'/'actors who perform like actors'.

[27]In the Rissone-De Sica archive, held at the Cineteca di Bologna, there is a letter to Enzo Staiola from two Scottish girls or women, dated April 1950. The senders say they saw the film seven times in Glasgow and express their admiration for the boy ('Io vi amare'), requesting a signed photo. The letter was enclosed within one to De Sica, asking him to pass it on to Staiola, but he clearly failed to do so, as the second envelope was unopened when placed in the archive. I am grateful to Valerio Coladonato for showing me this letter.

non-professionals out of their environment and then expecting them to return immediately to their old life, to the extent that the Argentine magazine *El Hogar* in 1950 held him up as a moral tale about the irresponsibility of using amateurs (in Halperin 2012: 131).

Maggiorani returned to work at the Breda arms factory in Rome after shooting the film. In 1949, however, he was made redundant, along with over half of the workforce. In an interview with *L'Unità* at the time, Maggiorani suggested that he might have been sacked because 'credevano fossi diventato un divo ... pieno di quattrini, con la voglia di smettere il mestiere dell'operaio'/'they thought I'd become a star ... loaded with cash, and wanting to stop working in the factory' (Morato 1949). He explained that the money he got from the film was just enough to redo their bedroom and to buy some nice clothes.[28] This interview is also important in positioning Maggiorani as a man of the people, a trade union member who is proud to stand with fellow workers against heartless bosses, and who insists that he is not a 'divo' upon being recognized by the journalist, who is there to cover the workers' protests. The caption of the photo the newspaper published of him to accompany the story delicately recasts his departure from the film industry as a personal choice: 'dopo aver lavorato sul film preferì tornare al suo mestiere di operaio'/'after making the film he preferred to return to his job as a labourer'. In fact, De Sica repeatedly said in interviews that he made Maggiorani promise to return to his job after the film, as if anticipating the latter's difficulties.[29] His attitude thus appears to have been consistent with his view that 'l'uomo della strada deve tornare ad essere l'uomo della strada (e noi registi dobbiamo aiutarlo in questo)'/'the man from the street must go back to being the man from the street (and we directors have to help him do that)' (Cristofani and Manetti 1956: 175), but Maggiorani's case certainly went on to test De Sica's sense of personal responsibility.[30]

Maggiorani's sudden redundancy exacerbated the issues of poverty and vulnerability that his casting as Antonio suggested. He turned to De Sica for help with getting another part: here there are various stories, which may all be true to some degree. By some accounts, he was put to work behind the scenes as an electrician, and/or De Sica gave him some money to start a shoe shop (Cristofani and Manetti 1956: 178). He did get some small parts

---

[28]In an interview with *Life* (Anon. 1950b), Maggiorani said he got 600,000 lire for the role, for six months' work. The average monthly salary for an industrial worker in 1950 was between 26,000 and 47,000 lire, depending on skills and experience. See Cova (2002: 116).

[29]In one interview, however, Maggiorani claimed that De Sica made him promise he would not act in anybody else's films (Hochkofler 1975: 210). Cecchi D'Amico, meanwhile (in E. Cost 2001), says that Maggiorani signed a contract agreeing never to act again, in order to stop him from reaching the sad end of other non-professionals.

[30]De Sica mentions his 'grossa responsabalità'/'great sense of responsibility', and that he personally got the factory manager to promise to hold Maggiorani's job open for him (Nuzzi and Iemma 1997: 102).

in films such as *Donne senza nome*/*Women Without Names* (Radványi, 1950) and *Achtung, banditi!*/*Attention, Bandits!* (Lizzani, 1951). By 1950, however, Maggiorani seemed embittered, and in the 1950 *Life* magazine interview, he and his wife talk of the eviction notice they have received, and are photographed doing laundry in their 'three-room apartment', while Maggiorani is pictured in his temporary bricklaying job (Anon. 1950b). Maggiorani's wife Giuseppina is said to have been 'filled with a longing for an actor's fame' and has named the turkey they are to eat for Christmas dinner 'De Sica' (ibid.)! The interview sub-heading, 'Hero of "Bicycle Thief" Finds Himself as Unlucky in Life as in Film That Made Him Famous' institutes a clear parallel between Maggiorani's life and the film's plot, and speaks to the degree of fascination that a figure like Maggiorani exerts, having joined the ranks of the misfits or 'spostati' (Cristofani and Manetti 1956: 174), caught between their old life and the promise of a glamorous new one.[31]

While it does appear that De Sica exerted himself to help Maggiorani in different ways, it is also clear that he wished simply for his former actor to return to paid manual labour. His desire for a clean and simple narrative regarding Maggiorani is evident, for example, in the statement that Maggiorani 'resta l'esempio di come un uomo possa prestare la sua opera in cinema per una volta e poi tornare ad essere quello di prima'/'remains the example of how a man can lend himself to the cinema once, and then return to being what he was before' (ibid.). But Maggiorani did not simply give up: whether he was driven by a genuine desire to act or by the economic despair of post-war Italy is rather unclear. For example, Maggiorani was the only actor present at the famous Parma conference in 1953 on 'Il neorealismo cinematografico'/'Cinematographic Neorealism' (see Castello 1953): was this out of a genuine interest in debates on neorealism, a networking opportunity, or both? Also in 1953, Maggiorani featured in a slightly humiliating advert, along with Staiola, for a new moped, the Paperino. In a *Settimana Incom* newsreel, the voice-over states as they pose with the bike that 'il piccolo attore Staiola ... con Maggiorani, prevede un nuovo film: *Ladro di ciclomotori*!'/'Staiola, the young actor ... with Maggiorani, is planning a new film: Moped Thieves!'[32] This is the advert mentioned by García Espinosa in the chapter opening as the nadir of Maggiorani's career.

---

[31]Maggiorani's out-of-placeness in the film industry is exemplified by the story of him and his family and friends turning up to the premiere of *Bicycle Thieves* in Rome in a 'rumoroso e malandato camion'/'noisy and broken-down truck', and disturbing the elegance of the occasion (Lughi 1989: 56). This heightens the sense of neorealism's unresolved contradiction between 'un'umanità "povera", e che si voleva reale, sullo schermo, e un pubblico in smoking'/'"poor" and supposedly real on-screen humans, and audiences in dinner jackets' (ibid.).

[32]*La Settimana Incom* 00935 (27 April 1953). Available at https://patrimonio.archivioluce.com/luce-web/detail/IL5000026208/2/la-magnani-sbarca-new-york-presentazione-del-film-luchino-visconti-bellissima-baia-inaugurato-nuovo-modello-motociclo-paperino.html

Yet he also monetized his 'celebrity' status in other interesting ways, for example, by acting as a judge in a beauty contest 'Miss Primavera' for the left-wing magazine *Pattuglia* in 1952. He was described in the contest blurb as 'l'indimenticabile operaio di *Ladri di biciclette* e di *Achtung, banditi*!'/'the unforgettable factory worker of Bicycle Thieves and Acthung, banditi!' and was announced alongside cultural figures such as writer Italo Calvino and director Carlo Lizzani.[33]

Maggiorani's precarious toehold in and near the film industry saw him pop up at various other leftist cultural events.[34] He also took small roles in a number of films, including in De Sica's *Umberto D.* (1952) and *Il giudizio universale/The Last Judgment* (1961). The extent to which Maggiorani functioned as a remnant of neorealism is clear in his brief appearance as a hospital patient in Pasolini's *Mamma Roma* (1962). When Mamma Roma's son Ettore steals his bedside radio, Maggiorani unleashes an outraged cry of 'Al ladro!'/'Stop thief!' just as his predecessor Antonio Ricci had. Rhodes (2007: 124) describes this moment as 'part homage, part parody', while Gaggiotti (2022: 183) argues that through this cinematic quotation, 'Pasolini retrospectively questioned (and mocked) the alleged sincerity and victimization of non-professional actors in Italian neorealism'. These fleeting appearances – like his later appearance in the Cittis' homage to Pasolini, *Ostia* (1970) – show him to be a bit-part player whose tenacity outweighs the desire expressed by many critics that non-professionals should have the 'discrezione'/'discretion' (Castello 1949) to withdraw from the film industry after one role.[35] Despite his lack of training and his identification with one major role, Maggiorani also attempted theatre, performing in Zavattini's play *Come nasce un soggetto cinematografico/How a Film Treatment Comes to Life* at the Piccolo Teatro in Milan in the 1959–60 season.[36] However, this was a one-off experience; meanwhile, another Zavattini project offers very significant insight into the 'afterlife' of Maggiorani.

---

[33]*Pattuglia*, 9 March 1952. I am grateful to Charles Leavitt for drawing my attention to this article.
[34]Maggiorani signed a petition against the atomic bomb (*L'Unità*, 27 July 1950), attended a debate about the future of cinema during a festival of contemporary culture in Turin (*L'Unità*, 9 February 1951), and was at the office of the left-wing magazine *Vie Nuove* for the award of the Italian prizes from the Karlovy Vary Film Festival (*L'Unità*, 10 October 1951).
[35]Maggiorani (in Hochkofler 1975: 210) also said that he had been offered roles in American films, but that these failed to materialize after he appeared on the cover of an Italian Communist Party publication.
[36]https://archivio.piccoloteatro.org/eurolab/repertorio.php?page=14

Tu, Maggiorani and the future memory of the non-professional

In May 1948, when *Bicycle Thieves* started filming, Zavattini wrote a treatment for a film called *Il grande inganno*/*The Great Swindle*, to star Maggiorani as himself (Zavattini 2006: 144). The project name then changed in 1950 to *Tu, Maggiorani*/*You, Maggiorani*, and the fact that it was planned contemporaneously with De Sica's film makes it both a premonition of what would happen to Maggiorani and a meta-reflection on his precarious professional status.[37] Zavattini called it an 'atto di accusa nei confronti dell'istituzione cinematografica radicale'/'radical accusation towards the institution of cinema' (ibid.: xxiii) and it creatively re-imagines Maggiorani's experience in the film and afterwards.

The proposed plot, in which Maggiorani appears in *Bicycle Thieves*, gets made redundant, and asks De Sica for help, mirrors his real experiences quite closely. Yet it also points beyond the temporality of the film itself, to a future that had already happened when Zavattini wrote the treatment. The treatment ends with Maggiorani walking in despair through the streets of Rome. He stops at a cinema where *Bicycle Thieves* is showing and watches the film, becomes emotional along with the audience at the screening, but when he steps outside nobody notices him. Zavattini's desire that Maggiorani function as a 'simbolo dei tanti eroi cinematografici che nel dopoguerra hanno cercato la soliarietà degli uomini'/'symbol of the many cinematic heroes who in the post-war period have sought human solidarity' (ibid.: xxiii) also highlights the disjunction between these stories of ordinary working-class Italians and the spectators who watch them, through the image of the patrons who hurry home past Maggiorani to their 'case riscaldate'/'warm houses' (2006: 143) after weeping at him on screen.

As he walks through the city, the treatment visualizes 'tutti i personaggi che hanno invocato in questo dopoguerra l'aiuto degli uomini, l'attacchino Antonio, il prete di *Roma città aperta*, i bambini di *Sciuscià*, il bambino di *Germania anno zero*'/'all the characters who invoked men's aid after the war: Antonio the bill-poster, the priest from *Rome Open City*, the boys from *Shoeshine*, the little boy from *Germany Year Zero*' (ibid.: 144). Maggiorani is just one of the many performers 'presi dalla strada'/'taken from the streets' and returned there, ignored by the 'folle che applaudono ... il personaggio fittizio e non fanno niente per il personaggio vero'/'crowds

---

[37]Interestingly, the trade press reported in February 1950 that two films about Maggiorani's life were being planned: one by Radványi, and another to be made in France by Henri Decoin and Alex Joffé. While neither was made, they show the wide impact of Maggiorani's story. See *Araldo dello Spettacolo*, 22, 16–17 February 1950: 2.

who applaud ... the fictional character and do nothing for the real person' (ibid.). Maggiorani's story, as it was reimagined by Zavattini for the unmade film, 'unfolds a poetics that links, though a series of indexical and symbolic slippages, spectator to actor, and actor to human being' (Margulies 2019: 56). Maggiorani is 'the real Antonio', but that fiction has become his own biography, in a manner typical of the non-professional.

Cinema cannot save Maggiorani, Zavattini makes clear, although for the screenwriter the responsibility for his plight should be levied at the broader problem of post-war unemployment (2006: 146) rather than at the cinema industry. For both Zavattini and De Sica, what befell people like Maggiorani afterwards was 'un problema angoscioso'/'a distressing problem' (De Sica 1975c: 280). Yet De Sica was also frank that 'non avendo nessuna qualità d'attore non lo scritturarono più'/'as he didn't have the qualities of an actor, nobody wanted to hire him' (2004: 103). Maggiorani unwillingly and unwittingly followed Zavattini's later prescription in his essay 'Alcune idee sul cinema'/'Some Ideas on Cinema' that 'il neorealismo richiede che ognuno sia attore di se stesso'/'neorealism requires everyone to be their own actor' (2002: 733); he excelled at one role only: that of himself, but that 'self' changed irrevocably after *Bicycle Thieves*.

So Maggiorani thus becomes a 'cautionary tale' of neorealism (McGurn 1950). Zavattini (2006: 146) writes somewhat sententiously in his gloss on *Tu, Maggiorani* that 'abbiamo il dovere di aprirgli gli occhi sulla verità delle sue doti e quindi sulle reali possibilità del suo avvenire, consigliandolo perciò di mettere da parte i soldi'/'we have the duty to open his eyes to the reality of his talents, and therefore to the real possibilities of his future, advising him therefore to save his money'. Yet his own treatment acknowledges the impossibility of this, as Maggiorani loses his job and is forced to spend his money on medical care for his sick son. The 'complex circuitry, which binds biography to representation and back again' (Gleghorn 2017: 222) in relation to the non-professional points to an infinite possible repetition of this scenario for Maggiorani.[38]

Zavattini pointed the finger somewhat at De Sica (and himself) in a 1950 article on the unmade film, saying that 'Forse è soltanto un moto egoistico che ci spinge verso certe azioni che tuttavia sono buone. Tutti ci lodano ma ci ha guidati il desiderio di queste lodi più che la bontà in sé' (Zavattini 1950: 3).[39] The tension between the ideal, one-off use of the non-actor, espoused by De Sica and other figures such as André Bazin, and the reality of

---

[38]In the early 1960s Zavattini planned a film about former Italian star Maurizio Arena, which would address the difficult aftermath of Arena's acting fame. He planned for a cameo by Maggiorani, 'humiliated and depressed by cinema' (Zavattini 2021: 334).

[39]'Perhaps there is an egotistical impulse behind certain of our actions that are, nonetheless, good. Everyone praises us, but we have been guided by the desire for praise rather than by goodness in itself'.

a need to return to the cinema industry for economic reasons is unresolved. The impossible future of the non-professional can only be secured, says Zavattini elsewhere, through professional training, thus echoing the debates we saw in Chapter 1: Maggiorani and others like Maria Fiore, Zavattini suggests (in Anon. 1954a), 'invece di essere gettati allo sbaraglio, vengano mandati in una scuola di recitazione'/'instead of being thrown away, should be sent to acting school'.

Absent this training, which for him happened only on the job in his various acting roles, Maggiorani retained a haunting quality in Italian cinema; this is visualized in *Tu, Maggiorani* through his wandering through Rome with the ghostly figures from neorealist films surrounding him, and in his fleeting film appearances, sometimes echoing his moment of glory. A 1949 magazine article (Cavassa 1949) in fact reproved Maggiorani, who, it asserted, had been spotted giving autographs instead of just remaining in his factory job. De Sica, who, as we have seen, did uncertainly try to take some responsibility for his actor, said in 1954 that the logic of stardom and the film industry was immoveable: 'il pubblico non va a vedere Lamberto Maggiorani, ma Sofia Loren, sì'/'audiences go to see Sophia Loren, not Lamberto Maggiorani' (1975e: 289).

Maggiorani's story is thus suspended, caught in a web of myths and anecdotes. However, it demands answers about the fate of non-professionals, as well as about the difficulties of reconstructing their lives, when nobody has written biographies of them, and they have often not had a chance to have their say. In May 2009, a plaque commemorating the centenary of Magggiorani's birth was unveiled at the Villaggio Breda, the workers' model village built during fascism for the Breda factory workers on the periphery of Rome where he had lived (Anon. 2009).[40] The ceremony was attended by Enzo Staiola, De Sica's son Manuel, and Maggiorani's surviving children. The plaque, on the wall of his house, reads simply:

In questa casa visse
LAMBERTO MAGGIORANI
1909–1983
ATTORE[41]

---

[40] See also the online piece by film scholar Flaminio Di Biagi (2009) who delivered an address at the commemoration. Di Biagi's information, presumably culled from family sources, includes such snippets as the fact that Maggiorani had played football for Viterbo, and began working at Breda in the early 1930s. Photos and an excerpt from the commemorative booklet for the event are available on the Facebook page of the Associazione Culturale 'La Fabbrica del Villaggio Breda'.

[41] *In this house lived Lamberto Maggiorani, actor.*

On a local level, at least, Maggiorani is remembered and celebrated as an actor.

La terra trema: Sicilian non-professionals as 'primitive' raw material

The dismissal of actorly agency, along with the difficult afterlife of the non-professional actor, is also relevant to *La terra trema*, which premiered at the Venice Film Festival a few months before De Sica's film came out. Like *Bicycle Thieves*, Luchino Visconti's 1948 masterpiece has been celebrated for its use of a non-professional cast (one of the few films of the period to use no professional actors whatsoever); however, it has rarely been examined from the perspective of its performers, the villagers and fishermen of the Sicilian village of Aci Trezza, who were essential to the film's critical success as they played the Valastro family, struggling against nature and against economic exploitation by those richer. As we will see, like Maggiorani, the Sicilian cast were chosen for their authenticity, but this proved challenging in the process of direction.

Visconti's plan to make a film of Giovanni Verga's 1881 novel *I Malavoglia* dates back to his experience with the group attached to the journal *Cinema* in the early 1940s, who were strongly attracted to Verga's works.[42] Visconti's attraction to the mythic, Homeric world of Verga's Sicily was first expressed in his 1941 essay 'Tradizione e invenzione'/'Tradition and Invention': 'la Sicilia di Verga era apparsa davvero l'isola di Ulisse, un'isola di avventure e di fervide passioni, situata immobile e fiera contro i marosi del mare Jonio'/'Verga's Sicily really seemed to be the island of Ulysses, an island of adventures and heated passions, immobile and proud against the breakers of the Ionian sea' (cited in Pucci 2013: 417). This timeless, primitive conception of Sicily must be interrogated in relation to Visconti's filmmaking practice there, to which, I argue, the casting is central.

Visconti visited the island in 1947 to scout locations for the film, which was financed by the Communist Party and intended as the first in a trilogy of documentaries (Miccichè 1998: 88).[43] As with De Sica, Visconti's casting approach was indexical: as he recounted of the scouting process in Aci Trezza, 'sono andato in piazza e ho detto: "ecco, questo è Ntoni, queste sono le due ragazze". ... Erano già lì, e io li avevo in testa'/'I went to the square, and said: "look, he's 'Ntoni, these are the two girls". ... They were

---

[42] See the essays by Alicata and De Santis (1941a and 1941b). Leavitt (2020: 25–7) discusses the modernist aspects of the revival of Verga.
[43] As is well known, Visconti ran out of money during filming, and eventually secured backing from the Catholic production company Universalia, led by Salvo D'Angelo. On the complex involvement of Universalia in the project's development, see Giori and Subini (2014: 10–13).

already there, as they were in my head' (in Rondi 2006: 283). The cast *were* the Valastros, or how he imagined them to be from Verga's novel. And, like De Sica with Maggiorani and Carell, Visconti brought them into being, or claimed them. As his friend Mario Alicata wrote (1949: 90), 'li ha fatti suoi durante il sopralluogo in Sicilia; ha scelto quelli più suoi'/'he made them his own during the location scouting in Sicily: he chose the ones who were most "his"'.

The story of the casting told by Antonio Arcidiacono, who played the lead role of 'Ntoni, also fits into the accidental or providential sighting of the non-professional that we saw with De Sica. Arcidiacono, in a 1981 interview, said that he was spotted by Visconti's assistant Anna Davini, who offered him a pack of Pall Mall American cigarettes (Mancini and Sciacca 1981: 74). Arcidiacono's response that he thought perhaps Visconti and his crew were part of the 'Banda Giuliano', the group of outlaws around legendary post-war Sicilian bandit Salvatore Giuliano, is telling in establishing his naïve distance from the glamorous culture of filmmaking.[44] Nella and Agnese Giammona, who played the sisters Mara and Lucia, were spotted by Visconti working in their parents' trattoria. Firstly, he stared at them, then convinced their parents to allow them to audition. The 'audition' was merely a photograph that he took (Verdesca 2016). According to them, Visconti knew as soon as he saw them that they were the sisters he wanted.

The casting on site, and its seemingly instinctive nature, adds to the discourse of naturalness that pervades accounts of *La terra trema*, a naturalness that is often conflated with problematic stereotypes about Southerners, as we will see. As with *Bicycle Thieves*, this discourse is at odds with the reality of the labour involved, both for the actors and for the production team, in trying to wrangle an 'unruly' cast, especially on a shoot that began on 10 November 1947 and was supposed to last only until January 1948, but which actually wrapped on 26 May 1948 (see Pucci 2013: 423). The length of the shoot, compounded by the financial problems of the production, took a toll on all involved, and the task of extracting performances from the non-actors, who had not even contemplated acting before, or presented themselves voluntarily for selection, was arduous.

The work of filming

Unlike *Bicycle Thieves*, we have quite extensive documentation of the production of *La terra trema*. Both Francesco Rosi and Franco Zeffirelli,

---

[44]There is an analogue here with the anecdote recounted by Giorgio Salvioni about the filming of *Paisà* in Naples, when Rossellini was mistaken for a 'bandito'/'bandit' (quoted in Aprà 1995: 95).

who worked as Visconti's assistants, wrote accounts of the filming. Rosi's 'diari di lavorazione'/'filming diaries' are particularly useful in documenting the tensions between cast and crew in several areas. The first concerns the complex process of creating dialogue, exemplifying what Rosi (2006a: 14) calls a kind of 'co-creation' between Visconti and the cast. Visconti had the treatment for the film which he used on set (Giori and Subini 2014: 23);[45] he would then ask the actors to suggest dialogue, via Zeffirelli, who taught himself Sicilian for the task (see Parigi 1993). The dialogue would then be further refined and rehearsals would take place before filming. The shooting style was strongly influenced by the non-actors: Rosi says that they used a 25mm lens because of the non-professionals, with 'inquadrature semplici, macchina da presa fissa'/'simple framings and a fixed camera' (1993: 21), and with cameras not following the actors. There was no improvisation permitted by the actors, despite rumours otherwise (see Armes 1971: 112): 'Visconti fixed the actors' responses in the script, to be as carefully rehearsed as a composed text in a controlled performance' (Steimatksy 2008: 106).[46] Thus their creative input ended with suggesting words for the dialogue.

In his diary of filming, Rosi repeats the word 'faticoso'/'exhausting' several times. Part of this 'fatica' was linked to Visconti's use of direct sound recording: unlike *Bicycle Thieves*, this meant that the moment of uttering the dialogue became 'il momento definitivo, immodificabile'/'the definitive, unchangeable moment' of performance (Rosi 2006a: 14). This led to up to thirty takes being needed sometimes (Rosi 1993: 22), as actors struggled to remember lines or to conquer nerves. For example, in December 1947 Rosi referred in exasperation to Antonio Arcidiacono's 'continue papere'/'constant mistakes' despite having practised the lines with Zeffirelli. 'Dice che s'impressiona per il ciak e per Visconti'/'He says that he's very nervous because of the filming and because of Visconti', he comments (2006b: 76), unsympathetically, and they have to postpone the scene till the next day.

The effort expended by the crew was not limited to getting actors to remember the dialogue. Rosi expresses frustration about their inability to behave like actors. This is frequently linked to the underlying idea that they do not really understand what they are being asked to do. Rosi acknowledges that Visconti was asking of them 'disciplina, e il dominio del mezzo che solo un attore professionista avrebbe potuto avere'/'discipline, and the control

---

[45]Though one of the Giammona sisters (in Verdesca 2016) claims that Visconti had with him on set only a copy of Verga's novel *I Malavoglia*, with parts underlined. This claim is not supported by others' testimony, however.
[46]'The discipline Visconti demanded from his non-professional performers was reiterated in the degree of preparation and control that he exercised on all planes of the image.' He rebuilt spaces to produce a 'deliberate and controlled theatrical order that would lend itself to the choreography of the actors' motions and blocking' (Steimatksy 2008: 107).

of their tools that only a professional actor could have had' (2006a: 14), and that they were, unsurprisingly, unable to provide this. When they do produce what is required, it is seemingly without full comprehension or control: "Ntoni senza saperlo, comincia a recitare'/'"Ntoni without knowing it, begins to act' (Rondi 2003: 593).

The villagers do not understand the basics of acting or filmmaking, it turns out. Numerous examples of this 'problem' are given by Rosi: these include performers turning up to reshoot the same scene the next day in different clothes, despite multiple warnings, men shaving between one take and the next, locals not understanding 'day for night' filming, fights breaking out between takes, children not turning up to film because they've gone off to *Carnevale*, an onion having to be used to extract tears from the actor playing Cola, and actors looking directly into the camera. As Visconti wrote in a 1948 letter to the film's editor Mario Serandrei, 'difficile poter portare uno di questi pescatori siciliani alla coscienza del meccanismo di una recitazione che, per quanto rudimentale, spontanea, ecc possa essere, è sempre recitazione' (Serandrei 1948: 50).[47]

In this litany of frustrations, what often emerges is a fundamental sense of the Sicilians' primitivism, linked to stereotypes of Southern backwardness. I will address this in more detail later, but it is clear that the power of the director is immensely enhanced in this process: Visconti is celebrated for his ability to elicit performances from this raw material. In his 1948 piece on the filming process, Gian Luigi Rondi (2003: 594) celebrated 'le commoventi vittorie ottenute da Visconti sul materiale umano che era andato a cercare in Sicilia'/'the moving victories obtained by Visconti over the human material he had sought out in Sicily'. What he calls the 'splendida materia plastica'/'splendid material to be shaped' (ibid.) represented by the Sicilians echoes De Sica's view of non-professionals as 'soft wax' to be shaped, and heightens the chasm between the expert director and the inert cast. Such is Visconti's skill, in fact, that he is described as having a 'maieutic' ability to create a performance and as being a kind of 'water diviner' (Parigi 1993: 143).

Control and exploitation

The idea that Visconti was faced with a resistant natural material to shape or extract is enhanced by the strategies he used to control his unruly performers. For example, performers were not allowed to look at rushes so as not to lose their 'semplicità'/'simplicity' (De Bernart 2006: 280). Girls

---

[47]'It is difficult to lead one of these Sicilian fishermen to an awareness of the process of acting, which, no matter how rudimental or spontaneous it might be, is still acting'.

in particular were controlled: Nella and Agnese Giammona recounted that Visconti did not want them watching any other films that might influence their acting (Kiss 2015: 32). However, they admitted to having watched the 1947 historical film *Genoveffa di Brabante/Genevieve of Brabant* and comparing themselves unfavourably to Harriet Medin.

> The sisters confronted Visconti with their observation. He had to convince them that in *Genoveffa di Brabante* when the main character's dramatic destiny was taken into account (Genoveffa is imprisoned and decides to live in the woods), Harriet Medin's invariably perfect hairdo and glossy lips did not match the story. (ibid.)[48]

This attempt to measure themselves against a cinematic model shows the girls' engagement in the world of cinema and complicates the assertion in *Oggi* at the time that most of the cast had never seen a movie (Anon. 1948a).[49]

Like De Sica, Visconti resorted to threats to get what he wanted: Rosi (2006a: 14) recalls his 'sfuriate'/'rages' when things did not go his way, and Aiace Parolin, assistant camera operator on the film, mentioned that Visconti shouted at the actors, called them 'mascalzoni'/'scoundrels', and physically threatened them (in Miccichè 1993: 243).[50] Visconti would become particularly enraged with the Giammona sisters when they appeared wearing make-up (Kiss 2015: 32), and Agnese Giammona says she was forced by him to look directly into a spotlight, and was blinded for twenty-four hours (ibid.: 29). She adds that these were the 'sacrifices' they made for the film, and it appears that she made them willingly.

The unruliness of the cast, which Visconti tried – sometimes in vain – to control, had another aspect too, an economic one: there were frequent protests from locals about the pay offered, and those who were not selected as extras kicked up a fuss on multiple occasions. On 21 November (ten days after filming started) Rosi records that already fishermen were refusing to do anything without getting paid. He wearily noted that these tussles over pay are 'la nostra perdita di tempo maggiore'/'our biggest waste of time'. Rosi repeats these references to pay demands: on

---

[48]American actress Harriet White Medin was credited in *Genoveffa di Brabante* as Harriet White, as in her appearance in the Florentine episode of Rossellini's *Paisà* (1946).
[49]This type of rhetoric around the non-professional's absolute innocence of film is very common. Interestingly, Zeffirelli (1993: 29) asserted that some of the locals were at first imitating the acting styles of the cinema or 'teatro popolare' that they were familiar with. They would also, of course, have been familiar with other types of performance such as opera, *sacre rappresentazioni*, radio, and puppet shows.
[50]De Bernart (2006) recalls that the girls were told that if they looked down the camera lens they would be thrown into the sea.

22 November he refers to a 'ressa per i pagamenti'/'rabble looking for payment', and on 26 January we learn that some locals are threatening to boycott the shoot if they don't get paid. Nino Valastro, one of the extras, on the same day demands money, and Visconti threatens to report him to the police in Catania, which shuts him up. On 18 February, it is noted that some of the villagers are refusing to lend the production props because they are not working every day (see Rosi 2006b, passim). One old man even spoiled a take (presumably in a protest about pay) by deliberately rowing across the background and had to be chased off by *carabinieri* (De Bernart 2006).

Rosi got more and more disenchanted with the locals, by late January and early February referring to them as a 'massa di boicottatori'/'mass of boycotters' (2006b: 96) and 'i soliti ricattatori'/'the usual blackmailers' (ibid.: 94). Part of his disdain seemed to derive from the fact that he felt the production was being taken advantage of by locals keen to make a quick buck: 'sono convinti che noi siamo gonfi di millioni da gettare via'/'they are convinced that we are swimming in money to throw at them' (ibid.: 108). Of course the financial difficulties of the production exacerbated these tensions, and in February 1948 Visconti had to go to Rome to secure the financing from Universalia. Yet Rosi seems rather unreflective on the financial situation of his actors, even when he records that the selection of extras is delegated to local 'capomaestri'/'foremen', in a situation that is presumably rife with inequality.[51]

As we have seen, the question of pay for non-professional actors is rarely critically discussed, as the prestige and recognition of taking part in a great film is often felt to be sufficient, fitting into neorealism's 'perfection of capitalist downsizing' (Kennedy 2005). But Nella Giammona (in Verdesca 2016) tells us that when the girls went to the Venice Film Festival with Visconti for the premiere in September 1948, they met Anna Magnani, whose first question to them was 'ma quanto vi hanno dato??'/'So how much did they pay you??' Magnani, the consummate professional, gets to the heart of the matter immediately. However, the possibility of exploitation lurks at the edges of the non-actors' accounts. The girls were initially contracted by Visconti, they say, for two weeks (they do not specify the rate of pay), but were required to be 'a disposizione'/'on call' at any time. As the shoot stretched on and on, it appears the contract was not renewed but that they were paid for the time they appeared on set only, and there were rumblings that their father should protest this. However, they maintain that Visconti was such a gentleman that they would not have rebelled against him. Their

---

[51]Miccichè (1998: 158) notes how both novel and film address the question of 'lavoro a giornata'/'day labourers', in which selection to go out in the fishing boats is a tool of control and humiliation. This practice resonates with the selection of extras for day work on the film.

'zero hours' contract was on top of the work they did in the family trattoria, and as Rondi (2003: 593) reported, they were effectively doing two jobs, with acting being their 'second shift'. One of them is quoted thus:

> 'Sono stanca, signuri', mi alzo alle 6, devo preparare la colazione per la mia famiglia, pulire la barca di mio padre e preparargli le reti. Poi vengo qui, 'per parlare nel cinema' e debbo far dieci o undici volte la stessa cosa. A mezzo giorno torno a casa per far da mangiare ai miei fratelli, torno qui di corsa: alle sette scendo sulla spiaggia perché papà torna dalla pesca e debbo portargli le reti. Poi la cena, poi lavo i piatti.'[52]

A more embittered figure is Arcidiacono, who wept in his 1981 interview and complained that he thought of Visconti as a father, but was then betrayed by him when Visconti did not help him financially after the film. He complains that 'non ci ha lasicato nemmeno un millione. Noi lo abbiamo fatto grande e ricco'/'he didn't leave us even a small amount [in his will]. We made him great, and rich' (Mancini and Sciacca 1981: 71). Arcidiacono also pointed out that the actors were uncredited in the film – they are named merely as 'pescatori siciliani'/'Sicilian fishermen' – and he wonders aloud if this was to prevent them from having royalties (ibid.: 74).[53] Whether this is remotely the case or not, it is certainly clear that the actors were not fully recognized, and their names unknown.[54]

Mancini opens the book of interviews and memories of the film with a reference to this lack of official credit and writes that 'questa nostra opera è almeno servita, per la prima volta, a restituire nella sua completezza il nome a un cast destinato al silenzio'/'our work has served, for the first time, to give a name to a cast that was destined to languish in silence' (1981: 5). He refers to it as a 'tenace documentazione di scomparse'/'tenacious act of documentation of those who have disappeared' and the noun 'scomparse' tellingly links both the repressions and ellipses of the actors' contribution and plays on their brief and unrecognized appearances (as 'comparse'/'extras') in a globally acclaimed masterpiece.

---

[52] 'I'm so tired, I get up at six, I have to get breakfast ready for the family, clean my father's boat, and prepare the nets. Then I come here, "to talk in the cinema" and I have to do the same thing ten or eleven times in a row. At midday I go home to make lunch for my brothers, then I rush back here: at seven I go down to the beach because Papà comes back from fishing and I have to bring his nets. Then dinner, then washing the dishes.'

[53] See Pitassio (2007: 157) on the opening titles which affirm the non-professional nature of the actors. He argues that these titles in neorealist film function as garanti della verità di quei corpi'/'guarantors of the truth of those bodies'.

[54] Viazzi (1949) reproduces a picture of Visconti with one of the Giammona girls at Venice, naming in the caption Visconti, the male critic Gadda Conti standing behind him, and 'one of the actresses from the film'.

Southernness and backwardness

As we saw in relation to *Bicycle Thieves*, there is often a difficulty in recognizing the work of non-actors as work. This is complicated in discussions of Visconti's film by a persistent discourse of *meridionalismo*, that is, a political interest in Italy's 'Southern Question' 'predicated on the assumption of southern Italy as a homogenous periphery examinable only within the framework of historical and social backwardness and stagnation' (Bouchard and Ferme 2012: xi).[55] Hence the idea of the 'natural' or 'primitive' south, and of actors who 'are' the characters (but who also have to have a performance brought out of them by a northern male genius), elides the painful labour of the process, which we have only been able to glimpse through Rosi's notes.

The question of primitivism is, as Fabbri asserts, central to the film's workings, in that it 'denies a proper rational agency to subaltern subjects by assimilating their revolts to natural events' (Fabbri 2016). The insistence on temporal backwardness and a sense of the events of the plot as part of an endless, fated cycle of exploitation leads Fabbri to argue that 'Visconti transfigures the story of a local insurgency into a Greek tragedy, an ancestral suspension of time that fixes human suffering in an ahistorical, archetypal dimension'.[56]

In some ways the production notes merely record some local cultural beliefs which seem somewhat anachronistic to the mainly northern team (though Rosi himself was Neapolitan). For example, the insistence on modesty on the part of girls and women is documented: the Giammona sisters talk of their family's fears that they might be 'perdute'/'ruined' after appearing in the film and might thus never marry (in Mancini and Sciacca 1981: 75). Rosi notes how 'le donne non vogliono assolutamente mostrarsi in piazza'/'the women absolutely do not want to put themselves on show in the piazza' (2006b: 64), which is somewhat similar to attitudes discussed in the next chapter, during the filming in southern Italy of Castellani's 1952 *Due soldi di speranza*. But there is an undoubtedly paternalistic tone to much of the coverage: De Bernart's references to 'stregoneria'/'witchcraft' (2006: 279), the description of Mara (Nella Giammona) as an 'animale naturale'/'natural animal' (Zagarrio 1993: 135), Rondi's mention of faces with 'i tratti marmorei dell'antica fissità siciliana'/'the rock-like characteristics of ancient Sicilian immutability' (2003: 593) all express

---

[55] In a 1960 essay, Visconti claimed the film was inspired by Antonio Gramsci's writings on the economic and historical basis of the Southern Question; however, Miccichè (1998: 85) shows that Visconti could not have been inspired by these writings, as they were not published until after he made the film.
[56] See Cassano's critique (2012: xxix) of *meridionalismo* as a conceptual schema in which 'cultural differences ... are transformed into temporal gaps'.

both a temporal and spatial distance from the 'raw material' of the film. Indeed, Zeffirelli (1993: 30) suggestively commented that the elegant and sophisticated Visconti was like a 'Martian' to the Sicilians.

In this regard, as is common with non-professionals, the emphasis on their out-of-placeness in the glamorous world of film was also played up, especially in coverage of the actors' trip to Venice for the 1948 Festival. Bazin wrote of the trip that 'this family was as much out of its element in the sumptuous reception Universalia gave in its honor at the Excelsior in Venice as the Farrebique family had been at its press party in Paris' (1971: 41), referring to the 1946 documentary by Georges Rouqier about Occitan-speaking peasants from the south of France. Actually, the Giammona sisters insisted that their experience was 'indimenticabile'/'unforgettable' (in Verdesca 2016), though Arcidiacono refers to going to Venice as going 'dalle stalle alle stelle'/'from the stables to the stars' (in Mancini and Sciacca 1981: 74), so it is clear that the notion of out-of-placeness may be extremely subjective, and that the voices of protagonists need to be heard more widely.

The question of otherness also regards an aspect of the film's style that has drawn much critique, which is the use of dialect: as mentioned, Visconti, drawing upon Verga's nineteenth-century text, asked locals to contribute dialogue in the local dialect. Sicilian writer and intellectual Leonardo Sciascia criticized the deliberate archaism of the result, which produced, for him, a form of dialect that was difficult to understand even for Sicilians. Sciascia's view of the wilful 'ritardatario romanticismo'/'out-of-date romanticism' (2003: 1212) of the language of the film aligns, albeit less harshly, with Fabbri's take (2016) that the language is 'an ideology-ridden folkloristic misconstruction'. In addition, the question of whether the villagers were actually all dialect speakers only is contested: the Giammona sisters mention that they knew Italian and some English from school, and acted as intermediaries between Visconti and the villagers (see Kiss 2015: 31). This omission contributes to the 'othering' of Sicily, and to the sense that the film is only 'capace di essere intesa dal regista stesso, dai suoi collaboratori, e da un piccolo gruppo di cineasti'/'capable of being understood by the director himself and a small group of cineastes' (Baldelli 1973: 1991).[57]

---

[57]Sciascia (2003: 1212) complained that Visconti's 'regressive' approach to language produced 'un vernacolo ... così stretto e concitato da riuscire, in parte, di difficile comprehensione agli stessi siciliani'/'a dialect ... so limited and rapid as to be difficult even for Sicilians to understand'. This is backed up by Sicilian responses to the film's Venice premiere: 'lo stesso impianto dialettale della *Terra trema* è fonte di ironie: un cronista presente a Venezia, che s'è intrattenuto con alcuni pescatori venuti da Aci Trezza per vedersi nel film, sostiene che essi parlano perfettamente l'italiano; e che, d'altra parte, nessuno dei siciliani seduti in sala, dal catanese Vitaliano Brancati allo stesso sindaco comunista di Venezia, il trapanese Giovanni Battista Gianquinto, ha capito una parola dei dialoghi'/'the dialect used in *La terra trema* is a source of irony: a journalist at Venice who spoke to fishermen who'd arrived from Aci Trezza to watch the film swears that they speak perfect Italian. And on the other hand, none of the

The dialect, in addition to being an index of a Sicily that is temporally and spatially removed from mainland Italy, is also part of the film's famed 'chorality'. The use of direct sound recording meant that unlike other neorealist films, the voices of the villagers and fishermen, their 'collaborative vocal activity' (Alsop 2014: 29) were registered as an important part of the film's narrative. Visconti's film, while denied major prizes at Venice for political reasons, was awarded a special prize for its 'valori stilistici corali'/'choral stylistic values' (see Giori and Subini 2014: 27). While this vocal effect works with the mise-en-scène to furnish an impression of 'choral spatiality' (Steimatsky 2008: 111), Steimatksy's suggestion that it 'gives humble subjects an eloquent voice' (ibid.: 116) might benefit from some nuance. As Alsop (2014: 28) has also pointed out, the choral use of voice in neorealism often 'performs a range of other rhetorical functions'; in this context, this might be to fuse individuals into a mass of 'pescatori siciliani'/'Sicilian fishermen' (as they are credited in the titles). Bazin's comment (1971: 41) that 'if festival juries were not what they are, the Venice festival prize for best acting should have gone to the fishermen of *La Terra Trema*' similarly elides individuals, but recognizes that 'valori corali'/'choral values' might reduce the actors to elements of the mise-en-scène, and negate their individual actorly contributions. A further overlooked, extra-diegetic, 'choral' factor, reading Rosi's production diaries, is his rendering of the fishermen as 'una massa di urlatori'/'a howling mass' (2006b: 96) as they complain about pay. His repeated disapproving mentions of their 'urla'/'cries' to the production team force us to consider not just the expressive and aesthetic quality of chorality but its ideological function in positioning the fishermen as an ungrateful, undifferentiated, noisy mass.

Visconti's beautifully staged mise-en-scène, with its elegant framing and 'deterministic theatricalization of space' (Steimatksy 2008: 108) has been similarly controversial in relation to the film's presentation of Sicily. From Bazin's comment (1971: 45) on Visconti's 'dangerous inclination to aestheticism' to Renzo Renzi's criticism of 'la estetizzante cura compositiva delle immagini'/'the aestheticizing care taken in the composition of the images' (1949: 67), to Franco Fortini's view (1973: 160) that the film 'peccava d'estetismo'/'committed the sin of aestheticism' many critics were uncomfortable with his indulgently pictorial approach to Aci Trezza.[58] Orson Welles famously claimed that cameraman G. R. Aldo's gorgeous

---

Sicilians watching the film, from Vitaliano Brancati [the writer from Catania] to the mayor of Venice, Giovanni Battista Gianquinto, from Trapani, understood a single word' (Ajello 1997: 217).

[58]Even Luigi Chiarini, who praised the film both at Venice and on its later release for its resemblance to the great Flemish painters, conceded that the limit of the film was its 'preziosismo estetico'/'aesthetic artifice' (1951a: 16). See Miccichè (1998: 97) for other contemporary examples of these negative views, with which Miccichè disagrees.

FIGURE 5 La terra trema: *The Sicilian actresses merge into the rocks of Aci Trezza.*

photography of the actors made them look like *Vogue* models rather than poor workers (quoted in Steimatksy 2017: 75).[59] The almost absurd beauty of the representation needs to be linked to the way that the characters are figured as part of the natural landscape, most particularly in the scene in which Mara and Lucia wait on the rocks for 'Ntoni's boat to return. The immobility of both characters and natural landscape, filmed with long takes and often static shots, fuses both into a timeless and despairing tableau of 'arcaica monumentalità'/'archaic monumentality' (Rondi, cited in Miccichè 1998: 91) (Figure 5).[60]

---

[59]Likewise, Tennessee Williams, who visited the set, remarked that the shooting stills were 'the most beautiful photographs of the most beautiful faces I have ever seen' (Williams 2006: 472). Aldo was celebrated for his use of *chiaroscuro*, apparently modelled on Caravaggio's paintings: see Ellero (1987: 8–9).
[60]The ASL of the film was 18.2 seconds, and Miccichè (1998: 91–2) notes that 70 per cent of the film's 527 shots are static. Miccichè, however, argues for a reading of the film in which its apparent slowness is complicated by the 'ricchissima dinamica dei piani'/'incredibly rich dynamics of the shots' (ibid.: 96).

Conclusion

In 1951, *Bianco e Nero* editor Luigi Chiarini (1951a: 16) declared that *La terra trema* marked the end of neorealism, and the beginning of its subsequent 'involution'. The year 1948, which also produced *Bicycle Thieves*, can be regarded as the zenith of the non-professional actor, although while De Sica's film was a box-office success, Visconti's was 'il più impopolare tra i film post-bellici'/'the most unpopular of the post-war films' (Miccichè 1998: 189). We have seen the differences in the way both directors handled their non-professionals: from De Sica's 'amalgam' of professionals and non-professionals to Visconti's rigorous focus on non-actors; from De Sica's emphasis on physiognomic performance with the knowledge the voices will be dubbed in later, to Visconti's careful blocking and setting up for live sound and its difficulties for the performers.

The similarities reside in the ideological functions and effects of the non-actors: what is common to both films and to their discursive surrounds is the fleeting insight we get into the experience of the performers themselves, and their own attitudes towards the work they did. As the case of the unmade film about Maggiorani literalizes, he became a meta-character in his own experience, and floated around the Italian film industry for years, a seemingly unwelcome reminder of the lability of the non-professional's career and the near-impossibility for it to become something more. While the cast of Visconti's film received less attention after the film, the production notes and elements of their interviews give insight into the frustrations of being treated like raw material in the production of a masterpiece. Visconti's idealistic conception of non-actors, expressed in his 1943 essay 'Anthropomorphic Cinema', praises their 'semplicità'/'simplicity' and 'qualità primitive'/'primitive qualities', because they are 'prodotti di ambienti non compromessi'/'products of environments that are not contaminated' and are thus 'spesso uomini migliori'/'often better men' (1943: 109). While this conception comes into conflict with the extra-diegetic reality of the needy humans who worked on the film, the film text itself preserves this sense of a pure and primitive grandeur of the ordinary person, imbricated in the natural environment.

We have seen that the debate on the value of the non-professional was still happening in the mid-1950s, albeit in much less heated form. A *Cinema Nuovo* editorial (Anon. 1955) lamented the poor state of the Italian acting profession, caused partly by the proliferation of non-professionals in various forms. Nevertheless, it concluded, the industry needed both stars like Anna Magnani and figures like the 'Valastros' and Maggiorani, both explicitly named. The fact that in the editorial the cast members are actually called by the name of their characters demonstrates the persistent and uninterrogated difficulty of integrating the (non)actors fully into accounts of these films, which have been so deeply analysed in nearly every other aspect. Whether the actors were exploited or not by the directors and production team, whether they felt that it had been a valuable experience or not, whether they felt they had had agency in the process clearly varies not just according to the person, but over time. One does not have to agree with Franco Fortini's 1952 critique of some neorealist films that they were representing 'una realtà ad un'altra realtà; una realtà di piedi nudi a platee di piedi di gente calzata'/'one kind of world to a different world: a world of bare feet to a well-shod audience' (1973: 157) to feel some unease at the way non-professionals were treated as curiosities and then left to fend for themselves.

Proletarian and peasant non-actors like some of the ones in this chapter were often regarded as curiosities and as strictly bound to the social and cultural reality they are filmed in. This is evident in a short newspaper article from 1949, in which the author excitedly and somewhat snidely reports that she saw one of 'the Valastros' from *La terra trema* in a nightclub in Rome (Cavassa 1949). The piece hits many of the usual notes of faux-concern: why is the young man (presumably Arcidiacono, who played 'Ntoni) drinking a fancy cocktail? Has he gone off the rails? Is he still speaking that incomprehensible dialect? Is he trying his hand at cinema, not realizing that Visconti was responsible for elevating him to that 'ignorante stato di grazia'/'ignorant state of grace' in the film? The journalist concludes her 'scandalous' squib by saying that she would much rather know that at 3.00 am he is out at sea, not in a bar (something that is, presumably, fine for her).

The same piece also mentions with sadness that Maggiorani has been spotting giving autographs, noted earlier. While De Sica was fond of saying that he 'borrowed' Maggiorani's face for the duration of the shoot, and then 'returned' it, he was left to manage the consequences of Maggiorani's refusal to leave the stage gracefully. While Maggiorani continued to haunt Italian cinema, like the return of neorealism's repressed, the cast of Visconti's film were forgotten about till many years later, when they were sought out to give interviews, and their names finally made public. Zavattini (2002: 731), in his polemic against the use of stars, pointed out that while the names of stars are embedded in cultural consciousness, 'all'anagrafe siamo tutti nominati'/'we are all named in the register of births'. However, with regard to both films, the 'circulation of anecdotal material' has acted like a kind of 'acoustic feedback' (Gleghorn 2017: 222), irrevocably conditioning how the films have been read, and foreclosing a more forensic analysis of the implications of their uses of non-professionals.

While neither Maggiorani nor the Sicilian cast were encouraged to continue acting, the testimony by the Giammona sisters (in Verdesca 2016) that *La terra trema* producer, Salvo D'Angelo, at the Venice Film Festival, told their mother 'lasci stare le sue figlie a casa'/'keep your daughters at home', instead of letting them work again, is particularly unsurprising, as the modesty *topos* came directly into play for them in a way that their male counterparts avoided. These tensions around non-professional female performance and stardom are the focus of the next chapter.

3

Girls, stardom, and the danger of cinema

Neorealism's use of the non-professional 'preso dalla strada'/'taken from the street' has a very particular resonance for girls. This chapter examines the phenomenon of girls aspiring to or attaining cinematic stardom in this period, whether short-lived or lasting: it will go beyond the well-trodden coverage which has focused on those like Sophia Loren, Gina Lollobrigida, and Lucia Bosè who gained sudden fame as actresses via beauty contests. While it places these girls in the broader context of press discourses around girls and cinema, from both left and right, it also traces a continuity between the beauty queens and those who were recruited by other means. I then go on to focus on two lesser-studied cases: Carmela Sazio (discovered by Rossellini in 1946 for *Paisà/Paisan* and then discarded) and Maria Fiore, who was recruited by Renato Castellani for his 1952 hit *Due soldi di speranza/Two Cents of Hope*, and who continued to work, but who is depicted in the press as full of regrets.

The chapter argues that there was a pervasive and moralistic Italian rhetoric that saw girls who pursued a career in cinema as both threatened by the immorality of cinema and a threat to its legitimacy, because of their lack of professional training, and also, crucially, because of the threat of feminization they carry. The very question of professionalism, the chapter argues, interpellates girls differently; the notion raises important questions of girls' vulnerability in the public sphere, and of their agency in a male-dominated industry and critical context, and the chapter shows how in the 1940s and 1950s, in patriarchal Italy, the profession of acting, for women, was often haunted by the spectre of sex work.

The first part of the chapter begins by examining the relationship of girls to the cinema industry in the post-war period, looking at their engagement with film via the popular press and *fotoromanzi* or photoromances, and at their involvement in beauty contests, which became a semi-official pipeline to the film industry. It investigates how this widespread engagement with cinema was accompanied by depictions of girls as uncritical consumers, whose morality was at risk through this fixation on film, and how girls and

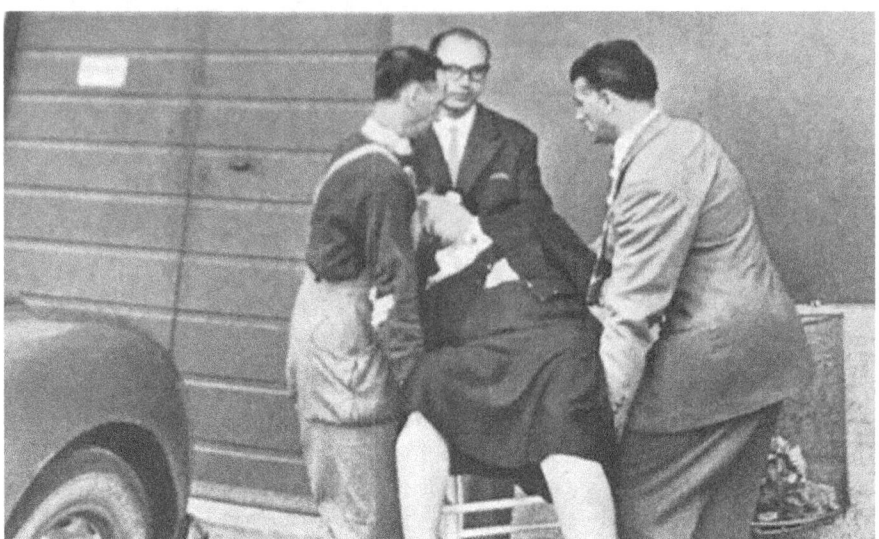

FIGURE 6 *A mother faints on hearing her daughter has not been given a part in* The Roof, *from* Cinema Nuovo, *1955. Author's own.*

young women who became stars were the object of attacks on their skills and professionalism. The second part then focuses on the case studies of Carmela Sazio and Maria Fiore, which provide a new perspective on the girl who is discovered by a powerful director, and whose 'Cinderella' stories illuminate the complex power dynamics and the struggle for agency that pervade these narratives.

Girls and cinema in post-war Italy

The above photo (Figure 6), published in *Cinema Nuovo* in 1955,[1] depicts a backstage moment in the search for the protagonists of Vittorio De Sica's film *Il tetto/The Roof*. The caption tells us that the fainting woman is the mother of one of the 300 hopefuls aged between 16 and 21 gathered for auditions at the Titanus studios in Rome, and that she has just learned that her daughter was not selected by the director. No further information is given, but I would speculate that the subtext of this mother's story is economic: in Italy's difficult post-war reconstruction, with poverty and unemployment rates still high (see Ginsborg 1990: 187), the appeal of work in the film industry was

---

[1]Martini (1955: 380).

obvious.[2] These economic stakes are underlined by Cesare Zavattini, writer of *The Roof*, whose diary records the case of a Neapolitan girl who offers herself to him to try to get a part. He notes her pathetic plea: 'mi faccia fare il provino: ho venduto la radio per comprarmi questo vestito'/'let me have a screen test: I sold my radio to buy this dress' (Zavattini 2002: 153). While Zavattini records other cases of being importuned by ordinary people desperate to work in his films, the case of the Neapolitan girl is particularly poignant, as it alludes to the trade-offs often implicit or explicit in engaging with the film industry. And while the mother of the aspiring girl in *The Roof* seems as desperate as her daughter to land the role, as we will see, the stigma still attached to cinema for girls and women made it potentially morally suspect, at the same time as it appeared lucrative and widely appealing. Zavattini seems to blame girls when he calls (2002: 140) the allure of cinema something 'per cui troppe donne sono pronte a tirarsi su le sottane appena lo sentono nominare'/'that too many women are ready to lift up their skirts for as soon as it's mentioned'. Examining these sexual trade-offs helps us consider the ramifications for young women of what Masi (2003: 336) has termed the 'mitopoesi del divismo come unico mezzo per redimere alla miseria schiere di fanciulle sognatrici'/'mythopoesis of stardom as the only means of redeeming from poverty these hordes of dreaming girls'.

In Chapter 1, we saw how competitions were used by production companies and magazines as recruitment tools and ways of encouraging girls' identification with cinema. Although most of these competitions encouraged the cinematic ambitions of girls, there are telling examples of mockery, such as the article from 1949 in the relatively highbrow film journal *Cinema*: '"Predive" col cuore a fumetti'/'"Pre-divas" with Comic-strip Hearts' (Giani 1949). These 'pre-divas' who aspire to stardom are described as narcissistic provincial girls who reply to magazine competitions, and whose pathetic attempts at stardom are the subject of mockery and moralistic judgment by the male journalist. We will see more of this when we come to consider specifically left-wing objections to young female stardom, but here these girls are portrayed as lower class and poorly educated ('non sanno scrivere perché di massimo nascono analfabete'/'they can't write because they're mostly illiterate' (ibid.: 526)) and as provincial (they are likened to Flaubert's Madame Bovary). The author gleefully quotes from a poorly written and hyperbolic letter from one of these girls as proof of their lack of education. Crucially, the author describes how with every notice of a casting call, the offices of production companies are 'invase da ragazze d'ogni genere'/'invaded by girls of every type' (ibid.: 524), figuring

---

[2]The image is a real-world analogue of the early shots of Visconti's *Bellissima* (1951), in which mothers anxiously watch their young daughters audition for a part in the film-within-the-film; one of the aspirational mothers later faints from stress and heat exhaustion while waiting for her child's turn. *Bellissima* will be discussed in detail in the next chapter.

these girls as a faceless mass, a trope that is commonly used to suggest their threatening presence.

In a 1961 piece on girls recruited to stardom and their regrets about it, journalist Lianella Carell, who appeared in *Bicycle Thieves* (1948), describes turning up to interview the director Vittorio De Sica and then being offered the part. De Sica, she is informed, was being assailed by girls who resembled 'belve inferocite'/'ferocious beasts'. Carell herself describes them as a 'sciame di stupide fanciulle'/'swarm of stupid girls' and a 'branco di ragazze esagitate'/'herd of frenzied girls' looking for parts (in Cavicchioli 1961a: 13–14).[3] Carell stresses that her journalistic career was more serious and respectable than the job of acting, which she describes as shameful and a torture (ibid.: 14). The ascribed stupidity and lack of individualism of girls in the cultural imaginary can be related to the 'tendency to represent and discuss girls as conformist rather than resistant' (Driscoll 2002: 11).[4] This resonates with what Hipkins (2016: 192) has termed the 'beauty trade-off' in this period: 'if cinematic visibility gives women power, this must be curtailed through their depiction as stupid, and quite possibly dangerous'.

The images of girls staring at a fortunate actress on the way into the film studios, seen in the contemporaneous shots from *La signora senza camelie/The Lady Without Camelias* (Antonioni, 1953) and *Siamo donne: episodio 'Quattro attrici una speranza'/We, the Women: Episode 'Four Actresses, One Hope'* (Guarini 1953), reinforce this sense that girls might overpower the film industry, and that some must be kept out (Figures 7 and 8).

This imagery also correlates with a broader cultural threat in the period, that of girls invading the workplace. Hipkins brings in a visual parallel with the film *Roma ore 11/Rome 11:00* (De Santis, 1952), in which a mass of female bodies is repeatedly shown, as desperate girls queue up on a staircase in a Rome building, looking for a job, until the staircase collapses under their collective weight. As Hipkins's analysis of De Santis's film (based on a true story) makes clear, cinema of the period commonly associates female work per se with prostitution, and it involves yet another trade-off: public visibility or praise versus the threat of sexual exploitation.

Yet, to return to the article on 'pre-divas', Giani's disdain (shown in the publication in the article of some of these girls' photos, accompanied by sardonic captions) has a (slightly) more sympathetic side, albeit laced with

---

[3]Luigi Cavicchioli, author of this feature on Carell and other accidental actresses, published a string of pieces in 1961 in the mainstream magazine *Oggi* decrying the dangers of acting for girls. See Cavicchioli (1961b, 1961c, 1961d, 1961e).
[4]See Siegfried Kracauer (1995: 76) on the dancing troupe The Tiller Girls as 'mass ornament', where he alleges that the spectacular 'indissoluble girl clusters' are a distillation of capitalism itself. Likewise, Bazin, in a 1946 essay 'Entomology of the Pin-Up Girl', describes them as 'manufactured on the assembly line, standardized by Varga' (Bazin 1971: 161). See also Lumby (2007: 342) on girls as historically in need of protection from mass culture.

FIGURE 7 *Lucia Bosè's character is stared at by girls entering Cinecittà in* The Lady Without Camelias.

FIGURE 8 We, the Women: *The visual threat represented by the mass of girls hoping for a film role in the episode 'Four Actresses, One Hope'.*

the moralism implied in the Madame Bovary reference. The girls are not entirely to blame, Giani suggests (1949: 526), because they are 'victims' of these competitions which exploit their hopes and dreams. This sympathy for girls who are in thrall to cinema is also visualized in the 1943 film *Apparizione/Apparition* (De Limur), in which Alida Valli plays a girl who is infatuated with star Amedeo Nazzari. Nazzari, playing himself, tries to lecture her about the dangers of cinema, and she angrily defends herself and all 'stupid little provincial girls' who have hopes and dreams. Yet the film cannot be too sympathetic to her, and so cannot resist moralizing and showing the danger of cinema: Valli's character runs off with Nazzari after her boyfriend gets angry at her love for the film star, and Nazzari resolves the problem by sexually threatening her in order to demonstrate the 'reality' of his glamorous world. When she agrees to return home, he is pleased that she has been 'healed' from her dreams, which can bring only bitterness and disappointment, he lectures.[5]

This uncertainty of tone and approach, by which girls are simultaneously prey and victim, both a natural and vulnerable resource to be captured on the streets of Italy and an invading horde, is very common.[6] It is reminiscent of the attitudes identified in the United States towards what Shelley Stamp (2000) termed the 'movie-struck girls' of the 1910s, avid readers of film periodicals and watchers of films, 'defined by biological youth, unbridled film consumption, and vapid longing for stardom' (Anselmo-Sequeira 2015: 1). As Anselmo-Sequeira points out (ibid.: 2), anxieties about the impact of women's unruly emotionality on the integrity of the cultural sphere can be read, since the mid-nineteenth century, as anxieties about an engulfing and feminized mass culture.[7] Similarly, in the Italian context, as elsewhere, ambivalence about whether to understand girls' enthusiastic participation in film culture as examples of excessive agency or as reckless actions that put them in moral danger can be understood, as Stamp (2000: 8) has shown, as ways of negotiating anxieties about women's film-going and participation in public life more broadly.[8] The line between agency and pathology was very

---

[5]The film ends with Nazzari receiving a phone call summoning him to the film studio early the next morning, and he takes up a script, showing the hard work and dedication required from his profession, which is to be contrasted with the facile perceptions of it that his fans have.
[6]See Zatterin (1949) who offers a story of a girl from Bari who has announced she is coming to Rome to work in *fotoromanzi* and has to be stopped by the editor. Interestingly, he also gives the example of a distressed mother whose son has given up his studies for the same reason. Both are placed under the heading of 'giovanotti malati di sogni proibiti'/'young people sick with forbidden dreams'.
[7]See Andreas Huyssens's (1986) foundational work on this subject. Marcus (2019: 173) notes the stigmatization of American 'matinee girls' who idolized male theatre stars in the 1890s, while Kenaga (2015) shows how girls who worked as extras in 1920s Hollywood were seen as desperate for stardom and, thus, as ripe for sexual exploitation.
[8]See the intervention by Monsignor Alfredo Maria Cavagna, whose 1945 book *Il Cinema: ieri, oggi, domani* argued that cinema was responsible for blurring social boundaries among girls

blurred: writer/director Mario Soldati wrote in his fictional 1935 account of a simple Roman girl seduced by cinema, that she was overcome by 'la mania del cinematografo ... una malattia nervosa'/'the mania for cinema ... a nervous illness' which he dubs 'filmopatìa'/'filmitis' (2003: 92).

As Lottini (2013: 152) shows, this disapproval of female hysteria around cinema-going was not new in Italian culture, with discussions circulating in the 1910s about this problematic nexus of young women, mass culture, and the public sphere.[9] However, it is evident that the phenomenon received broad attention in the post-war period, and that both mainstream and left-wing press were nervous about the 'invasion' of the film industry by unqualified girls, though for slightly different reasons. Later in the chapter I will look at the debate on unqualified actresses in the left-wing film journal *Cinema Nuovo* in 1953, but here I will briefly focus upon responses by the Communist Party-affiliated magazine *Noi Donne*.

Lucia Cardone (2009) has written of the moral panic around cinema for girls, as articulated in the pages of *Noi Donne* in this period: girls were deemed morally at risk due to the attractions of cinema, even though the magazine used cinema and mass culture extensively as a means of attracting female readers. Girls who wrote in inquiring about a movie career were reproved: for example, here are the thoughts of writer Renata Viganò in 1949, who responded to a girl asking advice on how to be an actress:

> Ecco un'altra candidata al cinema! Ma quanto siete, milioni? ... anche tu, questa estate, sulla spiaggia, fosti incoronata Miss-non-so-che, anche tu, adesso, ti senti pronta ad affrontare il cinema, e mi chiedi tranquillamente indirizzi di registi e produttori. Figliola mia, e se cominciassi con lo studiar qualcosa? ... una carriera cinematografica vera e propria io non la consiglio a nessuno che non abbia straordinaria forza di volontà, buona preparazione ed una fermezza di propositi incrollabile. (in Cardone 2009: 96)[10]

The opposition between easy fame and serious study is a recurring one, and girls are held to be permanently at risk due to their 'pericolose illusioni'/'dangerous illusions' (Cardone 2009: 13). Their impetuous desire to transfer small-scale recognition ('Miss non-so-che') to the national level

---

and for encouraging immoral behaviour in them such as smoking (cited in Dalle Vacche 2008: 189).

[9]See also Mazzei (2008) on this topic.

[10]'Here is another candidate for the cinema! Are there millions of you? ... This summer, on the beach, you were crowned Miss God-Knows-What, and now you feel ready to tackle the cinema, and you start to ask for addresses of producers and directors. My dear, perhaps start by studying? ... I wouldn't advise a cinema career to anyone without extraordinary force of will, a good level of competence, and an unbreakable firmness of intention'.

must be upbraided and contained. Similarly, in Fausta Cialente's article (1950: 3) she laments that:

> Appena una ragazza è ben piantata su due gambe dritte e snelle ed ha una grazioso visetto, eccola che sogna.. cinema e teatro, la notorietà prima, poi la celebrità, e onori, e lusso sfrenato, tutte altre donne morte d'invidia.. proprio come nei fumetti.[11]

Cialente's article was based on the case of Isolina Cipriani, a provincial girl who had come to Rome to break into cinema, and who, after supposedly being seduced by a film producer, committed suicide at seventeen. 'Non ha saputo resistere alle menzogne d'un mondo corrotto'/'She was unable to resist the lies of a corrupt world', says Cialente sadly. Rather than reflecting upon the economic conditions that drive this, or on the unbalanced gender order that punishes and sexually exploits girls with artistic ambitions, Cialente is sententious and says the story 'dovrebbe rammentare alle ragazze, alle mamme, alle famiglie, che invece di sognare le Anna Magnani e le Silvana Mangano, o addirittura le Ingrid Bergman, dovrebbero decidersi a rappresentarsi la vita teatrale e cinematografica quale essa è in realtà'/'should remind girls and their mothers and families that instead of dreaming of being Anna Magnani and Silvana Mangano, or even Ingrid Bergman, they should realize what theatre and cinema life is like in reality'.

The trope of suicide was very common in fictional accounts of girls lured by stardom: Luigi Malerba's *Le lettere di Ottavia/Letters from Ottavia*, fictional letters of a provincial girl who becomes an actress in Rome, published in *Cinema Nuovo* in 1956, features a suicide attempt by the vain and stupid protagonist (see Malerba 2018); in Amelia Del Frate's pulpy 1961 novel *Processo a Cinecittà/Cinecittà on Trial*, a similar protagonist, disgusted by her own corruption by the cinema industry, finally commits suicide, while at the same time another fresh-faced girl arrives at Cinecittà to take her place (Del Frate 1961).

The names of the stars chosen by Cialente as positive examples are interesting: Anna Magnani was of course an established and trained actress, who had performed for years in variety theatre and films before her big breakthrough in Rossellini's *Rome Open City*. Ingrid Bergman, Hollywood star, had arrived in Italy the previous year to make *Stromboli* with Rossellini and had proceeded to marry him. Silvana Mangano, an untrained actress, was a former beauty queen 'discovered' by Giuseppe De Santis on the

---

[11]'As soon as a girl has two slim and straight legs, and a pretty face she starts dreaming of cinema and theatre, wanting notoriety, then celebrity, and then awards, unbridled luxury, with all the other ladies dying of envy ... just like in the magazines'.

street in Rome, where he was 'thunderstruck' by her beauty (Faldini and Fofi 1979: 154). So Mangano was precisely the kind of beautiful, ordinary-girl-turned-celebrity that the *Noi Donne* readers might aspire to be.¹² Her star-making appearance in De Santis's *Riso amaro/Bitter Rice* (1949) also foregrounds the kind of serendipitous encounter that Mangano's character dreams of in the film, as she reads the *fotoromanzo Grand Hôtel*, and gets led astray by dreams of America.

The *fotoromanzo*, which featured photographic stories, sometimes adapted from popular films, is a specific sector of the popular press that is relevant for this discussion of the nexus of aspiring girlhood and cinema. The launch of *Grand Hôtel* in 1946 and *Bolero Film* in 1947 provided a point of identification and aspiration for the mainly young, lower-class, and poorly educated girls who read them; Cullen (2015: 291) notes that in one survey of readership in the 1950s over half had only an elementary school education.¹³ The links between the *fotoromanzi* and the cinema industry were consolidated by 'utilizzo in comune di attori, attrici, sceneggiatori e registi'/'the shared use of actors, actresses, screenwriters, and directors' (De Berti 2000: 115). For example, Sophia Loren and Gina Lollobrigida both got their starts as models for *fotoromanzo* stories and this kind of 'dialogo intermediale'/'intermedial dialogue' (ibid.: 110) between different media forms and figures shows the different possible routes for girls to access cinema: as avid readers and watchers, and as aspiring models and actresses.

The 'vernacular stardom' (Schneider and Hediger 2009; Hedling 2015) produced by the *fotoromanzi* is the object of the little-studied short film by Michelangelo Antonioni, *L'amorosa menzogna/Lies of Love* (1949). The film addresses the phenomenon of the *fotoromanzo* from the readers' perspective:

---

¹²Though the myth of Mangano's discovery on Via Veneto, the haunt of stars later immortalized in Fellini's 1960 *La dolce vita*, was undercut by De Santis himself who recounted that Mangano had already turned up for a screen test in her best clothes and wearing make-up, and had failed to impress. 'Vidi comparire davanti, sotto una pioggerellina fitta fitta, vestita in un leggero impermeabiluccio sdrucito e con la faccia del freddo ... Tra le mani aveva un fiorellino e i suoi capelli erano fradici. Rivederla così bella, dimessa, vera nella sua realtà di giovane donna non abbiente mentre quando si era presentata la prima volta aveva evidentemente indossato il vestito buono e si era aggiustata perdendo la genuinità, fu come una folgorazione'/'I saw her appear before me, in the heavy drizzle, dressed in a worn little coat and with a face red from the cold ... In her hands she held a flower, and her hair was damp. Seeing her again so beautiful and shabby, real, in her own lived experience as a poor young girl, while the first time she had come before me she had done herself up and had put on a good dress, losing her authenticity, was like being struck by lightning' (ibid.). The staginess of this epiphany cannot but reveal its terms: the rejection of 'artifice' through a contrived tableau of feminine authenticity.

¹³This demographic breakdown is, however, queried by Cardone (2004: 34) and Bonifazio (2020: 4), who argue that the readership was more middle class (and potentially more male) than has been commonly assumed.

Antonioni's camera, turning its back to the historic centre, follows *fotoromanzi* actors and their fans (working girls, delivery boys, soldiers on leave, housemaids, mechanics) around a city of workshops, warehouses, peripheral thoroughfares, tram stops, council housing estates, wine shops, hairdressers, dairies, and newsagents. (Benci 2011: 38)

This networked consumer desire (mainly, though not exclusively female) for the *fotoromanzi* shows the urban landscape to be a space of consumerism, of advertising, and of often female desire for stardom. The film places the stars of the *fotoromanzo*, Sergio Raimondi and Anna Vita, as heroes to the popular readership, who are deprived of glamour and excitement.

The scene in which Raimondi, a mechanic who acts in *fotoromanzi* parttime (and who went on to appear in a number of films), turns up outside a working-class apartment block and is besieged by girls of various ages demonstrates the strong popular appeal of these local stars. The cuts between close-ups of girls staring at him in appreciation cleverly speak to what Pitassio calls the new 'scopic regime' (2019: 209) produced in this period, and especially to the porous division between real life and stardom, as Raimondi is caught between his two jobs, and the *fotoromanzo* brings these stars into courtyards, living rooms, hairdressers' salons, and tram rides. The film ends with Anna Vita (who also went on to some limited film success)[14] reading a fan letter while standing on a very ordinary street (and missing her tram because of it) while the voice-over intones 'non ridiamo di questi personaggi'/'let us not laugh at these people', and links the *fotoromanzi* to a longer tradition of feminized reading such as the *letteratura d'appendice*.[15] The rupture from the ordinary that stardom provides is expressed by the writers of the fan letter, two sisters from Puglia, who say they have nothing else in their lives.

While Antonioni adopted a more satirical, though still gently humorous, attitude towards the female readers of *fotoromanzi* in the script he wrote for Fellini's film *Lo sciecco bianco*/*The White Sheik* in 1952, the starstruck protagonist of that film, the self-named 'bambola appassionata'/'passionate doll' (played by former non-professional Brunella Bovo) devoted to the fictional sheik, is still unable to tell fact from fiction.[16] As Morreale points out, 'il cinema dà un'immagine regolarmente negativa dei fotoromanzi'/'cinema gives a resolutely negative image of fotoromanzi' (2011: 154), with, for

---

[14] Vita and Raimondi are discussed in a 1949 *Oggi* article on the 'nuovo divismo'/'new stardom' represented by *fotoromanzi* stars (Zatterin 1949).
[15] See Bravo (2003) on this genealogy.
[16] Bovo was 'discovered' by Vittorio De Sica in a bar and cast in his *Miracolo a Milano*/*Miracle in Milan* (1950). See Cristofani and Manetti (1956: 176). Lancia and Poppi (2003a: 369) make the intriguing suggestion that Anna Vita turned down the lead role in Fellini's *The White Sheik* (1952) because it made fun of *fotoromanzi*.

example, the female protagonist of the film *Verginità/Virginity* (De Mitri, 1951) thinking she is going to break into the *fotoromanzo* world, only to be lured into white slavery. This is in tune with the moralizing of many of the *fotoromanzi* stories themselves, which often featured 'plotlines warning about the dangers of city life and consumption for young women' (Cullen 2015: 297).[17]

Yet the world of the *fotoromanzo* and of female-addressed media, importantly, produced a female stardom: Sophia, Silvana, and Gina, but also Anna Vita and many others. Maria LaPlace (1987: 146) writes of how the image and visibility of female stars, both on screen and in the magazines and gossip columns about them, can 'offer a representation of female power in the social world which contests the confinement of women to the family: the female star is visibly a woman whose work earns her large amounts of money and public acclaim'. The dream of being catapulted from poverty to riches and glamour was thus made visible in the new stars of the Italian film industry. Further, as Cullen (2015: 290) notes, many of the *fotoromanzi* stories themselves featured plots that depended upon a 'fairy-tale' twist typical of popular literature. Yet that Cinderella story is always laced with threat, moralizing, and a problematic focus on female ambition that needs to be neutralized. Girls are warned that they can monetize their physical appearance via the innumerable contests available, but that they should never forget their social place.[18]

Beauty queens and professionalism

By the mid-1950s, the Italian public was used to the success of stars such as Sophia Loren, Gina Lollobrigida, and Lucia Bosè who had emerged from beauty contests, as well as male stars like Raf Vallone and Franco Interlenghi who were also 'discovered' as non-professionals. Chapter 1 of this book discussed some of the various practices through which new faces were unearthed, including star searches, magazine competitions, beauty contests, and chance encounters on the street. The economic stakes were clear, as I have noted: for girls, the reputational stakes were higher, as the

---

[17]Cardone (2009: 99) gives the example of the story 'Il grido', by Silvio Micheli, published in *Noi Donne*, 2 May 1954, in which a working-class girl is chosen to appear in a film, only to find it a traumatic and alienating world.

[18]Bonifazio (2020: 113–39) notes the problem of stories with romantic happy endings for magazines of the left, in her study of political *fotoromanzi*. While some on the left argued that such 'Cinderella stories' ignored social class and offered romance and fame as a solution to problems of economic and class inequality, others defended the need for aspirations and escapism. Bonifazio also points out that we know little about how readers interpreted these stories or used them to make sense of their own lives.

ambivalence attached to women acting in this period was still considerable. The fact that a high-profile segment of the acting corps gained fame through a focus on their bodily perfection makes the beauty-queen-turned-film-star a figure of intense and uncertain attention.

The hyperbolic claim made by André Bazin in 1956 that Sophia Loren would probably kill neorealism (in Aristarco 1975: 77) speaks to several intersecting contemporary concerns, responding primarily to the endless debates over the involution of neorealism and its relation to stardom.[19] However, it also addresses the perceived threat of the untrained female star to the seriousness of Italian film production. By the early 1950s, Loren, Lollobrigida, Silvana Mangano, Silvana Pampanini, Lucia Bosè, and others were starring in some of the most popular Italian films.[20] Most of them emerged via beauty contests, as well as, in some cases, modelling for *fotoromanzi*. The so-called 'maggiorate fisiche' (physically well-endowed female stars) have been much discussed in terms of the new paradigm of female beauty they offered, the model of a popular Italian stardom that could compete with the American one; they are associated with a 'natural' femininity that has been linked to the renewal of the nation in the post-war period through visual analogies between the female body and the natural landscape.[21] Yet as we will see, this overdetermined 'naturalness' of the female performer has serious consequences when it comes to assessments of her professionalism.

The association between the female star and the natural landscape or environment is also facilitated by the widespread use of the term *popolana*, or woman of the people, to describe stars in this period such as Magnani, Lollobrigida, and Loren. As Sarah Culhane (2017b: 259) has shown, the term can be thought of as a superficial label, denoting authenticity, spontaneity, and down-to-earthness.[22] As a cultural cliché, it occludes many things, including the labour of the star, the crafting of her image, and her own role in her success, in favour of a natural or accidental emergence from 'the people'. It also forecloses any ambitious career planning on the part of the girls.

Some of the girls entering Miss Vie Nuove beauty contest in 1951, reports Zilioli (2019: 17), had little ambition to be actresses, and one (Miss Liguria)

---

[19] See also Dentice's argument (1953: 75) that neorealism was 'suffocated' by the actresses whom it cultivated, and who then 'devoured' it, possibly referring to Loren and Lollobrigida.
[20] Loren was a finalist in Miss Italia in 1950 at the age of 15; Lollobrigida came third in the 1947 pageant, which Bosè won (Gianna Maria Canale and Eleonora Rossi Drago also featured in that year's contest); Pampanini came a narrow second in the 1946 contest, while Mangano won Miss Rome in 1946. See Gundle (1995: 369–70).
[21] See Grignaffini (1988); Gundle (2007); Carman (2014).
[22] *Popolana* denotes a 'raw and primitive beauty', 'more natural' and not like the 'contrived and visibly constructed hyper-glamorous artifice' of American stars. Buckley (2008: 270–1).

admitted that even though she might be interested, 'morirebbe di vergogna a recitare'/'she would die of shame if she acted'. The idea of shame connected to the acting profession is a powerful one, as historically there has been a discursive slippage between the actress and the prostitute: as Kirsten Pullen (2005: 2) notes:

> At particular historical moments, the body of the actress (assumed to be an object onto which male desires were projected) and the body of the prostitute (assumed to be an object onto which male desires were enacted) slipped discursively into one: whore/actress.[23]

In the post-war period, as Hipkins (2016: 10) has argued, this 'borderline identity' for women was frequently invoked on screen, and the female prostitute haunts Italian post-war cinema, as a figure that marks out 'the hegemony of respectable femininities' (ibid.). This haunting also occurred off-screen, with shame, modesty, and disavowal of actorly ambition running through girls' stories of accessing cinema, as this quotation from Jean-Luc Godard also (Godard and Delahaye 1967: 16) indicates: 'All the people whom I have known, whom I have loved in actual life, and who have made cinema without being actors ... are people who ended badly. Either the girls became whores, or the boys killed themselves' Jean-Luc Godard (1966).[24]

For example, Lucia Bosè's story of being discovered by Luchino Visconti aged sixteen, and winning the 1947 Miss Italia contest, which led to her acting career, is couched in the language of a fairy-tale: Bosè recounts that Visconti came into the pastry shop she worked in, stared at her with piercing eyes, and said 'Lei farà del cinema'/'You will make films'. Not only did she have no idea who he was, she insists she didn't know what a film director was: 'Ero Cappuccetto Rosso, la bella addormentata nel bosco'/'I was Little Red Riding Hood, Sleeping Beauty in the woods' (in Faldini and Fofi 1979: 148). Her name was sent into the Miss Italia contest as a prank, she says, and her picture published in *Tempo*, whereupon her father, enraged, beat her and called her 'the shame of the family'.[25] Bosè was also pictured, in a photograph that was widely circulated, lying in bed in a negligee,

---

[23]See also Davis (1991).

[24]Another interesting example of this shame is the piece in *Cinema Nuovo* in 1956 on a *fotodocumentario* planned by Antonio Ernazza and Franco Pinna, about a contest for 13- to 14-year-old girls called *Le bellissime/Beautiful Girls*. Some girls were seamstresses, some shopgirls, others more middle class. While a few had already acted, the article states that the 'ragazze delle borgate'/'girls from the city's periphery' were 'meno fiduciose verso questo genere di avventure'/'less trusting towards this kind of adventure' (Anon. 1956: 260), suggesting a class-based reluctance.

[25]Likewise, Silvana Pampanini, in her autobiography, recalls that her mother was very reluctant to allow her to take part in Miss Italia in 1946, and her father slapped her when he heard (Pampanini 2004: 125).

smoking a cigarette. The provocative photograph both augmented her fame and cemented an association between female fame and sexualization (see Masecchia 2017a).

Bosè is clear that hers is not a Cinderella story, despite *Tempo* publishing a feature on her which showed her 'trying on her first evening dress' with photographs by Federico Patellani:[26] 'Mettiamoci nei miei panni. Pensiamo alle macerie della Milano 1947 e ai nomi e alle cose che ti gettavano in faccia. La fiaba di Cenerentola? Oh, non che avessi i denti lunghi, sogni o ambizioni. Ero ancora troppo ingenua'/'Put yourself in my shoes. Think about the ruins of Milan in 1947, and the names I was called. A Cinderella tale? I wasn't experienced, I didn't have dreams or ambitions. I was still too innocent' (ibid.). While the first part of her comment refers clearly to such a rags-to-riches narrative from bombed-out Milan to national celebrity, she is quick to disavow any ambition or intention to succeed.[27] Bosè's innocence is key to her presentation of herself, at least after the fact, and she also rejects the idea that Visconti 'created' her (Figure 9).

The image of Bosè winning Miss Italia at sixteen, still bearing, she insists, the bruises inflicted by her father, is a striking one: yet the role that most closely mirrors her experience, her performance as film star Clara in Antonioni's *The Lady without Camelias* (1953), refracts this experience in striking ways. Clara is a shopgirl discovered by a film producer, who marries her and makes her a star; she is thus untrained and inexperienced like Bosè was. Yet the film insists on her humiliation and degradation in this role.[28] Her entrapment in the world of cinema, within which she is profoundly uncomfortable, and in her own star image are the fascinating subjects of the film. The opening shows Clara lurking furtively on the street outside the cinema showing her melodramatic film *Addio signora!/Farewell Signora!*, pretending to study an advert as a couple exit the cinema, then finally entering. The scene, in one long take, sets up two ideas simultaneously: firstly, it acts as a reminder of Clara as the non-professional, plucked from the street, and the city therefore as this space of chance and possibility. Secondly, it establishes a clear visual suggestion of her as a prostitute, especially in the opening moment, when we only see her legs in the corner of the frame. Clara as streetwalker, which is an ambiguity the film holds until we see that when she enters the cinema she is also on screen, speaks to the 'borderline identity' that the actress inhabits. Antonioni reinforces this association at various points: Clara's husband polices her choice of film parts and asks her 'vuoi fare un film

---

[26]*Tempo*, 11 October 1947. The article also has photographs by Patellani showing Bosè hanging stockings out to dry, making her bed, and working in the shop, in true Cinderella style.
[27]We can see the enduring legacy of this conception of Bosè in the description of her as 'una diva per caso'/'accidental diva' in a 1997 newspaper headline. See V. Ca. (1997).
[28]Lollobrigida turned down the part of Clara because she felt it was degrading (Solmi 1953).

FIGURE 9 *Federico Patellani's photo of Lucia Bosè in her first evening gown, published in* Tempo, *1947. Photo credit: Federico Patellani © Archivio Federico Patellani – Regione Lombardia/Museo di Fotografia Contemporanea, Milano-Cinisello Balsamo.*

o della pornografia?'/'do you want to make a film or do pornography?', and she is presented with a film script in which a girl ends up becoming a prostitute. This self-reflexive address to cinema's preoccupations, and to what we might assume to be the fate of the non-professional girl, brings inside the diegesis what we see obsessively circulating in Italian culture.[29]

There is a kind of horror to *The Lady without Camelias*, as Bosè plays a character who is mocked for her inability to act, and it seems inevitable to interpret the film as a kind of narrative punishment for actresses like Bosè (not least because Antonioni admitted that he used to beat her to get her to perform adequately when he directed her in his previous film *Cronaca di un amore/Story of a Love Affair*).[30] Despite Bosè's extra-diegetic insistence upon disavowing any ambition, her character is shown as an empty image, especially when she watches, at the end of the film, a 'real' actress perform.[31]

Other beauty-queens-turned-stars enacted a similar disavowal of ambition to Bosè: Silvana Pampanini said her singing teacher sent in her photo to Miss Italia, and attributes her glittering career to 'puro caso'/'pure chance' (Faldini and Fofi 1979: 150). Eleonora Rossi Drago claimed (ibid.: 149) that she was 'persecuted' by beauty contest organizers to enter and eventually gave in. Gianna Maria Canale, runner-up to Bosè in 1947, achieved stardom after the competition, partly helped by her marriage to director Riccardo Freda. He saw Canale on the street, was 'thunderstruck' by her beauty, and followed her. He found out her phone number and rang her and she rejected his advances (ibid.). Although they eventually married (after Freda divorced his wife) and she made numerous films with him, Canale's story retains a sense of the threat that the street held for Italian girls, subjected to a constantly assessing gaze and potentially violent gaze. In a similar way, Gina Lollobrigida's first introduction to the film industry in 1946 was when she was accosted by a producer on Via Veneto, who insisted that she try acting. 'Pensai in un primo momento che si trattasse di uno dei soliti importuni

---

[29]These self-reflexive films are discussed by Casetti (1989–90 and 1992; Dagrada (2014).
[30]'Non aveva abbastanza mestiere per fingersi disperata: non era un'attrice. Per ottenere il risultato che volevo dovevo usare la violenza, psicologica e fisica. Insulti, frasi mortificanti, umiliazioni e schiaffi cattivi'/'She wasn't trained enough to pretend to be desperate: she wasn't an actress. To obtain the result that I wanted I had to use psychological and physical violence. Insults, degrading phrases, humiliations and blows'. Antonioni, quoted in Scandola (2020: 44).
[31]Other contemporary films figure the film industry, and the film studios, as hollow and ultimately to be rejected by girls: the Cinecittà-set *Il viale della speranza/The Avenue of Hope* (Risi, 1953) and *Bellissima* (Visconti, 1951), and the already-mentioned Titanus-set episode *Quattro attrici una speranza/Four Actresses, One Hope*. Earlier self-referential films such as *La stella del cinema/The Star of Cinema* (Almirante, 1931), *La signora di tutti/Everybody's Woman* (Öphuls, 1943), and *Inventiamo l'amore/Let's Invent Love* (Mastrocinque, 1938) also engage this question of the danger of the cinema environment for girls, as Mosconi notes (2002: 74).

della strada e gli risposi male'/'I thought first of all that it was just one of the usual episodes of street harassment, and I was rude to him' (ibid.: 151).[32]

The parallel I wish to draw here is with Zavattini's theory of *pedinamento*: this is the act of tracking a potential film subject on the street, observing his gestures and actions, and considering his mundane walk home itself a spectacle. In Zavattini's theorization of *pedinamento*, he resolutely genders the subject male, referring to 'the man Tonio' who will be followed (Zavattini 2002: 49). However, the theory or practice has a very different valence for women, given their unequal access to the public sphere, as Margulies's (2019: 56) definition of it as 'stalking cinema' suggests. Women's complicated relationship with the street as a site of harassment becomes clear in the episode in *We, the Women*, 'Four Actresses, One Hope'. Hipkins (2016: 192) notes the monologue of one aspiring actress during her audition:

> The glamorous and well-endowed Cristina Doria replies that she attracts too much attention in public spaces, re-creating a continuum between public space, sexual availability and cinematic ambitions that is a constant in this cinema. The problem of the 'maggiorata fisica' that she describes [is] 'non si può uscire in pace, ti seguono come poliziotti ... noi che abbiamo un po' di seno, non possiamo uscir di casa' ['you can't go out in peace, they follow you like policemen ... those of us with larger breasts can't leave the house'].[33]

The overdetermination of the body and physical beauty both in discourses of this period and in its cinema, as we will see, fatally undermines the credibility of the untrained female performer. Eminent film historian Gian Piero Brunetta described 'la prepotente apparizione di Silvana Mangano in *Riso amaro*'/'the powerful appearance of Silvana Mangano in *Riso amaro*' as the 'ponte tra neorealismo e il divismo delle maggiorate'/'bridge between neorealism and the stardom of the maggiorate' (cited in De Berti 2000: 122). The view that Mangano herself is the transition between neorealism proper and the so-called *neorealismo rosa* or pink neorealism, while a common one, has ramifications:[34] viewing the female star's body in this period as

---

[32]Pier Angeli – who later went on to American stardom – was also discovered on Via Veneto by De Sica, who introduced her to Léonide Moguy, who then cast her in his hit film *Domani è troppo tardi/Tomorrow Is Too Late* (1950). See Pavesi (2017).

[33]The connection between the street and predatory looking is made more concrete in the roughly contemporary *L'amore in città/Love in the City*, the portmanteau film conceived by Zavattini, in particular the episode directed by Alberto Lattuada, *Gli italiani si voltano/Italians Stare*. Rhodes (2017) astutely analyses how this short film stages neorealist practices of observation as predation, as dozens of girls (including budding actress Giovanna Ralli) are watched and followed on the streets of Rome. As Hipkins (2016: 189) notes, the film fuses *pedinamento* with the beauty contest, as the girls are unwittingly parading for a male gaze.

[34]See Reich (2004: 111); Minghelli (2020: 74).

a 'luogo culturale, lavorato dall'immaginario'/'cultural site, worked over by the imaginary' (De Tassis 1982: 26), an explanatory site that can bear multiple cultural, social, and historical meanings, neglects the possible agency of the performer, and how that might be able to resist or compete with the conceptions projected onto it by a masculinist critical culture.

The 'scandal' of the female performer

The displacement of blame onto the body of the untrained female star was very common in the film press at the time, as we saw in Chapter 1: in a 1949 piece on the problems presented by the non-professional, critic Giulio Cesare Castello singled out 'reginette di bellezza'/'little beauty queens' as partly responsible for the 'costume di improvvisazione'/'habits of improvisation' that threatened the entire film industry (Castello 1949: 54). The 'effetti perniciosi'/'pernicious effects' (ibid.) he feared include a general loss of acting quality and a 'de-professionalization of film acting' (Gundle 2019: 13). The yoking together of the non-professional and the beauty queen was quite common in the period: this is shown by a 1951 letter from the national actors' union (Anon. 1951b), complaining about the 'Miss' competitions, and urging union members not to participate as judges. Yet while Masi (2003: 337) argues that both the 'strada' and the 'concorso di bellezza' were part of the same 'serbatoio di realtà'/'source of reality', it is clear that they had a radically different status when it came to the legitimacy of the performer.[35]

A key case study of debate on the question of competence versus appearance for untrained Italian female stars was the polemical discussion in the left-wing film journal *Cinema Nuovo* in 1953: it was ignited by the editorial 'Lo scandalo delle curve'/'The Scandal of the Curves' (*Cinema Nuovo* editors 1953). The editorial was inspired by Vittorio De Sica's comments in London on the prominence in the industry of girls selected for their beauty: 'le bellezze italiane sono tutte curve: Lollobrigida, Mangano, Pampanini. Le loro capacità artistiche non possono davvero competere con i loro pregi

---

[35]See Parigi (2008: 257): 'Al teatro di prosa e al varietà, che hanno rappresentato i serbatoi privilegiati degli anni 30 – e che continuano a fornire buona parte del contingente maschile –, ora si aggiungono due nuove forme di selezione: la 'strada', contenitore metonimico e metaforico della tipologia del non professionista, da cui provengono gli innumerevoli bambini, oltre che molti personaggi adulti, dei primi film neorealisti; e i concorsi di bellezza, che forniscono la maggior parte dei miti femminili degli anni '50: Silvana Pampanni, Lucia Bosè,'Gina Lollobrigida, Silvana Mangano, Sophia Loren'/'to theatre and variety shows, the biggest sources of actors in the 1930s – and which continue to supply a lot of the male contingent – are now added two new forms of selection: the "street", the metonymic and metaphorical container of the non-professional, from which many children and adults are chosen for neorealist films; and the beauty contests, which supply most of the female stars of the 1950s'.

fisici'/'the Italian beauties are all curves: Lollobrigida, Mangano, Pampanini. Their artistic abilities cannot compete with their physical virtues' (ibid.). De Sica's insistence that Italian producers were intent on showing off the legs and 'opulent breasts' of starlets was backed by the editorial, which also disapprovingly commented on Lollobrigida's lack of humility in refusing to appear in the skewering of the phenomenon in *La signora senza camelie*. There followed a series of articles, all of which assert, according to Mandelli and Re in their insightful analysis of the debate, how for a certain masculinist cinephile discourse, 'bellezza fisica e doti attoriali sembrano essere non solo due dimensioni distinte, ma anche … inversamente proporzionali'/'physical beauty and acting talent seem to be not only two distinct dimensions but also … inversely proportional' (Mandelli and Re 2019: 258).[36] The editorial also included the harsh words of Visconti, from a 1951 interview, that 'Le Misses, in genere, non valgono niente. Non sanno parlare, non sanno muoversi; non hanno vere qualità di attrici'/'The "Misses", in general, are worthless. They can't talk, they can't move well: they have no real qualities as actresses', thus bringing the full weight of the auteurs of neorealism down against the insubstantial beauty queens.[37]

In the following issue of *Cinema Nuovo*, Michele Gandin's article ran: entitled 'Fanno il cinema guardandosi allo specchio'/'They Make Films Looking in the Mirror', it considered the 'problem of actresses' to be manifold. Gandin blamed producers for their modes of recruitment, the lack of adequate training – particularly at the national film school, the Centro Sperimentale di Cinematografia – and the problem that theatre actresses were not considered attractive enough for the screen. Gandin's view (1953b: 180) that beauty queens were only 'bei corpi'/'beautiful bodies' echoed the opposition between physical beauty and performing talent, but his statement that inevitably the girls 'perdono la testa – si rovinano come donne e come attrici'/'lose their heads – they are ruined as women and as actresses' makes text the subtext of the inappropriateness of acting for these women: that they will endanger themselves morally, again reinforcing the slippage between acting and prostitution.[38] He is echoing language used by Antonioni in the same period, who, while making *La*

---

[36] See also Mandelli and Re (2021) for an even more detailed analysis of *Cinema Nuovo*'s relationship to the female star image.
[37] Visconti had, as we saw, been closely involved in beauty contest juries, and addressed, in his 1951 film *Bellissima*, the consequences of acting for non-professionals, both through the trauma inflicted upon the little girl who tries out for a film part and in the character played by Liliana Mancini, non-professional star of Castellani's *Sotto il sole di Roma/Under the Roman Sun* (1948) who reflects bitterly on her experience.
[38] See the 1954 *Time* article cited in Gilardelli (2013: 83), which alludes strongly to the casting couch: 'An actress in Italy needs only two expressions: horizontal and vertical.' In *Four Actresses, One Hope*, Anna Amendola, the competition winner, is warned by her mother not to return home if she takes part in it, such is the moral dubiousness of the enterprise.

signora senza camelie, commented that untrained girls, once they 'withered', became 'rovinate'/'ruined' and 'viziate'/'spoiled', and ended up at the mercy of unscrupulous producers.[39] While Gandin blamed producers and the public for enabling these choices, his intense focus on conventional bodily appeal was of a piece with the dominant masculinist discourse.[40] It is also striking that there was no mention of the attractive male stars such as Raf Vallone and Franco Interlenghi who had emerged without training in the same period.[41] The element of moralizing and blame was continued by Fabrizio Dentice, who ironized over the fact that girls who had shot to fame for their beauty now wished to be recognized for their talent, asserting confidently that 'alle loro ridenti virtù fisiche non corrispondono eguali virtù di interpretazione'/'their delightful physical talents are not matched by their acting talents' (Dentice 1953: 75).

As Mandelli and Re (2019: 264) astutely point out, *Cinema Nuovo*'s disdain for sex appeal did not prevent it, however, from putting these actresses frequently on their covers, enacting a split between a 'discorso delle immagini'/'discourse of images' designed to attract male readers and a moralistic critical discourse inside the covers: the journal itself made visible the cultural fixation on women as public property, while disavowing the potential for female beauty to encroach upon high-culture values. What Mandelli and Re call the 'ambivalence' of the magazine, caught between a highbrow critical discourse and an emphasis on female beauty, is actually constitutive of cinephilia itself, as Geneviève Sellier has argued (2008: 29). Sellier's discussion of French post-war cinephilia resonates with the Italian context in many ways, not least in her assessment of the cinephile gaze as male, heterosexual, and fetishistic.

There are many other examples of similar interventions in this period, too numerous to mention.[42] The displacement of blame for the supposed decline of Italian cinema onto the body of the female performer routinely takes the form of a prurient, yet condemnatory rhetoric, such as the 1948 editorial in the journal *Cinema* by Adriano Baracco who said condescendingly

---

[39]Quoted in Solmi (1953: 39).
[40]Calendoli (1953: 141) also blamed the 'ignorant' public, who only want to see 'gambe di Miss Spreafico di sotto'/'the legs of Miss Spreafico di sotto'.
[41]One of the few references to the moral sacrifices male actors might make is given by producer Claudio Mancini: 'Gli uomini che a ogni costo volevano fare gli attori erano peggio delle donne, perché, in fin dei conti, le donne per riuscire andavano a letto, insomma davano in contropartita una prestazione abbastanza naturale. Gli uomini, invece, si sarebbero adattati a tutto, a qualsiasi forma di prostituzione, senza sottilizzare o dare peso ai compromessi'/'The men who wanted to be actors at all costs were worse than the women, because, at the end of the day, women just went to bed to get ahead, so they were performing a pretty natural service. But men would end up doing anything, any form of prostitution, without considering the nature of their compromises' (in Faldini and Fofi 1979: 153).
[42]A few examples: C. (1953); Gandin (1953a); 'Bert' (1954).

that he had nothing against beauty queens such as Bosè who get cinema contracts ('sono solide ragazze, provviste di seno generoso'/'they are solid girls, endowed with generous bosoms' ('B' 1948)), but that the problem was that they got film contracts even if they were better at playing *bocce* than at acting. While Claudio Varese's comments that the beautiful actresses recruited from contests are 'interchangeable' (1954: 108) seem predictable, the astonishing language used by Calendoli (1953: 141) to make a similar point is perhaps less so: 'Volti anonimi, eguali, immobili: ma il loro seno, quello sì, ha acquistato una personalità ed uno si distingue dall'altro, quale più rotondetto e turgido, quale più nervoso e guizzante, quale più opimo e riposante'/'The faces are anonymous, identical, immobile: but their breasts, those have a personality, they're distinct, one is more rounded and turgid, another is more twitchy and mobile, another is more abundant and restful.'

The idea of a 'performative' bosom serves to highlight how the assessment of performance itself is almost non-existent (apart from routine mentions of the great, and 'authentic', Anna Magnani as the exception to the current lack of serious actresses).[43] Francesco Callari in the same year in *Cinema* briefly broaches the subject of vocal performance: he uses the 'scandal' of Lollobrigida being awarded an acting prize for a role in which she was dubbed to argue that therefore her appeal, and that of other actresses, is merely aesthetic, and that they are 'corpi senz'anima'/'bodies without souls' (1953: 6).[44] This attitude thus justifies the reduction of former non-professional actresses to bodies, and aligns with the masculinist approaches to the subject in the period, despite the fact that dubbing was common for many actors in the period.

The discourses may be masculinist, yet a few of the rare female critics also participated: Marisa Rusconi wrote in 1966:

Our home-grown, well-stacked girls, from Gina to Sophia, embody a proletarian need for direct, obvious sexuality available to all. The comely girls of Ciociara and the shapely village women depicted on the screen spoke to the collective instincts of a mass population that was as yet unconcerned with Freudian and intellectualistic complications. But at the same time they were manoeuvred rather effectively by the puppeteers who held the strings of political life in a country that was still fundamentally fascist. The films based on the breasts of cheery peasant wenches are

---

[43]See Gandin (1953b: 181), who calls Magnani 'una delle poche attrici italiane con temperamento'/'one of the few Italian actresses with real artistic temperament'. Renzi (1956) says that the *maggiorata* is 'l'oca che ha fatto carriera, restando tale'/'*a silly bimbo who has made it*' and 'una caricatura rispetto a un'attrice come Anna Magnani'/'a caricature compared to an actress like Anna Magnani'.

[44]Lollobrigida (1954) indignantly responded to accusations of dubbing, saying she now acted only in films with direct sound, and defending her acting skills.

the sign of disengagement and social indifference that stands against the dangerous problematic of neo-realism and the first intellectual films. (quoted in Gundle 1999: 372)[45]

Rusconi's words make the female stars themselves and their screen presences complicit in a problematic lack of progressive commitment in Italy, with male actors again being elided. The overwhelming sense of the female body as spectacle, as a kind of suspect ideological container, assigns passivity to it and is enhanced by the pervasive discourses around these women as unskilled and as unable to offer anything beyond their bodies.

Further, the ideas of discovery and chance, central to the narratives of these 'accidental' actresses, reveal problematic underpinnings: discovery implies a quasi-colonizing and certainly proprietorial gaze. Chance is the central element in the Cinderella narratives that pervade the period, which can prevent girls from being positioned negatively as ambitious. As Noto (2011: 153) observes, 'le rielaborazioni del mito di Cenerentola (o di Pigmalione, a seconda dei punti di vista) presenti nei film dei primi anni Cinquanta fanno leva proprio su questa relazione ambigua tra aspirazione alla realizzazione personale e onorabilità femminile'/'the re-workings of the myth of Cinderella (or Pygmalion, according to your perspective) present in the films of the early 1950s leverage this ambiguous relationship between aspiration to personal fulfilment and female honour)'.[46]

Certainly, films such as *Miss Italia* (Coletti, 1950), in which Gina Lollobrigida plays a modest seamstress who accidentally wins Miss Italia, speak to this relationship; her character sews her own pageant winner's dress.[47] Yet it is striking that, extra-diegetically, Lollobrigida in this period was being called upon to defend her professionalism and her skills as a performer, and to counter the notion of having fame unjustly bestowed upon her. The accusations that these ersatz actresses lack professionalism (they haven't studied, they don't learn how to walk or speak properly, as De Sica is quoted as saying in the 1953 *Cinema Nuovo* editorial, they lack the 'order' and 'discipline' of Hollywood actresses) are the seemingly inevitable flip side to their appeal as pure nature or biology.

---

[45] Journalist Anna Garofalo wrote in *Cinema Nuovo* in 1956 'non basta un perfetto *guêpière* e un reggipetto scultureo pieni di grazia di Dio, per fare un'attrice'/'a perfect basque and a well-fitted bra full of God's graces, are not enough to make an actress'.

[46] In fact, in 1952 Orson Welles planned to make a film in Italy called *Operation Cinderella*, about an American film crew shooting a film near Naples, and recruiting a young girl as the film's star, whom locals fear will be led astray by Hollywood. Thirteen-year-old French girl (and future star) Marina Vlady was cast in the role, but the film was never made (see Anile 2013: 265–6).

[47] See the discussion of this film in Noto (2011: 381) and Hipkins (2016: 166–72).

As we have seen, it was not merely the accusations of unpreparedness or inability to act that were most dominant in contemporary critical discourse around girls chosen for their beauty, but the shadow of immorality that clings to them.[48] In an interesting 1946 piece in the film journal *Star*, a journalist interviews girls dancing in a low-rent variety show or *rivista* (Pinna 1946). The author describes the squalid nature of the theatre, as well as the 'turgid breasts' of the girls (accompanied by revealing photos of them); interviewed, they express a naïve wish to make it in movies and to appear in a film by the likes of Mario Mattoli (the director of popular weepies). Their dream of respectability, either via marriage or via a protector in the film industry, is doomed to failure, the author suggests, and all they can expect is a vulgar proposition from a drunk G.I.

A good number of girls did make the transition from *rivista* to minor roles in cinema (sometimes via radio): performers such as Luisa Poselli, Wilma Aris, Clely Fiamma, Giusi Raspani Dandolo, Isa Bellini, Vera Worth, and Wanda Osiris. And of course former variety star Anna Magnani is often invoked as the ur-example of, or transcendent exception to, this transition. However, pieces like the one above and a similar sneering article by Nanda Nobili (1945) imply that the line between public performance in variety shows and sex work is almost invisible, and it is the fault line that runs under most of the proclamations about non-professional girls in this period, while the division between respectability and its absence is very clear. These tensions will be explored further in the two case studies that follow.

Carmela Sazio: The wild southern girl

Fifteen-year-old Carmela Sazio was featured in the first episode of Rossellini's neorealist classic *Paisà/Paisan* in 1946. Her character Carmela was at the centre of the episode in which American soldiers land in Sicily during the Allied invasion in July 1943 and are welcomed by locals. Her character helps the soldiers, forges a tentative friendship with one, Joe, despite being unable to speak English, and eventually sacrifices herself to protect the G.I.s from the Nazis.

Carmela's story is significant, not merely because she appeared in an internationally acclaimed neorealist masterpiece with no training or preparation, but because of the language that was consistently used to describe her by those involved with the shoot and by critics. Firstly, there is her 'discovery', narrated in various accounts: journalist Giorgio Salvioni

---

[48]Masi's formulation (1987: 43) about the girls who were discovered in this period is revealing, when he talks of 'giovani attrici, raccolte a mo' di harem'/'young actresses, gathered into a kind of harem'.

wrote in his dispatch from the film's production that she was walking along the road near her village of Santa Maria la Bruna, about twenty kilometres from Naples. Rossellini, who was filming at nearby Maiori, on the Amalfi coast, spotted her walking with a basket on her head, 'malvestita, spettinata'/'poorly dressed and with uncombed hair' (Salvioni 1946: 3). She was frightened at the sight of Rossellini and ran away, only agreeing to speak to his female production secretary. Salvioni notes that Rossellini paid her family for her services and she agreed to act in the film.

Massimo Mida, Rossellini's assistant director, added a touch of local colour, when he recounted the same episode in a piece written in August 1946, which declared Santa Maria la Bruna a 'vero e proprio villaggio troglodita'/'an absolutely troglodytic village' (now in Aprà 1995: 92). Already we begin to see a narrative emerge around Carmela that centres primitivism and a particular kind of authenticity. Confirming this, already in January 1946 her face and 'discovery' were being used to promote the as-yet unmade film in the press, as an article in the magazine *Cinetempo*, accompanied by a photo of Carmela, shows: 'La protagonista sarà una semplice fanciulla scoperta ipso loco: una ragazzotta del Napoletano, tutta furia, dai tratti marcati, arcigna e rude'/'the protagonist will be a simple girl discovered on the spot, a sturdy girl from the Naples area, fiery, with dramatic features, coarse and scowling' ('M.T.' 1946). Mida emphasizes that she is 'assolutamente primitiva'/'absolutely primitive' (in Aprà 1995: 119).

The signs of Carmela's 'primitiveness' are everywhere: Salvioni referred to her as 'la ragazza selvaggia, ... una popolana semplice, scontrosa, che solo adesso scopre i segreti della "vita civile"'/'the wild girl] a simple, surly popolana, who is only now starting to discover the secrets of "civilization"' (Salvioni 1946).[49] I will come on to discuss the 'civilizing' of the *popolana* Carmela, but her wildness was attested by Rossellini himself, when he later said 'Carmela ... era come una specie di animaletto che non capisce, che si muove solo per impulso'/'Carmela ... was like a kind of little animal that doesn't understand anything, that acts by impulse alone' (in Aprà 1995: 105).[50] The animal analogy is striking and extends through the various accounts of Carmela. Mida's description here is telling: 'ragazzotta quindicenne, dai muscoli di cavallerizza, impegnava a testa bassa, veri e propri combattimenti taurini'/'a 15-year-old sturdy girl, with the muscles of a horse rider, she would lower her head and try to butt people like a bull'. It is a view echoed in the review of the film by *Time* magazine (Anon. 1948b), which refers to her as the 'half-savage' girl. These views of her wildness or savagery are also found in works by recent critics: Stefania

---

[49]He also calls her 'semplice, rustica, acerba, selvaggia'/'simple, rustic, immature, wild' (ibid.).
[50]He continued, 'È una caratteristica comune a migliaia di ragazze in Sicilia'/'it is a characteristic common to thousands of girls in Sicily', although she was from Campania, not Sicily.

Parigi talks of her 'selvaggia e quasi primordiale fisicità'/'savage and almost primordial physicality' (2005: 15), labels her an 'icona di una femminilità animalesca, istintiva e primitiva'/'icon of an animalesque, instinctive, and primitive femininity' (ibid.: 20), and as 'la selvaggia e istintiva Carmela'/'the savage and instinctive Carmela' (ibid.: 24–5). Meanwhile, Pierre Sorlin has described her as 'primitive and animal-like' (1991: 29).

These adjectives have several functions: they reiterate Carmela's untrained and unpolished nature, and thus her contrast with the world of showbusiness and spectacle, they align her with the natural and pre-modern world, and, relatedly, they inscribe her within existing discourses of *meridionalismo*, as discussed in relation to *La terra trema*. *Meridionalismo* is understood as 'a cluster of value-judgements that make the South seem like an irredeemable victim of its cultural and political backwardness, itself the result of a "history" that has been trasmuted into an essential "nature"' (Rosengarten 1998: 118). Mida recounts in horror that Carmela's 'troglodytic village' is removed from civilization: he asserts that it has been unchanged for centuries, and that 'bisogna vederlo per rendersi conto quanta parte dell'Italia è ancora da esplorare: luride stradette inondate di acqua stagnante, cassette con quattro pareti alte poco più di un uomo, una porticina e due buche per finestre'/'you have to see it to realize how much of Italy is still unknown: disgusting lanes overrunning with stagnant water, squat houses with four walls scarcely higher than six feet, a tiny door and two holes for windows' (in Aprà 1988: 139).

While emphasizing the primitive, Mida's recollection of seeing Carmela fetching water from the well also places her within a tradition of the picturesque, which as Dickie (1999: 83–119) noted has historically been the flip side to the focus on savagery in representations of Southern Italy: Mida calls her 'una figura di altri tempi, da letteratura dell'ottocento e da pittura napoletana'/'a figure from another era, from nineteenth-century literature and from Neapolitan paintings' (in Aprà 1995: 92). She becomes an archetype of a southern woman, with an essentialist focus on her body: 'Quel corpo tutto d'un pezzo, naturale del resto alle donne meridionali, larghe di fianchi'/'that solid, wide-hipped body, which was completely natural to southern women' (ibid.).

This dialectic between savagery and 'authentic' beauty underpins Carmela's representation outside the film. André Bazin called her 'an illiterate girl discovered on the dockside' (1971: 22), and Mida said 'Non sapeva né leggere né scrivere'/'she couldn't read or write' (in Aprà 1995: 119), even though, as we will see, she was able to write a letter to Rossellini after filming. Meanwhile, Salvioni (1946) focused on her natural beauty: 'senza sapere che cosa fosse il cerone o il più piccolo tocco di belletto'/'without the slightest knowledge of make-up or the faintest touch of rouge', and her skin had a 'straordinaria freschezza e luminosità'/'extraordinary freshness and luminosity', emphasizing her ignorance of all artifice.

The vision of Carmela as a wild, primitive, and unconventional beauty speaks to ideas that we saw in the last chapter around the Southern Italian non-professional lower-class actor in *La terra trema*. The idea that these performers do not understand what they are doing is asserted by Mida about Carmela, and he describes the 'torture' (in Aprà 1995: 119) that it was for her to learn her lines and what she was supposed to do, with Rossellini having to bully her to perform, so that the key scene where she talks to Joe in the tower took four days to film. This tracks with Barry King's observation (1985: 28) that:

> 'Good' acting is based on some concept of intentionality, or even authorship. It is taken for granted that the participation of the actor(s) in the process of signification should be an outcome of the deployment of a conscious and constitutive control at the point of performance.

Not only does Carmela clearly lack the ability to author her performance through intention or deliberate artistic choices, in the US pressbook for the film, one suggested promotional squib focuses on the 'peasant girl' star who has never seen a film before. As we know, this is a familiar way of locating the non-professional safely outside the sphere of professionalism and of craft.[51] Likewise, Salvioni recounts that Rossellini showed Carmela her screen test in the cinema in Maiori, and her reaction was spontaneous laughter and a pronouncement that it was all 'fesserie'/'nonsense', demonstrating her inability to comprehend her role in the production of what became seen as great art.

Carmela's 'wildness' is partly that of a child: Mida describes her 'bambinesca mentalità, retrograda'/'childlike, retrograde mentality' (in Aprà 1995: 93) and notes that at fifteen she seemed the same age as a city girl would be at ten. This focus on immaturity and unruliness contributes to the othering of her: as Lury (2010: 56) says of the child in film, 'innocent yet uncivilized child sexuality borders on the primitive with all its raced connotations'. Yet Carmela is also seen as a woman: at fifteen, while living with the cast and crew, she develops 'una femminilità ... naturalissima'/'a very natural femininity' (Aprà 1995: 92). And what emerges from the accounts of her is a kind of Pygmalion narrative, that is, that she was 'created' by Rossellini: 'Carmela si è poco a poco svezzata in mezzo alla troupe.. anche il suo passo si è fatto leggermente più spedito e meno pesante'/'Carmela was gradually weaned with the crew ... even her tread became lighter and more brisk' (ibid.). Salvioni (1946) concurs: 'Lentamente nella troupe di Rossellini è nata una "signorina" Carmela ... Carmela è nata veramente

---

[51]See *Paisà* pressbook (Mayer-Burstyn, 1948), New York Public Library for the Performing Arts, Billy Rose Theater Division.

solo qui'/'Slowly in Rossellini's crew, Carmela the young lady was born ... Carmela was truly born here'.[52] Carmela's contact with the film crew, in the small town of Maiori which Mida asserts seemed a 'paradise' compared to her primitive village, is cast as a civilizing process: 'Imparò a farsi il bagno, guardò le altre ragazze della compagnia con timore, prima, e poi con una curiosità morbosa, rimase lunghe ore ferme ad ammirare le coppie danzanti'/'she learned how to bathe herself, she watched the other girls in the company, first with fear, then with a morbid curiosity, and she spent long hours standing admiring couples dancing' (Aprà 1995: 92). She is thus tamed: 'la Carmela che ora si pettina con i capelli un po' sugli occhi, che mi regala una sua fotografia, la Carmela che ruba il profumo ad Annalena ... non è più la Carmela di prima'/'The Carmela who combs her hair over her eyes, who gives me a photo of herself, and who steals Annalena's perfume ... is not the same Carmela as before' (Salvioni 1946).

Carmela's uncertain status, in between childhood and womanhood, is emblematic both of the nature of adolescent girlhood itself, with its challenges to the stability of the boundaries of childhood and adulthood (Driscoll 2002: 6), and also of the prevailing culture in Italy, in which, as we have seen, girls from the age of fourteen or so were entering national beauty contests and being objectified in magazines. Both children and women exist as other and without agency in a patriarchal national structure: as Randall (2017: xxxiii) notes, 'children – particularly girls – are aligned with women in their uncertain categorization as "proper subjects"'.

The body of the girl and the threat of the real

Carmela's adolescent sexuality came under scrutiny: perhaps partly because she was dubbed into Sicilian dialect, her body became the focus of critical attention.[53] In addition to her wide (childbearing) hips, male critics have directed their gaze to her 'excessive' and perturbing adolescent physicality. Rondi (1956: 142) commented on 'il corpo gonfio, sgraziato di Carmela Sazio, quella massa arruffata di capelli, quegli occhi orlati dal nero delle immense occhiaie e la bellezza che si indovina segreta di quei lineamenti'/'the swollen, unattractive body of Carmela Sazio, that messy mass of hair, those eyes surrounded by large dark circles, and the secret beauty hiding in those features'. Amerio (1950: 18), meanwhile, included her in his account of neorealist actresses who have brought a new eroticism to Italian cinema.

---

[52]Mida also calls Carmela 'una delle numerose "invenzioni" di Roberto Rossellini'/'one of the numerous "inventions" of Rossellini' (in Aprà 1988: 139).
[53]Salvioni (1946) referred to her 'incomprehensible' Neapolitan dialect in person.

Yet there seems something almost threatening about the naturalism of Carmela's body. Robert Warshow says in his review of the film's US release in 1948 that her body is

> to an American eye almost repellent in its lack of physical charm, and at the same time disturbing in its persistent suggestion that charm is irrelevant. ... At the end, when this body is seen for a moment dead and sprawling on the rocks, hardly more ungraceful than when it was alive, it contains in its visible presence the dramatic meaning and conclusion of the episode. (Warshow 2001: 222–3)

The shock of the real represented by her body, so alien to Hollywood conventions of female beauty (and also so different from the *maggiorate* who were dominating Italian cinema) is clearly both thrilling and perturbing to Warshow and to a presumptively male viewer.

The persistent tying together of childlike primitiveness, realism, and discomforting sexuality is telling. As Randall (2017: 22) notes, the child, aligned with nature and wildness, 'can be aligned with the supposed

FIGURE 10 Rossellini's Paisan: *Carmela Sazio as Carmela, in a long shot highlighting her 'unruly' body.*

excessive, uncontrollable sexuality of the non-white other'. This threat was identified also by Peter Brunette in his discussion of the film (1996: 72):

> When we are involved in a conventional Hollywood-style picture, we unconsciously know (at least we did in 1946) that no matter how sexy its star might seem, there is a limit beyond which she will not go. We know, in other words, that her sexuality will necessarily be something faked. However, when the spectator (I am necessarily going to have to limit myself to what I take to be a male perspective here) is confronted with what seems to be a real woman on the screen, an unglamorous nonprofessional, a subliminal sense of *risk* is at some level re-established. ... it seems to me that the very presence of the girl – slovenly and directly sensual in a way no real actress would ever chance – gives an edge to her encounter with Joe that makes the film seem bracingly out of control. (my italics)

Brunette raises the question of risk here: as we saw, there is a broader context in post-war Italy within which girls are felt to be at risk in the cinema industry via a left-wing moral panic. Yet the 'risk' represented by Carmela is that she is 'too real' – is this a risk to the spectator? That the film might be somehow pornographic because of Carmela's lack of 'limits' (as a southern 'savage') and lack of actorly training?[54] Is it a risk to the girl, who assumes the 'borderline identity' of actress/sex worker, due to the 'contiguità tra carriera artistica e prostituzione'/'contiguity between an artistic career and prostitution' (Noto 2011: 152), itself reinforced by a naturalistic performance style?

The reading of Carmela in the film as an excessively sexual presence, despite the chastity of her character, is striking, as it once again positions the non-professional as not acting. The spectator knows that Carmela is not acting, or at least, her acting is not informed by any skill or training. Her image, as we saw, was already out there even before the film was made, and the extra-diegetic material conditions a reading of her performance as crude realism. This matching of type to role was confirmed by Mida (in Aprà 1995: 119) when he said that 'soltanto una ragazza così primitiva poteva essere credibile in quel ruolo'/'only such a primitive girl could have been so believable in that role'. As Gorfinkel (2012: 95) points out in her work on amateur sex films, in which acting performances can be read as 'failed', this kind of performance represents 'a realism that is inadvertently historicist, one that blurs the relation between the diegetic and extradiegetic aspects of cinematic experience and their relation to

---

[54]Rossellini said that they wrote a scene with Carmela being raped by German soldiers but never shot it (in Aprà 1995: 105).

spectatorial knowledge'. Again, we see the confusion between acting as work and acting as being, especially when the 'being' is an exoticized and unconventional female body.

The (male) spectatorial gaze on Carmela that sees her as excessively natural, or primitively sensual, brings in, then, a fusion of childlike, womanly, and animalesque characteristics. It is worth citing Gorfinkel's words (2012: 95–6) here:

> The marginality of nonprofessional actresses' labor, its compounding of particular inequities in aesthetic, cultural, social, and economic registers, manifests itself in content and form – the sex worker who is not, cannot be, working; the actress who is not acting but presenting for the spectator and for her employer her corporeal activity, made to collapse with her daily, actual, 'real', authentic self.

This 'marginality', here represented by a very young, poor, uneducated, and unprotected Southern girl presenting her 'corporeal activity', also brings to mind Bazin's words on the risks of acting for non-professionals, risks that he deemed particularly significant for children and 'native peoples' (1971: 24). He noted that the young star of Murnau's *Tabu* (1931) 'became a prostitute in Poland' (ibid.). Actually, Anne Chevalier, the sixteen-year-old Polynesian girl selected to star in the film, seems to have worked as a dancer and starred in a film in Poland (according to Egan 2020: 185). However, the shadow of prostitution that hangs over her career is significant, and, as we will see, Carmela faced exactly the same fate.[55]

Aftermath: 'A pitiful case'

The risk factor to the girl non-professional also means that the girl, untrained and unprotected in the industry, was vulnerable to being exploited by a director and crew who seemed to view her as a fond and exotic curiosity. But it also extends to the aftermath of the filming experience. For Carmela the aftermath was tough: Mida (in Aprà 1995: 93) reflects that

> Era un problema scottante: che cosa ne faremo di lei, una volta finita la parte. Con Rossellini ne parlammo come di un caso psicologico, caso

---

[55] The mixed-race Isabella Marincola, who started acting after working as an artist's model in Rome, appearing in De Santis' *Bitter Rice* (1949), recalls how her choices for survival were either acting or prostitution. She says that rumours circulated anyway about her being a prostitute, and it is clear that in her case racist assumptions were joined to sexist ones (see Amadei 2008).

umano, probabilmente irresolubile. Aveva incontrato un mondo nuovo, toccato con le proprie dita comodità e conforti.⁵⁶

Like Lamberto Maggiorani after *Bicycle Thieves*, Carmela did not wish to leave the scene gracefully. She had become close to the crew: Rose Nadell, secretary to producer Rod Geiger, commented that the real American soldiers playing themselves in the film had become very protective of her, and that she wept when they left (in Aprà 1995: 91). Mida (in ibid.: 92) also notes that Carmela had struck up an affectionate and possibly romantic friendship with fellow non-professional Robert Van Loon, who played Joe, the G.I. whom she saves.

Carmela wrote to Rossellini and Mida expressing her hurt and sadness at being left behind: 'Ci scrisse una lettera ... sgrammatica'/'she wrote us an ungrammatical letter' (ibid.: 93). Mida recounts that they did not know what to do about her, but were pleased that the supposedly illiterate girl had even picked up a pen: 'Aveva trovato con lo scriverci, il modo per sciogliersi, per consolarsi, per reagire all'incanto di una parentesi che sapeva di favola, e di proposito, decidemmo di non rispondere.. Forse era meglio'/'in writing to us she had found the way to unleash her feelings, to console herself, and to react to the enchantment of a brief episode that seemed like a fairy-tale. Thus we decided not to reply ... Perhaps it was better' (ibid.). The end of Carmela's 'fairy-tale' is deemed natural, and her Cinderella story is over, the production team decides. However, the fairy-tale has a coda:

> Carmela purtroppo diventò un caso pietoso. Così, tornata in famiglia nel suo borgo sperduto, non si riadattò alla più dura realtà del paese. Forse qualche giovanotto di poco scrupolo ne approfittò ... Qualche anno dopo venimmo a sapere che, tornata in mezzo ai suoi diseredetati, Carmela si era data alla vita. (ibid.: 120)⁵⁷

The subtext of Mida's note that some young man perhaps took advantage of Carmela when she returned home to her 'diseredetati' is that she was possibly viewed as 'contaminated' due to her role in the film. This speaks to the specific nature of the problems that acting might cause for girls, as we saw with the discussions on modesty in this and the previous chapter.

Mida refers to Carmela, sorrowfully and tellingly, as 'La prima vittima, dunque, del neorealismo. Purtroppo non fu la sola'/'the first victim,

---

⁵⁶'It was a burning problem: what to do with Carmela, once the role was finished? Rossellini and I spoke about her as a psychological case, a human case, which was probably irresolvable. She had entered a new world, and had touched with her own hands comforts and luxuries'.
⁵⁷'Sadly Carmela became a pitiful case. When she returned to her family in her god-forsaken village, she couldn't readapt to the harsh life there. Perhaps some unscrupulous young man took advantage of her ... Some years later we found out that, once she was back amidst those deprived people, she had become a woman of ill-repute.'

therefore, of neorealism. Sadly she was not the last' (ibid.). These accounts of her, wrapped in myth and anecdote, and in discourses of *meridionalismo*, as well as in the related discourses of positivism and racial pesudoscience that accompanied it, are of course written by men and are unverifiable. Carmela's story ends there: I haven't been able to find any trace of her at all after *Paisà*. The case of Carmela is an extreme one – however, it illustrates the connection between realism and the female body, and this fragile borderline between acting and prostitution. It also illustrates how difficult it was for any of these girls or women to participate in their own discursive representation, or to be redeemed by a narrative of craft or professionalism. Indeed, it highlights what Danielle Hipkins calls 'the usually repressed phantom of labour' (Hipkins 2017: 163).

Carmela, who was 'discovered' as an 'authentic' and primitive body, dies heroically at the end of her episode, but is tragically misrecognized by the American G.I.s who see her as a traitor and call her a 'dirty little Eyetie'. As Stefania Parigi argues (2005: 50), 'la morte di Carmela [nel film] è un sacrificio non riconosciuto'/'Carmela's death [in the film] is an unrecognized sacrifice.' Likewise, Carmela's extra-diegetic fate can be read as a sacrifice, albeit an involuntary one on her part. Carmela is the anti-celebrity, used to promote the film but with no future in the industry: the question of futurity, linked to that of protection, is key for the girl non-professional, as we will see in the case of Maria Fiore.

Maria Fiore: The 'Meteor'

I want to turn now to another girl, discovered at roughly the same age as Carmela six years later. Maria Fiore, like Carmela, made her debut playing a poor Southern Italian girl, another *popolana*, in Renato Castellani's *Due soldi di Speranza/Two Cents of Hope* (1952). While the trajectory that I will outline seems familiar (a paradigm of discovery by a director, a somewhat difficult but formative experience of shooting, and a rather traumatic afterlife for the non-professional), there are key differences. Fiore was able to construct a career in the film industry, which, if it never reached the heights of those of some of the *maggiorate*, included over fifty films, television shows, and a successful later career as a voice dubber.[58] And yet, her story, even in its apparent success, is revealing about the gendered dynamics of sudden stardom and about the construction of these non-professional girls

---

[58]Lancia and Poppi (2003a: 138) argue that she was 'forse l'unica attrice italiana che, giunta al cinema casualmente, riesce a continuare una carriera densa di soddifazioni'/'perhaps the only Italian actress who, having accidentally got into films, managed to continue a rewarding career'. This reading, however, neglects Maria Pia Casilio and, indeed, the likes of Sophia Loren!

in press discourse, although, as we will see, unlike Carmela Sazio, Maria Fiore did get to tell her own story.

As we learned in the first chapter, director Castellani conducted extensive press searches for the new face of his film, as he had done for his previous films. Indeed, Francesco Pitassio (2019: 273) points out how in promotion and trailers for his earlier films *Sotto il sole di Roma/Under the Roman Sun* (1948) and *È primavera/It's Forever Springtime* (1950), 'lack of professional training and youth were enhanced as production values in the films' advertisement', so that Castellani's recruitment of non-professionals became part of his 'brand'. *Two Cents of Hope* was his biggest commercial success, also picking up the Grand Prix at Cannes, although some critics accused it of either 'killing neorealism', via its emphasis on the comedic and folkloric, or of marking the passage to 'pink' or light-hearted neorealism.[59]

I've already outlined in Chapter 1 aspects of the casting of the film based on the production company documents: to focus on Maria, and on her experience on the film, we have an account written from a female perspective. French journalist Marie-Claire Solleville, who is credited as an assistant director on the film, wrote two articles for *Cahiers du Cinéma* on the production. The second focuses on Maria specifically and narrates Castellani's search for the female protagonist on the periphery of Rome.[60] Castellani and his team were in Quarticciolo, a fascist-era *borgata* or working-class district to the south-east of Rome city centre, having already seen hundreds of girls in schools and even in Displaced Persons camps (Solleville 1952b: 52).[61] As Solleville tells the story, fourteen-year-old Maria came to the casting session, wearing a string of fake pearls borrowed from her sister and resembling 'a bird in a trap' (ibid.: 53).[62] (However, the casting

---

[59]Spinazzola (1985: 104) calculates the film's box office take at 430 million lire, placing it just outside the top ten Italian box office hits in 1952–3, an impressive showing for a film with no stars, though far off the performance of the pink neorealist, Gina Lollobrigida-starring, *Pane, amore e fantasia/Bread, Love, and Fantasy* (directed by Luigi Comencini). While the film was crowned at Cannes, critical reviews in Italy were mixed: see Fortini's 1952 review that 'I guai del nostro cinema sono cominciati proprio da questo film'/'Italian cinema's problems began with this film (Fortini 1973: 156); Alberto Moravia (1954), while praising the film, said that it was the film that moved neorealism into dialect comedy, while Bonicelli (1953) argued that it was agreed upon as the film that killed neorealism.
[60]The male protagonist, the Calabrian fisherman Vincenzo Musolino, was discovered by Castellani, supposedly while doing his military service in Venice.
[61]Quarticciolo was built in the late 1930s and was designed for families with numerous children. An article in the newspaper *L'Unità* in 1944 noted that the area had no electricity, health services, or transport links (cited in Villani 2012: 255).
[62]While Solleville is explicit about Maria's age, other sources suggest differently. Lancia and Poppi record her birth year as 1935, making her instead fifteen or sixteen at the time of the casting in 1951. It is possible that Solleville, who spent a lot of time with Fiore, was engaging in a little myth-making about the youth of the prodigy they had discovered. This myth-making is reinforced in the piece on Fiore in the *Corriere d'Informazione* in 1952, which not only states

photographs previously discussed in Chapter 2 show Maria wearing a polka-dot sweater with no pearls.) Castellani reputedly thought that she wasn't 'savage' enough (ibid.) but then hired her anyway.

Maria's own account of her discovery differs, demonstrating once again the unreliable and anecdotal nature of these histories. In an interview given in 1961, she asserts that she was playing with some local boys, hitting them, 'scalcinata come una zingara'/'as shabby as a gypsy', when she was approached and asked if she wanted to be a film star. Her alleged response, 'Lassame, e va 'mmori'/'Get lost!' (Cavicchioli 1961a: 9) and her assertion that she had never heard of Castellani direct us to read this story, as with that of Lucia Bosè earlier, in terms of the valorization of chance and the denial of overt ambition. Fiore says she dreamed only of being a seamstress, and there is a reminder of this in the 1954 magazine advert she did for Necchi sewing machines.[63]

Further, Fiore fills in some of the details omitted by Solleville: she claims that when she went to the casting session, she was wearing a lot of make-up, and Castellani ordered her to go to the bathroom and wash it all off, presumably to experience her as an authentic and 'natural' girl, a figuration absolutely central to the film.[64] This resonates with the already-mentioned 'discovery' of Silvana Mangano by De Santis, when she came to a casting fully made up and left no impression, but who bowled the director over when he saw her fresh-faced in the rain in a simple dress on Via Veneto. Disentangling fact from myth is not the point here: rather, the key is to understand what elements of femininity are being privileged in accounts of these casting processes of non-professional girls.

Maria travelled to the small village of Boscotrecase in Campania, southern Italy, for the shoot, accompanied by her father as chaperone. The account given of the filming process in many ways recapitulates tropes we have seen earlier. These include Maria having to be both persuaded and threatened to perform adequately: Castellani deplored her 'Roman laziness' and on at least one occasion took down a tree branch to whip her, as she could not weep properly on cue (Solleville 1952b: 56). The director would berate her and call her an idiot, and Maria wept with rage (ibid.: 57).[65] Like Carmela Sazio, Maria is reckoned to have undergone a civilizing process

---

that she was fourteen but that she was discovered by chance by Castellani in Boscotrecase before filming (Art. 1952).

[63]The advert shows a smiling Fiore at a Necchi sewing machine, with a blurb claiming that she worked as a seamstress before becoming a star, and her dream was always to own a Necchi machine. *Oggi*, 7 January 1954, p. 42.

[64]Fiore's quote is telling here. She recalls Castellani saying 'cosa vuole questa bambina truccata come una. ...?'/'what is this child doing here, made up like a ...?' (ibid.).

[65]Solleville (ibid.) recounts 'sweets are stuffed into her mouth', presumably to placate Maria or shut her up.

during the filming: her name was changed (from Jolanda di Fiore to Maria Fiore), she was bought new shoes by the production team, she began to wear make-up, and according to Solleville, she 'became a woman' and got prettier (ibid.: 56).

As with *Paisà* and *La terra trema*, the filming location, a village about twenty kilometres south-east of Naples, is subject to an othering gaze, this time that of the French journalist parachuted in from Paris. In the first dispatch she sent back to *Cahiers*, Solleville reported 'some picturesque memories of the filming' (1952a: 33). She paints a picture of a backward, primitive location, where the locals, called upon to become actors, respond with varying degrees of ineptitude and rebellion. One is always drunk, another, the woman who plays the mother of the male protagonist Antonio, gets the better of Castellani by telling him she can't read and is thus allowed to improvise lines instead of sticking to the script.

While these picturesque anecdotes show the chaos on set, Solleville's quasi-anthropological gaze documents the gendered tensions of filming: while some mothers are anxious to get their children work on the film, most of the women are reluctant to appear on camera, due to the modesty issues we noted in Visconti's filming experience in Sicily.[66] This reluctance Solleville attributes to the fact that southern Italy is 'still very oriental' (ibid.: 36), and her view of southern backwardness is not helped by her revelation that the local women began to pester her for birth control tips, when they learned that she was married but had no children![67]

Although Maria was Roman, her youth, class background, and non-professional status allowed her to be easily conflated with the character she played, Carmela. What Castellani was looking for from her was youth, impetuousness, and an 'authentic' performance style that critics have reduced to nature: Luigi Chiarini, in his review of the film (1952), praised her 'esuberanza'/'exuberance', 'forza'/'force', and 'istinto'/'instinct', while Toschi (2015: 107) talks of her 'incontenibilità'/'irrepressibility'. As with other films discussed, the non-professional actors were dubbed by professional actors, so we do not hear Maria's real voice.[68] However, it is interesting that, unlike Carmela Sazio, Maria was not merely reduced by critics to her body.

Her character is defined by unruliness and rebellion: she insists on marrying her boyfriend Antonio against the objections of her parents. Maria said that Castellani said to her he was looking for 'la ragazza più impunita

---

[66] In Rome, however, Solleville is judgmental of mothers who attend casting calls and who are, in her view, attempting to 'sell' their children (1952b: 53).

[67] See also Martini (1952) who repeats many of these tropes in his account of the shoot. Orsitto (2017: 452) reads *Due soldi* as itself problematically part of a view of southern Italy as culturally and economically backward, typical of pink neorealism.

[68] Solleville (1952b: 57) refers to the 'incomprehensible *patois*' of the villagers, which was then dubbed into a Neapolitanized Italian.

FIGURE 11 *Maria Fiore in a customary dynamic moment of performance in* Two Cents of Hope.

di Roma'/'the most impudent girl in Rome' (Cavicchioli 1961a: 9), and her character spends much of the film shouting, running through the village, and gesticulating angrily. In this way, her 'frenesia locomotoria'/'frenzy of movement' (Toschi 2015: 107) has more in common with the 'unruly women' of the popular comedies and pink neorealism of the time, such as Sophia Loren and Gina Lollobrigida. Also, as opposed to Carmela in *Paisà*, who mainly stands alone, and ends the film as a figure of solitary and deathly resistance, Maria's character embodies the *popolana*'s 'everyday performance' (Culhane 2017b: 256), using the streets and squares as her stage to shout and sing (Figure 11).

Yet Maria's different physicality is important: her girlishness, and what Toschi calls her 'acerba fiscità'/'immature physique' (ibid.: 110) and 'corpo anomalo'/'anomalous body' (ibid.: 112) mark her out as an 'anti-diva' (ibid.: 110), by which Toschi seems to mean an anti-maggiorata, lacking curves. Interestingly, on the cover of the magazine *Tempo* in 1953 Fiore is pictured looking elegant with the caption: 'ha cambiato volto la scugnizza di *Due soldi di speranza*/'the tomboy of *Due soldi di speranza* has changed her look'. The reference to her desexualization shows how she has not been part of the arena of the sexualized stars, but as with accounts of Carmela Sazio, there is also a discursive emphasis on her maturation. A 1954 feature on her reveals a prurient fixation on her physical development:

> è cresciuta, non è più la quattordicenne scatenata e spettinata di *Due soldi di speranza*. Non è più la ragazzina impulsiva e ribelle che stupì il mondo intero con la sua grazia un po' acerba, con la sua fierezza selvaggia. È

diventata grande, e i suoi 18 anni ospitano ora una deliziosa ragazza (A.B. 1954: 62).[69]

Piera De Tassis argues for Fiore's uniqueness, saying (1982: 30) that she was 'forse la prima figura "diversa" del cinema italiano degli anni 50'/'possibly the first "different" figure of 1950s Italian cinema'. De Tassis labels Fiore a 'meteora'/'meteor' (ibid.), shooting across the filmic landscape of the 1950s. Despite sharing the verbal volubility of the *maggiorate* like Loren and Lollobrigida, as well as Magnani, to whom she was also compared, it seems hard for her to find a place in that landscape, as she is less objectified. This suggestion is borne out by the contemporary piece by Castello (1952: 14) in which he argued that Fiore's sex appeal is 'tanto diverso e più genuino di quello delle bellezze fatali fabricate in istudio'/'different from and more genuine than that of the femme fatale types fabricated in the studios'.

Aftermath: 'Et après?'

The upbeat ending of *Due soldi*, in which everything is resolved through the marriage of Carmela and Antonio, was not mirrored by the journalistic narrative around Maria. Solleville's piece on her ends with the journalist's visit to Maria three months after the end of shooting. At her home in Rome, Maria is discontented: her former friends treat her differently, calling her 'la star', while she herself has now changed: according to Solleville (1952b: 58), she is wearing high heels and has painted nails. This media portrait contradicts the interview before the film's release (Anon. 1951a), which breathlessly recounted how she bought her first-ever watch and a medal of Our Lady of Pompeii with her earnings.[70]

Solleville's article ends on an uncertain note: 'fera-t-elle d'autres films? un ou deux, peut-être. Le temps d'exploiter sa popularité d'un jour. Et après?'/'will she make other films? one or two, perhaps. Just enough to exploit her brief popularity. And afterwards?' (ibid.). That uncertainty was resolved by the time of her 1961 interview: by then Maria had made over two dozen films, mostly popular genre films, comedies and melodramas. As Lancia and

---

[69]'She has grown up, she is no longer the wild and unkempt fourteen-year-old of Due soldi di speranza. She is no longer the impulsive and rebellious young girl who astonished the world with her immature grace and her wild savagery. She has grown up, and is now a delicious eighteen-year-old'. Sergio Sollima's comments about young star Lea Padovani in 1945 also betray a fascination with this girl/woman dichotomy, noting that she had 'viso da adolescente su di un corpo esuberante di donna'/'an adolescent face on the exuberant body of a woman' (Sollima 1945).

[70]This modesty topos is reflected also in the piece in *Oggi* (Anon. 1954b) on stars' Christmases, in which Fiore, described as 'semplice e modesta'/'simple and modest', is pictured putting up a Christmas tree in the apartment she shares with her parents.

Poppi note (2003a: 138), many of these films reprised the Carmela-style character, the impulsive *popolana*, and led to her typecasting.[71] By 1961 she was embittered with the world of cinema: the interview she gave to Luigi Cavicchioli, part of his series of interviews with aspiring and established actresses on the evils of the cinema industry, is striking in this regard.

In the interview Fiore is jaded and disappointed with the film industry, which she terms her 'condanna'/'punishment'. She lists the films she has made and calls them 'filmetti dozzinali … che il pubblico più evoluto ignora completamente'/'second-rate films … which more sophisticated audiences don't even see' (Cavicchioli 1961a: 10). She expresses nostalgia for the girl from the *borgata*, wishing she could go back to dreaming of being a seamstress, and having her real name, Jolanda. Now, she says that she would tell Castellani where to go, in the manner of a good *borgata* girl. Unlike that innocent seamstress she dreams of being, there is also an undercurrent of loss of sexual innocence in the interview: Fiore miserably says she had an affair with a married producer, thus echoing the cautionary tales of *Noi Donne*, rather than the successful partnerships of Sophia Loren and Silvana Mangano with their producer husbands.

Fiore's Cinderella story is clearly written as a morality tale: Cavicchioli begins his piece (which interviews Fiore, Lianella Carell, and Madeleine Fisher) with the desire to 'sentire le testimonianze di alcune di queste attrici, giunte al cinema di colpo, per caso, quasi per magia, come Cenerentola al ballo a corte'/'listen to the testimonies of some of these actresses who got into films accidently, almost by magic, like Cinderella at the palace ball' (ibid.: 8). And Fiore's responses match perfectly the idea of the Cinderella illusion: 'era stato tutto troppo facile, inebriante, irreale: proprio come Cenerentola al ballo del principe. Ma in seguito ho aspettato invano che venissero a provarmi la scarpina di cristallo'/'everything had been too easy, intoxicating, unreal: just like Cinderella at the prince's ball. But afterwards I waited in vain for someone to put a glass slipper on me'. The reference to everything being 'too easy' presumably refers to the fact that she did not have to work to achieve her success, and that the dream world she entered was a temporary fantasy which expired quickly. She describes herself as now, at twenty-five, 'logorata, inutile, sfiduciata'/'worn-out, useless, discouraged', worn down by the industry of which she is a passive victim.[72]

The gendered aspect of this cinematic illusion is further highlighted when Fiore confesses that she is afraid she will never marry and is doomed to

---

[71] A caption on a 1954 photo of Maria in the newspaper *Corriere d'Informazione* calls her 'una delle più giovani e più attraenti bellezze popolane del cinema italiane'/'one of Italian cinema's youngest and most attractive popolana-style beauties', 26–27 October 1954, p. 8.

[72] Fiore actually went on to found a successful dubbing company and to pursue voice dubbing rather than appearing in front of the camera. The company is now run by her daughter: http://guide.supereva.it/doppiaggio_e_doppiatori/interventi/2008/09/339554.shtml

remain a spinster (ibid.: 10), reinforcing the pervasive and familiar idea of cinema rendering girls unfit for marriage. It is all the more striking that this rhetoric is being deployed (by Cavicchioli in his series of articles, and by Fiore and other actresses) in 1961, at the height of Italy's economic boom, when Fellini's *La dolce vita* had disseminated a vision of celebrity culture and industrial modernity. This idea is reinforced visually, through the two photos used for the *Oggi* feature: instead of Fellini's famed Via Veneto, Fiore is pictured in the article sitting on a waste pipe on a patch of wasteland, presumably in her childhood neighbourhood, defined only in the caption as 'un angolo della squallida periferia'/'a corner of the squalid periphery'. The other photo is a still from her first film. The photographs establish two levels of visual contrast, firstly between the younger Maria, with her unbrushed hair and plain dress in the film and her more composed and mature older self in the second photograph, and, in the second picture, between the demure pearl necklace and sweater-wearing girl and the industrial pipes signalling urban degradation (a shorthand for moral degradation?).

Conclusion

The paternalistic concern with out-of-placeness of the non-professional, and the simultaneous attraction of that, can also be seen in the image from the cover of *Oggi* (15 May 1952), with Maria Pia Casilio, the servant girl of De Sica's *Umberto D.*, when it was presented at Cannes. She was photographed alongside Princess Maria Francesca of Savoy with the caption: 'Una principessa e una "servetta"' al Festival di Cannes'/'A Princess and a "Serving Girl" at Cannes'. While Casilio actually went on to have a career in the Italian cinema industry, the Cinderella discourse demonstrates how this is an aberration; this temporary inhabiting of the star position, understood as an imitation or transient approximation of the star – whereby she is fortunate to get to Cannes and rub shoulders with royalty – announces the difficulty of constructing a 'girl future' (Harris 2004) in the form of an enduring professional career, relegating them to a space of unrepeatable fantasy.

To return to Michele Gandin's 1953 piece on the 'problem of actresses', the article is illustrated with a still of Maria Fiore and Vincenzo Musolino from *Two Cents of Hope*. However, the caption reads: 'Maria Fiore, rivelata da Renato Castellani. Di solito le attrici scoperte dai registi neorealisti appena diventate "dive" perdono la testa'/'Maria Fiore, discovered by Renato Castellani. Usually the girls who are discovered by directors lose their heads as soon as they become "dive"' (Gandin 1953b). Musolino, and by extension the male non-actor, does not appear in this narrative about knowing one's place and going astray, which is reserved for girls and women. Despite Fiore not being a beauty queen, she is still aligned with an idea of transgressing her station, a narrative she herself seems to buy into when she later discusses her experience in very negative terms. The girl who becomes a star is a figure of desire and unease: as Projansky (2014: 44) notes, 'given that "child" signifies sexual innocence but (female) "star" signifies erotic to-be-looked-at-ness, the girl star embodies the unresolvable contradiction of childhood sexuality'. The adolescent girls who undertook a 'Cinderella' journey to stardom instantiate this tension.

While Maria Fiore suffered from typecasting, a lack of training, and her own insecurities about the profession, Carmela Sazio clearly suffered in a way that went well beyond the parameters of the filmmaking experience. The critical focus on her as an excessively authentic body which somehow overwhelms the viewer runs alongside an othering gaze on her by the filmmakers themselves, and a neglect of her welfare after the film. Carmela's anecdotal fate seems to seal the association between the wild or primitive girl and an excessive sexuality, and she cannot survive the borderline identity of the actress, as an inexperienced young girl from the rural south. The non-professional may be the 'acteur idéal'/'ideal actor' in Jacqueline Nacache's (2005: 131) terms: passing through the film industry, poorly informed on the process of cinema, and docile. Yet this vulnerability of the non-actor is clearly gendered, as we have seen, and we can understand why some girls married producers or directors, which undoubtedly helped them navigate the industry. In fact, the self-reflexive films about cinema, as well as the persistent discourses around female stardom speak to what Ames identified in similar Hollywood films: 'an anxiety built into the male-female relationships of the studio system, in which the biggest stars were female and all the other powerful figures (director, producer, production chief) were male' (cited in Cohan 2019: 101). Female stardom and, by extension, female visibility and freedom are permitted as long as they are discursively disciplined.

The often celebratory critical attention given to the *maggiorate*, and to international stars like Loren, has obscured the broader picture of gendered access to the film industry, which I have sketched out here, although there are other cases that could be considered.[73] But taken together, the beauty contest winners, and Carmela and Maria, are representative, in their different ways, of a prevailing understanding of the non-professional girl as natural, in various senses. Just as the *popolana*, as Culhane (2017b: 259) argues, is 'often reduced to qualities such as naturalness, authenticity and spontaneity', the actress who embodies her, the non-professional girl or woman, is valorized as an Italian natural resource: she is associated with

---

[73]For example, both Maria Pia Casilio, discovered by De Sica for *Umberto D.* and who went on to make over 150 films, and Antonella Lualdi, who won a contest in *Hollywood* and went on to be a star, would make interesting case studies of success.

the natural environment, her body is inscribed into the landscape (even as the street is often the risky territory of the non-professional girl), her beauty is seen as artless, and she herself becomes a symbol of the potential for everyday stardom. The girl is capable of bearing all these meanings at once: as Adorno (1992: 179) writes, in relation to lower budget film which rejects the conventions of the mainstream, 'the flaws of a pretty girl's complexion become the corrective to the immaculate face of the star'. Thus the effect of authenticity is coded directly through the female body. Or as neorealist director and writer Carlo Lizzani (1978: 40) more crudely put it, 'il neorealismo ha fatto entrare le donne con la cellulite, le donne grasse, le donne brutte ma espressive'/'neorealism allowed into cinema women with cellulite, fat women, women who are ugly but expressive'.

Yet, as we saw, the girl also functions as a symbol of the mainstream itself and its threat to engulf high art. The Cinderella tales explicitly referenced by Lucia Bosè and Maria Fiore end differently, but Bosè's humiliation in Antonioni's film (itself read by Lollobrigida as an attack on her) and Fiore's bitterness at the industry which recycled her in popular genre films speak to this dichotomy between art and the mainstream. Meanwhile Carmela's contribution to a neorealist masterpiece has been shrouded in problematic ideas of her primitiveness, and she herself has been erased as a performer from film history.

The 'Cinderella' narratives we have seen have another element: that fairy-tale, accidental ascension to fame or notoriety always comes through an association with a powerful older male director or producer. Both Carmela and Maria were discovered, shaped, and 'civilized' by male mentors: in Fiore's case, we read in a contemporary piece (Anon. 1953) that Castellani 'l'ha fatta attrice, plasmando efficacemente la sua materia rozza ma autentica'/'made her an actress, moulding his authentic raw material effectively', even as the author wonders how she will fare without Castellani. As Tognolotti (2020) argues, in narratives of Italian actresses of the period, often Pygmalion and Prince Charming are fused, and so the stories, as we have seen here, commonly reinforce patriarchal ideas of actresses being created by male protectors, and lacking any agency, ambition, or design of their own. However (somewhat paradoxically perhaps) these girls are also thought, as we have seen, to threaten the integrity of Italian cinema itself; a 1955 newspaper article (Russo 1955) on the opposition by professional actors in Italy to the 'offence' represented by the number the non-professionals says 'delle nostre maggiori stelle (talvolta "doppiate") dalla Lollobrigida alla Loren, dalla Rossi Drago alla Mangano, alla Maria Fiore, quante di esse non sono state "prese dalla vita"?'[74] The Cinderellas, it seems, have taken over the palace.

---

[74]'How many of our biggest female stars (many of them "dubbed") from Loren to Lollobrigida, from Rossi Drago to Mangano, to Maria Fiore, weren't "taken from life"?'

As I have shown, the difficulty in reconstructing these cases is that we are often forced to rely on anecdote and gossip, as well as heavily slanted press accounts. The lack of reliable testimony by girls about their experiences leads to the recycling of well-worn stories about them, which are impossible to verify. However, if we think of anecdotes as offering not an unreliable history but a 'counter-history' or a secret history (Gossman 2003: 143) of the film industry, it might be possible to use them to understand the masculinist assumptions of the film industry. If in this chapter we saw how the untrained female body, whether glamorous, rebellious, or troublingly natural, can be hopelessly vulnerable to that industry, in the next chapter we will look at the experiences of child performers, in whom these questions of vulnerability and protection emerge even more strongly.

4

The non-professional child actor: Beyond *Bicycle Thieves*

Introduction

The figure of the child has loomed very large in accounts of post-war Italian cinema, partly because the films featuring children, such as *Sciuscià/Shoeshine* and *Ladri di biciclette/Bicycle Thieves*, which won Academy Awards in 1948 and 1950 respectively, were so internationally influential. Thus the transnational impact of neorealism has been manifested in these child-focused narratives, notably celebrated in auteur films heavily influenced by neorealism such as Buñuel's *Los Olvidados/The Young and the Damned* (1950) and Ray's *Pather Panchali* (1955).[1] Secondly, the child has almost always been understood as a symptomatic figure, often read as a symbol of lost innocence in the post-war period, of a desire for renewal of Italian society after fascism, and of (sometimes frustrated) futurity.[2] As Parigi writes (2014: 130), 'gli schermi dell'immediato dopoguerra assegnano alla figura infantile una centralità drammatica che non si è mai imposta in modo così incisivo e massiccio nella storia del cinema precedente'.[3] She argues that these child figures are both 'testimoni dell'apocalisse di una civiltà'/'witnesses of the apocalypse of a civilization' and 'i germogli della possibile rigenerazione'/'the seeds of a possible regeneration' (ibid.).[4]

This symptomatic reading of the child is closely tied, in my view, to the valence attributed to the child in the much-cited work by Gilles Deleuze on the 'time image' in post-war European cinema. Deleuze's view that neorealism in particular introduced 'a cinema of the seer [*voyant*] and no longer of the agent [*actant*]' (1989: 2), whose totemic figure was the child,

---

[1]See Biswas (2007); Halperin (2012); Gergely (2014); Krstic (2016: 97–9), among many others.
[2]See Leavitt (2018); Hipkins and Pitt (2014).
[3]'Cinema of the immediate post-war assigns to the child a dramatic centrality unprecedented in its scope and directness.'
[4]See the contemporary discussion by Pavesi (1950: 335) on the 'spicco singolare che figure di bambini sono venute assumendo nel cinema più recente'/'peculiar prominence that child figures have taken on in recent cinema'.

established a conceptual paradigm within which the act of witnessing became paramount. 'In the adult world, the child is affected by a certain motor helplessness, but one which makes him all the more capable of seeing and hearing' (ibid.: 3), he wrote, and the child was thus constructed as an admixture of passivity and a new optical awareness.

These readings foreground the child as symptom and symbol: however, they generally tell us little or nothing about the child as performer, rather than just as an effect of the mise-en-scène. Or to put it differently, we have ignored the 'enfant historique'/'historical child' (Tardy 1975: 171) in favour of a focus on the representational impact of the abstract child. An analysis is thus necessary which brings together accounts of the child performer in post-war Italian cinema with discussions of the performances themselves and their meaning. It is important to consider not merely what the child represents but how the child is presented or is presenting themselves as a performer.

Vittorio De Sica (quoted in Nuzzi and Iemma 1997: 102) pronounced that children are often understood as 'attori per eccellenza'/'actors par excellence' and are frequently seen as exquisitely *natural*. In his 1944 text on teaching children to act, De Sica positioned them as at the other end of the continuum from theatre actors (like himself), whom he deemed the least suitable for film acting. He wrote: 'per far recitare bene i bambini, insomma, bisogna voler loro sinceramente bene, affezionarseli, farseli amici, e poi affidare alla loro anima, al loro istinto, alla loro forza, ch'è la sincerità, il compito di essere vivi, veri'.[5] There is a contradiction here in the idea of children as 'natural actors': and as Karen Lury (2010: 151) has argued, 'the child actor confuses or threatens the understanding of what acting or performing is, and how it can be distinguished from non-acting or from "being"'. So if the child (non) actor challenges received ideas of acting and performance, analysing the work of the child in creating that performance, in tandem with the director and crew, is important in showing the variegated, agentic nature of their on-screen 'doing' rather than, or alongside, their 'being'.

Child actors were of course used in Italian cinema of the 1930s and early 1940s, with star searches conducted to find new faces, including Luciano De Ambrosis, the five-year-old star of Vittorio De Sica's acclaimed 1943 film *I bambini ci guardano/The Children Are Watching Us*.[6] However, as with the

---

[5] "To teach children to act well you need to have sincere affection for them, become fond of them, become their friend, and then entrust to their spirit, their instinct, and their sincerity, the task of being alive and real'. Letter to Silvio D'Amico titled 'Come insegno a recitare ai bambini'/'How I Teach Children to Act'. Rissone-De Sica archive, Cineteca di Bologna.

[6] See also Calvino (1940) who reports the result of a search to find the little girl star of Soldati's *Piccolo mondo antico/The Little World of the Past*. The winner was five-year-old Mariù Pascoli, chosen after a gruelling search, an audition at Cinecittà, and close observation on a trip to the zoo with the other little finalists.

searches for young female stars discussed in the last chapter, post-war Italian cinema, primarily that which can be labelled 'neorealist', is widely supposed to have produced a new kind of child performer. In the 1930s as Saponari (2020: 49–57) discusses, widespread Italian coverage of Shirley Temple in the Italian press led to numerous competitions for child actors, producing new little stars like Miranda Bonansea, known as 'the Italian Shirley Temple'.[7] In his review of Rossellini's *Germania anno zero/Germany Year Zero*, André Bazin (1997: 121) announced that 'the days of Shirley Temple ... are now over'. Although Edmund Moeschke, who played Rossellini's young protagonist, was of course German and not Italian, Bazin was placing him in the category of the new neorealist child performer, saying 'children in the cinema no longer look like china dolls' (ibid.). Bazin was also not above ascribing a natural and national characteristic to these young actors, in his essay on *Bicycle Thieves* (1971: 55): 'In Italy any little street urchin is the equal of a Jackie Coogan and life is a perpetual *commedia dell'arte*.'[8]

Beyond this rather problematic essentialization of Italian child acting, which still does not tell us much about the mechanics of performance, it is essential to remember that the child's performance work in these films is mirrored by the fact that they were workers themselves, in a post-war economic landscape that saw the child often as an economic resource. Examining the extra-diegetic conditions in which children created their performance allows us to trace these transmissions between on- and off-set conceptions of the child's work.

The chapter is not organized by case studies, although it begins with a consideration of Enzo Staiola, the most famous and acclaimed child performer of post-war cinema. Staiola's case allows us to reflect upon how the child's performance can be analysed, as well as on how the child star persona may be uniquely confining. But the chapter then moves through various thematic areas, which permit a discussion of particular child actors, some of them in films considered classically neorealist, others not. Firstly, looking at acting as work, the chapter considers both the work of acting and also how films such as *Shoeshine*, *Proibito rubare/Hey Boy* (Comencini, 1948), and *Abbasso la miseria!/Down with Misery* (Righelli, 1945) insert

---

[7]Bonansea starred in *La cieca di Sorrento/The Blind Woman of Sorrento* (Malasomma, 1934) and *Fermo con le mani!/Hands Off Me!* (Zambuto, 1937). She also dubbed Temple's voice in multiple films (Lancia and Poppi 2003a: 40).

[8]There was a deliberate attempt to imitate Chaplin and Coogan, with Borghesio's 1950 film *Il monello della strada/Street Urchin*, starring young Sicilian boy Ciccio Iacono alongside well-known comic Macario. The film, however, was panned as too derivative of Chaplin. Iacono was apparently spotted by director Pietro Germi when he was shooting in Sicily and then offered a three-year contract by producer Luigi Rovere, who also supposedly sent him to boarding school when he was not filming (Anon. 1950c).

their actors into a post-war landscape in which work and crime are indistinguishable.

The final two sections deal with the child as an element of the Bazinian 'amalgam' with the non-professional, and with the child as a figure of nature, aligned with animals or, more problematically, with non-whiteness. Studying interactions between children and adult stars such as Anna Magnani and Vittorio De Sica, in *Bellissima* (Visconti, 1951) and *L'oro di Napoli/The Gold of Naples* (De Sica, 1954), reveals how the child non-actor often functions as a key element in the unstable collaboration between professionals and non-professionals that Bazin held to be essential to neorealism's effect. Finally, the alignment of the child with pure nature in the form of animals or, more controversially, of a notion of non-whiteness understood as primitivism is important to interrogate: the example of Angelo Maggio, the mixed-race child star of *Il mulatto/Angelo* (De Robertis, 1950), shows how the racialized child operates to exacerbate the notion of the child performer as both natural and unnatural, as an object of fetishistic curiosity, and as a literal scandal.

Overall, the chapter argues that the child actor is not merely a particularly intense form of the non-professional, as De Sica suggested, but that s/he is an under-investigated dramatic performer and economic labourer, who is capable of producing an on-screen 'expressive act' that is not necessarily conscious, but which is made ostensive in the circumstances of its recording and dissemination.

Enzo Staiola: 'Uncursed by any of the regrettable qualities of the child actor'[9]

Enzo Staiola was internationally acclaimed for his role in the Academy Award-winning *Bicycle Thieves*, shot while he was only eight. American critic John Mason Brown's comment that he was 'uncursed' by the usual child actor mannerisms is typical of press responses to his performance. Another US critic (Jacobson 1949) writes that 'I have been fooled too many times to risk even guessing that Enzo is giving a performance in the accepted sense', thus getting to the heart of what is felt to be the alchemy of Staiola's appearance in the film – is he even performing? While, as we will see, this uncertainly extends generally to all non-professional child performance, Staiola's 'exceptionality' on many levels will be discussed here.

As we saw in Chapter 2, Staiola was cast on account of his face, with De Sica calling him a gift from Saint Gennaro. His 'magical' or 'supernatural' appearance on set just in time to be cast reinforces both the 'romantic

---

[9]Mason Brown (1950: 32).

narrative' of actor selection and the idea of him as a kind of freak of nature, as being 'the one' or having 'It' (Lury 2010: 153, 179). But there has been little analysis of his performance in *Bicycle Thieves*, in tune with the lack of discussion of acting in general in relation to neorealism and post-war cinema. The performance has mainly been measured by its effects: as the *New York Times* review wrote, 'Enzo Staiola plays his small son with a firmness that fully reveals the rugged determination and yet the latent sensitivity of the lad' (Crowther 1949a).[10]

As seen in Chapter 2, the focus on bodily expressiveness in criticism of the film, on Staiola and Maggiorani's movements as they walk in tandem across Rome, while useful in expanding our sense of performance, still fails to think about these actors as authors of performance, as critics generally prefer to attribute the credit to De Sica.[11] This failure is exacerbated by the famous anecdotes surrounding Staiola's treatment by De Sica to get him to cry. We have already seen how the various stories about how De Sica operated (using public humiliation, or using the more standard technical expedient of glycerine) negate Staiola as a deliberate producer of complex emotion. If glycerine is administered, his reaction is purely automatic or somatic. If humiliation is involved, with De Sica publicly reminding Staiola of his own lowly socio-economic status by accusing him of scrounging cigarette butts, or reminding him of his family's poverty, then Staiola's reaction is a real inhabiting of emotions, but his own, rather than those of the character of Bruno.

Staiola, as we have seen, was far from the only non-professional who was hit or humiliated to extract an appropriate performance style from them. Franco Interlenghi, for example, whose performance in De Sica's *Shoeshine* I will come to discuss later, cheerfully recounted how De Sica slapped him before a take (in Miccichè 1994: 34). The non-professional, generally cast for their appearance or air rather than acting ability, is often not thought of as capable of consciously authoring a performance. As Bazin wrote (1971: 56) of films like *Bicycle Thieves* and *La terra trema*:

> In these films the very concept of actor, performance, character has no longer any meaning. An actorless cinema? Undoubtedly. But the original meaning of the formula is now outdated, and we should talk today of a cinema without acting, of a cinema of which we no longer ask whether the character gives a good performance or not, since here man and the character he portrays are so completely one.

---

[10] While American critics praised the actors, as we have seen, Italian critics more or less ignored the performances. Guido Aristarco's long review of the film in *Cinema* (1949: 221) only briefly mentions Staiola, Maggiorani, and Carell to say that they are non-professionals.

[11] See Dalle Vacche (2020: 123) on how De Sica got non-professionals to 'discover and perform imaginary and immanent alter egos that they already have inside themselves'.

Pace Bazin, these performances raise fascinating questions of intention: however, as Elizabeth Marquis (2013: 45) has pointed out, when it comes to performance, 'arguing intention is an uncertain task of limited use in any case, particularly because textual meanings may far outstrip the aims of their authors and meaning-making ultimately rests in the process of interaction between spectator and text'. Professionals as well as non-professionals have relied on glycerine, for example; while children may be ill-equipped for method-type approaches that rely upon a 'developed subjectivity' as well as a 'mature inner self' and an ability to access that self via specific training and memory exercises (Lury 2010: 156), we as scholars draw upon a range of extra-textual sources to inform us about a performer's practice. So once we 'know' that Staiola was humiliated and burst into tears, we assess his performance accordingly. If we didn't know that (and sources conflict anyway) how would we assess this moment, which is the emotional climax of the film?

To assess Staiola's performance mode in the film, it is helpful to contrast it with a later one. Staiola was one of the few child non-actors of the period to develop some sort of star persona, albeit one that was limited to *Bicycle Thieves*. For example, he was one of the subjects of a newsreel in 1950 on child actors returning to school (along with Angelo Maggio and Pier Angeli). The clip refers to him as a 'piccolo divo'/'little star' now transformed back into an elementary school kid.[12] Similarly, in the 1953 promotion for a new motor scooter, discussed in Chapter 2, Staiola is pictured signing autographs for fans, and we have already seen how he was sent fan letters. Staiola's face also appeared on a 1988 Italian stamp (featuring him looking up at Maggiorani in a still from the film). This rather marginal star persona ensured that Staiola, unlike many of the other child performers discussed in this chapter, did not disappear after one film. He went on to appear in a further twelve films before his 'retirement' in 1954, including international co-productions such as *I'll Get You for This* (Newman, 1951), in which he played a homeless shoeshine boy, and *The Barefoot Contessa* (Mankiewicz, 1954).[13]

As Paolo Noto has observed (2011: 143), Staiola's subsequent film appearances in some cases repeat and repropose his star-making role, although in others, such as *Penne nere/Black Feathers* (Biancoli, 1952), he occupies a space apart in the narrative, which also emphasizes the pathos of his character, tying him again to *Bicycle Thieves*.[14] A comparison of

---

[12]'Riaprono le scuole anche per i giovani attori e per i bambini prodigio'. *La Settimana Incom*, 20 October 1950, https://patrimonio.archivioluce.com/luce-web/detail/IL5000016014/2/riaprono-scuole-anche-i-giovani-attori-e-i-bambini-prodigio.html?startPage=0&jsonVal=

[13]On the poster for *I'll Get You for This*, Staiola is credited (ninth) thus: Enzo (*Bicycle Thieves*) Staiola.

[14]Staiola's part in *Vulcano/Volcano* (Dieterle, 1949) is small and includes a couple of brief scenes with Anna Magnani.

performance styles is instructive: in *Cuori senza frontiere/The White Line* (Zampa, 1950) Staiola plays Pasqualino, the little brother of Gina Lollobrigida's character. Set in a small town on the north-eastern border of Italy, the characters are caught up in a territorial dispute between Italy and Yugoslavia after the war, which divides the community. Pasqualino tragically dies at the film's end, highlighting the absurdity of this adult geopolitical dispute.

Firstly, Staiola's performance in this later film is striking because of the amount he *talks*. His character's garrulousness in *The White Line* highlights the importance of silence to his performance in *Bicycle Thieves*. There are many scenes in the earlier film in which Staiola says nothing, watching his father, and his facial expression dominates, 'il suo volto di bimbo fatto uomo troppo presto dalla miseria'/'his face that of a child turned man too quickly by poverty' (Pavesi 1950: 335), accompanied by the sentimental score of Alessandro Cicognini.[15] Bruno's silence exposes what Karen Lury (2010: 165) refers to as the association of 'proper acting' with speech, and with the ability to master and remember complex dialogue and deliver it convincingly, and encourages us to expand our definition of performance well beyond speech. Likewise, Wojcik (2004: 8) reminds us that 'performance includes cultural codes of body language as well as unique gestures and mannerisms attributed to the individual actor's idiolect, or personal employment of body language or other sign systems'.

In *The White Line*, on the other hand, Staiola talks a lot. His character delivers a number of monologues and is often placed with a group of other boys, all of whom are speaking. The singularity of Bruno, or his dyad with his father, contrasts with his presentation in a group here and is accentuated by the very different dubbing. In Zampa's film he is dubbed using a much more middle-class and geographically vaguer voice, which produces a much less striking effect. Thus the climactic scene for Staiola in this film is a deathbed scene in which he begs forgiveness of his community: as he delivers the lines 'non sono stati loro... sono stato io, papà! Io!'/'it wasn't them ... it was me, papa! Me!', he is given an opportunity for 'spectacular acting', in which 'framing, camera movement and editing all work to isolate and center the star as an object of attention' (McDonald 2012: 63). However, despite the melodramatic orchestral score by Carlo Rustichelli, the delivery is curiously breathy and affectless, and Staiola's eyes are dry. Meanwhile, in *Bicycle Thieves*, the emotional climax of the scene comes when Bruno weeps at his father's humiliation, and then looks up at him and takes his hand as they walk off together. As we saw, the source of the tears Staiola produced is debatable; likewise, as he looks forward resolutely but sadly, with his father's hand in his, he stumbles slightly. This little stumble, which is

---

[15]On Cicognini's evocation of pity in the film, see Dyer (2006: 35).

followed by another one a few seconds later, reinforces the contingent nature of his performance, which has the effect of accident. This example of what Schoonover (2012a: 151) terms neorealism's use of 'bodily contingency' in order to generate authenticity is powerful in its seemingly unorchestrated nature.

A final aspect of difference between the two performances is a simply biological one: Staiola's face as a ten-year-old in *The White Line* has changed slightly from two years earlier. His cheeks are slightly less chubby, and there is a subtle but real difference in his face, the site of so much of his performative appeal. The inevitable physical changes that children go through are one of the reasons, of course, that child stardom often does not translate to adulthood: another example is that of Vito Annicchiarico, young star of *Rome Open City* (the focus of a later section of this chapter), who claimed (in Aprà 1995: 38) that Rossellini wanted him also for the part of the Neapolitan boy in *Paisan*, eventually played by Alfonso Bovino, but that he had got too fat!

Staiola thus evaded Bazin's prescription against the re-use of the non-professional, about whom he had pronounced 'indispensable as are the factors of inexperience and naïveté, obviously they cannot survive repetition' (1971: 24).[16] However, he remained largely trapped within the role he had created: Staiola, now in his eighties, has continued to do interviews centred on his seminal role, going so far as to say, as we saw in the introduction, that for him neorealism never ends. Staiola's odd position now, as a veteran of Italian cinema who retired in 1954 but who is one of the few witnesses left to De Sica's masterpiece, makes him a living embodiment of neorealism.[17] This talismanic status was cemented in 2018 when he was invited to be present at the start of filming of a feature film, *Frammenti/Fragments*, funded by the Italian government and written and starring children from a school in the *borgata* of Val Melaina in Rome, where part of *Bicycle Thieves* was shot.[18]

A piece on *Bicycle Thieves*' 70th anniversary presentation at Cannes includes the comment that Staiola frequently recycles anecdotes about the film, with the somewhat condemnatory take that 'l'episodio fa parte dei ricordi che Staiola rispolvera a ogni intervista ... e spesso per raccontare la sua breve vita di attore chiede di essere pagato' (Marucci 2018).[19] The

---

[16]See also Quinn (1990: 156) on how the '"newest young ingenue" is by definition excluded from enduring fame, because the extent to which she exemplifies her type will correspond to the rate of her disappearance'.

[17]Interestingly, in the 1063 questionnaires on post-war cinema memories circulated by the *Italian Cinema Audiences* project in 2013, the only mentions of non-professional actors are several respondents who explicitly say how much they were moved by and identified with the child protagonist of *Bicycle Thieves*. See Treveri Gennari et al. (2020).

[18]http://www.alvearecinema.it/frammenti-batte-il-primo-ciak-il-29-aprile-nei-luoghi-di-ladri-di-biciclette-sul-set-anche-lattore-bambino-del-film-di-de-sica/

[19]'The episode is part of the memories that Staiola dusts off in every interview ... and often he asks for payment to recount his short career as an actor'.

scandal, for this journalist, that Staiola might demand payment for his tales of De Sica's film, suggests several things about the non-professional: firstly, that he should be grateful to share his experiences for free (reinstating an opposition between art and commerce that always has the non-professional fall on the former side). And secondly, it repeats the misconception that the work of interviews or promotion is not actually work at all. The invisible, 'immaterial labour' of these paracinematic activities, which have continued for Staiola long after his career in cinema was over, works against the common idea of Staiola, and other child non-professionals, as merely having engaged either in some kind of joyful play or in being simply themselves.

Work, delinquency, acting

While Staiola's image has been largely tied to one celebrated role, there were also a large number of other children who worked in the cinema industry in this period, many of them uncredited, as we will see. This substantial recruitment of non-professional child actors has to be set within the context of child labour more generally in the Italian Republic. The Italian constitution, promulgated in December 1947, explicitly protected the rights of minors: Article 37, which groups together women and children, has a provision for a minimum age for paid work, and pronounces: 'La Repubblica tutela il lavoro dei minori con speciali norme e garantisce ad essi, a parità di lavoro, il diritto alla parità di retribuzione'/'The Republic protects the work of minors by means of special provisions and guarantees them the right to equal pay for equal work.'[20]

That the new Republic inscribed child labour as a right to be protected demonstrates its taken-for-granted nature in Italy in the post-war period. It is also in tune with the first 'principio fondamentale'/'fundamental principle' of the new nation, articulated in the opening words of Article 1 of the constitution: 'L'Italia è una Repubblica democratica, fondata sul lavoro'/'Italy is a democratic Republic founded on labour.' The sacredness of work is thus enshrined at the heart of the new nation. However, in the post-war period the law that protected children's rights was still the fascist one of 1934: that law established a minimum working age of fourteen, and prohibited under-eighteens from night work. But it also had a series of loopholes, such as allowing the over-twelves to work in certain cases, provided they had finished elementary school. Further, while Article 6 of the 1934 law declared that under-sixteens must not be allowed to work in the 'preparazione of spettacoli cinematografici'/'preparation of cinematographic spectacles', the law also allowed the local police chief to authorize this kind

---

[20]https://www.senato.it/documenti/repository/istituzione/costituzione.pdf

of work, even for under-twelves, without parental consent, as long as the work was not dangerous or at night.[21]

There is no trace in the documentation or interviews that I have studied of any official monitoring of or adherence to these laws, nor of much adult supervision of child performers.[22] The concern for the 'salute e moralità dei fanciulli'/'health and morality of children' that Article 6 of the 1934 law claims is paramount does not seem to be particularly reflected in working practices on the ground. It is also important to note that while there were various organizations and unions for actors, it was only in 1960 that the major union, the Società Attori Italiani (SAI), was founded.[23] In addition, it is clear that in the post-war period, child labour was normalized: the example of Vito Annicchiarico, who was discovered in late 1944 by Rossellini for *Rome Open City* while shining shoes for American GIs on the streets of Rome, aged ten, is particularly telling in this respect. Annicchiarico's telling of the story (in Ramogida 2015: 21–3) – in which Rossellini lured him by asking him to shine forty pairs of shoes and then brought him to the production office while little Annicchiarico excitedly questioned him on the material the shoes were made out of, so he could procure the right polish – illustrates perfectly the continuum of labour that structured these children's existence at the time.

Annicchiarico's memories emphasize both the collective nature of the work that children his age in Rome were often doing, as he talks (in ibid.) about being part of a large group of boys who roamed the streets, having stopped going to school, and the variety of work they did: in addition to shining shoes, they would gather cigarette stubs to sell (exactly what De Sica supposedly accused Staiola of shamefully doing) and sell American newspapers to the G.I.s.[24] Annicchiarico's immediate calculation that the film role would be better paid than what he was doing made up his mind. He was paid 1,200 lire a day for the role, plus food and clothes, as compared

---

[21]https://www.normattiva.it/uri-res/N2Ls?urn:nir:stato:legge:1934-04-26;653
[22]Alfonso Bovino (in O'Rawe, Boccuti, and Geri 2023: 193) does say that when he was brought to Naples by Rossellini for *Paisan* he was looked after by an older lady, who stayed with him in his hotel room. Ten-year-old orphan Vittorio Manunta was to be accompanied on the set of *Imbarco a mezzanotte*/*Stranger on the Prowl* (Losey, 1952) by his guardian, Lady Mary Berkely. However, documents in the production file show discussions only about the fee she would get for Manunta, and nothing about protecting his welfare. See Archivio Centrale dello Stato, Direzione Generale dello Spettacolo Files, CF1260.
[23]SAI was founded by Gino Cervi, Giancarlo Sbragia, Enrico Maria Salerno, Saturnino Manfredi, Arnoldo Foà, and Marcello Mastroianni (see Small 2009: 23). On actors' associations in theatre and early cinema in Italy, see Di Lasscio and Ortolani (2010: 61–2). In 1955 the union FISAP: Fed Ital. Sindacati Attori Professionisti was formed (Angeli 1979: 59).
[24]In the photo-reportage that accompanies De Sica's 1945 article on the shoeshine boys on whom he will base *Shoeshine*, we see a small boy shining shoes with the caption telling readers that even at five years old 'lavorano come uomini'/'they are working like men' (De Sica 1945: 5).

to what he might earn during a day's work as a shoeshine boy (perhaps 150 lire).

Annicchiarico says (in Aprà 1995: 38) that he was asked to recruit the boys who played the other members of his child gang in the film, who were paid 500 lire each per day. This anecdote illustrates how the working children of post-war Rome were viewed as a cinematic resource upon which to draw, and is backed up by the testimony of Franco Interlenghi, who noted that the casting call for De Sica's *Shoeshine* the following year was packed, because of the 'spaventosa miseria'/'frightening poverty' and that kids were desperate to earn a few lire (in Miccichè 1994: 31).[25] The fact that *Shoeshine*, as well as films such as *Ok John!* (Fasano, 1947), *Paisan* (Rossellini, 1946), and *Hey Boy* all drew on the real-life experiences of their child protagonists shows how the young actors functioned as a material resource for filmmakers.[26] It also shows us, as Michael Lawrence (2011: 104) reminds us with reference to post-war Indian cinema, itself highly influenced by neorealism, how the failure to remove the child from the national workforce can leave its trace in film texts. While Lawrence (ibid.) goes on to note that 'this failure reminds us of the differences that exist between a universalized (originally Western) model of childhood and the actual experience of particular children around the world', it is important to consider the particularity of the post-war Italian socio-economic context, and the position that the child – as actor and as worker – occupied within it.

Children's work and participation in the informal economy that was widespread in cities like Rome, which were still full of American soldiers and subject to rationing, also shows how the border between legal and illegal work was very blurred in this period. As we will see in examining representations of child work, and in thinking about the child's labour on set as work, the child (non)actor occupies a particularly uncertain status and the nature of their performance as an 'effortful approximation' (ibid.) of a fictional child often goes uninterrogated.

Shoeshine

By 1950, critic Mario Verdone was arguing that cinema had a role to play in discouraging juvenile delinquency and providing better role models, as children were identifying with child actors. Verdone (1950) stated that

---

[25]Children were not attending school then anyway because of the wartime bombings, said Rinaldo Smordoni, who played the other lead in *Shoeshine* (in Verdesca 2016). Smordoni went on to say that he left school at the age of twelve or thirteen to begin work, and only later in life attended evening school to make up his missed learning.

[26]Annicchiarico (in Ramogida 2015: 30) says that Sergio Amidei, who co-wrote both *Rome Open City* and *Shoeshine*, would quiz him on the set of the first film about his lifestyle, and then used that material for the second film.

current cinema was contributing to this problem, and it is possible he was thinking of the Italian films, as well as US ones, in saying this. The fixation on and anxiety about child delinquency in post-war films is perhaps unsurprising: the disruption caused by the war, by the German occupation and the Allied liberation, and the poverty and rationing associated with the wartime and post-war period, saw a sharp rise in crime. Crimes (as defined by the penal code) had doubled between 1940 and 1945 (Canosa 1995: 8), and in January 1946 the official government report on public security noted a worrying rise in 'delinquenza minorile'/'juvenile crime', with 'numerose schiere di fanciulli traviati, che, specie nei grandi centri, vengono indotti, se non costretti a mendicare ed a offrire umili servizi, talvolta anche immorali' (cited in ibid.: 14).[27] These boys, the report concluded, were often involved in petty thefts, but also in burglaries and even murders (ibid.: 15). The widespread anxiety about delinquency was matched by an equally widespread humanitarian concern for children in the post-war period: various initiatives were launched to protect orphans, homeless, and poverty-stricken children, including the foundation in 1946 of an organization to protect 'troubled youth', the Ente nazionale per la protezione morale del fanciullo (Patriarca 2015: 557), and a 1953 parliamentary enquiry into poverty (see Maida 2019; Allasia et al. 2019).[28]

These groups of boys roaming the streets of cities are a focus of the films I examine in this part of the chapter.[29] The most well-known is of course De Sica's *Shoeshine*, about shoeshine boys in Rome who engage in petty crime, released in April 1946, and planned and scouted in the immediate post-war period. De Sica's original piece on the film, 'Sciuscià, giò?', dates from June 1945 and tells the story of its casting.[30] De Sica based his film on the experiences of two twelve-year-old Roman street boys, Giuseppe and Luigi: he met the boys at the horse-riding area in Villa Borghese, where they hired horses for 300 lire an hour. In 'Sciuscià, giò?', De Sica is disturbed by

---

[27]'Numerous gangs of lost boys, who, especially in big cities, are lured, if not forced, into begging and offering small services, sometimes even immoral ones'.
[28]A 1948 documentary directed by Amedeo Castellazzi and sponsored by the National Veterans Association, *I figli delle macerie/Children of the Ruins*, also addressed the crisis produced in cities by abandoned and orphaned children.
[29]See Fisher (2001: 100) on how post-war German films often depicted a 'youthful mob that comes to form a kind of a youth public sphere, both primitive and overactive', as a sign of collapsing social relations.
[30]The film at that point was to be called *Ragazzi/Boys*. Zagarrio (1994: 65) outlines its genealogy, noting a possible precursor in Perilli's lost 1934 film *Ragazzo/Boy*, in which a delinquent orphan (Costantino Frasca) is rescued from crime by being absorbed into fascist youth organizations. Parigi (1994: 89–90) adds several other possible influences, including the Soviet-inspired *Gli ultimi della strada/The Lowest on the Street* (Paolella, 1939), and a short film closing the inaugural Luce Nuova newsreel in 1945, called *Sciuscià*. On the influence on neorealism of Soviet films about children, see Hicks (2016: 155).

the prostitution he sees but the boys deny stealing, and Luigi tells him that he washes dishes in a trattoria. They and the other street boys De Sica talks to are reluctant to speak, distrusting him, and they are 'terrorizzati'/'terrorized' (De Sica 1945: 4) at the thought of appearing in the press, which is constantly discussing boys like them. When in 1954 De Sica recounted the gestation of the film again, things had changed somewhat: the boys were now called by the nicknames *Cappellone* (Long Hair) and *Scimmietta* (Monkey) (see De Sica 1975c: 279).[31] The boys worked as shoeshine boys on Via Veneto, De Sica specifies, and after the film Cappellone was arrested for theft and spent time in prison.

If in casting *Bicycle Thieves* a few years later De Sica felt that the children being brought in for his consideration were too conventionally cute (see Chapter 2), in the case of *Shoeshine* the opposite held true. Scimmietta and Cappellone, De Sica admitted, were unsuitable to appear in the film loosely based on them because they were 'troppo brutti, quasi deformi'/'too ugly, almost deformed' (ibid.: 279). Cappellone in particular had a 'grossa testa deforme di rachitico'/'large head deformed by rickets' (ibid.) and also went around naked apart from a large cloak.

Cappellone and Scimmietta did not appear in the film at all, and it seems they received no compensation for providing the inspiration for the film, though De Sica says that he gave Scimmietta some money to go off and become a shepherd. However, the film is full of other boys, who have not received the same kind of attention that the two leads, Franco Interlenghi and Rinaldo Smordoni, did. In particular, the film is often regarded as a kind of origin story for Interlenghi, who went on to sustain film stardom.[32] Thus a kind of teleological reading has prevailed, whereby the film and its events are read for signs as to why one boy, Interlenghi, became a star, and the other, Smordoni, did not.[33] We also have some familiar tropes in the casting of the two boys: Smordoni was discovered by accident by producer Paolo William Tamburella who almost knocked him over in his car (see Miccichè 1994: 35), while Interlenghi used his cunning to convince De Sica he could

---

[31]However, De Sica's daughter Emi says (in Verdesca 2017) that their real nicknames were the highly colloquial *Chiappe d'oro* ('Golden Buttocks', connoting luck) and *Merda liscia* (untranslatable, but literally 'Smooth Shit') but that it was impossible to print these, so other nicknames were invented, pointing to De Sica's sanitization of these boys' reality.

[32]Interlenghi appeared in films such as Emmer's *Domenica d'agosto/Sunday in August* (1950) and Fellini's *I vitelloni* (1953), as well as numerous international co-productions (see Gundle 2019: 314–15). His marriage to star Antonella Lualdi in 1955 also brought him sustained press attention.

[33]Smordoni insists (in Miccichè (1994: 36)) that despite being cast first by De Sica while the director was dubious about Interlenghi, he was unable to proceed with acting beyond a few small parts due to his lack of proper diction and inability to speak standard Italian well, while Interlenghi, who was better educated, got some theatre parts before doing more films. Thus a class-based distinction is very apparent.

box when in reality he couldn't (ibid.: 31), neither knew what cinema really was, and they got paid very little (250 lire a day, a quarter of what the crew got, says Interlenghi (ibid.: 34)).

Yet the contribution of the boys who make up most of the juvenile cast has gone unexamined.[34] The rhetoric surrounding the mostly unnamed boys recruited from the streets of Rome, and reproduced in interviews and press accounts, emphasizes their wildness and criminality. Interlenghi (in Miccichè 1994: 33) recalls that most of them were 'teppisti'/'hooligans', and that the production director would shout at them 'Statevi bboni, brutti fiji de 'na mignotta!'/'Behave, you little sons of bitches!' but says it was necessary to treat them like this. Smordoni (in Verdesca 2017) says that 'erano tutti delinquenti'/'they were all petty criminals' and that at least half of them came out of the juvenile reformatory in which the film is set, while a contemporary article on the casting (Dragosei 1945) says that one of the boys was discovered while robbing a truck in the centre of Rome and was afraid that the production team were policemen. A later piece (Dragosei 1946) claims that the boys staged a revolt in the studio, destroying dressing rooms and even firing a gunshot.[35]

The idea of the boys running wild on set like 'bestie selvatiche'/'wild beasts' (ibid.) is matched by the description of them by critic Antonio Pietrangeli (1946) on the film's release as 'pezzi di natura'/'natural specimens': they are both close to nature and transgress the deep humanism the child is felt to instantiate. As Malkki notes, the child is 'central to widely circulating representations of "humanity" that are foundational to the whole affective and semiotic apparatus of concern and compassion for "the human" that underlies practices of humanitarian care' (cited in Lawrence 2019a: 15). The child on screen ought to function as a kind of fantasy mirror to the adult spectator in the sense that 'we [adults] are thus seeking to contemplate ourselves in them ourselves plus the innocence, awkwardness and naïveté we lost' (Bazin 1997: 121).

---

[34] A 1946 interview with the two main protagonists plus two others, Aniello Mele (who played Raffaele) and Bruno Ortensi (Arcangeli), draws a clear distinction between these clean and polite boys (Mele's grandfather is a well-known surgeon) and the 'irrequieti, rissosi'/'boisterous, unruly' real *sciuscià* of the film (Dragosei 1946).

[35] The Dragosei piece in *Star*, published a year before the film's release, highlights that it stars 'autentici ragazzi di strada, sciuscià, ladruncoli, venditori di "nazionali zigrinate"'/'authentic street kids, shoeshine boys, petty thieves, and sellers of hand-rolled cigarettes' (Dragosei 1945). The piece also twice uses the noun 'rastrellamenti'/'round-ups' to describe the process of recruiting the children, presumably loading them up in a lorry to bring them to casting sessions. The noun, also used by Castellani in the Introduction, is here even more disturbing for its dehumanizing connotations, partly as it gives the sense of the boys as a mass, but also as it is used shortly after the end of the German occupation of Rome, which saw multiple infamous *rastrellamenti* of Romans, particularly partisans and Jewish citizens.

The street boys quickly became experts in the language of filming: a report from the set in October 1945 records that they had to be told how to hit their marks and not to pick their nose on camera, but that one of the boys also asks De Sica eagerly, 'A commendato'! me lo fa er primo piano?'/'Hey, *commendatore*! Can you do me a close-up?' (quoted in Melani 1945: 1). However, disciplining them was paramount, especially as the boys had other work to do, with one boy asking 'be' se sbrighiamo? devo anna' a venne le sigarette'/'can we hurry this up? I need to go and sell some ciggies'. Such was the realism of the shoot that several times production was apparently halted as police took boys in for questioning (according to Interlenghi in Miccichè 1994: 34), with the boys' status as criminals bleeding into their work on set. The way that publicity around the film promoted this kind of anecdote is in tune with the broader branding of the film which emphasizes its authenticity and the 'real' threat its cast carries. This is something that has carried over into the coverage of other films about delinquent youths: for example, press discourse on 1980s films about Brazilian street children starring protagonists taken from that environment similarly plays on this kind of fascination.[36]

Proibito rubare/Hey Boy

The influence of *Shoeshine* was huge, not least because of its positive critical reception in the United States, and, later, a famous 1961 review of it by *New Yorker* film critic Pauline Kael, which asked 'if people cannot feel *Shoeshine*, what *can* they feel?' (Kael 1965: 102). The film inspired other Italian examples dealing with youth criminality, especially Luigi Comencini's Naples-set *Hey Boy* (1948), which Morreale (2014: 123) refers to as a 'spostamento di certi aspetti di *Sciuscià* verso la commedia'/'displacement of certain aspects of Sciuscià towards comedy'.[37] However, the other important influence on Comencini was the hugely successful American film *Boys Town* (Taurog, 1938), starring Spencer Tracy as the real-life priest who founded a sanctuary for homeless boys: at one point in the film a character asks of the priest's desire to set up a sanctuary for street boys, 'sarebbe questa la vostra Città dei ragazzi?/'is this your version of a Boys Town?'[38] Comencini had already made the documentary *Bambini*

---

[36]See Reimer (2012); Gleghorn's point about the 'complex mediatic processes' (2017: 210) in which the non-professional becomes implicated in such films' generation of authenticity can be applied to the post-war Italian films also.
[37]*Proibito rubare* was released in the United States as *Guagliò* (Neapolitan slang for 'guaglione' or boy), but also had a release as *Hey Boy*.
[38]Due to the boycott of the Italian market by the Hollywood majors *Boys Town* was not released in Italy until 1946. It was followed by a sequel, *Men of Boys Town* (1941), released in Italy in 1948.

in città/*Children in the City*, set in war-ravaged Milan in 1946.[39] He was then offered the chance by Carlo Ponti of Lux to make a version of *Boys Town* that combined neorealism with Lux's production values and a sense of optimism (Seregni 2019: 91).[40]

The credits name the children merely as '"scugnizzi" napoletani'/' Neapolitan street urchins', and Comencini insisted upon their authenticity as part of the film's neorealism (in ibid.: 92).[41] This collective identity is common to other films of the period featuring children: the poster for Fasano's *Ok John!* (originally titled *Sciuscià in paradiso*/*Shoeshine Boy in Paradise*) lists among the cast 'autentici ragazzi della strada', while the little-known and unavailable film *Soli per le strade*/*Alone on the Streets* (Siani, 1953), set near Naples, credited a group of 'ragazzi della strada'/'street kids'.[42] In Comencini's case, the use of 'authentic' kids brought a refreshing spontaneity to the set, with improvisation by the boys – for example, calling lead actor Adolfo Celi 'zi' prévete' (a bastardization of 'zio prete'/'uncle priest') – being kept in (Solmi 1947: 21).

However, tales of the boys' disruptive behaviour quickly emerged from the shoot, with director of photography Aldo Tonti saying that the twelve 'scugnizzi veri' found by Comencini disliked being taken away from their life of petty theft and sleeping on the streets, and could not adjust to being put up in a comfortable convent (in Seregni 2019: 92). Cinematographer Aldo Tonti (1964: 128) recalled that by the end of shooting they had transformed into 'creature umane'/'human creatures' who could eat in fancy restaurants, but this civilizing narrative is upended, as we discover

---

[39]Comencini (1975: 123) spoke of the influence of *Shoeshine* and its absolutely new use of children on *Bambini in città*, and said that for De Sica, the boys became not '"piccoli attori" detestabili'/'detestable little actors' but 'testimoni semplici e spontanei'/'simple and spontaneous witnesses', thanks to De Sica's masterful ability to direct children.

[40]See the review of the film by *The New York Times*' Bosley Crowther (1949b), who wondered aloud: 'some say it should be labeled "the Italian *Boys Town*", some say "the answer to *Shoe Shine*", and some say "the Naples *Dead End Kids*"'. The Dead End Kids were young actors who starred in *Dead End* (Wyler, 1937), *Crime School* (Seiler, 1938), and *Angels With Dirty Faces* (Curtiz, 1938). Kohlert (2014: 867) points out that although the boys were professional actors, having appeared in the Broadway version of *Dead End* in 1935, Warner Bros. 'positioned them as products of the slum'.

[41]Marlow-Mann (2011: 92–3) points out that the *scugnizzo* has been a recurrent figure in Neapolitan cinema ever since Gennarino, the child star of Elvira Notari's silent films. He traces a genealogy of the cinematic *scugnizzo* that passes through Comencini and goes on to *Vito e gli altri*/*Vito and the Others* (Capuano, 1991). I would add a recent Camorra-themed film like *La paranza dei bambini*/*Piranhas* (Giovannesi, 2019) to that tradition. However, an alternative genealogy links the *scugnizzo* not to criminality but to resistance, shown in photos of the *scugnizzi* defending Naples during its liberation, published in *Life*, 8 November 1943 (Forlenza and Thomassen 2016: 194).

[42]A lesser-known film about a gang of orphan boys is *Gli angeli del quartiere*/*The Five Angels* (Coletti, 1951), featuring Enzo Cerusico, the boy deemed too cute by De Sica and Zavattini to act in *Shoeshine*, as well as Ciccio Iacono.

that when the crew later returned to Naples two of the boys were in jail. Tonti labelled the boys 'scugnizzi simpaticissimi'/'likeable urchins' and 'fior di canaglie'/'total scoundrels' (ibid.: 126) but also admitted that there was a price to be paid for their unfamiliarity with cinema, namely, that the bright lights hurt their eyes.

As with other films featuring children in the period such as *Paisan*, *Shoeshine*, and *Rome Open City*, the boys are often depicted not just as a group but as a swarm, and the soundtrack marks this with pronounced scenes with indistinguishable noise emanating from them. This sonic indiscipline reflects their anarchic natures, and in some moments overwhelms the visual track.[43] Yet there are a few moments of individual 'spectacular performance': in one of these the priest walks in on the boys as one of them is dancing on a table, wearing the priest's hat, while the others sing along. The little boy's dance, shimmying his hips, is interestingly more akin to that of a Hollywood female star, like a Rita Hayworth, and it would be useful to know if this was another of the film's improvised scenes (Figure 12).[44]

The elision of work and crime which we glimpsed in *Shoeshine* is made more apparent in *Hey Boy*: from the opening scene when the boys cleverly steal the suitcase of the priest Don Pietro, the film foregrounds the nature of their livelihoods as stealing. The fact that this moment was apparently based on real experience (see Solmi 1947) demonstrates the fragile professional identity of the 'delinquent' child actor, whose filmic appearance becomes entwined with often tragic 'extra-cinematic folklore' (Gleghorn 2017: 215). Diegetically, the film reproduces the confusion between work and criminality, when Don Pietro asks for the mayor's help, saying that he wants to resolve the 'problem' of the boys' lives through their work: 'in fondo hanno sempre lavorato. Invece di raccogliere le cicche, si dedicheranno a un'attività più utile e più redditizio'/'after all, they've always worked. Instead of gathering cigarette ends, they'll dedicate themselves to a more useful and lucrative activity'. The contrast between the boys' previous work, picking up cigarette butts to take out the tobacco and resell it, and their new activity, helping the Naples 'boys town' to flourish, is striking.[45] While the boys end up comically in jail at the end of the film, Don Pietro secures their release by arguing that

---

[43]See Whittaker (2020: 135) on 'the distinctive sonorities of the delinquent voice' in Spanish films of the 1980s. However, the disorderly and slang-filled soundtracks he discusses were predominantly recorded with direct sound.

[44]This moment aligns with how the character actor, often presented as a 'de-individualised stock type' (Thomas 2013: 39) can get a brief star moment in which their uniqueness is contemplated by the spectator.

[45]There is also a reference in the film to one of the boys having been taught by his parents to pimp women out to soldiers.

FIGURE 12 *The undifferentiated and uncredited group of 'scugnizzi' in* Hey Boy.

the reformatory is not the solution to their problems. Instead, collective work is presented as the answer.

The naturalization of 'good work' is interesting and is justified in the film by a contrast between Italy and the United States, represented by the American photojournalist who is there to take photos of street kids for a sentimental reportage on their plight. The journalist claims that the American government has resolved the problem of street children: 'c'è stato qualcuno che ha pensato per loro'/'there was someone else who thought about them', presumably a reference to the New Deal and the kind of social assistance programmes it developed. The othering gaze on Naples, noted by one of the boys ('prima ci vengono a fotografare e poi ci sfottono'/'first they come and take our photos and then they make fun of us') is matched by a paternalistic view which holds that Naples is also racially other to the Italian nation. Don Pietro is supposed to be en route from northern Italy to missionary work in Africa, when he is forced to stop over in Naples by the theft of his suitcase, and realizes the extent of the boys' poverty. His missionary work thus becomes that of saving the *scugnizzi* and inscribes them within a long tradition of *meridionalismo* which, as we have already seen, characterized 'the Italian South – and Naples as its ultimate expression – as an uncivilized and barbaric place, in thrall to poverty and crime' (R. Glynn 2019: 263).

Paisan

This association between Naples, juvenile crime, and race echoes what was seen in Rossellini's *Paisan* two years earlier. In the Naples episode, Alfonso Bovino as Pasquale is caught selling cigarettes and stealing from a truck with other *scugnizzi* by the African American GI, Joe. He also warns the drunk Joe not to fall asleep, or he will steal his boots. The famous dénouement of the episode, when Joe (Dots Johnson) follows Pasquale to the cave where he lives, only to be horrified by the conditions of the orphans living there, contributes to what Bayman (2014b: 171) terms the '"melodramatization" and "idealization" of the child in post-war Italian cinema, through a presentation of them as victims even when they commit crimes'.

Bovino has already effectively developed his character's combination of innocence, bravado, and knowingness at the opening of the episode when, a tiny figure in a patched military jacket, cap, and bare feet, he acts as a barker for a little pal who is doing cartwheels.[46] Bovino's Pasquale assures the street audience that the boy is risking his life, a claim made more laughable by their proximity to a fire-eater across the street. When a G.I. exposes the paucity of their efforts by easily performing several backflips, the boys are left without money. But Pasquale immediately moves on to the next mark, and as he walks along the narrow street in the centre of Naples, his eyes are moving along the ground until he finds a cigarette end, picks it up, and asks another boy for a light. He then becomes embroiled in the 'buying' of the drunk Joe, using his ingenuity to make the other boys flee by pretending the police are coming, which leads to him stealing Joe's boots and a few days later being apprehended by him while robbing a truck (Figure 13).

I will consider the playing of the relationship between Pasquale and Joe in a later section, but here I want to highlight Bovino's ability to incorporate objects into his performance (when apprehended by Joe he quickly offers him a cigarette, and when Joe angrily refuses, waits a beat, and then produces another packet from a different pocket, grinning all the while). Knowing of Rossellini's penchant for permitting or encouraging improvisatory moments (Muscio 2004: 35), the scene reads like a spontaneous set of gestures, which have, as Naremore (1988: 1) would argue, an 'ideological importance' in

---

[46]Wagstaff (2000: 43) highlights the importance of costume, noting how Joe misreads Pasquale's oversized sweater and interprets him as an adult. Bovino says he wore his own clothes.

FIGURE 13 *Little Alfonso Bovino, wearing his own military-style jacket in Paisan.*

convincing us both of their realism and of their appropriateness to that character.[47]

Bovino, who was seven or eight at the time of filming, later called his salary for the film 'una fesseria'/'rubbish' (Iaccio 2006: 47), which was deemed fitting of course to his status as a poor, unknown, untrained child.[48] Yet the versatility of his performance is striking, as is his ability to combine pathos and humour, even in the moving scene where he tells Joe about his parents' death. Rossellini begins with a long shot from Joe's POV of the

---

[47]Bovino himself said there was no script, and that he used his 'spontaneità'/'spontaneity' (in Iaccio 2006: 44). However, he contradicted himself in a 2021 interview, saying he followed the script strictly (see O'Rawe, Boccuti, and Geri 2023).

[48]Bovino went on to appear in several films: the British-Italian production *La madonnina d'oro/ The Golden Madonna* (Carpentieri/Vadja, 1949), where he played a Neapolitan *scugnizzo*, and was apparently credited as Alfonsino Bonino, and the French-German co-production *Au revoir M. Grock/Farewell Mr Grock* (Billon, 1950). Iaccio (2006: 44) also mentions a French film called *Hallo Paisà*, though no record of it can be located. *Paisan*'s credits have him as just 'Alfonsino' and numerous sources list him incorrectly as 'Alfonsino Pasca'. Bovino says that he might have continued acting but that Rossellini didn't want him to work for other directors (in ibid.: 47).

squalid Mergellina caves housing the refugees; he then cuts back to Pasquale, whose face falls as he sees his living conditions through Joe's eyes, but whose gaze simultaneously tracks the boots Joe is holding, clearly hoping to get them back to resell. As Joe quizzes Pasquale about his parents' fate, the boy is forced to keep moving round to face Joe, looking up at him in a way that emphasizes the vast difference in stature between them, although Rossellini resists a standard two-shot until the climax of the scene.[49]

As Wagstaff points out, the whole episode relies upon a disjunction between the way Joe first understands Pasquale, as a hardened little thief, and the reality of Pasquale's life, which is slowly revealed to us. The bravado and expertise of the early sequences give way to the pathos of the revelation of Pasquale's status as an orphan living in abject poverty. Yet even that revelation is softened by Bovino's humour: as Joe gazes around after Pasquale's statement that his parents are dead, Pasquale's voice continues while the camera is still focused on Joe's face. He continues, 'Boom boom! capisci? 'e bombe. Boom boom!'/'Boom, boom! Do you get it? Bombs. Boom boom!' The tone here, which echoes a child's playful imitation of war, works against the camerawork and the dramatic, swelling score by Renzo Rossellini, to continue the uncertain characterization of Pasquale as on the border between childhood and adulthood.[50] When Joe drops the boots abruptly and runs off, overwhelmed by what he has seen, Pasquale picks them up immediately, but simultaneously gazes after him, with a hint of a tear in his eye, before the camera cuts to Joe speeding away.

Bazin's view (1971: 65) that in employing a non-professional, 'ignorance of theatrical technique [is] less a positively required condition than a guarantee against the expressionism of traditional acting' would seem to apply to Bovino and other children. It also refers, as Lury noted, to a view of the child who acts as somehow blurring the boundaries between acting and being. While Bovino's family were very poor, he specifies that he was from Maiori on the Amalfi coast, not Naples, and they were not bombed. He admits that as children they used to go out stealing – 'andavamo a rubà' – but that they stole fruit from orchards, a more wholesome and pastoral image than that of little Pasquale and his friends surviving the urban jungle.[51]

The idea that Bovino is somehow inoculated against expressionism, and is merely performing a version of himself, reflects the critical view of these non-professional children as both innocent victims of war and cunning, if accidental, juvenile criminals. Here, what Drake terms (2006: 84) 'the

---

[49]See Wagstaff (2000: 44–5) for a careful reading of this scene, but one which is not focused on performance.
[50]See Wagstaff (2007: 205–6) on most of *Paisan* being recorded with direct sound. It seems probable but not certain therefore that this is Bovino's voice. Bovino confirms this in O'Rawe et al. (2023), but his recollection may not be reliable.
[51]See the 1983 interview here: https://www.youtube.com/watch?v=cDUQYutkduc

epistemological frames through which screen performance makes sense' are those of authenticity, and also of a particular cultural view of children in this period in Italy and beyond.[52] This epistemological frame also encourages us to ask 'what is a child?' in this historical moment, when cultural representations of them are so ambiguous. Zelitzer (1994: 55) argues that 'child labor is a paradox': that when a child works they cease to be a child, but that is self-evidently not the case in post-war Italy.

Abbasso la miseria!/Abbasso la ricchezza!

This ambiguity around the child, labour, and criminality extends to a more evidently comic film like *Abbasso la miseria!/Down with Misery* (Righelli, 1945).[53] The film stars Anna Magnani as a Roman *popolana* who adopts a Neapolitan child, Nello, played by Vito Annicchiarico, who had famously played her son in *Rome Open City* in the same year. Nello, described as a 'bastardello napoletano'/'little Neapolitan bastard', has lost his mother and is taken in by Magnani's husband Giovanni (Nino Besozzi). Annichiarico's Roman accent was dubbed into Neapolitan for the character, who is presented as a black market veteran.[54] He generates comedy through his adult behaviour: he confidently sells lighters, swindles a G.I., and is able to inform Giovanni that the *pietrine* or flints that he has bought to make lighters with are fake, laughing 's'è fatto fregare pure da un negro!'/'he got swindled by a black man!' Nello is also able to do maths quickly in his head, and these survival skills, signalled by his early response to Giovanni as to how he survives, 'm'arrangio'/'I get by', are approvingly noted by Giovanni's business partner, who tells him that he might make it into the Italian cabinet.

This recognition of the 'unnatural' circumstances of post-war Italy, where childhood has become synonymous with adulthood, matches the performative register used by Annichiarico. Like Pasquale, his productiveness and quick thought, shown by business with his hands, when he steals a fish from a market stall and hides it behind his back and when, ordered by Magnani to get rid of the dog he carries, stuffs it up the back of his shirt, are seen as now naturally 'belonging' to children. His smart replies mirror Magnani's own famous verbal volubility, and we will see in the next section, on the 'amalgam', how productive and rich these child–adult actorly exchanges can be.

---

[52]See Lawrence (2019a) and Fisher (2007) on other contemporary films about orphans in European and Hollywood cinema.
[53]The film, released three months after *Roma città aperta*, came fourth at the Italian box office in 1945.
[54]Annicchiarico recalls that Righelli always threw away his cigarette ends without fully smoking them, and that he would think what a waste this was, as Annicchiarico could have sold them (Ramogida 2015: 146).

In the follow-up film, *Abbasso la ricchezza!/Peddlin' in Society*, also directed by Righelli and released in late 1946, Annicchiarcio is reunited with Magnani. However, just as she plays a different character, another *popolana*, but this time one who has gone up in the world, Annicchiarico plays not a Neapolitan but a Roman boy, Tranquillo. The film again engages with the contemporary topic of black market contraband;[55] Annicchiarico's character Tranquillo has a scene with Vittorio De Sica, playing a kindly aristocrat, in which he is first reprimanded for swearing, then is revealed to be hiding various black market items up the back of his sweater ('just some cologne, chocolate .... oh and a chicken').[56] The matter-of-fact way that Annicchiarico lifts a cooked chicken with one finger, and gazes soberly at De Sica, both refers back to his character in the previous film and creates a 'behavioural architecture' (King 1985: 33) that engages De Sica as straight man in place of Magnani (Figure 14).

This continues when De Sica complains about the noise upstairs and Annicchiarico raises his eyes and says disapprovingly 'questi cornutacci'/'these assholes'. De Sica begins to repeat his words, then glares at him, whereupon Annicchiarico giggles childishly, disturbing our impression of his uncanny adulthood.[57]

But there is a further layer both to Annicchiarico's performance and to its reference to his own limited star persona (he had been described in a review of *Rome Open City* as 'un Mickey Rooney italiano'/'an Italian Mickey Rooney' (M. C. 1945)). So when pressed by De Sica on where he got the goods from, he says that it is 'materiale del nemico'/'materials belonging to the enemy' and declares 'io so' partigiano'/'I'm a partisan'. His character's black market activity is therefore framed as a continuation of his wartime activities when apparently he used to sabotage German trucks, and he repeats this assertion to Magnani later in the film. This moment asks to be read as an intertextual 'ghosting' (Carlson 1994) of an earlier performance, Annicchiarico's role as Marcello in *Rome Open City*, in which he and other children formed a little partisan gang, sabotaging German attacks.[58] This 'self-reflexive moment' (McDonald 2012: 67) encourages the audience

---

[55] See Lanocita's sniffy review (1947) that 'ci spiace che la Magnani attiri quasi simpatia sulla spregevole categoria dei rivendugloli che di questi tempi vanno arricchendosi con truffe e con esosi guadagni'/'it is unfortunate that Magnani is almost sympathetic as a disreputable black marketeer, a category of people who are currently enriching themselves through swindles and extortionate profits'.

[56] He also steals some food expertly from a maid's tray, stuffing it down the front of his sweater, and then walking away casually without being spotted.

[57] Similarly, in *Down With Misery!* he interrupts an adult row by blowing a raspberry, rupturing the film's construction of him as a mini-adult.

[58] The gang, including ringleader Romoletto (Giacomo Cottone), was apparently based on the 1935 film *I ragazzi della Via Paal/The Boys of Via Paal* by Mondadori and Monicelli (Leavitt 2018: 361).

FIGURE 14 *Vito Annicchiarico as Tranquillo outfoxes Vittorio De Sica in* Peddlin' in Society!

to notice performance commonalities. For example, Annicchiarico's appropriation of an adult register was important to his performance in *Rome Open City*, as tiny Marcello seriously informed Don Pietro (Aldo Fabrizi) that 'dobbiamo formare un blocco compatto contro il comune nemico'/'we must form a compact unit against our mutual enemy'. Again, the comic force of Annicchiarico's interactions with the adult performer derive from his own inhabiting of an unlikely maturity.

Although there is another famous comic moment in *Rome Open City* when Annicchiarico gleefully praises Don Pietro in Roman dialect for the whack he gives an ailing old man with a saucepan in order to conceal weapons in his bed ('All'anima Don Piè, che padellata che j'ai dato!'/'Oh my word, Don Pietro, what a whack you gave him!'), his character Marcello in the film has been defined by the tragedy he endures, in seeing his mother, Pina, killed and in witnessing Don Pietro's execution at the film's climax.[59] Annicchiarico's screaming and bodily flailing as he rushes to his mother's body only to be pulled away by Don Pietro and the quiet witnessing of

---

[59]Wagstaff (2007: 106) discusses the fact that Annicchiarico couldn't get this frying pan line right so they had to cut from him to Don Pietro and get him to dub it later.

Don Pietro's murder, followed by Marcello being comforted by another boy as they walk away towards Rome, have great affective power; the child character(s) in the film have thus been interpreted exclusively as bearing what Parigi (2014: 134) calls 'il peso luttuoso della storia'/'the mournful weight of history'.[60]

The critical inattention to performance in the film, apart from that of Magnani as Pina, is typical, as Magnani is one of the few actors whose performance style has received very detailed attention in recent years.[61] The prevailing sense that Magnani overwhelms any film she is in has intriguing implications for the relationship between her characters and others; more broadly, performative dynamics between adult (professional) actors and child non-actors are deserving of study, and I will turn to them now.

The 'Amalgam'

Vito Annicchiarico and Magnani

The amalgam was outlined by André Bazin, in his 1948 essay 'Le réalisme cinématographique et l'école italienne de la Libération' ('Cinematic Realism and the Italian School of the Liberation'). It is striking that despite the voluminous attention that film criticism and film philosophy have devoted to Bazin, his views on acting are rarely discussed (in tune with the general neglect of acting in film studies till quite recently).[62] In the section on 'L'amalgame des interprètes/'The Amalgam of Actors', Bazin draws on the chemical metaphor of the alloy of mercury with another metal to form a harder but malleable composite. Bazin's definition refers not just to the conjunction of professional actors or stars and non-professionals, as is often

---

[60]Leavitt (2018) reads the child in Rossellini's film as an emblem of witnessing and hope. See the documentary by Laura Muscardin *I figli di Roma città aperta*/*The Children of Rome Open City* (included as an extra on the 2005 Arrow Films DVD of *Roma città aperta*) which follows a now-seventy-year-old Annicchiarico around some of the sites of the film. In a striking, and perhaps too-unlikely coincidence, he and the crew bump into an elderly man entering the palazzo in Via Montecuccoli where some of the film was shot. The man turns out to be the boy who put his arm around Marcello in the final sequence of the film. The moving moment, in which the two men reminisce and ruefully note how age has changed them, still leaves the other man unnamed, as do the film's credits. However, Ramogida (2015: 43) names him as Bruno Pinci.
[61]See the special issue of *Journal of Italian Cinema and Media Studies* (2018) on the film, in which performance goes unmentioned apart from the contributions by Pitassio and Rigoletto, both on Magnani. See also Carluccio et al. (2022).
[62]For example, the volumes on Bazin by Joubert-Laurencin and Andrew (2011) and Dalle Vacche (2020), in which acting and performance are barely mentioned.

thought, but also to the use of professionals against audience expectations. The 'law of the amalgam', which Bazin stressed was not new to neorealism, thus resulted in 'the rejection of the star concept and the casual mixing of professionals and of those who just act occasionally. It is important to avoid casting the professional in the role for which he is known' (Bazin 1971: 23).[63]

The amalgam, in Bazin's formulation of it, is fragile and unpredictable: 'When the amalgamation comes off – but experience shows that it will not unless some "moral" requirements are met in the script – the result is precisely that extraordinary feeling of truth that one gets from the current Italian films' (ibid.: 24). The amalgam is thus a kind of magical result: it is also necessarily short-lived and, according to Bazin (ibid.), contains within itself the principle of its own destruction:

> The chemical balance of the amalgam is of necessity unstable, and nothing can prevent it evolving to the point at which it reintroduces the aesthetic dilemma it originally solved – that between the enslavement of the star and the documentary without actors.

The amalgam is a useful concept, I believe, because it offers the sense of fragility and unpredictability that comes with the pairing of professionals and non-professionals. In the moment of performance, something happens, Bazin suggests, and the metaphor gets at the difficulty of analysing and penetrating that 'something' for critics. The instability and unpredictability of the amalgam is intensified when it refers to an acting partnership between a professional (adult) actor and a child non-professional, given the inherent 'risk in production terms' that the child represents (Lury 2010: 146) because they may not know how to behave on set.

The metaphor of the amalgam is also useful for me because it denotes both a process (the coming together of professionals and non-professionals) and a product (the effect of authenticity miraculously produced by this conjunction).[64] Looking first at the use of the amalgam in relation to Magnani, critics have noticed how her *popolana* persona is produced through the frequent positioning of her among a crowd of women, often visually literalized by having her emerge from or merge with a crowd of extras. This has various functions: it expresses a 'collective truth' through her persona, according to Rigoletto (2018: 390), who argues that 'the notion of the individual as the repository of a truth – a truth that is unique to that

---

[63] As Elena Dagrada has pointed out (2017: 211), Bazin wrote this essay in late 1947 and had not seen, for example, *La terra trema*. She notes that in the section on the amalgam he cites only three films, *Rome Open City*, *Paisan*, and *Shoeshine*, and that the theory seems developed specifically around the work of Rossellini.

[64] This resonates with Sergio Rigoletto's discussion of Magnani's authenticity 'both as a construct and as a performative effect' (2018: 392).

individual – crucially shapes our modern understanding of the concept of authenticity; in the case of the neorealist star, this truth was often expected to be a collective, historically specific one'. The device also aligns Magnani very strongly with the neorealist 'chorus', which in Elizabeth Alsop's (2014) terms expresses a group identity, not an individual one, and finally, it establishes a dialectic between Magnani as an 'extraordinary individual' and the 'anonymous chorus', the group or class, in Franceso Pitassio's (2018: 373) terms.

However, her performative relationship with individual children has not been studied: if acting style is ideological (Mur 2015: 49), Magnani's has always been identified with instinct and naturalness, which itself aligns her with the child performer.[65] The three films Magnani made with Vito Annicchiarico (*Rome Open City*, *Down with Misery*, and *Peddlin' in Society*) established a relationship which, says Annicchiarico, led to Magnani asking to adopt him, something his mother refused (Ramogida 2015: 69–70). While Annicchiarico (ibid.: 60–1) suggests that Aldo Fabrizi resented him as he feared he was stealing his scenes, and insisted on the child's face being shot in profile, his collaboration with Magnani is described as organic, due to the almost maternal relationship she had developed with the boy.

Magnani's iconic death scene in *Rome Open City*, in which as Pina she runs towards the truck taking away her lover Francesco and is gunned down by Nazis, has been immortalized by critics and poets;[66] but little attention has been paid to the acting of Annicchiarico in the scene. Magnani's propensity for histrionic, voluble performance is well known, as is the tendency for her films to emphasize this by creating 'spectacular acting' moments. These moments have inevitably tended to eclipse what other performers are doing.

In this scene, then, what Annicchiarico is doing in the background is important. While Magnani runs towards the truck, uttering her famous cry of 'Francesco!', Marcello – dressed as an altar boy – is kicking the German soldier who is attempting to restrain him. A cut to Pina running is followed by a cut to Don Pietro holding Marcello and covering his face as he anticipates what is to come. When the gunshots ring out, and Pina falls to the ground, Marcello escapes the priest's grasp and runs towards her screaming 'Mamma! Mamma!' While Wagstaff (2007: 126) notes how

---

[65] According to Pitassio (2019: 376): 'Magnani's association with childhood was iterated again and again ..., as the mother of many children in *L'onorevole Angelina* (*Angelina*) (Zampa, 1947), or a nun discovering her need for motherhood, in *Suor Letizia* (*The Awakening*) (Camerini, 1955). This association was magnified in *Vulcano* (*Volcano*) (Dieterle, 1950), by coupling Magnani with the prime example of neorealist children, Enzo Stajola, who previously had played Bruno in *Ladri di biciclette*.'

[66] Pier Paolo Pasolini's famous 1961 poem 'La ricchezza' foregrounds the affective power of 'l'urlo della Magnani'/'Magnani's cry'. See O'Rawe (2017) on poetic reflections on Magnani's cry. Marcus (2008) calls the scene a 'synecdoche' (426) and 'scena madre' of neorealism (428).

'out-of-control' Magnani seems in this scene, which was shot using three cameras, the visual and aural tumult is augmented by the child performance. Magnani's traditional 'vocal dominance' (Chiappetta-Miller 2015: 372) is contested by Francesco's shouts, and then by the gunshots, the cries of Marcello, and the non-diegetic music by Renzo Rossellini that strikes up. While Marcello lies on top of his mother's body, Don Pietro immediately pulls him off and hands him over to a policeman, as Marcello again kicks and screams to be released. The scene ends with the famous *Pietà* image, of Don Pietro cradling Pina, while Marcello has disappeared from the shot. The star duo of Fabrizi and Magnani are left to carry the overdetermined weight of the death of Pina.

However, it is interesting to focus for a minute on Annicchiarico. His performance here is rarely mentioned at all: yet he is a crucial element in one of the most famous sequences in Italian cinema. His combination of physicality and vocal passion can be read as imitative of Magnani's: like her, he runs and shouts despairingly. Yet there is a disjunction in his performance, as the dubbing of his cries of 'mamma!' is noticeably poorer than that of Magnani.[67] It is also competing against the musical soundtrack. The vocal effect is one of curious contradiction: it combines what Sisto (2014: 86) terms the 'spacelessness' of Italian post-synchronization in the period, which feels removed from the street shooting, and yet offers an intensity of volume that creates a sense of proximity to the spectator, despite the lack of sonic realism.[68]

Wojcik (2006: 78) emphasizes that 'despite the seeming integration of voice and body in film performance, film performance occurs in multiple time segments – multiple and repeated moments of actors' performances in production, postproduction, and exhibition'. Here Annicchiarico's bodily performance (anger turning to desperate grief, demonstrated via bodily movements) is yoked to his post-synchronized, excessively loud cries, and the orchestration of editing, sound, and performance makes of Annicchiarico a key and overlooked avatar of the film's melodramatic emotionality, even though he is swept aside to make room for the star duo of Magnani and Fabrizi. Annicchiarico himself said (in Ramogida 2015: 67) that he wept for half an hour after shooting the scene, so great had his immersion in it been, and it is notable how he accesses this frantic emotional register, in addition to the humour he deploys in scenes with Fabrizi and the calm affection he demonstrates towards stepfather Francesco (played by amateur actor Francesco Grandjacquet).

---

[67]See Wagstaff (2007: 106) on the film's poor synchronization. He also says that most of the actors dubbed themselves, including Annicchiarico.
[68]There are also extremely interesting reflections on neorealism's use of sound and dubbing in Sisto (2021).

If children are 'dispositivi utilissimi dal punto di vista narrativo'/'very useful tools from a narrative point of view' (Scandola 2020: 54), when deployed in an 'amalgam' with an established star, they can have multiple effects: they can highlight different acting styles and their effects (why do we remember 'Francesco!' and not 'mamma!'? Is one cry more 'authentic' than the other?), they can allow a star's training and professionalism to flourish, or conversely, as we will see with the case of Pietro Bilancione, they can, through their untrained nature and its mode of presentation, allow us to reflect upon the magical effect produced by a child with no formal preparation, who can outshine even an experienced star. And, as we will see now, turning to Tina Apicella and her performance with Magnani in Visconti's *Bellissima*, the child's performance, when juxtaposed with that of an actor like Magnani, famed for her own authenticity and spontaneity of style, allows us to question just what 'good acting' is. As Schoonover (2012a: 44) points out, 'amateurs destablise the aura of actors', and this can be even more the case when they are children.

Tina Apicella and Magnani

Visconti's *Bellissima* (1951) has been regarded as a deliberate act of destruction of the poetics of neorealism (see Miccichè 1998: 198). The story of Maddalena, a woman of the people (Magnani), who enters her daughter (Tina Apicella) into a competition to find 'the most beautiful little girl in Rome', with the prize a film part, the film attacks, 'i sistemi di reclutamento degli attori neorealisti'/'the systems of recruitment of neorealist actors' (Parigi 2014: 171), particularly the contests that pitted girls against one another to succeed. It also takes aim at the illusions created by the cinema industry, represented here by Cinecittà and by veteran director Alessandro Blasetti, and the exploitation of non-professionals, represented by the appearance of Liliana Mancini, star of Castellani's *Sotto il sole di Roma/Under the Roman Sun* (1948).

Mancini appears as 'herself', that is, a former neorealist actress now turned film editor, who confesses to Magnani that cinema has created so many unfortunates like her, and issues a stark warning: 'o esse' attori sul serio, de professione, o meglio non illuderti per niente, e avere un mestiere'/'either be a serious actor, a professional, or it's better not to have illusions, and get a real job'.[69] This critique of neorealist casting processes, from which

---

[69]Mancini herself, a seamstress who was discovered on the street by Castellani (see Cristofani and Manetti 1956: 178), went on to appear in several films, including as a calque of her *Under the Roman Sun* character in Castellani's *Vent'anni/Twenty Years* (1949). Mancini herself claimed that she and her former co-stars were all quite satisfied with post-acting experiences (see Cristofani and Manetti 1956: 178).

Visconti of course benefitted in *La terra trema*, and of the commodification of authenticity by the cinema industry, is very clear.[70] Yet it is worth focusing upon the relationship the film creates between Magnani and Apicella, the famous actress and the unknown little girl, playing, respectively, a woman seduced by cinema and the child she is determined to make successful.

Karen Lury's brilliant analysis of *Bellissima* (2010: 159) highlights the way that the film deliberately contrasts the simplicity of five-year-old Apicella's performance with the artistry of Magnani. Yet she also notes (ibid.) how the film exploits the 'freakish' capacity of Apicella to cry on command. Visconti himself (in Gandin 1951: 293) thought that Apicella had 'istinti non comuni'/'uncommon instincts' and that 'dopo 15 giorni conoscerà tutti i trucchi del mestiere'/'after a fortnight she knows all the tricks of the trade', sometimes leaving the crew 'perplessi'/'perplexed' by her abilities. Apicella is thus seen as a 'natural', yet one who is somehow unnerving in her precocious abilities. This is reflected diegetically, when during little Maria's screen test one of the producers mockingly asks if she isn't really a 'twenty-five-year-old dwarf', such is her uncanny appearance. She is also directly contrasted with the other little girls auditioning, one of whom performs a discomfortingly provocative Betty Grable impersonation (see Aristarco 1952: 19).

The film sets up a tension between Maria's instinctual performance, which is recognized by the great director Blasetti when his expression changes as he watches her screen test even as others mock it, and the ideological orthodoxy of the film that only work can produce success: Maria is dragged to various lessons and her dance teacher opines that the only route to success is to 'studiare, studiare, studiare'/'study, study, study', as well as 'sudare'/'hard work'. This matches what Visconti declared about Apicella (who made only this film), that if she wanted to make it in the film industry she needed to train herself properly (Gandin 1951: 294). The importance of 'lavoro'/'work' is emphasized again at the film's ending, when Maddalena rejects the offer for Maria to appear in the film, and her husband agrees that their new house will have to be built through his work and sacrifice, not their daughter's.

And yet the contradictions inherent in Visconti's approach to acting are obvious: Maria and Apicella both succeed (temporarily) due to their uncommon aptitude, regardless of the film's condemnation of the film industry.[71] Meanwhile, the contrast between Magnani and Apicella operates

---

[70]Gundle (2019: 3) notes that the film 'comments on the neorealist practice of non-professional casting while also itself being cast in part in this way'. See also Zagarrio (2000), Masecchia (2017b), and Casetti (1989–90; 1992) on the film's self-reflexive aspects.

[71]Aristarco (1952: 18) calls the film a 'condanna di un mondo, quello di Cinecittà'/'a condemnation of a world, that of Cinecittà'. Noto (2017) argues, however, that the film is ultimately a defence of the rigid hierarchies of the film industry, against the undisciplined mass that neorealism had allowed in.

in a complex fashion: Magnani the 'diva', who was also seen as an 'anti-diva' via a carefully produced 'illusion of authenticity' (Landy 2004: 92) herself incarnates contradictory ideas about stardom and performance.[72] Magnani's extensive experience, professionalism, and training were often obfuscated: Bazin, for instance, took Rossellini more or less at his word that he had practically 'discovered' Magnani in casting her for *Rome Open City* – in a 1946 interview with Georges Sadoul, Rossellini had declared 'ho fatto debuttare Magnani'/'I gave Magnani her debut', while calling her (in Rossellini (2006: 51) 'un'attrice di avanspettacolo che aveva avuto delle particine in qualche operetta, ma che nel cinema era stata solo utilizzata come una figurante intelligente'/'a variety actress who had had some small theatre parts, but who in the cinema had only been used in minor roles'. Bazin (1971: 22) goes along with this idea, calling Magnani 'admittedly a professional but from the world of the café-concert' and 'a singer of popular songs'.

In *Bellissima*, Magnani, who was due to star in Visconti's ground-breaking *Ossessione/Obsession* (1943) until her pregnancy resulted in the part being given to Clara Calamai, inevitably draws the spectator's attention: 'for all its critical thrust, the film is something of a star vehicle' (Gundle 2019: 3). This 'star vehicle' which critically reflects on Magnani's *divismo* is, as Marcus (1999: 10) notes, 'meta-performative', as Magnani's character addresses the borders of acting and being, borders which her persona both inhabits and habitually problematizes. Her character muses on these borders, as she gazes in the mirror and wonders if she herself could have succeeded as an actress ('in fondo, che è recita'? se io mo' mi credessi di esser un'altra, se facessi finta di esser un'altra, ecco che recito'/'in the end, what is acting? If I thought now I was someone else, if I pretended to be someone else, I'm acting, see?') This process of simultaneous deconstruction and mystification of acting and stardom is augmented by the use of the 'amalgam' of Magnani and Apicella. While little Maria is given Stanislavskian acting lessons by the ridiculous former actress Tilde Speranzoni, these fail because, as we have seen, the Method relies on what children lack: a complex subjectivity and an ability to excavate one's inner life and memories.[73]

What Maria, whose speech impediment prevents her from delivering speeches effectively, *can* do is cry instinctively. Her repeated crying fits in the film have an effect, both on the extra-diegetic spectator and on the director within the film, who decides to cast her. Like Magnani, Maria/Tina blurs boundaries: as Williams (2012: 461) notes, 'the child who can cry on cue ...

---

[72]Pitassio (2018: 382) argues that 'Magnani conflated what might today seem to be contradictory issues, i.e. authenticity and artistry, spontaneity and technique, nature and culture'. See also Culhane (2017b), O'Rawe (2017), and Rigoletto (2018) on these aspects of Magnani's star persona and performance style.
[73]See also Jandelli (2013) on this point.

traverses the unclear line of real/performance'. The uncomfortable nature of Maria's tears (are they real? Was the child threatened, as we have seen in other examples of child performers?) seems to operate on a different register to Magnani's spontaneity and naturalness and work to highlight it, and her own somewhat unnatural precociousness.

It is interesting that Visconti (in Gandin 1951: 293) admitted that, in order to get a performance from Apicella he would leave the camera running before and after the take, a process which also helped Magnani, who loved to improvise (ibid.). He also noted that Magnani both put herself on the same plane as the non-professionals, and lifted them to her level: this is what Bazin (1971: 19) called the perfect 'osmosis' of the amalgam: 'the technical inexperience of the amateur is helped out by the experience of the professionals while the professionals themselves benefit from the general atmosphere of authenticity'.

Bellissima, of course, forms part of the contemporary awareness of cinema as a possible exit from poverty, especially for girls, as discussed in the previous chapter, and the film's publicity played on this, with adverts for it before its release billing Apicella, perhaps hyperbolically, as having been chosen from among four thousand children. The protagonist's rejection of this exploitation of her daughter constitutes a reassuring finale as domestic harmony is restored, and Maddalena lets Maria be 'una ragazzina come tutte le altre'/'a little girl just like any other'. It is impossible to find out what happened to five-year-old Apicella after her one cinematic turn. She seems to have left no public trace. However, in another intriguing meta-cinematic moment, in October 1951 the popular magazine *La Settimana Incom Illustrata* ran a competition to meet the stars of *Bellissima* at Cinecittà: the short newsreel documenting this ends with Magnani entering to meet the competition winners, carrying little Apicella.[74] The camera closes in on Apicella as the male voice-over announces: 'Finita la pellicola, la piccina avrebbe terminata di essere "bellissima". Ma lei non accetta'/'now that the film is over, the little girl is no longer "Bellissima". But she rejects this', as Apicella makes a face to camera and says 'no!'[75] Apicella's 'no!' can be read as an embrace of her futurity within the film industry, and the fact that she did not achieve that thus becomes a disappointing failure. Apicella, the uncannily expert actor at five years old, left her mark in her collaboration with Magnani and Visconti even though she, like Maria, returned to being 'una ragazzina come tutte le altre'.

---

[74]According to Governi (1981: 158), as with Annicchiarico, Magnani wanted to adopt Apicella but the girl's family refused! A 1952 piece suggested that Apicella's father had left the family, and returned on reading in a magazine about his daughter's success. https://alla-ricerca-di-luchino-visconti.com/2016/01/13/bellissima-la-censura-e-il-miracolo-di-tina-apicella/

[75]'Cinecittà: i vincitori del concorso indetto dalla "Incom Illustrata" incontrano gli attori e il regista del film "Bellissima"', 25 October 1951. https://tinyurl.com/dcwsstcd

Vittorio De Sica and Pierino Bilancione

In Zavattini's early outline for *Bellissima*, there is a scene where Vittorio De Sica appears at Cinecittà and, impressed by Maddalena's face, asks her if she would like a part in his film (in Jandelli 2013: 59). She immediately slaps him. This reference to De Sica's casting practices, already amply discussed in this chapter and in Chapter 2, brings us back to De Sica's work with non-professionals, particularly with children. However, in addition to his masterful work directing children, I would like to focus briefly on his work as an actor. For that reason I will analyse an episode of De Sica's anthology film *L'oro di Napoli/The Gold of Naples* (1954); the episode, 'I giocatori'/'The Card Players', features De Sica as an impoverished, hen-pecked count, who regularly compels the young son of a doorman to play cards with him.

Much of the episode's humour stems from the fact that we gather that the middle-aged count regularly loses to young Gennarino, who would much rather be playing with his friends. Yet there is considerable comic play also generated by the performance style of young Pierino Bilancione, who played Gennarino. Ten-year-old Bilancione, De Sica said, was cast when he served the crew coffee at a bar (De Sica 1975e: 289);[76] he added, intriguingly, that casting the boy himself was an extreme example of 'amalgamare l'attore professionista con l'improvvisato'/'creating an amalgam of the professional and the non-professional' (ibid.). De Sica was of course famed as a consummate theatre and screen actor for his pre- and post-war work: André Bazin (1971: 72) commented that 'as an actor he has a quality of presence, a light which subtly transforms both the script and the other actors to such an extent that no one can pretend to play opposite De Sica as he would opposite someone else'.

The 'clash' of acting styles between the former matinée idol and the Neapolitan street kid operates along a dialectic that we have already seen, whereby the child takes on adult qualities which generate humour through incongruity. As Parigi (1994: 93) notes, 'il vecchio e il bambino si invertono i ruoli: laddove il primo crea infantilmente la finzione del gioco, il secondo ne accetta le regole con una supponenza e un fare annoiato da adulto'.[77] Bilancione's untutored performance has been widely praised: De Sica (1975e: 289) said approvingly that 'vi sfido a dire chi è più "attore" di noi due'/'I challenge you to say which of us is more of an "actor"', while Parigi (1994: 94) comments that 'pur scelto dalla strada, Pierino Bilancioni [sic] è un attore a tutti gli effetti'/'although he was plucked off the street, Pierino Bilancioni [sic] is an actor in every sense'. But what is it that Bilancione *does*

---

[76]De Sica (ibid.) noted that the boy supported his whole family with his busboy wage of 500 lire a day.

[77]'The old man and the child invert their roles: the former childishly creates the fiction of the game, the latter accepts the rules with the arrogance and bored air of an adult'.

in this episode to demonstrate that he is an actor on a par with the great De Sica?

The majority of the episode is a two-hander between De Sica and Bilancione as they face off across a card table. However, before this, we see Gennarino's father grabbing him off the street where he is playing with his pals, and dragging him off to fulfil this obligation, upon which, it is to be understood, his father's job might rest. Gennarino cries as he ascends the stairs to the apartment, but once he enters it he is immediately solemn and unnervingly composed. The scene is shot as a back and forth between the two, through the use of shot–reverse shot, with De Sica's anxious and enraged facial expressions contrasting with Bilancione's preternatural composure as he wins almost every hand. Bilancione's seemingly effortless work in the scene extends to his handling of the cards, as he expertly shuffles and deals them multiple times. This professionalism came naturally to him, as De Sica (1975e: 289), himself also famously an inveterate real-life gambler, attested that the boy was an excellent card player.

This naturalness, both in card-playing and in performance, is so noticeable as to appear almost uncanny; as Lebeau (2008: 176) writes, 'the child makes the familiar strange, the domestic uncanny', and here the uncanniness is generated by Bilancione's adoption of behaviours that do not 'belong' to him, as they are properly those of an adult. This idea of an almost excessive naturalness is picked up diegetically, as the furious count demands to know how the boy is such an expert, to which he merely replies, infuriatingly: 'la carta sa dove deve andare'/'the cards know where to go'. Similarly, De Sica's rather baroque performance – singing, laughing, exclaiming – comes up against the boy's calm and seemingly effortless acting: he is restrained, merely tapping his fingers impatiently as he waits for his cards, or opening his eyes slightly in bafflement at De Sica's histrionics (Figure 15).

The clash between the characters, which is also one of class (shown in the contrast created between De Sica's elaborate suit, with its ostentatious handkerchief, and Gennarino's plain sweater) is resolved by Gennarino winning the game. Unable to bear the humiliation of losing to a child, the count threatens the boy's father with 'si mette a fare il maestro!'/'he thinks he can teach me how to play!' and his father begs Gennarino to concede it was pure luck or chance. Gennarino refuses, defending his skill and professionalism as his only resources. In the scene's coda, having witnessed his father's humiliatingly obsequious behaviour towards the count, he returns to being just a child, gazing at his catapult, and picking up his cat and stroking it mournfully, underlined by Cicognini's score. The coda effectively highlights the episode's clever presentation of Gennarino as an exploited and vulnerable child, whose method of self-defence is his ability to gamble and to understand cards, but who is nevertheless left unprotected, despite the humour inherent in much of the scene. The episode title is suggestive: the 'players' are not playing, as for De Sica too much is at stake, and for the boy,

FIGURE 15 The Gold of Naples: *Pierino Bilancione as Gennarino boredly displays his card-playing skills.*

he is compelled to be there to save his father's job, looking out the window wistfully as he hears his friends laughing. Bilancione himself inhabits an uncertain middle ground between work and play, between professional skills and startling organic talent.

Bilancione wrote a letter to De Sica the year after the film was released, in which he asked whether having praised his acting in the film so much, De Sica might not give him a *raccomandazione* to the national acting school at the Centro Sperimentale di Cinematografia.[78] There was presumably no reply to this letter, and Pierino made no more films, becoming instead a well-known master ice-cream maker in Posillipo, Naples. In 1998 Neapolitan director Antonio Capuano approached Bilancione to appear in his *Polvere di Napoli/The Dust of Naples*, which was to be a self-reflexive take on De Sica's film. Bilancione would have played the son of his original character, in a reworking of 'I giocatori'. Bilancione ultimately declined, despite having done a screen test, and the part went to someone else (a.t. 2000). Capuano mused wistfully that 'però aveva ancora gli stessi occhi, era straordinario'/'but his eyes were just the same, it was remarkable' (ibid.); however, Bilancione's

---

[78]In the letter he endearingly writes 'mi hanno detto che a Roma esiste un centro sperimentale, un tipo di collegio dove i giovani vengono appunto preparati alla carriera di attori'/'I've been told that there is a training centre in Rome, a college where young people are prepared for an acting career'. *Cinema Nuovo*, 3 October 1955, p. 162. It is unclear what role *Cinema Nuovo* played in this letter, as they printed a photo of Pierino writing the letter, and another of him playing cards with his father.

performance ultimately proved to be a memorable one-off, like Apicella's, and conformed to Bazin's desire for the 'unrepeatable' amateur performance.

Race and the child

Bazin had warned of the impossibility of replicating the amalgam, the miraculous and unstable product born of the conjunction of the star and the non-professional. This magical combination is partly predicated upon the unrepeatability of the non-professional performance, as well as the ineffable alchemy generated by the fusion of the two types of actor. In the case of the child, as we have seen, it is also predicated upon a figuration of the child as irreducibly spontaneous and natural, someone who 'is' and does not act, in Lury's terms. While close analysis certainly undermines this negation of the child as accomplished actor, the question of the child as 'pure nature' (Taylor 2011: 423) is one that is often disturbingly racialized, as we will see.

The Western conflation of the child with nature is, as Taylor (ibid.) demonstrates, a legacy of Rousseau's opposition of the 'natural' child, linked in an essentializing fashion to the primitive natural world, and the rational adult, a product of civilization, and marked by loss of innocence and purity.[79] This 'mutually constituting relationship between childhood innocence and pure nature' (ibid.: 429) is refracted often in theoretical works on children and acting. Bazin, for example, problematically aligned the pure and uncorrupted child performer with the indigenous person, asserting in his discussion of the amalgam that the unrepeatability of these amateur performances 'can be observed most dearly and quickly in children's films or films using native peoples' (1971: 24). This leads to his formulation that 'indispensable as are the factors of inexperience and naïveté, obviously they cannot survive repetition' (ibid.).

This concept of the child and the more 'primitive' peoples as sharing an essential short-lived performative appeal based on 'naïveté' reveals a fear of their contamination by cinema. As Bazin (ibid.) argues, 'we all know what happens to children raised to stardom by their first film', reflecting a widespread view of the child actor as offering a 'deviant version of childhood' (O'Connor 2008: 1). Béla Balázs went further, in his 1924 thoughts on 'natural actors', praising the 'fresh and not yet compromised' (2011: 108) gestures and facial expressions of peasants and non-Western peoples. He declared (ibid.) that in films such as *Moana* (Robert Flaherty's 1926 account of a Samoan family) or *White Shadows in the South Sea*, Flaherty and W. S. Van Dyke's 1928 Tahiti-set drama, 'the naive, childlike acting ability to which I am referring is found more frequently among exotic

---

[79] See also Randall (2017: xi–xlix) on this aspect.

races'. These non-white non-actors, Balázs argued (ibid.), did not engage in 'theatrical acting' but were 'more like children at play: a kind of trance, a daydream. Now, is this art or nature? It is an intermediate state which, like hallucination and the dream, is undoubtedly closer to nature.'[80]

Balázs and Bazin were merely making more explicit ideas that run through conceptions of non-professional performers, and this alignment of children and the 'primitive' means that the child becomes a signifier of otherness. As Lury (2010: 11) argues, we recognize how in adult actors their performances as 'conscious intending subjects (as human)' produce 'a subjectivity that is self-conscious, coherent and legible, in contrast to the unconsciousness, incoherence and illegibility of the "something else" manifested by the animal and in the child'.[81] This otherness carries with it traces of the non-human: another foundational European film theorist Siegfried Kracauer (2004: 22) linked the child and the animal as performers, saying that 'Flaherty calls children and animals the finest of all film material because of their spontaneous actions'. Edgar Morin (2005: 125) also performs the same conjunction, linking the non-professional, the child, and the animal as three points of a triangle of natural, untrained, and effective performers, 'unspecialized raw material' for directors.

The association of the child and the animal is evident in *Shoeshine*, where the two boys are aligned with the white horse which acts as an avatar of a fairy-tale innocence destroyed (see Miccichè 1994: 53). This reference is explicitly picked up in the acclaimed recent film by Jonas Carpignano, *A Ciambra/The Ciambra* (2016), in which a young Calabrian Romani boy (non-professional Pio Amato playing himself) experiences a poetic moment of reverie in which he sees his dead grandfather's white horse. Carpignano's film, with its multiply marginalized young protagonist, who is excluded from the nation and from whiteness as a southern, criminal, Roma child, will be discussed further in the next chapter. This relation between neorealism, whiteness, and the 'primitive' south can, however, be profitably explored by examining closely a somewhat neglected film, *Il mulatto/Angelo* (De Robertis, 1950).

Il mulatto, set on the island of Ischia, off the coast of Naples, is the story of five-year-old Angelo, whose father was an African American G.I. His mother's husband, Matteo, gets out of prison and discovers with horror that 'his' son is Black. The film traces the growing bond between Matteo (Renato Baldini) and the boy. At the film's end, Matteo decides to allow Angelo to go to the United States with his paternal uncle, who wants to bring the boy 'home'. Shelleen Greene (2012: 121) has written of the film that 'it

---

[80]See Lawrence's (2019b) pertinent discussion of questions of naturalness and the primitive in the Indian child actor Sabu, 'discovered' by Flaherty.
[81]See also Grosoli (2011) on this point.

presents the resolution of racial ambiguity as central to the nation-building project'. *Il mulatto* joins films which depict the Black G.I., such as *Paisan*, *Vivere in pace*/*To Live in Peace* (Zampa, 1947), *Tombolo, paradiso nero*/*Tombolo* (Ferroni, 1947), and *Senza pietà*/*Without Pity* (Lattuada, 1948), in displacing questions of Italy's own recent colonial past in Africa and the status of the mixed-race subjects born there onto the American soldier.[82] The symbolic representation of Angelo's eviction from the Italian body politic has been linked astutely by Greene to the racialization of the Italian south before and after unification (ibid.: 126–7), and the film makes of the mixed-race child a spectacle of otherness, within a region that is itself other to the nation. This is accomplished in the film by making Angelo a spectacle, a kind of freakshow, as he is put on display during his musician father's performances of traditional Neapolitan songs. Compared to a monkey (ibid.: 135), his own racial identity is problematically offered as an element of the film's deployment of comedy and melodrama, typical of the post-war 'Neapolitan formula'.[83]

Yet a closer look at the both the film and the 'real' Angelo can illuminate further the ways that performance and the familiar discourses of the non-professional are racialized in this very particular case, one of only two post-war Italian films to feature a non-white child as a leading protagonist.[84] The 'real' Angelo, who is credited in the titles as 'il piccolo Angelo'/'little Angelo', but was legally known as Angelo Maggio, was a product of an interracial relationship. A 1950 profile in the magazine *Oggi* (Zatterin 1950) asserted that his father was 'un gigantesco negro di Chicago, eternamente ubriaco'/'a giant drunken negro from Chicago' who had a brief encounter with a 'biondissima ragazza romana'/'very blonde Roman girl', producing Angelo, who blends the 'feline' features of his father with the blonde curls of his mother, and is thus an 'anomaly' for a 'mulatto'.[85] Angelo, who was actually Roman, was adopted by the well-known Neapolitan actor Dante Maggio when his son apparently found him, sick, on the street and brought him home.[86]

---

[82]See also Harris (1999; 2001) and Giovacchini (2012; 2015) on this theme.

[83]See Marlow-Mann (2011: 41–70) on the characteristics of the 'Neapolitan formula'.

[84]The follow-up, *Angelo tra la folla*/*Strange Witness* (De Mitri, 1950), was set in Rome and featured Angelo as an orphan who witnesses a murder. Unfortunately the film is unavailable.

[85]See also Patriarca (2022: 98) who reports attention to Angelo from African American newspapers in 1952.

[86]Dante Maggio had already appeared in a film produced by the Scalera production company, *La grande aurora*/*The Great Dawn* (Scotese, 1947) so it seems probable that he was instrumental in the casting of Angelo in the Scalera-produced *Il mulatto*. A copy of the contract for the subsequent film, *Angelo tra la folla*, suggests the child and his father come as a pair: they will be paid 3.5 million lire and Maggio agrees to 'loan' Angelo to the production company for the shoot. See Archivio Centrale dello Stato, Direzione Generale Cinema Files CF1042.

The *Oggi* profile, written while Angelo was making his second film, is a strange mixture of racist assertions – calling him a 'scimmietta'/'little monkey', the above-mentioned description of his father – problematic statements by Dante Maggio comparing his adopted son to a little cat, and saying that if cinema doesn't work out he will put him in his variety show, and an attribution to the young child of troubling statements (ibid.).[87] For example, the real Angelo apparently hates 'negroes' – he pummels a child who calls him the child of a negro, refuses to meet other Black people for fear they will dirty him, won't work with a make-up artist who wants to darken his skin, and explains his colour by saying he forgot to wash; this last statement recalls a moment in *Il mulatto* when kindly Don Gennaro wishes aloud that they might be able to rub Angelo's skin hard and reveal a white layer underneath.

Contrasted with this focus on Angelo's exceptionality is a more conventional trope in describing the non-professional, which is that of work. Angelo is depicted as loving to work (aged five!) and the article sub-heading says that 'il mulatto biondo' 'non ha altra passione che quella di lavorare'/'the little blond mulatto has no passion other than work'. His motto is, in Romanesque dialect, 'Annamo a lavora"/'Let's go to work!', and he demands to get to work early, asserting that he understands better than the director how to shoot a scene. His professionalism, like that of Tina Apicella, is uncanny, and he supports his biological mother with his salary, although now he regards Dante Maggio's wife as his real mother (Figure 16).

Angelo's performance in the para-cinematic event that is the interview thus blends together his status as a racial fetish (it is reported that he is an object of curiosity in the Quadraro area of Rome where he lives), his animalesque qualities, and his work ethic. If work is represented as giving his life value and cementing his inclusion in the Maggio family, within the film *Il mulatto*, his 'work' as a kind of freakshow helps Matteo's own attempts to integrate back into society through his musical job. However, unlike the real Angelo, who is painted as a garrulous and aggressive child, in the film Angelo's performance is often mute.[88] He is not given much dialogue to speak; he is often either reacting or being the object of others' reactions, and the film relies heavily upon his unusual appearance, which causes either horror (when Matteo first sees him) or fascination.[89] His 'novelty' status

---

[87]It appears that Angelo appeared in at least one Neapolitan-themed variety performance with his adoptive father, *Napoli non è milionaria* (1951), according to Lancia and Poppi (2003b: 11).
[88]Patriarca (2015: 545) says that Angelo's silence makes it seem like he is even younger than he is, just a 'cute bundle of needs and feelings'. She herself seems under the impression that he is younger than his real age of five.
[89]Parigi (2014: 138) calls him a 'una sorta di bambino extraterrestre con la pelle scura e i capelli biondi'/'a kind of extraterrestrial child, with his dark skin and blond hair'.

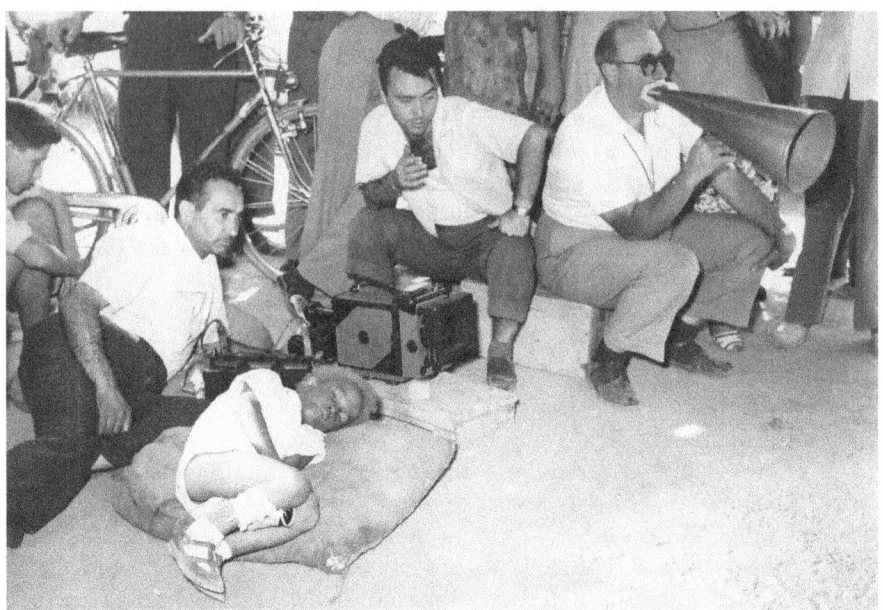

FIGURE 16 *Angelo Maggio on the set of* Strange Witness *(De Mitri, 1950). Photo Credit: colaimages/Alamy Stock Photo.*

(Greene 2012: 135) does not require words and verges on the uncanny, as when he laughingly puts a safety pin in his mouth without being hurt, and Don Gennaro exclaims 'questo non è un mulatto, è un fakir!'/'He's not a mulatto, he's a fakir!'. Even when the film operates a kind of calque of *Bicycle Thieves*, in a sequence where Angelo disconsolately walks behind his angry father, the comic pathos generated in De Sica's film by the disparity in stature between adult and child is here intensified by the racial disjunction, as Angelo's blond hair glints in the sunlight and offers a deliberate contrast with his dark skin.

Angelo's appearance generates comedy, as do his physical actions, often in a duo with Don Gennaro, played by well-known character actor Umberto Spadaro: Don Gennaro humorously tries to teach Angelo how to eat spaghetti but he gets it all over his face, demonstrating his 'uncivilized' ways. He puts mud on his face and Don Gennaro has to tell him severely to wash it off. When Don Gennaro tries to teach him how to sing the traditional Neapolitan song 'Santa Lucia', Angelo comically shouts out of tune instead of imitating the melody. This musical incompetence seems to suggest that he is not a 'natural' Neapolitan, based on clichés about their southern musicality. Yet when his African American uncle arrives there is an interesting face-off: at the welcome dinner, Matteo performs a Neapolitan song while Angelo watches solemnly, but when his uncle (H. Mohammed

Hussein) later begins to improvise an energetic jazz-blues fusion with the house band, complete with 'wild' howling, Angelo is immediately alert, eyes widening. When his uncle then segues into a rendition of the African American spiritual 'Deep River Jordan', Angelo is magnetically attracted to the song, fixing his gaze on his uncle, and he walks up to the stage and joins him in singing along. Thus Angelo's prior musical ineptitude is revealed merely as a lack of the 'natural affinity' (Greene 2012: 147) that he instinctively displays for the African American musical idioms. Angelo's innate musicality has been unlocked by these forms, reinforcing the 'romantic notion of black music as an authentic Other unobtainable by whites' (Radano 1995: 75), and the film's logic dictates that he must leave Ischia and accompany his father to the United States, overcome as he is by his 'intrinsic blackness' (Greene 2012: 120).

Angelo Maggio's career in film was truncated: after his second film he has only three further credits listed.[90] The lack of information about him after 1950 is connected to the relegation of *Il mulatto* to the margins of neorealism.[91] Just as the film could not find a way to accommodate Angelo within the national body politic, Italian film history has not quite found a way to accommodate Angelo and his films. Their hybrid genre status is one reason; another is that the mixed-race child is perhaps not able to contribute effectively to the critical narrative of neorealism as 'the touchstone of civically responsible cinematic practice and nation building' (Duncan 2008: 205). The body of Angelo, so visually fetishized by the film and the journalistic discourse around it, stands as a signifier of otherness and racial difference, and the framing and performance strategies emphasize this (see Ellena 2015: 25). He is also, as Greene has argued, made to stand as an emblem of Italian victimhood: it is explicitly mentioned that his mother was raped in the film, and this victimhood effaces Italy's own very recent colonial guilt.

The mixed-race child is also briefly glimpsed in another southern-set film of the period, *Campane a martello/Alarm Bells* (Zampa, 1949); star duo Gina Lollobrigida and Yvonne Sanson play prostitutes who arrive on Ischia and get embroiled in looking after a group of orphan girls. One of the young girls is played by ten-year-old Vittoria Febbi, a mixed-race Italian-Eritrean child born in Asmara, and Hipkins (2016: 116–17) notes how the question of whiteness is conflated both with southernness and with deviant

---

[90] In *Il grande addio/The Great Farewell* (Polselli, 1954) he played another 'mulatto', this time the son of John Kitzmiller's G.I. – the film, co-starring both Dante Maggio and his other son Enzo, seems to be based on Angelo's own life.

[91] The magazine *Oggi* ran another feature on Angelo a few months after the first one, with more pictures of him at home. His parents say he is about to start school and they fear for his bad temper when he faces inevitable abuse there (Anon. 1950d).

sexuality, as we are left to recognize the child as a product of probable colonial aggression.[92]

The suturing of Angelo Maggio (really a proud Roman, as he declares in the *Oggi* profiles) into the rural south is a similar way of aligning the southern and the non-white. Revisiting *Paisan* in the light of *Il mulatto*, the pairing of the white child and the Black man can be further explored: if Angelo is placed as naturally drawn to Black musical idioms, and therefore as authorizing the film's climactic bittersweet expulsion of him, the two-hander between little Alfonso Bovino and the Black G.I., played by professional actor Dots Johnson, plays out somewhat differently.[93] When Joe, drunk and melancholy, begins to sing an African American spiritual, 'Nobody Knows the Troubles I've Seen', at first little Pasquale attempts to accompany him on his harmonica. Pasquale's musicality (his somewhat clumsy playing causes Joe to follow him) is eclipsed by Joe, who continues to sing mournfully, before slipping into a fantasy monologue about the heroic welcome awaiting him on his return to America.

The equivalence between Pasquale and Joe is strongly suggested by a cut to a solemn reaction shot of the boy when Joe sings the line 'nobody knows my sorrow' and reinforces the notion that the spiritual carries with it a 'folkloric idea of authenticity' (Radano 1995: 83). However, unlike in *Il mulatto*, their communion is undercut almost immediately by Pasquale beginning to argue with Joe, and his comic and uncomprehending interjections into Joe's monologue. The pairing of the Black soldier and the white child, Giovacchini (2012: 144) argues, was following in the 'narrative direction fashioned by Hollywood films (the most recent and famous example at the time being the pairing of Shirley Temple and Bill "Bojangles" Robinson)'. Yet, as we have seen, not only is the neorealist child the supposed antithesis of the saccharine Temple, but Pasquale's Neapolitan whiteness can be questioned, both historically and diegetically, through the pairing with Joe, reminding

---

[92]Vittoria Febbi, who moved to Rome aged around eight, had followed a course on working in radio before the film, and later became a well-known voice dubber (see http://www.encicl opediadeldoppiaggio.it/index.php?title=Vittoria_Febbi). An important casting precursor is Ali Ibrahim Sidali, a Somali child who featured in the colonial epic *Sentinelle di bronzo/Sentinels of Bronze* (Marcellini, 1937) and then as a 'good savage' in the Rome-produced *Piccoli naufraghi/ The Little Adventurers* (Calzavara, 1939), a colonial adventure film for children. See Tonti (1964: 67).

[93]Although Rosssellini claimed Johnson was not a professional actor (Dagrada 2009: 110; Parigi 2005: 20), Gallagher (2006: 244) says: 'he was an actor, not a real soldier. He had … played two or three years in the American Negro Theater, been Canada Lee's understudy in *Anna Lucasta*, and was touring Canada in *Hasty Heart* when [Rod] Geiger's father hired him after Lee, for whom "Naples" had originally been scripted, became unavailable. Rossellini's improvisatory style of non-acting was initially quite difficult for Johnson to get used to'. In this sense, Johnson was unlike African American G.I. John Kitzmiller, a non-actor and former G.I. who forged a career in Italian films. See Anon. (1954c) and Giovacchini (2015) on Kitzmiller.

us that whiteness can be thought of as a 'racialized position' rather than a skin colour (Duncan 2008: 200). As Greene (2012: 32) notes, 'the Naples sequence achieves a destabilizing of "blackness" as a signifier for the shared historical oppression of people of African descent in the Western world, and transfers this signification onto the Neapolitan people'. The performance of Bovino, oscillating between empathy for Joe and inability to understand him, demonstrates how the Neapolitan child occupies a peculiar racial space, and his active performance allows him to escape being a mere spectacle, as is the case with Angelo. In performance terms, the use of music, with both Angelo and Pasquale reacting emotionally to an adult performer, positions the child as a foil to highlight both the Blackness of the African American and the precarious whiteness of (southern) Italians, with the south, once again, functioning as a 'synecdochal red flag' (Verdicchio 2007: 266).

To conclude this section, in 2008, Spike Lee made *Miracle at St. Anna*, a film which in many ways rewrites the post-war Italian narrative of the African American G.I. The Black soldier, Train (Omar Benson Miller), and the young Italian boy Angelo (Matteo Sciabordi) form a 'spiritual bond despite both being unable to speak the other's language' in a deliberate evocation of *Paisan* (Greene 2012: 164). Lee declared that 'the crucial role for this film was the kid. That was a wild card. We had to get the right kid. If you look at the great films of Italian neorealism … all those films are in some aspect about the effect of the war on children'.[94] Lee's insistence on the centrality of the child and his encounter with the G.I. (and the 'miraculous' casting of Sciabordi (ibid.)) demonstrates the enduring legacy and attraction of the neorealist child performer. Again, neorealism's association with the white child is striking, and the amalgam of professional adult actor and child non-actor is also part of that heritage.

Conclusion

Angelo Maggio's career ended after only a few films. While it is unsurprising that the racist Italian film industry had no room for him once he was no longer a cute little child, in many ways Angelo's dilemma was common to all child performers of the era. He was trapped biologically, as the passing of time inevitably lessened his appeal, and in his case his skin colour made him acceptable for only a limited number of roles, even with the patronage of his adoptive father, the established and well-connected actor Dante Maggio. The lack of information about his life after the films he made leaves a void.

---

[94]*Miracle at St. Anna* pressbook (Touchstone Pictures, 2008). https://web.archive.org/web/20160806081702/https://www.mediatecatoscana.it/img_rassegna_stampa/COMUNICATI_STAMPA_2008/57.MIRACLE_engl.pdf

In this way, I am reminded of Saidiya Hartman's words (2019: 260) on one of the early-twentieth-century African American girls whose life she tried to reconstruct: 'she falls into the black hole; she is the black hole, a person of no account'.

The problems for the non-professional child actor have been outlined in this chapter: these are both material (what do they earn? Can they continue to support their family? Can they adapt to working on a set?) and conceptual: how do they know what they are doing? Are they producing a conscious performance? I have tried to demonstrate in this chapter my belief that they are in fact agentic performers, not natural beings who are merely being filmed as themselves. Whatever the limits of the performers, and their understanding of the process of filmmaking, we have seen a range of performance modes and styles, which allow for a broader consideration of performance work in the period, as well as thinking about these children, some as young as five, as workers. As Lawrence (2011: 116) puts it, in relation to post-war Indian cinema, by 'treating screen performance as a representation of work' we remember the work of the real child, who is often a member of the national workforce at that time. Performance is, to them, another form of work, albeit alien to the kind of work many were already doing: 'acting naturally is a skill – it is work. The child actor cannot be child*ish* – that is, irresponsible and unprofessional – about appearing to be child*like*' (Lury 2010: 152).

These screen performances can also tell us much about the values attached to childhood, beyond what the child has commonly been held to represent in the post-war period. Zelitzer's argument (1994: 3) that the United States in the early part of the twentieth century saw the 'emergence of the economically "worthless" but "priceless" child' due to the elimination of child labour does not hold for Italy in the 1940s, where screen representations of working children were often mirrored in the life conditions of their portrayers. Meanwhile Angelo Maggio supporting his mother aged five, or Pierino Bilancione being the family breadwinner aged ten, remind us of the economic value of the child, and the responsibility that might bring. A 1955 report on casting for a Lattuada film confirms this, as a mother is reported as hitting her child who is unable to audition, and saying that a role as an extra in the film would have brought in a day's wage, crucial to them as they are still living in a Displaced Persons camp (Mattia 1955: 35).

As we have seen, children have been highly valued in studies of this period for their symptomatic function, and it is clear that many of the films addressed here point to the widespread anxieties of the post-war: the large number of orphans, the risk of criminality, fears of exploitation and abuse, and anxieties that children are called upon to act as adults. While the hopes of the new Republic may have been pinned to the idea of the child, it is important to remember the trauma that many of these child performers had already gone through, and which directors wished to harness. A couple of lower-profile examples will suffice, such as young Giuliano Cabbia, star of the long-forgotten *La mascotte dei diavoli blu/The Mascot of the Blue Devils* (Baltieri, 1947). Cabbia was blinded during the German occupation of northern Italy, and several years later appeared as himself in a film that positions him as both heroic and pathetic. Vittorio Manunta, meanwhile, was described by *Life* magazine very unsympathetically in a 1952 feature as a 'war orphan' who nevertheless behaved like a 'savage' during US promotion of the film *Peppino e Violetta/The Small Miracle* (Cloche and Smart), in which he played a little orphan. The magazine (Anon. 1952) blamed ten-year-old Manunta's violent behaviour on exhaustion, but it is debatable how much cinema itself might have retraumatized him as well as offered him opportunities; more gravely, for the German boy Edmund Moeschke, filming Rossellini's bleak *Germania anno zero/Germany Year Zero* in 1947 may have contributed to a mental breakdown (Gallagher 2006: 305).

While I have focused in this chapter on portrayals of children who are poor, delinquent, or in some way othered, I might have also offered analysis of 'good' children on screen in this period: the children who police the morality of their parents in Matarazzo's melodramas, for example (see Bayman 2014b), or religious children, such as the portrayal of St Maria Goretti by Inés Orsini in Genina's 1949 *Cielo sulla palude/Heaven over the Marshes*.[95] There is clearly much more research to be carried out on this topic: one thing hampering this research is the lack of information on some of these children. While this is a problem that goes with the territory in researching non-professional performers, who might never give interviews, and leave behind no archive, it is radicalized in the case of child performers, who are rarely profiled and about whom it is very difficult to establish even the basic facts, bar the exceptional ones who go on to stardom, like Franco Interlenghi or Carlo Dalle Piane, who worked solidly for decades after appearing in Coletti's *Cuore/Heart* (1947).[96] This leaves the scholar in the position of writing only about the effects of the child performance, and not the process, which has been the case with the many symptomatic readings of children in post-war Italian cinema. While the young protagonists seen here are rooted very solidly in the economic and cultural humus of post-war Italy, marginalized or traumatized child and adult non-professionals continue to be a staple of world cinema until the present day, as the next chapter discusses.

---

[95]See Vitella's (2018) fascinating account of the promotion of the non-professional Orsini as a Catholic star.
[96]For example, Vito Annicchiarico says he worked on *Ok John!* but was not credited.

5

The non-professional in contemporary global cinema

Introduction

In 2009 *New York Times* critic A. O. Scott used the term 'neo-neorealism' to discuss recent independent US productions. These films, featuring 'fictional characters most often played by nonactors from similar backgrounds', were, he argued, part of a direct lineage from post-war Italian cinema, citing De Sica and Visconti to support his argument. Apart from the use of location shooting, Scott (2009) did not identify other shared formal features of this new wave of films: instead he described neorealism itself as an 'impulse' or 'ethics' that has 'migrated' to other cinemas, very much in tune with many other critics who have seen it as a type of approach to cinema, rather than a school (see Leavitt 2020: 4). This type of amorphous yet discursively potent categorization begs to be unpacked: while the recourse to neorealism as 'ineluctable centre' of Italian film history has been critiqued (O'Leary and O'Rawe 2011: 110), it seems clear that the very use of non-professionals in global arthouse cinema reflexively triggers this comparison, despite the uses of the non-professional in other cinematic practices.[1] Similarly, when Indigenous non-actor Yalitza Aparicio was nominated for the Best Actress Oscar in 2019 for her role in Alfonso Cuarón's *Roma*, critics were quick to align the film with neorealism and to present her 'Cinderella story' as intrinsically linked to its poetics of the non-professional (see Gleiberman 2018; Hastie 2019; O'Rawe 2019; Merjian and Welch 2020).

I will come back to Aparicio in the second half of this chapter, but in the first half I wish to examine the 'migration' or circulation of 'neorealist' practices to other cinemas, and to interrogate some of the key elements of this circulation, specifically the non-professional actor, who appears to

---

[1] See Dalle Vacche's (2018) discussion of Sean Baker's *The Florida Project* as 'American neorealism'. Jordan Schonig (2021) in his video essay on *Tangerine* (Baker, 2015) uses the term 'digital neorealism' to denote recent films shot on digital devices. He does not pick out the non-professional actors in Baker's film as important to its neorealism, however.

be both central and overlooked in the history of these transmissions and legacies. I will examine the perceived influence of neorealism on global film movements (Latin America, India, Iran, etc.), working to identify the role of the non-professional within that influence. I will then address the supposed resurrection of neorealism in Italian cinema in the 1990s, when the term *neo-neorealismo* gained currency. I will examine the practices of realism in this period, focusing on how the widespread use of marginalized protagonists to address difficult social realities both lays bare social inequalities and risks essentializing these inequalities within the bodies of the non-professional protagonists. I will then consider how current Italian cinema and television adopt more varied tactics, using genres such as comedy, and enabling a more diverse set of non-professional figures to appear.

In Part Two of the chapter I move on to the study of casting practices in contemporary global arthouse cinema, in which the non-professional features strongly. While also considering uses of the non-professional outside of the arthouse world I will elucidate how this talismanic figure is frequently deployed to offer an effect of authenticity which enhances a film's cultural capital, particularly through mechanisms such as the festival circuit. As the promotional blurb for the film series 'The Non-Actor' at New York's Lincoln Center in 2017 stated, 'the non-actor has emerged time and again as a totem of renewal, central to many of film history's most consequential movements', and this enduring totemic quality will be explored here.[2]

Neorealism's legacy

The global influence of post-war Italian cinema has been endlessly analysed: as Hallam and Marshment (2000: 40) note:

> Neorealism is regarded by film historians and scholars as one of the most significant filmmaking legacies to emerge from the debris of the Second World War, at the core of developments in cinematic modernism, influencing practitioners as far apart as Spain, Japan, France, Poland, India, Greece, Latin America, Britain and the USA.

This canonical view of neorealism as the 'core' or radiating centre of what becomes a 'global style' (Sklar and Giovacchini 2012: 12) obviously can be and has been challenged by film historians on multiple levels. Nagib (2017: 312), for example, argues against a view of simple transmission that would 'place Europe as the gravitational centre of world/modern cinema

---

[2]https://www.filmlinc.org/daily/the-non-actor-a-historical-survey-spanning-over-40-films-begins-november-24/

and in irrevocable opposition to Hollywood and all other so-called classical/commercial cinemas'. She affirms a positive notion of 'circulation' rather than 'transmission' (Nagib 2006: 30), drawing on the anti-Eurocentrism of Shohat and Stam (1994). Nonetheless, ultimately she does not dislodge neorealism from its status as the 'ethical and aesthetic centre' (O'Leary and O'Rawe 2011: 107) of European and global cinema. Similarly, Sklar and Giovacchini's claim (ibid.: 12) that 'through a process of adaptation and creolization, neorealism – the hybrid, Italianized output of an international conversation about realist cinema that began in the 1930s – was absorbed with varying results into national cinemas' inevitably keeps neorealism at the centre of the conversation.

The amorphous nature of neorealism and the difficulty of defining its practices given the variegated nature of the films that compose the original cluster lead Hallam and Marshment to define it as a 'vacant signifier' and a 'flexible container for a range of non-classical practices' (2000: 40 and 41). Nagib (2017: 316) settles on terming it a 'mode of production', characterized by broadly anti-industrial practices: 'the physical engagement on the part of crew and cast with the profilmic event; the near identity between the cast and their roles; real location shooting; the audiovisual medium's inherent indexical property; and the engagement with works of art in progress within the film'.[3] Without becoming too embroiled in an endless definitional game, what seems to be agreed on by critics of all types is that one of the core features of this mode of production is the non-professional actor. Indeed, it seems to operate as a kind of genre marker: where there is a non-professional actor, we have realism, or a certain type of global arthouse cinema.

The totemic presence of the non-professional can thus potentially be read as what Altman (1984: 10) would term 'one of the semantic elements which make up the genre', part of its vocabulary, as opposed to its syntax, or 'meaning-bearing structures' (ibid.: 11). If a genre's vocabulary 'is thus generated by this syntactic relationship, and not vice versa' (ibid.), the non-professional as a symbolic figure as well as a central element of the mode of production is therefore generated by the supposedly ethical approach of neorealism. As we will see, despite the divergences and adaptations of the neorealist format, the non-professional is one of the elements that persists.

In recent years there have been two important attempts to systematize and map the influence of neorealism on global cinema: the books edited by Ruberto and Wilson (2007) and Sklar and Giovacchini (2012). The volumes perform the valuable function of documenting these ebbs and flows, although despite valiant efforts to complicate the notion of a unidirectional outward flow of neorealism, generally they cannot help ultimately restating it. The

---

[3] See Sklar and Giovacchini (2012: 11) on neorealism as 'mode of production' and, in the Italian context, Farassino (1988).

critical orthodoxy that neorealism is a fundamental source of inspiration for politically engaged cinema movements has often focused on Latin American cinema: direct contacts between practitioners like the Argentinian Fernando Birri and the Cuban Julio García Espinosa, both of whom studied at the Centro Sperimentale in Rome in the early 1950s, have solidified this idea of a direct transmission of neorealist practice.[4] While 'twenty-eight Latin American directors earned diplomas at the Centro Sperimentale in the 1950s and 1960s' (Francese 2007: 431), as Salazkina (2012: 110) notes, it was particularly Zavattini who was a 'consistent interlocutor for the emerging critics and filmmakers of the New Latin American cinemas and an active participant in the festival circuits promoting in particular the development of the Cuban film industry'. It is no coincidence, I would argue, that Zavattini was the privileged interlocutor of Latin American theorist and directors, since, as we have seen in earlier chapters, he was the most vocal of the neorealist cineastes in insisting on the centrality of the non-professional actor to the project of neorealism. The neorealist mode of production was adopted by many Latin American directors 'because it had produced superior films at low cost and without famous stars' (Francese 2007: 432), thus addressing both budgetary and aesthetic concerns. To quote Brazilian director Nelson Pereira dos Santos, 'the most important lesson of neorealism to Third World filmmakers was to prove that cinema could exist with very few resources, forgetting big studios, stars and elaborate sets. The idea was to go to the streets and film the people' (cited in Creus 2011).

Thus in tracing the neorealist influence on movements such as New Latin American cinema and Brazilian Cinema Novo, many scholars have identified the use of non-professionals as a core element of this influence, albeit without devoting much specific attention to it.[5] While there has been some pushback against the Eurocentrism of much of this view (see Schroeder Rodríguez 2016: 162), and identification of ways in which neorealism intersected with national practices of filming 'real people' already in use (see Halperin 2012: 127), the Eurocentric narrative has tended to prevail. This narrative has, in turn, been traced through to African cinema, albeit indirectly via the influence of Latin American directors. Niang (2012: 196) identifies the use of non-professionals as a key factor of African cinema of the 1960s and 1970s, both in order to offer authenticity to performances and as a direct result of the lack of training and infrastructure for cinema actors. Yet again, as Gabara (2007: 200) notes, such automatic critical labelling of these practices in directors such as Ousmane Sembène as 'neorealist' 'limits the terms of discussion to the vocabulary of the European canon and, whether as praise or critique, functions to pull Sembène toward it'.

---

[4] See Mestman (2012); Chanan (2004: 147–50); Gabara (2007: 192–3).
[5] See Johnson and Stam (1995: 32); Traverso (2007).

My intention in this section has not been to offer an exhaustive listing of the extent of the global neorealist influence, but rather to nod towards its centripetal discursive pull. This has also, of course, been identified in relation to Iranian cinema (see Naficy 2012), Chinese Sixth Generation films (Lu 2014), and Indian cinema (Biswas 2007; Majumdar 2012), to name but two; however, in each case, again, it is important to excavate local and national antecedents and practices, such as the role of the Indian 'Social film' (Biswas 2007: 78) or the complex role played by British colonial documentary, as Lawrence's (2019b) work on Sabu, non-professional peasant star of Flaherty's 1937 *Elephant Boy* (1937) illuminates.

It is clear that neorealism achieved a canonical status in its imbrication with Latin American cinema, to the extent of later appearing fossilized and inadequate to address the conditions of the late 1960s, as Fernando Solanas and Octavio Getino's manifesto on 'Third Cinema' elaborated (see Solanas and Getino 1970–1). Their dismissal of the then-superseded European art cinema or 'Second Cinema' speaks to the ways in which elements such as the non-professional actor – as a function of a certain low-budget mode of production, and as the offshoot of an ethical impulse towards an 'authentic' representation – had become a synecdoche for a whole approach to cinema. This figure is, as I have argued here, essential but overlooked: in most of the studies I have cited, actors are mentioned only briefly, without deep consideration of their contribution of their relation to the film industry. As we will see later in this chapter, attention is generally paid to the non-professional in global cinema either when they achieve a degree of mainstream recognition, or as part of a 'where are they now?' narrative. An example here can suffice: the 2013 film *Apur Panchali* by Kaushik Ganguly traced the story of Subir Banerjee, the child protagonist of Satyajit Ray's globally celebrated *Pather Panchali* (1955), which was heavily indebted to De Sica's *Bicycle Thieves*. The film makes this connection clear through its trailer, with a picture of Enzo Staiola as Bruno in De Sica's film; it is dedicated to 'the journey of a forgotten child actor', speaking to the enduring link in the cultural imaginary between neorealism, global arthouse cinema, and the non-professional.

Neo-neorealismo in Italy

The currency of neorealism is, as we have seen, enduring, and of course, in Italy this term has been weighted with symbolic baggage since the 1940s, with the 'rebirth' of neorealism in the 1990s being an important example of this. After what has been, somewhat hyperbolically, termed the Italian cinematic 'genocide' of the 1980s (Brunetta 2003: 350), the so-called rebirth of Italian cinema in the late 1980s and 1990s was marked by politically engaged films which reflected upon Italian identity by directors such as

Marco Risi, Gianni Amelio, Carlo Mazzacurati, and Ricky Tognazzi, leading critic Gian Piero Brunetta (ibid.: 190) to term it a 'nuova Resistenza'/'new Resistance'.

This movement was labelled *neo-neorealismo* (see ibid.: 397); works like *Amore tossico/Toxic Love* (Caligari, 1983), *Mery per sempre/Forever Mery* (Risi, 1989), and *Il ladro di bambini/The Stolen Children* (Amelio, 1992) clearly demonstrate their neorealist heritage, both through the use of cinematographic techniques of realism (long takes, the long shot in deep focus) and scripts that are dialectal, colloquial, and which give an effect of immediacy and spontaneity.[6] However, for these films, the non-professional actor acts as a genre marker: in Caligari's film, which depicts the gritty environment of drug addicts on the outskirts of Rome, the characters were all played by current or former addicts with no acting experience. Meanwhile in Risi's film trans actress Alessandra di Sanzo as the titular Mery was a memorable protagonist, flanked by a number of Sicilian boys from underprivileged backgrounds who played the other pupils in the juvenile reformatory school in which the film is set. In Amelio's film, which won the Grand Prix at the 1992 Cannes Film Festival, well-known Sicilian actor Enrico Lo Verso starred alongside two Sicilian children, Valentina Scalici and Giuseppe Ieracitano. The film is set against a backdrop of child abuse and forced prostitution, and therefore both films situate their protagonists in a familiar working-class context, as we saw in the last chapter, marked by marginality and exploitation. Risi's film, in particular, uses the mechanism of what Morreale (2020) terms the 'amalgama coloniale' or 'colonial amalgam', 'con attori professionisti "nazionali" calati in un contesto di non professionisti o di professionisti locali'/'with nationally recognized professional actors plunged into a context of local non-professionals or professionals'. Michele Placido was already well known for his role in the TV series *La piovra/The Octopus*, and the film operates an effective contrast between Placido's suave and polished persona and the rough edges of the reformatory kids (Figure 17).

Alessandra di Sanzo was one of the first trans actors to make a mark on Italian cinema; although she went on to appear in several films, including Risi's sequel to *Forever Mery*, *Ragazzi fuori/Boys on the Outside* (1990), in a recent interview (Rocca 2020) she was frank about the extent to which her career was both enabled and stifled by her iconic role as Mery, as well as by the notoriety she gained for her trans status, at a time when such a thing was regarded as extremely transgressive in Italy.[7] She calls her

---

[6]Zagarrio (2012) gives as an example of what he calls 'New-New Italian Cinema' or *neo-neorealismo* the little-seen films by Luigi Faccini, *Notte di stelle/Starry Night* (1991) and *Giamaica/Jamaica* (1998), both of which star boys from the peripheral areas of Rome.
[7]Colombian trans actress Juana Jimenez has made a career in Italian cinema ever since her casting by Ponzi in *Besame mucho* in 1998. See De Marco (2018).

FIGURE 17 *Alessandra di Sanzo (Mery) and Michele Placido (Marco) face off in* Forever Mery.

notoriety a 'gabbia'/'cage' and even argues that it 'castrated' her, due to her excessive recognizability for that one role. Di Sanzo's erratic career in TV, film, and theatre, punctuated by periods of return to different types of non-performing work, seems to point to this difficulty of carving out a space that is not simply replicating her own presumed marginality as a gender non-conforming person: 'Sono stata etichettata sempre nei soliti ruoli'/'I was always boxed into the same roles' (in Errico 2011). Her trajectory speaks to the question that Saidiya Hartman (2019: 261) has posed, in the very different context of lost histories of African American girls and women in early-twentieth-century US cities: 'was her fate to remain trapped within the impoverished realm of realism, or worse, confined in the sociological imagination that could only ever recognise her as a problem?'

Yet as we have seen in previous chapters, Di Sanzo's case is merely a very particular instantiation of the dilemma of the non-professional. Watson (1999: 139) argues that 'the use of actual former reformatory inmates in *Forever Mery* in particular, follows Zavattini's preference for the authentic iconicity of non-actors in given roles'. Like Di Sanzo, the boys who were cast, mainly from the streets of Palermo, to play the other 'delinquents' can be read, I argue, not as tragic 'where are they now?' case studies, but as examples of a desire to break free from the Zavattinian prescription that the non-actor is only capable of representing themselves. Evidence of this is the career of Francesco Benigno: his casting by Risi to play hardened young criminal Natale in *Mery* followed the traditional route of a fortuitous encounter between director and non-professional (Benigno attended the audition solely to accompany his friend), and his subsequent career in film and television, often playing similar roles to the one that brought him fame, might be read as the usual evidence of an inability to break away from the template in which the casting had secured him. However, we can read in Benigno's career a narrative of the pains and triumphs that the negotiation of non-professional fame brings.

Benigno himself has discussed his challenging journey to establish himself in the film industry, culminating in his directorial debut with *Il colore della vita/The Colour of Pain* (2020). The award-winning low-budget film, part-financed by the Sicilian Film Commission, is based on Benigno's autobiography, and recounts his difficult childhood before his casting in Risi's film. Casting Palermitan Alessandro Alicata as his young self, Benigno operates a kind of *mise-en-abyme* which speaks to and instrumentalizes the blurred boundaries between himself and his roles. While he himself uses the language of conversion and redemption to speak of how Risi saved him from a life of crime, and offered him a 'new life' (Anon. 2019), it is his own labour in a multitude of projects, including music and reality television appearances, that has allowed him a public profile, not just the miraculous rescue of him by Risi. Benigno is working as a director very much in the neo-neorealist style of his mentor but his trajectory is also a lesson in the precarity of the film industry, even for those with a professional formation. In that sense he is far from exceptional.

While Benigno has attempted to make of his identification with Risi's film a selling point in order to construct a lasting career as actor and director, others have been allowed less agency. While some of the boys appeared in the downbeat drama *Vite perdute/Lost Souls* (Greco, 1992) and a number of them (Maurizio Prollo, Stefano Termini, and Alfredo Li Bassi) went on to forge acting careers, it is notable that they have been reunited for appearances in music videos such as the video for the song 'Pensa' by Fabrizio Moro (2007), directed by Marco Risi. The video, with its anti-mafia message, is shot in what appears to be an ex-prison, and the carceral motif, while obviously addressing Risi's canonical film, also speaks, I feel, to the potentially imprisoning effect of non-professional microcelebrity.

Another music video shot by Risi in 1990 for the song by Pierangelo Bertoli, 'Chiama piano', featuring 'i ragazzi di Mery per sempre'/'the kids from Mery per sempre', also, perhaps unwittingly, reproduces this indivisibility of the actor and role as the members of the cast wander disconsolately around the urban landscape of Milan. This musical paratext, like Moro's later one, cements the cast as 'from the streets' and the rejection of glamour is on a par with the downbeat aesthetics of cinematic neo-neorealism. The video also features the final appearance on screen of young Roberto Mariano, who played Antonio in *Mery per sempre* and *Ragazzi fuori*. Not long after filming it, Mariano was killed in a plane crash, aged twenty-one, while emigrating to Switzerland to look for work. Newspaper discussions of Mariano's death emphasized the tragedy of someone who had turned their life around after juvenile prison being killed so young. His uncle is quoted as saying (in Rosso 1990): 'Cercava di inserirsi, in modo stabile nel mondo dello spettacolo. Non voleva essere uno di quegli attori usa e getta, che recitano una o due volte in qualche film di successo e poi scompaiono dalla scena. Ora, purtroppo, tutto è finito'/'He was trying to find a solid position in the film industry. He didn't want to be one of those disposable actors, who appears in one or two successful films and then disappears. Now, sadly, everything is over.' Yet the narrative of the tragic non-professional ultimately dominates: in a 1991 article (Anon. 1991) Mariano is listed as the fifth actor from Risi's 'cursed' film to die, his death a mere footnote confirming the determinism associated with this type of protagonist, fated to meet a doomed end, or to return to a life of crime.

According to Morreale (2020), the same casting agency was responsible for finding protagonists for both *Forever Mery* and Amelio's *The Stolen Children*. The Palermo-based agency run by Enzo Castagna has supplied local actors and extras for many years: 'La figura di Castagna è indicativa di una fase pre-industriale del casting locale, in cui la conoscenza del territorio costituisce il principale capitale cui le produzioni nazionali devono fare riferimento'/'The figure of Castagna is indicative of a pre-industrial phase of local casting, in which knowledge of the region constitutes the principal asset that national productions have to acknowledge.'[8] The two children selected through the Castagna agency for the co-lead roles in *Il ladro di bambini* were eleven-year-old Valentina Scalici and nine-year-old Giuseppe Ieracitano. Both children were cast, apparently, 'because they looked like "authentic" southerners' (Papalia 2010: 103), thus contributing to the discursive reification of a north-south divide, also seen in previous chapters. We have seen how the process of casting based on specific regional physiognomic characteristics is reminiscent of a certain Lombrosian essentialism, in which physical traits, especially facial ones, are indexical markers of southernness, itself since Italian unification associated with criminality and backwardness (see Gibson 1998). As with many other of the films we have encountered, critical discussion of the film rarely mentions the actors, beyond a cursory note that the children are non-professionals. While Giuseppe Ieracitano made several further films, Valentina Scalici disappeared, despite winning, with her on-screen brother, a David di Donatello special prize for acting. Scalici is one of the many figures in this book about whom there simply does not appear to exist any information in circulation.

The film formed part of a wave of films in the 1990s and 2000s addressing endangered or damaged children, generally identified with a (neo)neorealist

---

[8]See the documentary about Castagana directed by Ciprì and Maresco, *Enzo, domani a Palermo!/Enzo, Tomorrow in Palermo!* (1996).

filmmaking tradition (see Sutton 2005; Pitt 2012). This use of the endangered child can be seen particularly in the *filone* of films about Neapolitan street kids, films in which, as Marlow-Mann (2011: 94) notes, the child progresses from *scugnizzo* to *muschillo* (from street child to mafia gang member). Examples by director Antonio Capuano such as *Vito e gli altri/Vito and the Others* (1991), *Pianese Nunzio, 14 anni a maggio/Sacred Silence* (1996), *La guerra di Mario/Mario's War* (2005), and Salvatore Piscitelli's *Baby Gang* (1992) recapitulate some of the themes of the post-war films analysed in the previous chapter in a strikingly realist key. However, like Amelio's film, they place a greater emphasis on personal trauma such as child sexual abuse or exploitation. This is significant in terms of the young non-professional protagonists being asked to participate in difficult dramatic material. Pitt (2012: 155) points out that in the scene in *The Stolen Children* in which we see young Rosetta, played by Scalici, being forced by her mother to entertain a male client, 'meticulous camera work ensures ... that what we "see" as spectators, is not what her abuser "sees", that the child's image is not focalized by him'. He goes on to note how 'the careful positioning of the camera corresponds to the filmmaker's determined aim to desensationalise Rosetta's abuse and avoid her commodification as its victim', but it is also true that the scene is staged so that the only signal of the abuse about to take place is the shot of Rosetta's hand on the bed being caressed by the man's large hand. This 'desensationalizing' is thus also perhaps an attempt to protect the untrained child performer who is not placed in the position of acting out something they do not even understand.

As Pitt asks (ibid.): 'How does a director balance the competing aims of protecting the integrity of his child actor whilst ensuring the dramatic impact of these scenes for his audience?' While Amelio may have resolved that question here, the ethical implications of using underage non-professionals for delicate scenes are clear. Many of the films involving children, especially those by Capuano, involve children witnessing abuse or abusing others. For example, in *Pianese Nunzio*, young non-professional actor Emanuele Gargiulo has to narrate to police a (false) accusation of sexual abuse, complete with details. In *Vito e gli altri*, the child protagonist is a victim of sexual abuse and there is a scene where he also has to simulate sex, before the film's climax where he carries out a murder.[9] This staging of child criminality is replicated in other films such as *Certi bambini*, but also continues in more recent critically acclaimed films such as *Gomorra/Gomorrah* (Garrone, 2008), *La paranza dei bambini/Piranhas* (Giovannesi, 2010), and *A*

---

[9]Though see Marlow-Mann (2014: 279) on how the young actors collaborated on the situations and dialogue. Young Nando Triola, who played the eponymous Vito, and also appeared in *Pianese Nunzio*, ended up in prison several times after the films, a fact treated by local press with depressing resignation, although he did reappear in 2003 in Francesco Patierno's film *Pater familias*, (yet) another gritty tale of urban degradation in Naples.

Ciambra/The Ciambra (Carpignano, 2016) among many others. As Lury (2010: 182) notes, audiences' obsession with child suffering on screen inevitably brings to the fore 'the element of exploitation inherent to (screen) performance itself'. Indeed, in cases such as *A Ciambra*, set in the run-down Ciambra area of Gioia Tauro in Calabria, in which a young Romani boy, Pio Amato, plays a version of himself and the audience watches him stealing and visiting prostitutes, to what extent are we being invited to fetishize the boy's own difficult experiences, or to voyeuristically observe the 'public ritual re-enactment of their personal distress?' (Upton 2011: 216).[10]

It has been impossible to find information for these films pertaining to how the director or production team worked to safeguard their child non-actors or the extent to which they considered the ethical implications of their employment of the child.[11] However, in recent years the figure of the on-set acting coach working with child performers and non-professionals has become more common in Italy.[12] As we have seen in previous chapters, the potential trauma for the non-professional is rarely considered in their encounter with the cinema industry, even though there are multiple high-profile examples of the need for careful handling of the child both on set and off. Beyond Italian cinema, a film such as *Slumdog Millionaire* (Boyle, 2008) notably raised controversy because of the negative attention it brought to its child actors, recruited from the slums of Mumbai. Despite director Danny Boyle's efforts to protect the interests of his young charges Rubina Ali and Azharuddin Mohammed Ismail by setting up trust funds for them, and paying for their schooling (Khan 2009), stories continue to circulate regarding financial difficulties for the now-adult stars, family disputes, and drug addiction (Malavade and Mishra 2020).

On the subject of sexual exploitation of child non-actors, the case of Dominique Swain, who was selected at the age of fifteen to play the titular role in Adrian Lyne's 1995 adaptation of Nabokov's controversial *Lolita*, and the difficulties she encountered in the promotion of the movie, is just one example.[13] These salutary tales, which predate what we might perhaps hope is a more enlightened, post-#MeToo attitude towards workers in the film industry, are not restricted to girls and women. The recent documentary *The Most Beautiful Boy in the World* (Lindström and Petri, 2021) charts the trajectory of Björn Andrésen, cast, also at fifteen, to play Tadzio in Luchino Visconti's *Morte a Venezia/Death in Venice* (1972). Labelling Visconti

---

[10] It is notable that Italian cinema has only just begun using intimacy coordinators: see Brocardo (2020).
[11] An example of this lacuna is Labate's *Domenica* (2001) with the eponymous heroine played by young Neapolitan girl Domenica Giuliano, on a quest to track down her rapist. I have not been able to find any information about how Giuliano was guided through the filming.
[12] See Pierini (2015) and Morreale (2021).
[13] See https://actedby.com/dominique-swain-remembers-lolita/

ambiguously as a 'cultural predator', and stating that the role and the sexual attention he received 'screwed up my life', Andrésen's case is a reminder that both inside and outside the genre of realism, the problematics of a child non-professional's navigation of the film industry persist, and may only come to light years later, if they are given a chance to tell their story.

Contemporary Italian cinema and television

As noted, there are multiple examples in contemporary Italian cinema of the deployment of the marginalized non-professional within the mode of realism. There is little point in listing all of these, as the risk of saturation is obvious.[14] However, I would like to focus briefly on one exceptional use of the marginalized child protagonist, in Agostino Ferrente's 2019 documentary *Selfie*, before moving on to explore the ways in which Italian cinema and television might now offer a somewhat different take on race and ethnicity in the casting and use of the non-professional.

As I noted above, the figure of the *scugnizzo*, or *muschillo*, is familiar in contemporary films such as the critically acclaimed *La paranza dei bambini/Piranhas*, winner of the Silver Bear for Best Screenplay at the Berlin Film Festival in 2019. The story of teenage boys inexorably drawn into the Camorra's web of criminality in Naples, it attracted many comparisons to *Gomorra*, written by the same writer, Roberto Saviano. However, at Berlin at the same time another Italian film was presented with less fanfare: Agostino Ferrente's *Selfie*, shot by two sixteen-year-old Neapolitan boys on iPhones given to them by the director. The film, shot in July 2017, charts how the boys, Alessandro Antonelli and Pietro Orlando, navigate the neighbourhood they live in, the tough Rione Traiano, trying to stay out of trouble, find work, and avoid the lure of organized crime.

What is striking about the film is both its resistance to the clichés of the Neapolitan drama of criminality, as both boys adhere to a desire for legitimate work (Alessandro is a barista, Pietro dreams of being a barber), and also its attempt to give agency and voice to these non-professional protagonists. Ferrente, in fact, talks of how he wanted to use this documentary to 'dare la parola'/'give voice' to the kids who are normally viewed from a sociological perspective.[15] The stylistic choice by which the entire film hangs, Alessandro and Pietro narrating their own lives by recording themselves selfie-style in

---

[14]A few examples should suffice: *Saimir* (Munzi, 2004), *Cesare deve morire/Caesar Must Die* (Tavianis, 2012), *Alì ha gli occhi azzurri/Alì Blue Eyes* (Giovannesi, 2012), *Fiore* (Giovannesi, 2016).
[15]Open Roads (2019).

the place they live, thus has deep resonance. In addition to guaranteeing them near-invisibility when they shoot, which would not be possible with a video camera, it also asks questions about the performing self in our contemporary digital world, as well as, in my view, inviting reflection on the representational possibilities available to the marginalized non-professional actor in contemporary cinematic realism.[16]

Hearing from the two young protagonists, in their own words, is vital and allows the viewer access to their subjectivity. The metacinematic structure of the film – we see auditions by other would-be protagonists, squabbles between the boys over how to narrate and frame the film, and discussions about an appropriate soundtrack – also ensures a feeling of privileged insight into a milieu that is normally narrated in more conventional neorealist style with all the potentially voyeuristic pitfalls I have noted.[17] The boys assert their agency both as 'attori sociali'/'social actors' (Ravesi 2019: 128) and as creatives, when they confidently declare themselves directors, or when Pietro insists on playing a piece of classical music rather than the Neapolitan neomelodic music which he laments is generally associated with their milieu. Ferrente, however, is reluctant to give up his own agency and in interviews has repeated that not only was he the director but that for each take he and the crew were present but unseen.[18] He also, tellingly, describes how the kids in the neighbourhood regarded the crew as their last chance for help, and as 'liberatori'/'liberators' (Open Roads). This tension between agency, as the boys film quite assuredly with familiar technology, and the infrastructure, funding and prestige of Ferrente and his backers that can garner an international audience far beyond what they could ever aspire to through their own Instagram posts, points up important contemporary questions regarding performance and digital media.

---

[16]In Ferrente's earlier documentary (1999), made with Giovanni Piperno, *Intervista a mia madre/Interview With My Mother*, the four young Neapolitan protagonists sometimes film their own families as well as being interviewed. The follow-up, *Le cose belle/Beautiful Things* (2013), tracks the same people years later, and showcases the 'intimate collaboration' (Centorrino 2018: 226) between directors and subjects that we see expanded in *Selfie*.

[17]In fact, Ferrente emphasized how he wanted to avoid the danger of 'spettacolizzare la miseria'/'turning poverty into a spectacle' (Open Roads 2019) and notes how filmmakers often produce an 'effetto safari'/'safari effect' in working with this kind of material: 'vado, vedo, filmo personaggi grotteschi e torno a casa mia'/'I come, I see, I film grotesque characters and I leave' (Finos 2019).

[18]'Non avevo intenzione di subappaltare, anche solo in parte, la regia del film, non cercavo un documentario "partecipato": ho solo chiesto ai miei protagonisti di essere al tempo stesso anche cameraman, col compito di auto-inquadrarsi, da me guidati, guardandosi sempre nel display del cellulare come se fosse uno specchio'/'I had no intention of sub-contracting the direction of the film, even partially; I wasn't looking to make a collaborative documentary: I merely asked my protagonists to be also be cameramen, with the job of framing themselves, guided by me, and looking at themselves in the phone screen as if it were a mirror' (in Tantillo and Carlino 2019: 121).

The boys' self-filming in 'selfie mode' highlights the ways in which social media platforms such as Instagram have institutionalized the idea of a constantly performing self. The 'techno-social performativity' (Leeker et al. 2017: 10) produced by the imbrication of self and technology means that we are now performing subjects in all our everyday experiences. The registers of self-conscious behaviour that the boys traverse in the film – as, for example, when they argue over its narrative direction – expose the illusion of the natural or authentic self in a digital age. As Leeker (2017: 33) argues, 'the production of self within digital cultures now relies on a self-illusion, which obscures its technological operations, while at the same time binding the human to them'.[19]

This 'regime of digital performativity' (Leeker et al. 2017: 11) that we inhabit, which aims at the effortful production of a naturalistic self, mirrors a new attention to the idea of performance within documentary film. As Marquis (2013: 45) notes, 'in discussions of non-fiction film-making, the issue of performance has often been given short shrift', meaning that rather naïve ideas of documentary protagonists as subjects directly captured by the camera have tended to prevail. Performance itself constitutes the dividing line between fiction and non-fiction, according to Bruzzi (2000: 153): 'performance has been treated with suspicion because it carries connotations of falsification and fictionalisation, traits that traditionally destabilise the non-fiction pursuit'. The 'presentational' mode of performance in non-fiction noted by Marquis is encouraged by a film such as *Selfie*, with its acknowledgement of the camera, its direct address, and incorporation of modes such as rapping; even the snippets of the auditions we hear such as when two young girls shockingly narrate how they are prepared to marry *camorristi* and spend years being faithful to their imprisoned husbands could be considered through this lens of performance.[20] To what extent do the girls say this because they think it is what is expected in order for them to appear in a film about their neighbourhood? Meanwhile Alessandro and Pietro take aim at the visual and narrative clichés surrounding representations of Naples (Busetta 2022: 11).

Ultimately, Alessandro and Pietro's close friendship seems to have been threatened by the film: Pietro announces at the end that he is taking time away in order to reflect upon the different directions they want for the film. Both boys are still in Naples: according to their Instagrams, Alessandro is still a barista, while Pietro seems to have achieved his desired goal of working

---

[19]The inclusion of CCTV footage in the film, both that relating to the murder in 2014 of the boys' friend Davide Bifolco and snippets of contemporary footage, offers a different register of complete unself-consciousness against which to read the selfie-style commentaries.
[20]Marquis is drawing on Waugh's binary of 'presentational' and 'representational' performance modes, where the first addresses the camera, and the second fosters a naturalism by refusing to acknowledge it (Marquis 2013: 51).

as a barber.[21] While Ferrente said that the Berlin Film Festival offered to pay for both boys to take a directing course (Finos 2019), I haven't been able to ascertain whether this actually happened. While I will say more in the next section about the importance of the non-professional in the economy of the film festival, it is telling that in the videos online from festivals and screenings, it is always Ferrente who is talking about the film and the boys. They are absent from press conferences and the discussions of the film, even though they are its co-creators. This absence illustrates powerfully the gatekeeping role of film press and festivals in eliding the non-professional, even as their labour is celebrated in the very touching end product. The main record of the boys' promotion of the film is, fittingly, Alessandro's Instagram account, on which could still, until recently, be found his excited visual account of their trip to Berlin.

Beyond marginality and realism?

While new technologies and platforms have enabled a shift in modes of representation, as we have seen with *Selfie*, the mode of realism is far from exhausted in contemporary Italian cinema. Non-professionals are still routinely cast in productions as part, for example, of a general commitment to the unflinching representation of migration. As De Franceschi (2013: 192) has argued, the tendency since the 1990s to cast untrained performers in these films of social denunciation has produced 'una recitazione immedesimata o mimetica'/'a style of acting that is mimetic or based on the identification between actor and role'. He notes (ibid.: 194) that migrant non-actors have generally been cast alongside professional Italian actors, in a kind of one-way amalgam where the non-professional is nearly always the non-Italian or non-white person. This deprofessionalization of the non-white or non-Italian actor in Italy raises many questions:

> Per quale motivo, verrebbe da chiedersi, tanti registi e produttori italiani, quando si tratta di attribuire il ruolo di un personaggio di migrante (o non-italiano), anche da protagonista, fanno ricorso spesso a non professionisti? Forse perché costano meno? Perché, trattandosi in larga parte di tipi sociali, tutto sommato possono essere alla portata anche di attori presi dalla strada? (ibid.: 195)[22]

---

[21]See https://www.instagram.com/pietro__orlando__/?hl=en and https://www.instagram.com/_ale_17.9_/
[22]'One might wonder why so many Italian producers and directors, when it comes to casting a migrant or non-Italian role, even a leading one, often use non-professionals? Perhaps because they are cheaper? Or because, being just social types, the roles are within the abilities even of untrained actors?'

De Franceschi notes that these acting experiences have nearly always been one-offs, with performances such as those by Thywill Amenya in *Pummarò* (Placido, 1990), Kalubi Kabongo in *Dall'altra parte del mondo/From the Other Side of the World* (Catinari, 1993), Mounir Ouadi in *Riparo/Shelter* (Puccioni, 2007), and Said Sabrie in *Good Morning Aman* (Claudio Noce, 2009) lacking a follow-up. More recently, the lack of training and support for Black Italian actors was noted in the documentary *Blaxploitalian: 100 Years of Blackness in Italian Cinema* (Kuwornu, 2016). Expedients that producers and directors have had recourse to instead of casting non-white professional Italian actors include casting non-Italian actors of colour, such as Thandiwe Newton in Bertolucci's 1998 *L'assedio/Besieged*, or asking Italians to play non-Italian migrants: for example, Sicilian actor Giovanni Martorana played both a Tunisian migrant in *Io l'altro/I, the Other* (Melliti, 2006) and a Maghrebi character in Marco Tullio Giordana's 2003 *La meglio gioventù/The Best of Youth* (see De Franceschi 2013: 197).

More recent acclaimed films such as the diptych by Jonas Carpignano formed by *Mediterranea* (2015) and *A Ciambra/The Ciambra* (2017) also cast non-professionals: Burkinabé migrant to Italy Koudous Seihon and Calabrian Romani child Pio Amato star in both films, thus allowing some sort of performance development. Seihon, in fact, won Best Actor prizes at several film festivals for *Mediterranea*. While critics praised the neorealist qualities of *A Ciambra* in particular, comparing the casting of Pio to Staiola in *Bicycle Thieves* (see O'Rawe 2018), Carpignano's close collaboration with his actors and the fact that he is deeply embedded in their community in Calabria also suggest a more progressive dimension to casting.[23] Questions remain, nonetheless, about the potential for trauma in asking Seihon to relive his experiences as a migrant crossing the Mediterranean to Italy. While 'Carpignano has talked about the trauma the actors experienced reenacting the scenes of the crossing' (Duncan 2020: 199, n. 6), a documentary film such as Antonio Tibaldi's *[S]comparse/[Dis]appeared* (2011) explicitly critiques this process of traumatic re-enactment, making visible the emotional and physical labour of the African migrant extras.[24]

While the recourse to neorealist techniques and the critical prestige of neorealism as a legitimating trope continue, it is important to examine alternative modes of representation, which are perhaps reinvigorating the use of the non-white non-professional in Italian film and television. Recognizing neorealism as a genre or mode like any other (see O'Rawe 2008), rather than as the only way of representing social reality, allows us to evaluate its representational strategies alongside those of other genres involving

---

[23]Both Seihon and Amato also appear briefly in Carpignano's latest film *A Chiara*, which had its premiere at Cannes in July 2021.
[24]See O'Healy (2014). *[S]comparse* documents the filming of Emanuele Crialese's fiction film *Terraferma* (2011) on the island of Linosa.

non-professional actors. One of the most interesting genres to study is the romantic comedy: its mainstream appeal and address to a broader audience can work intriguingly with the unknown and inexperienced protagonist. It will suffice to examine briefly two instances here: *Io Rom romantica/I, a Romani Romantic* (Halilovic, 2014) and *Bangla* (Bhuiyan, 2019).

Io Rom romantica was directed by Bosnian-Italian Romani director Laura Halilovic and was funded by the Torino and Lazio Film Commissions as well as the Italian Ministry for Culture (Ministero dei beni e delle attività culturali, or MiBAC). The typical 'MiBAC film' is socially committed and politically engaged (see Manzoli and Minuz 2017), and Halilovic's tale of a Romani girl from the outskirts of Turin, which cast many of its actors from a local Roma camp (see Cotticelli 2014), fit the bill by addressing traditional restrictive gender roles and anti-Roma prejudice. However, despite the predominance of non-professionals aligning the film with the 'discorso antidivistico'/'anti-star discourse' of the MiBAC film (Minuz 2017: 43) the use of genre conventions consistent with the rom-com allows the film to evade the representational clichés of the realist gaze on the Roma.[25] As Hope (2016) notes, filmic takes on the Roma in this mode are often interlaced with tropes of criminality; Halilovic's film explicitly takes this on, by having the protagonist Gioia, played by teenager Claudia Ruza Djordjevic, humorously express her boredom at the idea of being filmed for a documentary on the Roma by a well-meaning director, and demanding to make a romantic comedy in the vein of Woody Allen's *Manhattan*.

While the film did not achieve mainstream success, it points towards possible avenues for the use of the non-professional actor in more diverse genres outside of the dreary universe of sociological investigation. It also slyly calls out the realist or documentary style of engaging with marginalized groups: Gioia overhears her director acquaintance saying he wants to include interviews with the Roma in her proposed feature because 'con i rom quanto ci può costare?'/'how much can the Roma cost?' What might happen therefore if more non-actors from underrepresented groups were cast in star-driven genres such as romantic comedy?

Bangla takes a somewhat similar route, deploying rom-com tropes in its account of its Italian-Bangladeshi protagonist and his relationship with a white Italian girl. The film, shot on location in the director/star Phaim Bhuiyan's native Tor Pignattara area of Rome, is a comic look at second-generation Italians, and Bhuiyan availed himself of street casting from his community in order to generate authenticity (see Gamberini 2020). A key difference between his film and that of Halilovic is its greater success, both

---

[25]The film does deploy a well-known actor in an interesting example of the 'amalgam': Marco Bocci, who achieved stardom through his role in the television series *Romanzo criminale* (2008–10), plays Gioia's love interest.

commercially and critically, as it gained several Italian film industry awards. One reason for this, beyond better distribution, may be due to Bhuiyan's director/actor persona: although this was his first real acting role, he is aligned by one critic (Ulivi 2019) with star director Nanni Moretti's early comic acting roles, in which he played a thinly veiled version of himself (Woody Allen might also spring to mind here, interestingly). This kind of autobiographical persona that produces the effect of a deliberately amateur or unpolished performance style (and is more associated with male actor-directors) has an undeniable critical cachet.[26]

Significantly, Bhuiyan came to prominence before *Bangla* via his internet videos, indicating one of the important new reservoirs of talent for the film and television industry. Young Italian YouTube stars such as Riccardo Dose and 'Favij' (Lorenzo Ostuni) have been cast in movies, presumably partly in the hope that their millions of viewers will accompany them to the big screen. Italian television in particular is thus drawing upon new pools of talent in order to provide new and diverse faces for its fiction programming. In this context, two recent Italian series have received extensive attention for their more diverse casting: *Summertime* (2020–22) which has had two seasons to date, was screened on Netflix internationally, as was the first season of superhero series *Zero* in 2021.[27] The star of *Summertime*, Coco Rebecca Edogamhe, is a Black Italian teenager with no acting experience who was cast via an open casting call alongside her younger sister Alicia, who plays her sister in the series. *Zero*, meanwhile, is the first Italian series to feature an almost entirely Black main cast and for this has been hailed as revolutionary (see e.g. Vivarelli 2021). The main protagonist, Omar or 'Zero', is played by Giuseppe Dave Seke, who was working in a warehouse in Padua when he saw the casting call (Anon. 2021). Two of the other young cast members were also non-actors: Dylan Magon was a rapper, and Madior Fall a model.

While much more attention needs to be paid to the politics of casting in Italy and its mechanisms, it is striking that *Summertime* seems to have been 'blindcast', in that Edogamhe insists (in Bellamy 2020) that the producers were not looking for a Black girl as lead.[28] Coupled with the all-white writing team for the series, it seems that here the non-professional may just be inserted as part of a 'visual landscape of difference' (Warner 2021), especially as Summer's racial identity is not really explored in the series. *Zero*, meanwhile, based on a novel by Black Italian writer Antonio Dikele Distefano, harnesses its young cast in order to tell a very specific story, about

---

[26]Bhuiyan developed the film into a TV series, produced by Rai Fiction and Fandango in 2022, and later shown on Netflix Italia.
[27]*Summertime* was produced by well-known production company Cattleya, while *Zero* was produced for Netflix by Fabula Pictures and Red Joint.
[28]See Renga (2020) on casting in Italian quality television.

Black identity in contemporary urban Italy. While both series use different modes – *Summertime* the romance, *Zero* the superhero genre – the contrast between them can usefully illustrate Warner's point (2017: 35) that racially diverse bodies on screen can function as mere 'visual identifiers for specific demographics' rather than as fully three-dimensional and culturally rooted characters.[29]

As we have seen throughout this chapter, the non-professional is crucial to the debates over agency, institutional gatekeeping, and the problems of representing a 'complex personhood' (Wanzo 2006: 136) when it comes to marginalized subjects. Concurrently, as the documentary *Blaxploitalian* has made clear, the severely limited opportunities for Italian actors of colour to receive professional training and to be hired in anything other than stereotypical roles must be urgently addressed. The frequent use of the non-professional as a visual shorthand of difference needs to be reconsidered in the light of any aspiration towards a more freighted complexity of representation. This is strikingly evident when we turn our gaze beyond the confines of Italian cinema.

The non-professional in contemporary global arthouse cinema

In 2016 and 2017 the Italian films nominated for consideration for the Academy Award for Best Foreign Language Film were, respectively, Gianfranco Rosi's *Fuocoammare/Fire at Sea*, and Carpignano's *A Ciambra*. Despite the fact that neither film was eventually selected as an official nominee by the Academy, their international trajectories are revealing about the mechanisms through which Italian films without well-known directors acquire legitimacy, and the role played by neorealism in this process. Both *Fuocoammare* and *A Ciambra* were embedded in the festival circuit: *Fuocoammare* won the Golden Bear at the Berlin Film Festival in 2016; *A Ciambra* was presented out of competition at Cannes in 2017, in the Quinzaine des Réalisateurs. There it was sold in a deal negotiated by the super-agency William Morris Endeavour, with US rights being picked up by IFC Sundance Selects, no doubt aided by having Martin Scorsese as one of its executive producers.[30] The films' positive reception was due largely to the connections between festival promotion, with film festivals operating

---

[29]Dikele Distefano subsequently wrote and directed the film *Autumn Beat* (2022), starring first-time actor Hamed Seydou and rapper Abby 6ix. The film, billed as the first with an entirely Black Italian cast, was made for Prime Video, suggesting the importance of streamers in supporting more diverse casting in Italy.
[30]See Obensen 2017.

as an enduring 'site of cultural legitimation' (de Valck 2016), and a critical reception that linked them to the prestige of Italian neorealism.[31] The recourse to neorealism by critical reviews, and a focus on the figure of the non-professional boy actor is hardly surprising, given the movement's totemic values outside Italy, and the failure of most of Italy's popular cinema to circulate internationally. The discussion of the non-professional as an aspect of neorealism functions, of course, as a legitimating trope: *The New York Times* wrote that *A Ciambra* 'provides fresh evidence of the continued vitality of the neorealist impulse. … The actors are nonprofessionals playing versions of themselves', and compared it to the work of the Dardenne brothers and Bresson (Scott 2018). Other comparisons recur to De Sica and Visconti (see Bradshaw 2018). *The Guardian*'s review of *Fuocoammare*, reproduced in much of the film's promotional material, declares that 'I'm tempted to say Samuele is a descendant of Enzo Staiola as young Bruno in De Sica's *Bicycle Thieves*' (Bradshaw 2016). Both Pio and Samuele are thus read as avatars of the boy non-professional of neorealism, and of Italian film heritage itself.

This discussion can profitably be extended to encompass some of the other Italian films to get international distribution via appearances at high-profile festivals: Alice Rohrwacher's *Lazzaro felice/Happy as Lazzaro* (which won the Best Screenplay prize at Cannes in 2018) centres on a non-professional actor, Adriano Tardiolo). Her earlier film, *Le meraviglie/The Wonders*, won the jury Grand Prix at Cannes in 2014, while *Corpo celeste/Heavenly Body* was presented there in 2011. Both films featured girl non-professionals alongside professional actors. Meanwhile, the last Italian film to win the Grand Prix before Rohrwacher's was Matteo Garrone's *Reality* in 2012, also featuring a non-professional actor, Aniello Arena.

Looking a little more in-depth, we can count other Italian films featuring non-professional actors that have succeeded in the 'intangible mechanisms of the "prestige economy"' (Cucco 2018) such as *Gomorra/Gomorrah* (Garrone, 2008) (Grand Prix winner in 2008); *Fiore* (Giovannesi, 2016) – nominated for the Queer Palm at Cannes; Rotterdam International Film Festival winner *Bellas mariposas/Pretty Butterflies* (Mereu, 2012), Karlovy Vary Grand Prix winner in 2004, *Certi bambini/A Children's Story* (Frazzi brothers), and Berlin Golden Bear winner *Cesare deve morire/Caesar Must Die* (Taviani brothers, 2012).[32] At the 2019 Berlinale, several Italian

---

[31] As Johnson (2019: 49) notes, 'from neorealism to auteur cinema, Italian film appears to be a key example of a national cinema that depends upon film festivals for its international prestige and circulation and, moreover, one that instantiates and provides the origins for many of the tropes through which European A festivals construct art cinema more generally'.

[32] Two of these films, *Fiore* and *Caesar Must Die*, are set in prisons, a familiar setting for dramas of marginalization. The latter film, along with *Tutta colpa di Giuda/Freedom* (Ferrario, 2009), features real inmates putting on performances, and both films explicitly dramatize the performative aspect present within the observational documentary mode. I am grateful to Ellen

films were singled out by the press, including *Selfie*, Federico Bondi's *Dafne/Daphne*, starring Carolina Raspanti who has Down's syndrome, and *Piranhas* directed by Giovannesi, featuring a non-professional cast, again, from the streets of Naples, his adaptation of Roberto Saviano's book on junior *camorristi*.

These Italian examples are illustrative of the fact that one of the ways that arthouse films may acquire visibility internationally, and pick up distribution, is through the deployment of non-professional actors. As a marker of distinction and of symbolic and cultural capital, the non-professional can be interpreted as a sign of resistance against an economy of global stardom, and as such is often a welcome presence on the festival circuit. As Cindy H. Wong (2011: 85) argues: 'Nonprofessional actors tend to provide the festival films more legitimate claim to authenticity, to substantiate the claim that a serious filmmaker does not want the audience to be distracted by the glamour of the familiar faces of the actors.' If glamorous international stars (who dominate much of the coverage of festivals) 'overtly signal the presence of a culture of international commodity flow' (Harbord 2012: 70), the unfamiliar non-professional actor offers what seems to be a visible disruption to that.

The non-professional actor, who does not expect or desire global stardom, in many ways seems to offer what Anna Tsing (2004) suggests is a friction that disrupts the idea of global interconnectedness as a well-oiled machine, reintroducing the local and the particular (often in terms of voice, accent, language, or dialect). Many of the festival performances (and it is important to think of festival appearances and other 'para-cinematic events' – both interviews and red carpet posing – as performative) of these individuals would seem to support this. As Chaplin (2019: 540) argues, 'peripheral' events like photocalls often overshadow the prizes themselves at festivals such as Cannes.[33]

Edgar Morin, in his classic 1955 article on the sociology of Cannes, identified four types of pose or attitude adopted by stars in press photos at the festival: however, along with nearly all other critics, he does not consider how non-stars might fit into this publicity landscape. I argue that one of the key tropes visible in the presentation of non-professionals at festivals is 'out-of-placeness' where their sometimes awkward or unsure presence functions to 'aestheticize that which is commercial' (Morin 1955: 2279). An interesting recent Italian example of this can be found in the featurette included in the DVD release of *A Ciambra* (Ifc Independent Film, 2018). The short film is called 'Dalla Ciambra a Cannes'/'From the Ciambra to Cannes',

---

Nerenberg for this point. I would also point to an interesting film like *Grazie ragazzi/Thanks Boys* (Milani, 2023) that fictionalizes and reflects on this process of bringing incarcerated non-actors to acting.

[33] See also Schwartz (2007) on coverage of para-cinematic events at Cannes.

FIGURE 18 *Pio Amato, star of* A Ciambra, *looks uncomfortable on stage at the Cannes Film Festival, 2017.*

and presents a rags-to-riches story of the Romani boys who star in the film driving to Cannes in 2017 from their impoverished Calabrian community and getting dolled up for the red carpet. Pio Amato, the fourteen-year-old star of the film, is visibly overawed and seems uncomfortable with the attention (see Figure 18). We see how the festival is presented as a kind of tourism for its unknown protagonists, who are expected to be excited and grateful for the opportunity to be there. Similarly, images circulated globally of the young protagonist of *Fuocoammare*, Samuele Pucillo, on the red carpet at Berlin, and meeting Italian president Sergio Mattarella at the Quirinale while showing off the Golden Bear the film won. While Pucillo looks more at ease than Amato, he is incorporated into the spectacle of the festival, his tiny size and large grin alongside the head of the Italian state acting as an unexpected element in the festival iconography.

The non-professional, especially when associated with certain genres, is often the object of voyeuristic press discourse. This is the case of the press calls for Giovannesi's *Piranhas* at Berlin, as the following journalistic quotes demonstrate:

> The large ensemble cast of Claudio Giovannesi's *Piranhas* (*La Paranza dei Bambini*) sprawled into the audience at the press conference for the competition film. Many of the boys were street-casted in Naples and their tenacity of spirit sparkled in the room. (Harvey 2019)

> Quasi l'intero cast è arrivato a Berlino per presentare la pellicola in concorso, un esercito di giovanissimi attori ha invaso le zone del festival portando, non si può non ammetterlo, una ventata di aria fresca tra i vari

impegni lavorativi. Durante il photocall si sono presentati tutti sorridenti e, seppure un po' impacciati, hanno posato per le foto senza risparmiarsi. (Sciammana 2019)[34]

Here the boys are represented as a welcome breath of fresh air, who, by definition, do not belong in this environment. This voyeurism can also be accompanied by a certain shock value, as when *Reality* star Aniello Arena was unable to go to Cannes as he was in prison, which *Vanity Fair* excitedly described as 'a Cannes plot twist' (Miller 2012).[35]

This idea that the non-professional on the red carpet or at a festival press conference might be functioning as a kind of fetish or totem for a cinephile audience is heightened when we note that often the director will speak for them at press conferences: see, for example, the 2019 Cannes press conference for Mati Diop's *Atlantique/Atlantics*, where non-professional Senegalese actress Mama Sané had to be translated into French as she speaks only Wolof – and press coverage inevitably emphasized how she couldn't speak for herself, and was totally ignorant of cinema (see Sotinel 2019). This silencing of the non-professional is also present in the already-mentioned documentary about Björn Andrésen, *The Most Beautiful Boy in the World*, which documents the boy's appearance at Cannes in 1971 to promote *Death in Venice*: unable to speak French, he was spoken for by Visconti at the press conference, who made a nasty joke to journalists that the then-sixteen-year-old boy had aged, and was no longer the beauty he had been the year before. Andrésen sits there, looking uncomfortable, and in the documentary reveals that he was 'terrified' by the Cannes circus, which sealed his burgeoning global fame and what he felt to be his sexual exploitation.

Festivals are not always, of course, places of discomfort for non-professionals: the young female cast of the Turkish hit *Mustang* (Ergüven, 2015) appeared whooping and excited at Cannes in 2015 as they leapt into a sponsored Renault car and chatted in French, as well as dancing along to Pharrell's 'Happy'.[36] However, I argue that the apparently disruptive or incongruous presence of the non-professional in a space populated by practised cinephiles and glamorous stars can actually be thought of as strategic, if we consider Janet Harbord's view (2016: 78) that 'accidental occurrences secure the time of the festival as an unrepeatable event', and that the accidental or contingent is necessary: 'the festival is in need

---

[34]'Almost the entire cast has come to Berlin to present the film, an army of young actors has invaded the festival spaces, bringing a breath of fresh air to the normal work duties of the festival. They appeared at the photocall all smiles, and although a little awkward, they posed for photos uncomplainingly.'
[35]See O'Rawe (2020b) for a more detailed examination of the non-professional actor on the festival circuit.
[36]https://www.youtube.com/watch?v=SzqCPZOIreA

of disruption'. Thus these seemingly improvised or spontaneous public performances by non-professionals, including interviews where they may be unable to discourse learnedly about their film or role, can be considered part of the unquantifiable value of publicity, which, as Turner et al. (2006: 796) argue, 'always appears to be something else'.

Red carpet appearances are of course taken as the apogee of the trajectory of the non-professional's 'Cinderella story'. To return to Yalitza Aparicio, the public followed her Cinderella-style journey to the red carpet at Venice and other film festivals and award ceremonies, culminating in the Oscars. This fairy-tale comparison was reinforced by her stylist, who commented on Aparicio's 2019 Golden Globes dress: 'Cinderella on her way to the ball in Miu Miu'.[37] Aparicio's negotiation of her sudden fame has seen her lauded for her style (Ortiz 2018) and devoting much of her energy to activism on behalf of domestic workers in Mexico, like her character Cleo in Cuarón's film (Aparicio 2020; Báez 2021), even as she waited for a second film role. The ambivalence that traditionally subtends non-professional notoriety is enhanced both by Aparicio's race, and by her rare achievement in being nominated for an Academy Award for her first role, with no training. The acclaim she achieved was thus accompanied by antipathy from some quarters, as her nomination was viewed as a threat to 'legitimate' actors, and, typical of the non-professional, she was felt to be only playing herself.[38]

Acting nominations or awards for non-professionals thus bring into focus their peculiar status: there was much attention in the Italian film press to seventeen-year-old Swamy Rotolo, who won the David di Donatello Best Actress Award in 2022 for her eponymous role in Jonas Carpignano's 'Ndrangheta drama *A Chiara*.[39] As I noted in the Introduction, the shock felt at Cannes in 1999 when three amateurs were given acting awards both bolstered a divide between trained and untrained actors, and ultimately reinforced the status of the directors who were able to elicit a performance from an untutored individual. As Austin (2004: 253) comments: such awards 'challenge the star system but not the auteur system'. This power differential is reflected upon by Céline Sciamma: for her critically lauded film *Bande de filles/Girlhood* (2014), the lead girls were found at a funfair after director had been searching for faces and bodies for months. She freely admits that part of the reason for working with non-professionals was to do with power: 'working with non-professionals helped me figure

---

[37] https://www.instagram.com/p/BsUF8FZBtjA/
[38] See De la Mora (2019) on the racist verbal attacks on Aparicio by fellow Mexican actors.
[39] Rotolo's win makes her only the second non-professional ever to win a David di Donatello award in an acting category, the other being Ilenia Pastorelli who won in 2016 for *Lo chiamavano Jeeg Robot/They Call Me Jeeg* (Mainetti). Pastorelli was fresh from an appearance on Italian *Big Brother*, but had no acting experience. As noted, Valentina Scalici and Giuseppe Ieracitano were given a joint special prize at the 1992 ceremony.

out what kind of director I wanted to be, what my method would be, without destroying the hierarchy with actors. You know, the actors being more powerful than me or me more powerful than them' (in Phillips 2015). The film secured a prestigious César nomination in France for newcomer Karidja Touré, but the power dynamic between a white director and Black girls recruited from the streets of Paris perhaps bears more scrutiny, as Niang (2019: 233) observes: 'the recruitment of non-professional actresses, who are ultimately being asked to perform their everyday lives, raises the question of an essentialization of bodies that are confused with the milieu they come from'.[40]

In mainstream US cinema, Somali-American Barkhad Abdi, who shot to notoriety with his sensational performance opposite Tom Hanks in *Captain Phillips* (Greengrass, 2013), was nominated for Best Supporting Actor at the Oscars, losing to Jared Leto, and won the BAFTA award in the same category. He has continued to work in film and television, although the revelation (in Walker 2014) that he was paid the industry minimum ($65,000) for his scene-stealing role in the multi-million dollar-grossing movie points to the inevitable lack of power of someone like him in the industry. Indeed, Abdi's lasting popularity as an online gif (representing the moment where he utters the now-iconic line 'I'm the captain now') speaks to the persistent association between the non-professional and their star-making role, allowing them little potential for growth and change.

Non-professional 'success' obviously exists, whether that is calculated by acting awards, a longer career, or monetary security. However, such success can also act as an unforgiving discursive peak from which the non-professional star can only descend rapidly. As we saw in our examination of Italian post-war non-professionals, the 'where are they now?' narrative is a familiar one. The 'fall from grace' of the Cinderella figure is also a deep-rooted media trope: one example of how the Cinderella effect sours for girls who are brought to stardom via non-professional acting is Katie Jarvis: director Andrea Arnold cast seventeen-year-old Jarvis as the protagonist of *Fish Tank* in 2009 when she saw her arguing with her boyfriend at a train station, and knew she was right to play the bolshy lead in the film, an anecdote recycled in nearly every feature about the film. Jarvis went on to do a role in the soap opera *EastEnders* but found herself in the spotlight recently, firstly when she was seen working in a shop (P. Glynn 2019), then more seriously when she was convicted of a racist attack in 2022.

Jarvis's fall from Cinderella figure to disgraced failure can be read as merely a heightened version of the 'where are they now?' trope. For

---

[40]See also Higbee (2019) on the casting of *Girlhood* and the subsequent careers of the young actors. Touré contributed to the polemical collective essay by Black French actresses *Noire n'est pas mon métier/Black Is Not My Job* in 2018.

example, the stars of Sean Baker's acclaimed *Tangerine* (2015), who were trans women of colour who had been doing sex work, and were 'discovered' working a Los Angeles corner, also fall into this discursive paradigm. While Mya Taylor, who won several awards for her portrayal of Alexandra in the film, continued to pursue a career in film, her co-star, Kitana Kiki Rodriguez, whose character was significantly called Sin-Dee Rella, is discussed by Gardner (2016) in terms of the potentially tragic non-professional girl/woman: 'Why Has "Tangerine" Star Been MIA During Awards Season?'

The rise of *casting sauvage* or street casting has seen French films such as *Divines* (Benyamina, 2016) and *Brooklyn* (Tessaud, 2014) gain prominence, or *Rocks* (Gavron, 2019) in the UK context, all featuring young Black non-professional girls. Notably, however, in *Divines*, director Houda Benyamina cast her younger sister in one of the lead roles, and *Rocks* director Sarah Gavron forged a collaborative and mentoring relationship with the London girls she cast.[41] Likewise in the Egyptian film *Souad* (2021), the director Ayten Amin developed the script through extended conversation and improvisation with her teenage girl protagonists.[42] We can read these strategies as attempts to protect young non-actors, and to lessen their risk of exploitation, as well as to elicit superior performances.

Yet the element of risk attached to casting the non-professional, which Lury identified as the creative unpredictability they bring to a film set, extends also to their reputation or life through the spotlight that is shone on them. One does not have to appear in a film with the huge global success of *Slumdog Millionaire* to experience some unwelcome attention, and arthouse films have also ended up placing their actors in difficulty. The Spanish film *Carmen y Lola/Carmen & Lola* directed by Arantxa Echeverría was presented at Cannes in 2018. The story of a lesbian relationship between two Roma girls in Madrid, it cast two Roma girls – Zaira Romero and Rosy Rodríguez – who admitted that they experienced the discomfort of their community due to the film's representation of homosexuality, and also commented (in Pérez de las Heras 2019) on their own lack of preparation for taking on these challenging roles. An analogous situation occurred around the Kenyan film *Rafiki* (Kahi, 2018), banned in Kenya due to its depiction of a lesbian relationship, which posed challenges for the non-actors who starred in it, Samantha Mugatsia and Sheila Munyiva (see Greenwood 2018).

Exposure to sexual content for young non-actors can be problematic: the global controversy around the French film *Mignonnes/Cuties* (Doucouré, 2020) is exemplary in this regard. The film provoked outrage among viewers and politicians who decried its alleged promotion of child sexuality,

---

[41]See Newland (2020) and Azimi (2017). Nineteen-year-old *Rocks* star Bukky Bakray was named the BAFTA Rising Star in 2021 for her performance.
[42]See Khan (2021).

mainly due to Netflix's unfortunate promo poster (see Brody 2020). While the director Maïmouna Doucouré took the brunt of this criticism, thirteen-year-old star Fathia Youssouf was dragged into the polemic, although her parents had given her permission to participate in the film.[43] Youssouf won the César for Meilleur Espoir Féminin (Rising Female Star) in 2021 for her role, but the particular vulnerability of girls to charges of immodesty or sexualization is clear, as we saw also in Chapter 3.

A final example can illustrate this: the Afghan film *Osama* (Barmak, 2003) starred fourteen-year-old Marina Golbahari. Found by the director begging for food on the streets of Kabul, the illiterate Golbahari's compelling performance as the cross-dressing lead character won acclaim, and seemed to have provided the girl with an escape from poverty.[44] A 2003 profile mentions how she used the money from the film to buy her family a house, and that she now attended school (Wagner 2003). Yet this simple redemption story is complicated by subsequent events: press reports in 2016 stated that a picture of her circulating with head uncovered at the Busan Film Festival had led to accusations of immodesty and even death threats in her home country. She and her husband fled to France and were reported to be living in a shelter for asylum seekers, with Golbahari afraid to go out in public. Director Siddiq Barmak notes (in Anon.: 2016) that 'when you are an actor or actress in Afghanistan, or part of a film, you are accused of being an infidel, you are always in danger'. The complicated trajectory of Golbahari signals, albeit in extreme fashion, the tensions inherent in the integration of the non-professional actor into the global arthouse circuit, and the double-edged sword that visibility and success can represent in certain contexts, especially for girls and women.[45]

Here Anita Harris's identification of opposing media discourses about the 'at-risk girl' and the 'can-do girl' in postfeminist neoliberal culture is significant: these models position young womanhood as exemplars of either success or failure, a site of either possibilities or problems (Harris 2004: 14). While neoliberalism suggests that hard work and buying into narratives of resilience and self-curation will offer success, we can see how the entrance into the film industry both offers that promise but cannot secure it. Significantly, Sarah Projansky (2014: 7) observes that 'the can-do girl is usually white, while the African American or Latina girl is usually

---

[43] Youssouf was named among the 'best actors of 2020' by *The New York Times*, alongside veterans such as Viola Davis and Sophia Loren. See Morris and Scott (2020).
[44] A compelling account of the casting process and Golbahari's difficulties in learning the lines is given in Landrigan and Omar (2012).
[45] In the 2003 documentary *Joy of Madness*, fourteen-year-old Hana Makhmalbaf captures the casting for her sister Samira's film *At Five in the Afternoon*, a lengthy and frustrating process during which both Afghan men and women express discomfort, leading Samira to exclaim 'cinema is not a sin!'

at-risk'. It is interesting to think about the non-white non-professional girl, as risk is central to the non-professional category per se, because of the unpredictability they are felt to introduce into a film production. I would argue that the non-professional troubles the can-do/at-risk binary, though it does not collapse it completely. Race and ethnicity also clearly play a key part in the narratives around non-professionals, as do questions of class, where those who are sought are the more marginalized and precarious: as we have seen, the fortuitous 'discovery' by a director is rarely enough for an individual to overcome the institutional and race- and class-based barriers to a successful film career.

Conclusion

This chapter has identified the legacy of neorealism in the still-widespread use of the non-professional. We have seen how in both Italian and global cinema the use of marginalized non-professional actors continues, with familiar patterns emerging. While I noted in the Italian context a focus on delinquent and adolescent children, as Vieira points out (in Randall 2017: 139), films about children from impoverished urban are now a true transnational genre; an international success like *Cidade de Deus/City of God* (Meirelles, 2002) showed the Brazilian *favelas* as 'a privileged locus for exoticism, mystery and danger', and the more recent Mexican film *Ya no estoy aquí/I'm No Longer Here* (Frías de la Parra, 2019), which got a global Netflix release, did the same for Monterrey's violent suburbs, and brought teen Juan Daniel García Treviño to global recognition. Treviño's comment 'I walk in two worlds' (in Linthicum 2021) about his liminal status between an old and new, post-success life, sums up in many ways the predicament of the marginalized non-actor.

If I have dwelt on the complexities and difficulties inherent in the visibility that the non-professional suddenly gains, as well as the dynamics of fetishism present in media discourses, it has also tried to recognize the advantages that movie fame can bring to a small group of non-actors. A final example will illustrate the complexity at work: Zain Al Rafeea, a twelve-year-old Syrian refugee, was cast in the critically acclaimed Lebanese film *Capernaum* (Labaki, 2018). The illiterate Al Rafeea was found by director Nadine Labaki in the 'slums' of Beirut, as journalists repeated, and contributed his own improvised dialogue to the film. His journey to stardom took in a standing ovation at Cannes, and culminated in him and his family being resettled in Norway, where he now attends school.[46] Zain's story is a

---

[46]See Abou Khaled and Mawad (2019): https://www.unhcr.org/neu/24594-syrian-boy-takes-incredible-path-from-refugee-to-red-carpet.html

triumph, and the director is recognized as playing a humanitarian role as well as an artistic one.

The film can profitably be read in relation to Karl Schoonover's work (2012a) on Italian neorealism as 'brutal humanism', in which suffering was put on display for the benefit of a global audience, who would be moved to pity and aid by such distress. The heart-warming individualized experience of Al Rafeea, who has now hopefully been 'saved' by arthouse cinema from poverty and the trauma of exile, represents an unequivocal success. Yet his trajectory, and those of others, remind us that we still live in a world in which, as in post-war Italy, 'the impoverished must perform their neediness in order to earn our benefaction' (ibid.: 182), and must expose their suffering to the pitying gaze of the global cinematic spectator.

Conclusion

In finishing this book, I am struck by the difficulty of finishing it: I could go on listing examples of interesting non-professional performers and their biographies forever. When I have presented on this material people have often been eager to share fascinating cases and films with me, some of which I have ended up including, others which I have not been able to see. This leads to two related issues of process and method: the first is the risk of omission. Obviously this book cannot aim to be exhaustive: while I have striven to range widely across genres, I haven't, for instance, discussed some prominent post-war Italian films using non-professionals such as Rossellini's *Germania anno zero/Germany Year Zero* (1948), *Stromboli terra di Dio/Stromboli* (1950), *Francesco, giullare di Dio/The Flowers of St. Francis* (1950), and *La macchina ammazzacattivi/The Machine to Kill Bad People* (1952), or De Sica's *Miracolo a Milano/Miracle in Milan* (1951).[1] Hopefully these gaps can be rectified later, by myself or by others.

The second methodological issue raised is one that has been at the heart of my thinking on this project: I have wanted to avoid the book becoming a list of interesting examples of non-professionals, even if at times it might feel like that! There is a governing tension in the book between the desire to tell the forgotten or never-heard stories of these people who appeared in the films – what Dever et al. (2010: 110) call 'search-and-recover missions' – and close analysis of performance and how these appearances were shaped by directors and by the cinematic apparatus: on the one hand a kind of 'distant reading' of the non-professional actor in Italian cinema, in which broader patterns and systems are traced, and on the other, a close engagement with the signs of performance in the text. As O'Leary writes (2017: 18), drawing on the work of Franco Moretti, we need to try to 'deploy the effort of being exhaustive to reconfigure knowledge rather than merely to accumulate detail', and so this '"toggling" of scales from the very largest to the very smallest' (ibid.) allows us to mix quantitative and qualitative, and to locate details within a more expansive patterning. We might even think, recklessly,

---

[1]The reworking by Rossellini of Ingrid Bergman's Hollywood star persona in *Stromboli* and other films is discussed in detail in Gelley (2012: 78–102).

of this book as offering a (partial) history of post-war Italian cinema from the point of view of the actor, so inverting the customary film-historical perspective, which has been on great male directors. And in many places, because of lack of evidence, the desired historical rigour has had to give way to 'the frisson of the anecdotal rupture, the flash of the undiscernible real' (Gallagher and Greenblatt 2000: 67).

While the non-actor is a focus of attention because they are unbranded and lacking a star persona, what have we learned about the little-studied area of acting and the non-professional? It is hard to try to sum up the variegated approaches and acting styles of the post-war period, but we need to pay attention to practices of rehearsal and coaching (up to and including the not-infrequent recourse to violence!). I've also dwelt at times in the book on technical elements such as use of voice and dubbing that cause the viewer to question where performance is located. Gesture, body language, and the way the body occupies space also vary, from the static framing of Visconti in *La terra trema* to the kineticism of *Two Cents of Hope*. The alienation effects later produced by Pasolini or Straub-Huillet in their work with non-actors also point up the obsession with 'natural' acting that has frequently characterized discussions of neorealism.

While it is important to avoid value judgments, we can reflect upon what our perception of 'bad acting' might tell us: from the high point of expressivity of an Enzo Staiola, who moves us by virtue of his facial expressions or ability to cry on command, we might look at a recent example such as the protagonists of Clint Eastwood's 2018 thriller *The 15:17 to Paris*. The film was based on the accounts of three American men who foiled a 2015 terrorist attack on a train from Amsterdam to Paris. Eastwood cast the men – Anthony Sadler, Spencer Stone, and Alek Skarlatos – as themselves, a rare move in a mainstream Hollywood film by a major director.[2] The reception of the film often repeated the critique that the acting was wooden and insufficiently dramatic, apart from, that is, the climactic fight scene when the men take on the attackers, which is the only time the film really comes alive. The men suddenly inhabit the scene with vigour, almost as if a muscle memory has been activated. Indeed Stone recounted how filming that traumatic scene both triggered a flashback for him and allowed him to act in a way that felt vertiginously like 'the real thing': 'That was reality. That wasn't fiction. That was us two years ago' (in Siegel 2018).

This question of re-enactment has lingered throughout the book: I have considered the ways that non-professionals have often been invited to re-present their own conditions of marginalization on screen, foreclosing alternative possibilities, or indeed, the possibility of being seen as actors.

---

[2]*The Hollywood Reporter* says it is 'the first time in decades that a major film studio has taken a risk on real-life protagonists leading a moderately budgeted film' (Siegel 2018).

And the traumatic potential of re-enactment has historically been, and still is, justified by the artistic achievements of the films, and the presumed transformative effect of portraying these experiences. Farrier (2008: 223) points to the trope of chiasmus as inherent in screen re-enactment, as it operates a transformation through 'repetition and reversal'. As Sedgwick notes of chiasmus (1985: 15), 'the subject of the beginning of the narrative is different from the subject at the end, ... the two subjects cross each other in a rhetorical figure that conceals their discontinuity'. The figure of chiasmus thus stands for the personal and cultural value of the re-enactment, which compensates for the psychological difficulties caused to the performer.

This view of cultural production generally, as we have seen, is a top-down one, which doesn't really interrogate the costs to the individual. Even a 'success story' like Antonythasan Jesuthasan, Sri Lankan star of Audiard's Cannes Palme d'Or-winning *Dheepan* (2016), whose character's experiences are like his own as a former Tamil Tiger and asylum-seeker in France, might give us pause once we hear his story. He was stopped on trying to return to France after attending the Toronto Film Festival due to his lack of papers, had to sleep at the airport, and thereafter decided not to risk travelling again to festivals (in Donadio 2016). The transformative impact of Jesuthasan's story thus has hard limits (the securitized borders of Europe), and he refused to offer his totemic presence on the festival circuit as a guarantor of the film's authenticity.

I am aware, as the above vignette shows, that I haven't resolved the problem of becoming myself discursively entrapped in a success/failure binary when it comes to writing about non-professionals, or in a binary construct of trauma and agency, when of course the reality is more complex than that. While I have tried to locate actorly agency in my accounts of their performances, and in reproducing their own words about their experiences as far as possible, I acknowledge that these are people who have been placed within a media system that has treated them generally as workers with fewer rights and creative licence than trained and experienced actors. So 'the antagonistic relations of labor practices' (Clark 1995: xi) and the oppressive dynamics of race, ethnicity, gender, class, and sexuality have a particular weight in these contexts, and position the non-actor as a vulnerable subject in need of protection and in the eternal present of their lived body.

An example of a different type of non-professional might help think through these issues: this is the 'crossover star', the star who moves into acting from another discipline, normally music. There are endless examples of this figure, whom Lobalzo Wright (2017: 2) has shown to be central to Hollywood cinema: Elvis, Sinatra, Cher, Lady Gaga, Ice T., Bowie, Jennifer Hudson, the list goes on ... While these freshman actors are still carefully judged as proficient (or not – as the rumbling controversies in the summer of 2022 around Harry Styles's performance in Olivia Wilde's *Don't Worry Darling* attested) they are definitely classified differently to the non-professionals that have been my primary focus.[3] Crossover stars carry a star image from their previous careers with them, disqualifying them from being 'anonymous bodies' (Distelmeyer 2012: 152). They are also professional performers, possessing skills felt to be transferrable from one discipline to another, as singers, dancers, and comedians are expert in what Naremore (1988: 34) terms 'the physics of movement and gesture [in performance] that makes signs readable'. When an athlete/performer like The Rock takes up acting, therefore, it is felt to be a case of an established performer deploying a performative mode (in this case, personification) in a different media context.

Another type of non-professional to explore would be the reality TV or social media star: the performance of the self that has become routine on television and on social media platforms in the last two decades has implications for ideas of non-professional acting. The work of performing and constructing one's identity is now inextricable from the branding of the self (Wood 2017), and points to the shift that has taken place since the post-war, when seeing one's image reproduced was relatively infrequent. My discussion of Ferrente's *Selfie* in the last chapter illustrates this shift on the big screen. We have established that questions of authenticity have always haunted the non-professional, most famously in neorealism's 'instrumentalization of bodily contingency as a rhetoric of authenticity' (Schoonover 2012a: 151). However, the commodification of this authenticity, now imbricated in a deep familiarity with the media apparatus, has placed us in a new position of uncertainty, caught between a desire for the real and an endless knowledge that we are all constantly performing.

Authenticity itself is of course a problematic cultural construction, and in looking at the filming of non-actors we are often reminded of the ways that the 'film camera has been used to primitivize, facilitate racializing processes, and produce the expectation of radical cultural alterity' (Shankar 2020). I hope that future work on the non-professional will account for all these avenues, as well as going well beyond the Western focus of this book. The reduction of the non-professional to a bodily symptom manipulated by a director has been challenged here, but there is much more work to do.

Tying together the intangible and ineffable product of performance labour that is film acting with the biography and lived experience of the non-professional has been important; by digging into the lives of the non-actors who were plucked from obscurity I have sought to illuminate how their contributions might be both the products of their own experiences and artistic interventions into the cultural climate of the time. Bazin (1971: 60) famously pronounced in relation to *Bicycle Thieves*, 'no more actors, no more story, no more sets, which is to say that in the perfect aesthetic illusion

---

[3]On Styles's lack of acting ability, see e.g. Sims (2022).

of reality there is no more cinema'. But cinema of course continues, and despite the lack of material evidence of their lives, the non-professional remains there, on screen, with the richest evidence of their actions being their roles in these films. While octogenarian Enzo Staiola might sigh that, for him, neorealism never ends, in a more transcendent key we remember Martin LaSalle in the documentary on Bresson's *Pickpocket* smiling wistfully as he says 'we're still there, immortal'.

WORKS CITED

A. B. (1954), 'Maria Fiore è diventata grande', *L'Europeo*, 480: 62.
Abou Khaled, L., and D. Mawad (2019), 'Syrian Boy Takes Incredible Path from Refugee to Red Carpet', 22 February. https://www.unhcr.org/neu/24594-syr ian-boy-takes-incredibleran-path-from-refugee-to-red-carpet.html.
Adorno, T. (1992), 'Transparencies on Film', in J. Bernstein (ed.), *The Culture Industry*, 178–86, London: Routledge.
Agnoletti, B. (1952a), 'Anche i produttori hanno una testa', *Cinema*, 95: 173.
Agnoletti, B. (1952b), 'Portare l'attore dall'uomo della strada. Intervista con Eduardo De Filippo', *Cinema*, 84: 199–200.
Ahmed, S. (2013), *The Cultural Politics of Emotion*, London: Routledge.
Ajello, N. (1997), *Intellettuali e PCI 1944–1958*, Bari: Laterza.
Albritton, D., A. Melero and T. Whittaker (2016), 'Introduction', in *Performance and Spanish Film*, 1–15, Oxford: Oxford University Press.
Alicata, M. (1949), '*La terra trema*', *Bianco e Nero*, 10(7): 90–2.
Alicata, M., and G. De Santis (1941a), 'Verità e poesia. Verga e il cinema italiano', *Cinema*, 127: 216–17.
Alicata, M., and G. De Santis (1941b), 'Ancora di Verga e del cinema italiano', *Cinema*, 130: 314–15.
Allasia, C., B. Maida, and F. Prono (2019), 'Introduzione', in *Infanzia e povertà: storie e narrazioni nell'Italia del dopoguerra (1945–1950)*, 7–12, Turin: Edizioni Sinestesie.
Alsop, E. (2014), 'The Imaginary Crowd: Neorealism and the Uses of Coralità', *Velvet Light Trap*, 74: 27–41.
Altman, R. (1984), 'A Semantic/Syntactic Approach to Film Genre', *Cinema Journal*, 23(3): 6–18.
Amadei, A. (2008), 'Quale razza?' Interview with Isabella Marincola. https://www.youtube.com/watch?v=ivqZeYkMCm0.
Ambrosino, S. (1989), 'Il cinema ricomincia: Attori e registi fra "continuita" e "frattura"', in A. Farassino (ed.), *Neorealismo: Cinema italiano 1945–49*, 61–6, Turin: EDT.
Amerio, P. G. (1950), 'Erotismo e sex-appeal nel cinema italiano', *Follie*, 3(10): 15–18.
Andrews, N. (2018), '*Roma* – a Modern-day Neorealist Classic from Alfonso Cuarón', *Financial Times*, 28 November. https://www.ft.com/content/2529a cd6-f30a-11e8-9623-d7f9881e729f.
Angeli, O. (1979), 'Strutture produttive, contratti, organizzazione sindacale', in A. A. V. V. (eds), *La città del cinema. Produzione e lavoro nel cinema italiano 1930–1970*, 49–63, Rome: Napoleone.

Anile, A. (2013), *Orson Welles in Italy*, Bloomington: Indiana University Press.
Anon. (1945), 'Un nuovo grande concorso: *Star* Ambrosia Film', *Star*, 2(29): 3.
Anon. (1948a), '*La terra trema*', *Oggi*, 18 July: 17–18.
Anon. (1948b), 'Review of *Paisan*', *Time*, 19 April.
Anon. (1950a), 'Schermi e schermaglie', *Araldo dello Spettacolo*, 24 August: 1.
Anon. (1950b), 'Fame Mocks a Movie Star', *Life*, 23 January: 56–60.
Anon. (1950c), 'Pietro Germi in collegio', *Araldo dello Spettacolo*, 15–16 September: 3.
Anon. (1950d), 'Angelo in famiglia', *Oggi*, 23 November: 8–9.
Anon. (1951a), 'Divenuta attrice si è comperata il primo orologio della sua vita', *Oggi*, 18 October: 1.
Anon (1951b). 'Pronunciamento degli attori contro le "Misses"', *Araldo dello Spettacolo*, 7–8 November: 3.
Anon. (1952), 'Revolt of an Angel', *Life*, 2 June: 53–8.
Anon. (1953), 'Gli attori, questi sconosciuti', *Teatro Scenario*, 17(2): 39.
Anon. (1954a), 'Risposte a un giovane attore', *Cinema Nuovo*, 7: 7.
Anon. (1954b), 'Il loro Natale', *Oggi*, 20 December: 6.
Anon. (1954c), 'Italy's Movie Boom for Negro Actors', *Jet*, 13 May: 60–2.
Anon. (1955), 'L'albo degli attori', *Cinema Nuovo*, 71: 367.
Anon. (1956), 'Le bellissime', *Cinema Nuovo*, 56: 257–64.
Anon. (1991), '"Mery" film maledetto muore un attore, il quinto', *La Repubblica*, 10 August. https://ricerca.repubblica.it/repubblica/archivio/repubblica/1991/08/10/mery-film-maledetto-muore-un-attore.html.
Anon. (2009), 'Omaggio a Lamberto Maggiorani protagonista di *Ladri di biciclette*', *Il Tempo*, 11 May. https://www.iltempo.it/roma-capitale/2009/05/11/news/omaggio-a-lamberto-maggiorani-protagonista-di-ladri-di-biciclette-683557/.
Anon. (2013), 'Intervista a Enzo Staiola. L'attore bambino più famoso del neorealismo'. 8 October. http://blog.triworldcinema.com/it/intervista-enzo-staiola/?fbclid=IwAR2Pl3ooBXEeohVfOdlIEK3fjL4pLOTm-MHNkH_p2vt7F4Tmc6y0U-a7hGw.
Anon. (2016), 'Afghan Film Star in French Exile After Death Threats', *The Local France*, 5 May. https://www.thelocal.fr/20160505/afghan-film-star-in-french-exile-after-death-threats/.
Anon. (2018), 'L'ora del pasto. Il ladro bi biciclette', 23 November. https://www.tuttobiciweb.it/article/2018/11/23/1542902307/l-ora-del-pasto-il-ladro-di-biciclette-marco-pastonesi-enzo-staiola-tuttobiciweb.
Anon. (2019), 'Da *Mery per sempre* alla regia, la nuova vita di Francesco Benigno', *Il Tempo*, 5 December. https://www.iltempo.it/cultura-spettacoli/2019/12/05/news/francesco-benigno-colore-del-dolore-mery-per-sempre-cinema-regista-palermo-1251583/.
Anon. (2021), 'Giuseppe Dave Seke, chi è l'astro nascente della (seconda) generazione Netflix', *Wired*, 23 April. https://www.wired.it/play/televisione/2021/04/23/giuseppe-dave-seke-protagonista-serie-zero-netflix-intervista/.
Anselmo-Sequeira, D. (2015), 'Screen-Struck: The Invention of the Movie Girl Fan', *Cinema Journal*, 55(1): 1–28.

Aparicio, Y. (2020), 'In Mexico, *Roma* Lit a Fire for Workers' Rights', *New York Times*, 23 May. https://www.nytimes.com/2020/05/23/opinion/roma-mexico-workers-rights.html.
Aprà, A. (ed.) (1988), *Rosselliniana: bibliografia internazionale, dossier 'Paisa'*, Rome: Di Giacomo.
Aprà, A. (ed.) (1995), *Il dopoguerra di Rossellini*, Rome: Cinecittà International.
Aristarco, G. (1948), 'La terra trema', *La critica cinematografica*, 12: 10–11.
Aristarco, G. (1949), 'Ladri di biciclette', *Cinema*, 7: 220–1.
Aristarco, G. (1952), 'Film di questi giorni: *Bellissima*', *Cinema*, 78: 17–20.
Aristarco, G. (1956), 'Il tetto', *Cinema Nuovo*, 2: 217.
Aristarco, G. (ed.) (1975), *Antologia di Cinema Nuovo, 1952–1958*, Florence: Guaraldi.
Aristarco, G. (1983), *Il mito dell'attore. Come l'industria della star produce il sex symbol*, Bari: Dedalo.
Armes, R. (1971), *Patterns of Realism*, London: Tantivy.
Art. (1952), 'Cronache del cinema. Grazie a Maria Fiore', *Corriere d'Informazione*, 11–12 April: 2.
a. t. (2000), 'Addio bimbo prodigio dell'*Oro di Napoli*', *La Repubblica*, 13 January. https://ricerca.repubblica.it/repubblica/archivio/repubblica/2000/01/13/addio-bimbo-prodigio-dell-oro-di-napoli.html.
Auriol, J. (1949), 'L'autore svaluterà l'attore', *Cinema*, 9: 237–40.
Austin, G. (2004), 'The Amateur Actors of Cannes 1999: A Shock to the (Star) System', *French Cultural Studies*, 15(3): 251–63.
Azimi, N. (2017), 'Houda Benyamina, the French Filmmaker Who Brought the Banlieues to Hollywood', *New Yorker*, 9 April. https://www.newyorker.com/culture/persons-of-interest/houda-benyamina-the-french-filmmaker-who-brought-the-banlieues-to-hollywood.
'B'. (1948), '"Dive" prefabbricate e d'importazione', *Cinema*, 4: 101.
'B'. (1952), 'Bilancio', *Cinema*, 99–100: 285.
Báez, J. (2021), 'Beyond *Roma*: Yalitza Aparicio on the Global Media Stage'. Talk given at the University of Toronto Cinema Studies Institute (online), 11 March.
Balázs, B. (2011), 'The Close-Up', in E. Carter (ed.), *Early Film Theory: Visible Man and The Spirit of Film*, 97–111, London: Berghah.
Baldelli, P. (1973), *Luchino Visconti*, Milan: Mazzotta.
Baldini, G. (1944), 'Afoso pomeriggio al Centro Sperimentale', *Star*, 1(5): 4.
Balio, T. (2010), *The Foreign Film Renaissance on American Screens, 1946–1973*, Madison: University of Wisconsin Press.
Baracco, A. (1950), 'Etichette mortali', *Cinema*, 48: 197.
Barbaro, U. (1937), 'L'attore cinematografico', *Bianco e Nero*, 1(5): 8–39.
Barbaro, U. (1951), 'Che succede al Centro Sperimentale di Cinematografia?', *Rinascita*, 8(1): 48–9.
Barbaro, U. (1975), 'Influsso del cinema sovietico', in G. Aristarco (ed.), *Antologia di Cinema Nuovo 1952–1958*, 212–14, Florence: Guaraldi.
Baron, C. (2007), 'Acting Choices/Filmic Choices: Rethinking Montage and Performance', *Journal of Film and Video*, 59(2): 32–40.
Baron, C., and S. Carnicke (2008), *Reframing Screen Performance*, Ann Arbor: University of Michigan Press.

Barthes, R. (1981), *Camera Lucida: Reflections on Photography*, trans. R. Howard, London: Farrar, Straus and Giroux.
Battisti, C. (1955), *Come divenni Umberto D*, Rome: Edizioni della Cineteca Scolastica.
Bayman, L. (2014a), *The Operatic and the Everyday in Post-war Italian Film Melodrama*, Edinburgh: Edinburgh University Press.
Bayman, L. (2014b), 'Something Else Besides a Man: Melodrama and the *Maschietto* in Postwar Italian Cinema', in D. Hipkins and R. Pitt (eds), *New Visions of the Child in Italian Cinema*, 169–88, Bern: Peter Lang.
Bazin, A. (1971), *What Is Cinema?* Vol. II, trans. H. Gray, Berkeley: University of California Press.
Bazin, A. (1975), *Qu'est-ce que le cinéma?*, Paris: Éditions du Cerf.
Bazin, A. (1997), 'Germany, Year Zero', in B. Cardullo (ed.), *Bazin at Work: Major Essays and Reviews from the Forties and Fifties*, 121–4, New York: Routledge.
Beccalossi, C. (2017), 'Italian Sexology, Nicola Pende's Biotypology and Hormone Treatments in the 1920s', *Histoire, médecine et santé*, 12, http://journals.open edition.org/hms/1173.
Bellamy (2020), 'Chi è Coco Rebecca Edogamhe, la giovane stella di *Summertime* su Netflix?', *Afro Italian Souls*, 7 May. http://www.afroitaliansouls.it/vi-facci amo-conoscere-coco-rebecca-edogamhe-la-giovane-stella-di-summertime-su-netflix/.
Benci, J. (2011), 'Identification of a City: Antonioni and Rome, 1940–1962', in L. Rascaroli and J. D. Rhodes (eds), *Antonioni: Centenary Essays*, 21–63, London: Bloomsbury.
Ben-Ghiat, R. (2015), *Italian Facism's Empire Cinema*, Bloomington: Indiana University Press.
'Bert' (1954), 'Attori in cifre', *Cinema*, 126: 50.
Berti, G. (1953), 'Sette storie segrete', *La Settimana Incom Illustrata*, 16: 28–30.
Bettetini, G. (1975), 'Altro professionismo', *Bianco e Nero: Special Issue on Vittorio De Sica*, 36(9–12): 111–13.
Bianco e Nero editors (1949), 'Stile e maniera', *Bianco e Nero*, 10(12): 3–7.
Birri, F. (1999), 'Natale e Luisa: dalla strada allo schermo', in G. De Santi and M. De Sica (eds), *Il tetto di Vittorio De Sica. Testimonianze, interventi, sceneggiatura*, 25–7, Rome: Associazione Amici di Vittorio De Sica.
Biswas, M. (2007), 'In the Mirror of an Alternative Globalism: The Neorealist Encounter in India', in L. Ruberto and K. Wilson (eds), *Italian Neorealism and Global Cinema*, 72–90, Detroit, MI: Wayne State University Press.
Bolchi, S. (1951), 'Gli attori di teatro italiano nei loro rapporti col cinema', *Cinema*, 58: 135–7.
Bonicelli, V. (1953), 'Molta carne al fuoco che De Sica ha acceso di notte', *Tempo*, 15(7): 21–3.
Bonifazio, P. (2020), *The Photoromance: A Feminist Reading of Popular Culture*, Cambridge, MA: MIT Press.
Borselli, A. (1945), 'Il concorso *Star* Ambrosia Film - un mese dopo', *Star*, 2(34): 5.
Bosco, U. (1949), 'Tipo e individuo nel cinema e nel teatro', *Bianco e Nero*, 10(7): 3–9.

Bouchard, N., and V. Ferme (2012), 'Translator's Introduction: On Franco Cassano's *Southern Thought*', in F. Cassano (ed.), *Southern Thought and Other Essays on the Mediterranean*, ix–xxvi, York: Fordham University Press.
Bradshaw, P. (2016), '*Fire at Sea* Review – Masterly and Moving Look at the Migrant Crisis', *The Guardian*, 9 June. https://www.theguardian.com/film/2016/jun/09/fire-at-sea-review-masterly-and-moving-look-at-the-migrant-crisis
Bradshaw, P. (2018), '*The Ciambra* Review – Rush of Storytelling and Style', *The Guardian*, 13 June. https://www.theguardian.com/film/2018/jun/13/the-ciambra-review-rush-of-storytelling-and-style.
Bragaglia, C. (1937), 'Narrazione e documento', *Cinema*, 31: 222–3.
Bravo, A. (2003), *Il fotoromanzo*, Bologna: Il Mulino.
Brecht, B. (1964), 'Two Essays on Unprofessional Acting', in John Willett (ed.), *Brecht on Theatre: The Development of an Aesthetic*, 148–53, New York: Hill and Wang.
Brennan, N. (2012), 'Marketing Meaning, Branding Neorealism: Advertising and Promoting Italian Cinema in Postwar America', in R. Sklar and S. Giovacchini (eds), *Global Neorealism: The Transnational History of a Film Style*, 87–102, Jackson: University Press of Mississippi.
Bresson, R. (1991), 'Notes on the Cinematographer', in J. Butler (ed.), *Star Texts: Image and Performance in Film and Television*, 80–7, Detroit, MI: Wayne State University Press.
Brocardo, E. (2020), 'Intimacy coordinator, una professione del futuro (almeno in Italia)', *Vanity Fair Italia*, 15 August. https://www.vanityfair.it/mybusiness/annunci/2020/08/15/intimacy-coordinator-nuova-professione-tv-cinema-come-funziona-chi-puo-farlo.
Brody, R. (2020), '*Cuties*, the Extraordinary Netflix Début That Became the Target of a Right-Wing Campaign', *The New Yorker*, 8 September. https://www.newyorker.com/culture/the-front-row/cuties-mignonnes-the-extraordinary-netflix-debut-that-became-the-target-of-a-right-wing-campaign.
Brody, R. (2021), 'Ingrid Bergman in "Stromboli" and the Power of Nonprofessional Actors', *The New Yorker*, 5 March. https://www.newyorker.com/culture/the-front-row/ingrid-bergman-in-stromboli-and-the-power-of-nonprofessional-actors.
Brunetta, G. P. (1969), *Umberto Barbaro e l'idea di neorealismo (1930–1943)*, Padua: Liviana.
Brunetta, G. P. (1982), *Storia del cinema italiano: dal 1945 agli anni ottanta*, Rome: Riuniti.
Brunetta, G. P. (1995), *Cent'anni di cinema italiano*, Vol. I, Bari: Laterza.
Brunetta, G. P. (2003), *Cent'anni di cinema italiano*, Vol. II, Bari: Laterza.
Brunette, P. (1996), *Roberto Rossellini*, Berkeley: University of California Press.
Bruni, D. (2022), *De Sica: Ladri di biciclette*, Rome: Carocci.
Bruzzi, S. (2000), *New Documentary*, London: Routledge.
Buckley, R. (2008), 'Glamour and the Italian Female Film Stars of the 1950s', *Historical Journal of Film, Television and Radio*, 28(3): 267–89.
Busetta, L. (2022), 'Do you Want to Film Yourself? Narrating the Personal and Rewriting Reality in Agostino Ferrente's *Selfie* (2019)', *Studies in Documentary Film*, 1–16.

Butler, I. (2022), *The Method: How the Twentieth Century Learned to Act*, New York: Bloomsbury.
C. (1953), 'Et Bubbius Dixit', *Cinema*, 119: 189.
Cabitza, M. (2011), 'How Bolivian Juan Carlos Aduviri Won Big Film Role', 1 February, https://www.bbc.co.uk/news/world-latin-america-12276026
Caldiron, O. (1975), 'Il serpente e la colomba', *Bianco e Nero: Special Issue on Vittorio De Sica*, 9–12: 5–13.
Caldiron, O. (2002), '1948, nasce un capolavoro', in *Millenovecento*, 1(1): 88–95.
Caldiron, O., and M. De Sica (eds) (1997), *Ladri di biciclette di Vittorio De Sica. Testimonianze, interventi, sopralluoghi*, Rome: Pantheon.
Calendoli, G. (1952), 'Gli attori neorealisti', *Filmcritica*, 4(19): 182.
Calendoli, G. (1953), 'Critici a congresso', *Cinema*, 117: 141–2.
Callari, F. (1953), 'Cosa si premia?', *Cinema*, 113: 5–6.
Calvino, V. (1940), 'Si è trovata 'Ombretta. Mariù diventa diva', *Film*, 38: 4.
Camerini, C. (1983), 'La formazione artistica degli attori del cinema muto italiano', *Bianco e Nero*, 54(1): 7–43.
Caminati, L. (2011), 'The Role of Documentary in the Formation of Neorealist Cinema', in R. Sklar and S. Giovacchini (eds), *Global Neorealism: The Transnational History of a Film Style*, 52–67, Jackson: University Press of Mississippi.
Campanella, M. (1956), 'Vecchi come il cinema i "presi dalla strada"', *Cinema*, 184: 127–9.
Campbell, T. (2017), *The Techne of Giving: Cinema and the Generous Form of Life*, New York: Fordham University Press.
Canosa, R. (1995), *Storia della criminalità in Italia dal 1946 a oggi*, Milan: Feltrinelli.
Cardone, L. (2004), *Con lo schermo nel cuore. Grand Hôtel e il cinema (1946–1956)*, Pisa: ETS.
Cardone, L. (2009), *Noi Donne e il cinema*, Pisa: ETS.
Carlson, M. (1994), 'Invisible Presences: Performance Intertextuality', *Theatre Research International*, 19: 111–17.
Carluccio, G., and A. Minuz (2015), 'Nel paese degli antidivi', *Bianco e Nero*, 581: 10–11.
Carluccio, G., F. Mazzocchi, G. Muggeo and M. Pierini (eds) (2022), *Effetto Magnani. Sguardi sull'attrice e sulla diva*, Imola: Cue Press.
Carman, E. (2014), 'Mapping the Body: Female Film Stars and the Reconstruction of Postwar Italian National Identity', *Quarterly Review of Film and Video*, 31(4): 322–35.
Carnicke, S. (1999), 'Lee Strasberg's Paradox of the Actor', in A. Lovell and P. Kramer (eds), *Screen Acting*, 75–87, London: Routledge.
Carpenter, B., L. Goldblatt, and L. Hanson (2021), 'Unprofessional: Toward a Political Economy of Professionalization', *Social Text*, 39(1): 47–67.
Carrigy, M. (2021), *The Reenactment in Contemporary Screen Culture: Performance, Mediation, Repetition*, New York: Bloomsbury.
Casetti, F. (1989–90), 'Specchio su specchio, autoriflessività nel cinema italiano degli anni Cinquanta', *La scena e lo schermo*, 2(3–4): 196–212.
Casetti, F. (1992), 'Cinema in the Cinema in Italian Films of the Fifties: *Bellissima* and *La signora senza camelie*', *Screen*, 33(4): 375–93.

Casetti, F., and L. Malavasi (2003), 'La retorica del neorealismo', in C. Cosulich (ed.), *Storia del cinema italiano, vol. VII (1945–1948)*, 177–90, Venice: Marsilio.
Cassano, F. (2012), *Southern Thought and Other Essays on the Mediterranean*, New York: Fordham University Press.
Castellani, S. (1945), 'Città aperta a porte chiuse', *Star*, 37: 2.
Castelli, R. (2018), 'Scrittori-registi e film-inchiesta: un esperimento di cinegiornale d'autore nell'Italia degli anni Cinquanta', in L. Battistini et al. (eds), *La letteratura italiana e le arti, Atti del Congresso dell'ADI*, Rome: ADI. https://www.italianisti.it/pubblicazioni/atti-di-congresso/la-letteratura-italiana-e-le-arti/ADI_Napoli_Castelli.pdf.
Castello, G. C. (1949), 'Processo al "non-attore"', *Bianco e Nero*, 10(3): 54–6.
Castello, G. C. (1952), 'Alfabeto del sex-appeal', *L'Eco del Cinema*, 37: 14–16.
Castello, G. C. (1953), 'Il neorealismo è vivo', *Cinema*, 123: 317–19.
Castello, G. C. (1957), *Il divismo. Mitologia del cinema*, Turin: ERI.
Cavassa, L. (1949), 'Il cinema ha fatto girare la testa al pescatore di Luchino e all'operaio di De Sica', *Il Mattino dell'Italia Centrale*, 9 November: 3.
Cavicchioli, L. (1961a), 'La storia di tre attrici famose che hanno pagato un solo trionfo con molte amarezze', *Oggi*, 17 April: 8–14.
Cavicchioli, L. (1961b), 'Gli indegni trucchi per indurre le ingenue a svestirsi nella speranza d'una particina', *Oggi*, 4 May: 2.
Cavicchioli, L. (1961c), 'Suggerimenti d'un regista alle aspiranti dive per non smarrirsi nella giungla di celluloide', *Oggi*, 10 April: 12.
Cavicchioli, L. (1961d), 'Disavventure d'attrici che rifiutarono di seguire le vie facili ma pericolose', *Oggi*, 11 May: 48.
Cavicchioli, L. (1961e), 'Anche nel cinema non c'è bellezza che valga se non è accompagnata da un po' di talento', *Oggi*, 18 May: 26.
Centorrino, C. (2018), '*Le cose belle*: On the Aesthetics of Becoming in Documentary Film', *L'Avventura*, 4(2): 225–42.
Chanan, M. (2004), *Cuban Cinema*, Minneapolis: University of Minnesota Press.
Chaplin, F. (2019), 'Stars and the Off-Screen Spectacle of Film Festivals: Charlotte Gainsbourg at Cannes', *Celebrity Studies*, 10(4): 533–42.
Chiappetta-Miller, T. (2015), 'Projecting the Diva's Voice: Anna Magnani in Visconti's *Bellissima*', *Italian Studies*, 70(3): 364–76.
Chiarini, L. (ed.) (1938), *L'attore: saggio di antologia critica*, *Bianco e Nero*, 2(2–3).
Chiarini, L., and U. Barbaro (1941), 'L'attore cinematografico e i suoi mezzi espressivi', *Bianco e Nero*, 5(1): 105–42.
Chiarini, L. (1948), 'Cattivi pensieri sul realismo', *Cinema*, 1: 11.
Chiarini, L. (1951a), 'Discorso sul neorealismo', *Bianco e Nero*, 12(7), July: 3–27.
Chiarini, L. (1951b), 'La crisi c'è', *Filmcritica*, 1(5): 147–50.
Chiarini, L. (1951c), 'Opera di collaborazione e corsi di insegnamento', *Cinema*, 59: 162–3.
Chiarini, L. (1952), 'Esuberanza di Carmela e sette peccati capitali', *Cinema*, 86: 260–1.
Chiaromonte, N. (1949), 'Rome Letter: Italian Movies', *Partisan Review*, 14(6): 621–30.

Chiti, R., and R. Poppi (1991), *Dizionario del cinema italiano. I film, vol. 2: dal 1945 al 1959*, Rome: Gremese.
Cialente, F. (1950), 'Un triste "fumetto" vero', *Noi Donne*, 41: 3.
Cicognetti, L., and L. Servetti (1996), '"On Her Side": Female Images in Italian Cinema and the Popular Press, 1945–1955', *Historical Journal of Film, Radio and Television*, 16(4): 555–63.
Cinema Nuovo editors (1953), 'Lo scandalo delle curve', *Cinema nuovo*, 6: 135.
Clark, D. (1995), *Negotiating Hollywood: The Cultural Politics of Actors' Labor*, Minneapolis: University of Minnesota Press.
Cohan, S. (2019), *Hollywood by Hollywood: The Backstudio Picture and the Mystique of Making Movies*, Oxford: Oxford University Press.
Colless, E. (2009), 'The Possessed', *Continuum: Journal of Media & Cultural Studies*, 5(2): 235–46.
Comand, M. (2020), *Ephemera: Scrapbooks, fan mail e diari delle spettatrici nell'Italia del regime*, Venice: Marsilio.
Comand, M. (2022), *Elsa De' Giorgi. Storia, discorsi e memorie del cinema*, Milan-Udine: Mimesis.
Comencini, L. (1975), 'Li capiva', *Bianco e Nero: Special Issue on Vittorio De Sica*, 36(9–12): 122–4.
Corsi, B. (2001), *Con qualche dollaro di meno. Storia economica del cinema italiano*, Rome: Riuniti.
Cotticelli, A. (2014), '*Io rom romantica*, la regista dal campo nomadi alle case popolari di Torino', *Il Fatto Quotidiano*, 3 August. https://www.ilfattoquotidiano.it/2014/08/03/io-rom-romantica-la-regista-dal-campo-nomadi-alle-case-popolari-di-torino/1075477/.
Cova, A. (2002), *Economia, lavoro e istituzioni nell'Italia del Novecento*, Milan: Vita e Pensiero.
Creus, T. (2011), 'Poverty, Violence and Children: The Influence of Italian Neorealism in Brazilian Cinema from Cinema Novo until Today', paper given at the Symposium of Portuguese Traditions, UCLA, https://www.academia.edu/5719579/Italian_neorealism_and_its_influence_on_Brazilian_cinema
Cristofani, P., and Manetti, R. (1956), 'Processo al non-attore', *Cinema Nuovo*, 79: 173–80.
Criterion Collection (2016), *Bicycle Thieves*. DVD.
Crowther, B. (1949a), 'Vittorio De Sica's *The Bicycle Thief*, a Drama of Post-War Rome, Arrives at World', *The New York Times*, 13 December.
Crowther, B. (1949b). '*Guaglio*,' Italian Film on Style of 'Boy's Town,' New Feature at the Avenue Playhouse', *The New York Times*, 19 May.
Cucco, M. (2018), 'The Academy Award in the Promotion of Italian Films'. https://www.italiancinema.it/the-italian-submissions-to-the-academy-awards-and-their-foreign-digital-distribution/.
Culhane, S. (2017a), 'Beyond "belle e brave": Female Stars and Italian Cinema Audiences (1945–1960)', PhD diss., University of Bristol.
Culhane, S. (2017b), 'Street Cries and Street Fights: Anna Magnani, Sophia Loren and the *popolana*', *The Italianist*, 37(2): 254–62.
Cullen, N. (2015), 'Changing Emotional Landscapes? *Grand Hôtel* and Representations of Love and Courtship in 1950s Italy', *Cultural and Social History*, 11(2): 285–306.

Czach, L. (2012), 'Acting and Performance in Home Movies and Amateur Films', in A. Taylor (ed.), *Theorizing Film Acting*, 152–66, London: Routledge.
Dagrada, E. (2009), 'L'attore bambino nel cinema di Rossellini', *L'Asino di B.*, special issue on 'L'attore tra teatro e cinema', 11(12): 101–11.
Dagrada, E. (2014), 'Contro il neorealismo? Michelangelo Antonioni e *La signora senza camelie*', in L. Cardone and S. Lischi (eds), *Sguardi differenti. Studi di cinema in onore di Lorenzo Cuccu*, 129–38, Pisa: ETS.
Dagrada, E. (2017), 'Non solo Ingrid. Attori di professione, interpreti occasionali e "legge dell'amalgama" secondo Bazin e Rossellini', in G. Carluccio, E. Morreale, and M. Pierini (eds), *Intorno al neorealismo. Voci, contesti, linguaggi e culture dell'Italia del dopoguerra*, 209–17, Milan: Scalpendi.
Dalle Vacche, A. (2008), *Diva: Defiance and Passion in Early Italian Cinema*, Austin: University of Texas Press.
Dalle Vacche, A. (2018), 'American Neorealism? Sean Baker's *The Florida Project*', *Cinergie*, 13. https://cinergie.unibo.it/article/view/8275/8133.
Dalle Vacche, A. (2020), *André Bazin's Film Theory*, Oxford: Oxford University Press.
Davis, T. (1991), *Actresses as Working Women: Their Social Identity in Victorian Culture*, London: Routledge.
De Bernart, E. (2006), 'Luchino pazzo di Acitrezza', in S. Gesù (ed.), *La terra trema: un film di Luchino Visconti*, 279–80, Comiso: Salarchi.
De Berti, R. (2000), *Dallo schermo alla carta. Romanzi, fotoromanzi, rotocalchi cinematografici: il film e i suoi paratesti*, Milan: Vita e Pensiero.
De Certeau, M. (1988), *The Practice of Everyday Life*, trans. S. Rendell, Berkeley: University of California Press.
De Franceschi, L. (2013), 'L'attorialità come luogo di lotta. Africani e afrodiscendenti nel cinema italiano post-1989', in L. De Franceschi (ed.), *L'Africa in Italia: per una controstoria postcoloniale del cinema italiano*, 189–206, Rome: Aracne.
De la Mora, S. (2019), '*Roma*: Reparation versus Exploitation', *Film Quarterly*, 72(4). https://filmquarterly.org/2019/06/07/roma-repatriation-vs-exploitation/.
Del Frate, Amelia (1961), *Processo a Cinecittà*, Rome: Canesi.
Deleuze, G. (1989), *Cinema 2: The Time-Image*, trans. H. Tomlinson and R. Galeta, Minneapolis: University of Minnesota Press.
De Marco, M. (2018), 'Juana Jimenez, the trans Diva!', *Rome Central*, 24 May. https://www.romecentral.com/en/intervista-con-juana-jimenez/.
Dentice, F. (1952), 'Attori bambini in un cinema adulto', *Cinema*, 96: 205–7.
Dentice, F. (1953), 'Risorgono le dive sulle rovine del realismo?', *Teatro Scenario*, 17(5–6): 75–6.
De Santi, G., and M. De Sica (eds) (1999), *Il tetto di Vittorio De Sica. Testimonianze, interventi, sceneggiatura*, Rome: Associazione Amici di Vittorio De Sica.
De Santis, G. (1951), 'È in crisi il neorealismo?', *Filmcritica*, 1(4): 109–12.
De Sica, V. (1945), 'Sciuscia, giò?', *Film d'oggi*, 1(3): 4–5.
De Sica, V. (1975a), 'Volti nuovi per il cinema italiano', *Bianco e Nero: Special Issue on Vittorio De Sica*, 36(9–12): 253–4.
De Sica, V. (1975b), 'L'America è tutta una lampadina', *Bianco e Nero: Special Issue on Vittorio De Sica*, 36(9–12): 266–70.

De Sica, V. (1975c), 'Gli anni più belli della mia vita', *Bianco e Nero: Special Issue on Vittorio De Sica*, 36(9–12): 275–81.
De Sica, V. (1975d), 'Gli anni più belli della mia vita: il pianto di Chaplin', *Bianco e Nero: Special Issue on Vittorio De Sica*, 36(9–12): 281–5.
De Sica, V. (1975e), 'Gli anni più belli della mia vita: Farò ancora l'attore per pagare i miei film', *Bianco e Nero: Special Issue on Vittorio De Sica*, 36(9–12): 285–9.
De Sica, V. (2004), *La porta del cielo. Memorie 1901–1952*, Cava de' Tirreni: Avagliano.
De Tassis, P. (1982), 'Corpi recuperati per il proprio sguardo', *Memoria*, 3(6): 24–31.
De Valck, M. (2016), 'Fostering Art, Adding Value, Cultivating Taste. Film Festivals as Sites of Cultural Legitimization', in M. de Valck, B. Kredell, and S. Loist (eds), *Film Festivals: History, Theory, Method, Practice*, 100–16, Amsterdam: Amsterdam University Press.
Dever, M., S. Newman, and A. Vickery (2010), 'The Intimate Archive', *Archives and Manuscripts*, 38(1): 94–137.
Di Biagi, F. (2009), 'Cinema/personaggi/Il Gary Cooper dei poveri', http://oggi7.info/2009/09/03/2375-cinema-personaggi-il-gary-cooper-dei-poveri.
Dickie, J. (1999), *Darkest Italy: The Nation and Stereotypes of the Mezzogiorno, 1860–1900*, Basingstoke: Palgrave Macmillan.
Didi-Huberman, G. (2009), 'People Exposed, People as Extras', *Radical Philosophy*, 156: 16–22.
Di Giammatteo, F. (1949), 'Agonia dell'attore', *La fiera letteraria*, 4(4): 6.
Di Lasscio, A., and S. Ortolani (2010), *Istituzioni di diritto e legislazione dello spettacolo. Dal 1860 al 2010, i 150 anni dell'Unità d'Italia nello spettacolo*, Milan: FrancoAngeli.
Distelmeyer, J. (2012), 'Frames for Ambivalence: Acting Out Realism in Italian Neorealism and the Films of Christian Petzold', in J. Sternagel, D. Levitt, and D. Mersch (eds), *Acting and Performance in Moving Image Culture*, 145–57, Bielefeld: Transcript.
Donadio, R. (2016), 'For Its Star, *Dheepan* Was the Role of His Lifetime', *New York Times*, 20 April. https://www.nytimes.com/2016/04/24/movies/for-its-star-dheepan-was-therole-of-his-lifetime.html.
Donahue, D. (1985), 'Cambodian Doctor Haing Ngor Turns Actor in the Killing Fields, and Relives His Grisly Past', *People*, 4 February: 43.
Dragosei, I. (1945), 'Cinema senza Cinecittà', *Star*, 2(43): 2.
Dragosei, I. (1946), 'Non siamo sciuscià!', *Film d'oggi*, 2(19): 10.
Drake, P. (2006), 'Reconceptualizing Screen Performance', *Journal of Film and Video*, 58(1–2): 84–94.
Driscoll, C. (2002), *Girls: Feminine Adolescence in Popular Culture and Cultural Theory*, New York: Columbia University Press.
Duncan, D. (2008), 'Italy's Postcolonial Cinema and Its Histories of Representation', *Italian Studies*, 63(2): 195–211.
Duncan, D. (2020), 'Trans-regional Optics and Queer Affiliations in the Work of Jonas Carpignano', in J. S. Williams (ed.), *Queering the Migrant in Contemporary European Cinema*, 188–200, London: Routledge.

Durney, E. (2022), 'Johnny Depp's Former Agent Testified That Movie Studios Were "Reluctant" to Hire Him Because of His "Unprofessional Behavior" on Set', *BuzzfeedNews*, 14 May. https://www.buzzfeednews.com/article/ellendurney/johnny-depp-agent-unprofessional-testimony.
Dyer, R. (1987), *Heavenly Bodies: Film Stars and Society*, London: Macmillan.
Dyer, R. (1998), *Stars*, London: BFI.
Dyer, R. (2006), 'Music, People and Reality: The Case of Italian Neorealism', in M. Mera and D. Burnand (eds), *European Film Music*, 26–40, Farnham: Ashgate.
E. Cost. (2001), 'Cecchi D'Amico: più crudo del nostro film', *Corriere della Sera*, 5 December: 38.
Eaton, S. (2019), 'To Catch a Bicycle Thief: David O. Selznick's Failed Attempt to Co-Opt the Neorealist Classic', *The Italianist*, 39(2): 222–30.
Egan, D. (2020), *America's Film Legacy: The Authoritative Guide to the Landmark Movies in the National Film Registry*, London: A & C Black.
Ellena, L. (2015), 'Geografie della razza nel cinema italiano del primo dopoguerra 1945–1955', in G. Giuliani (ed.), *Il colore della nazione*, 17–31, Florence: Le Monnier.
Ellero, R. (1987), 'Protagonista di una stagione indimenticabile', in R. Ellero, M. Gottardi and A. Marzo (eds), *Aldò: tra cinema e fotografia*, 8–9, Venice: Comune di Venezia. Assessorato alla Cultura.
Errico, L. (2011), 'Alessandra Di Sanzo a *Verissimo*: "Ci sono trans cattivissime"', *Conto Corrente*, 14 October. https://www.newnotizie.it/2011/10/14/alessandra-di-sanzo-a-verissimo-ci-sono-trans-cattivissime/.
Eugeni, R. (2006), 'Il dibattito teorico', in O. Caldiron (ed.), *Storia del cinema italiano, vol 5 – 1934–1939*, 521–36, Venice: Marsilio.
Fabbri, D. (1949). 'Neorealismo italiano: segno di contraddizione', *Rivista del Cinematografo*, 1(22): 10–11.
Fabbri, L. (2015), 'Neorealism as Ideology: Bazin, Deleuze, and the Avoidance of Fascism', *The Italianist*, 35(2): 182–201.
Fabbri, L. (2016), 'Chrono-Maps: The Time of the South in Antonio Gramsci, Luchino Visconti, and Emanuele Crialese', *Senses of Cinema*, 81. http://sensesofcinema.com/2016/feature-articles/chrono-maps-the-time-of-the-south-in-antonio-gramsci-luchino-visconti-and-emanuele-crialese/.
Faldini, F., and G. Fofi (1979), *L'avventurosa storia del cinema italiano: raccontata dai suoi protagonisti 1935–1959*, Milan: Feltrinelli.
Farassino, A. (1988), 'Il costo dei panni sporchi. Note sul modo di produzione neorealista', in V. Zagarrio (ed.), *Dietro lo schermo. Ragionamenti sui modi di produzione cinematografici in Italia*, 135–43, Venice: Marsilio.
Farassino, A. (2003), 'Gli attori neorealisti', in C. Cosulich (ed.), *Storia del cinema italiano, vol. VII (1945–48)*, 340–1, Venice: Marsilio.
Farrier, D. (2008), 'The Journey Is the Film is the Journey: Michael Winterbottom's *In This World*', *Research in Drama Education*, 13(2): 223–32.
Ferreri, G. (1944), 'Passo d'addio al Centro Sperimentale', *Star*, 1(14): 4.
Finos, A. (2019), '*Selfie*, amicizia e camorra nel cellulare. Il regista: "Gli attori, il realismo che fa impallidire i sociologi"', *La Repubblica*, 9 February. https://www.repubblica.it/spettacoli/cinema/2019/02/09/news/_selfie_-218721859/.
Fiore, I. (1948), 'I milioni del neo-realismo', *Rivista del cinematografo*, 21(11): 14–15.

Fisher, J. (2001), 'Who's Watching the Rubble-Kids? Youth, Pedagogy, and Politics in Early DEFA Films', *New German Critique*, 82: 91–125.

Fisher, J. (2007), 'On the Ruins of Masculinity: The Figure of the Child in Italian Neorealism and the German Rubble Film', in L. Ruberto and K. Wilson (eds), *Italian Neorealism and Global Cinema*, 25–53, Detroit, MI: Wayne State University Press.

Forlenza, R., and B. Thomassen (2016), *Italian Modernities: Competing Narratives of Nationhood*, New York: Palgrave Macmillan.

Fortini, F. (1973), *Dieci inverni 1947–1957. Contributi ad un discorso socialista*, Bari: De Donato.

Fortmueller, K. (2016), 'Encounters at the Margins of Hollywood: Casting and Location Shooting for *Bhowani Junction*', *Film History*, 28(4): 100–24.

Fortmueller, K. (2021), *Below the Stars. How the Labor of Working Actors and Extras Shapes Media Production*, Austin: University of Texas Press.

Francese, J. (2007), 'The Influence of Cesare Zavattini on Latin American Cinema: Thoughts on *El joven Rebelde* and *Juan Quin Quin*', *Quarterly Review of Film and Video*, 24(5): 431–44.

Gabara, R. (2007), '"A Poetics of Refusals": Neorealism from Italy to Africa', in L. Ruberto and K. Wilson (eds), *Italian Neorealism and Global Cinema*, 187–206, Detroit, MI: Wayne State University Press.

Gaggiotti, M. (2019), *Nonprofessional Performance in Fiction Film: Historical Perspectives and Contemporary Approaches*. PhD diss., University of Bristol.

Gaggiotti, M. (2021), 'The Non-Professional Actor in European Cinema', in G. Gergely and S. Hayward (eds), *The Routledge Companion to European Cinema*, 243–51, New York: Routledge.

Gaggiotti, M. (2022), 'The Corruption of Non-professional Performance: Pasolini and *Salò*', *Screen*, 63(2): 182–205.

Gallagher, C., and S. Greenblatt (2000), *Practicing New Historicism*, Chicago: University of Chicago Press.

Gallagher, T. (2006), *The Adventures Of Roberto Rossellini: His Life and Films*, New York: Da Capo Press.

Gamberini, F. (2020), 'Intervista a Phaim Bhuiyan, regista e protagonista di "Bangla"', *Parole a colori*, 6 August. https://www.paroleacolori.com/intervista-a-phaim-bhuiyan-regista-e-protagonista-di-bangla/.

Gandin, M. (1951), 'Storia di una crisi in *Bellissima* di Visconti', *Cinema*, 75: 292–5.

Gandin, M. (1953a), 'Diamo agli attori scuole e insegnanti', *Cinema Nuovo*, 37: 8–10.

Gandin, M. (1953b), 'Fanno il cinema guardandosi allo specchio', *Cinema Nuovo*, 7: 180–1.

Gandin, M. (ed.) (1956), *Il tetto di Vittorio de Sica*, Bologna: Cappelli.

Gardner, C. (2016), 'Why Has *Tangerine* Star Been MIA during Awards Season?', *The Hollywood Reporter*, 27 February. https://www.hollywoodreporter.com/movies/movie-news/why-has-tangerine-star-been-868538/.

Garofalo, A. (1956), 'L'inflazione delle curve', *Cinema Nuovo*, 74: 110.

Garofalo, P. (2002), 'Seeing Red: The Soviet Influence on Italian Cinema in the Thirties', in J. Reich and P. Garofalo (eds), *Re-Viewing Fascism: Italian Cinema, 1922–1943*, 223–49, Bloomington: Indiana University Press.

G. D. (1954), 'Hanno eletto Caterina', *Cinema Nuovo*, 28: 43.

Gelley, O. (2012), *Stardom and the Aesthetics of Neorealism*, New York: Routledge.

Geraghty, C. (2000), 'Re-examining Stardom: Questions of Texts, Bodies and Performance', in C. Glpedhill and L. Williams (eds), *Reinventing Film Studies*, 183–202, London: Arnold.

Gergely, G. (2014), '*Los Olvidados/The Young and the Damned* (1950): A Damning Verdict on Neorealism's Aesthetic and Moral Positions', in D. Hipkins and R. Pitt (eds), *New Visions of the Child in Italian Cinema*, 103–28, Bern: Peter Lang.

Giani, R. (1949), '"Predive" col cuore a fumetti', *Cinema*, 17: 524–6.

Gibson, M. (1998), 'Biology or Environment? Race and Southern "Deviancy" in the Writings of Italian Criminologists, 1990–1920', in J. Schneider (ed.), *Italy's 'Southern Question': Orientalism in One Country*, 99–116, Oxford: Berg.

Gilardelli, A. (2013), 'Lollo vs. Marylin. La rappresentazione del corpo femminile nel cinema e sulle riviste degli anni Cinquanta', *Immagine. Note di storia del cinema*, 7: 73–96.

Ginsborg, P. (1990), *A History of Contemporary Italy: Society and Politics: 1943–1980*, London: Penguin.

Giori, M., and T. Subini (2014), 'Questioni aperte su *La terra trema*. Ipotesi preliminari intorno ad alcuni nuovi documenti', *Cabiria*, 176: 4–36.

Giovacchini, S. (2012), 'Living in Peace after the Massacre. Neorealism, Colonialism, and Race', in R. Sklar and S. Giovacchini (eds), *Global Neorealism: The Transnational History of a Film Style*, 141–59, Jackson: University Press of Mississippi.

Giovacchini, S. (2015), 'John Kitzmiller, Euro-American Difference, and the Cinema of the West', *Black Camera*, 6(2): 17–41.

Gleghorn, C. (2017), 'A Star is Born: The Rising Profile of the Non-professional in Recent Brazilian Cinema', in T. Bergfelder, L. Shaw, and J. Luiz Vieira (eds), *Stars and Stardom in Brazilian Cinema*, 210–26, London: Berghahn.

Gleiberman, O. (2018), 'Film Review: *Roma*', *Variety*, 30 August. https://variety.com/2018/film/reviews/roma-review-alfonso-cuaron-1202919033/.

Glynn, P. (2019), 'Katie Jarvis: Ex-EastEnders Actress Felt "Degraded" by Job-shaming Story', 22 October. https://www.bbc.co.uk/news/50125396.

Glynn, R. (2019), 'Decolonizing the Body of Naples: Elena Ferrante's Neapolitan Novels', *Annali d'italianistica*, 37, 261–88.

Gobbato, E. (2011), 'Non accreditata. Goliarda Sapienza invisibile protagonista del cinema italiano', in L. Cardone and S. Filippelli (eds), *Cinema e scritture femminili*, 106–18, Guidonia: Iacobelli.

Godard, J.-L., and M. Delahaye (1967), 'The Question, Robert Bresson Interview', *Cahiers du Cinéma in English*, 8: 5–27.

Goodridge, L. (2022), 'Professionalism as a Racial Construct', *UCLA Law Review*, 38: 39–54.

Gordon, R. S. C. G. (2008), *Bicycle Thieves*, London: BFI.

Gorfinkel, E. (2012), 'The Body's Failed Labor: Performance Work in Sexploitation Cinema', *Framework*, 53(1): 79–98.
Gossman, L. (2003), 'Anecdote and History', *History and Theory*, 42(2): 143–68.
Governi, G. (1981), *Nannarella*, Milan: Bompiani.
Grande, M. (1992), 'Attore', in G. Moneti (ed.), *Lessico zavattiniano: parole e idee su cinema e dintorni*, 31–8, Venice: Marsilio.
Graver, D. (1997), 'The Actor's Bodies', *Text and Performance Quarterly*, 17(3): 221–35.
Greene, S. (2012), *Equivocal Subjects: Between Italy and Africa – Constructions of Racial and National Identity in the Italian Cinema*, New York: Bloomsbury.
Greene, N. (2017), *Pier Paolo Pasolini: Cinema as Heresy*, Princeton, NJ: Princeton University Press.
Greenwood, D. (2018), 'Meet the Stars of Kenya's Banned Lesbian Drama', *i-D Magazine*, 14 May. https://i-d.vice.com/en/article/zm8eaj/meet-the-stars-of-kenyas-banned-lesbian-drama-rafiki.
Grespi, B. (2015), 'Italian Neo-Realism between Cinema and Photography', in S. Hill and G. Minghelli (eds), *Stillness in Motion: Italy, Photography, and the Meanings of Modernity*, 183–216, Toronto: University of Toronto Press.
Griffith, B. (1995), 'Italian Cinema in the Thirties: *Camicia nera* and Other Films by Giovacchino Forzano', *The Italianist*, 15(1): 299–321.
Grignaffini, G. (1988), 'Female Identity and Italian Cinema of the 1950s', in G. Bruno and M. Nadotti (eds), *Off Screen: Women and Film in Italy*, 111–23, London: Routledge.
Grignaffini, G. (1989), 'Lo stato dell'unione: appunti sull'industria cinematografica italiana, 1945-1949', in A. Farassino (ed.), *Neorealismo: cinema italiano 1945–1949*, 37–44, Turin: EDT.
Grosoli, M. (2011), 'The Privileged Animal: The Myth of Childhood and the Myth of Realism According to André Bazin', *Red Feather Journal*, 2: 59–67. http://nebula.wsimg.com/f6352bdd1c57237a5d628d12515a7c1e?AccessKeyId=F0152308703B0C3D5115&disposition=0&alloworigin=1.
Guarini, A. (1953), 'Il neorealismo e l'industria', *Cinema*, 123: 320–3.
Gundle, S. (1995), 'Sophia Loren, Italian Icon', *Historical Journal of Film, Radio, and Television*, 15(3): 367–85.
Gundle, S. (1999), 'Feminine Beauty, National Identity and Political Conflict in Postwar Italy, 1945-1954', *Contemporary European History*, 8(3): 350–78.
Gundle, S. (2000), *Between Hollywood and Moscow: The Italian Communists and the Challenge of Mass Culture, 1943–1991*, Durham, NC: Duke University Press.
Gundle, S. (2002), 'Hollywood Glamour and Mass Consumption in Postwar Italy', *Journal of Cold War Studies*, 4(3): 95–118.
Gundle, S. (2007), *Bellissima: Feminine Beauty and the Idea of Italy*, New Haven, CT: Yale University Press.
Gundle, S. (2013), *Mussolini's Dream Factory: Film Stardom in Fascist Italy*, London: Berghahn.
Gundle, S. (2019), *Fame Amid the Ruins: Italian Film Stardom in the Age of Neorealism*, London: Berghahn.

Hallam, J., and M. Marshment (2000), *Realism and Popular Cinema*, Manchester: Manchester University Press.
Halperin, P. (2012), '"With an Incredible Realism That Beats the Best of the European Cinemas". The Making of *Barrio gris* and the Reception of Italian Neorealism in Argentina, 1947–1955', in R. Sklar and S. Giovacchini (eds), *Global Neorealism: The Transnational History of a Film Style*, 125–40, Jackson: University Press of Mississippi.
Harbord, J. (2012), *Film Cultures*, London: Sage.
Harbord, J. (2016), 'Contingency, Time, and Event: An Archaeological Approach to the Film Festival', in M. de Valck, B. Kredell and S. Loist (eds), *Film Festivals: History, Theory, Method, Practice*, 69–82, London: Routledge.
Harris, A. (2004), *Future Girl: Young Women in the Twenty-First Century*, New York: Routledge.
Harris, C. (1999), '*Nero su bianco*. Examining the Presence of the African-American Soldier in Rossellini's *Paisà*', in D. Ashyk, F. Gardaphe and A. Tamburri (eds), *Shades of Black and White: Conflict and Collaboration between Two Communities*, 211–17, New York: American Italian Historical Association.
Harris, C. (2001), 'Nero su bianco: the Africanist Presence in Twentieth-century Italy and its Cinematic Representations', in S. Matteo (ed.), *ItaliAfrica: Bridging Continents and Cultures*, 281–303, Stony Brook, NY: Forum Italicum Publishing.
Hartman, S. (2018), 'On Working with Archives. An Interview with Writer Saidiya Hartman. From a Conversation with Thora Siemsen', *The Creative Independent*, 18 April. https://thecreativeindependent.com/people/saidiya-hartman-on-working-with-archives/
Hartman, S. (2019), *Wayward Lives, Beautiful Experiments: Intimate Histories of Social Upheaval*, New York: Serpent's Tail.
Harvey, C. (2019), '*Piranhas (La Paranza dei Bambini*) press conference with Claudio Giovannesi, Roberto Saviano and Francesco Di Napoli', *The Upcoming*. 13 February. https://www.theupcoming.co.uk/2019/02/13/piranhas-la-paranza-dei-bambini-press-conference-with-claudio-giovannesi-roberto-saviano-and-francesco-di-napoli/
Hastie, A. (2019), 'The Vulnerable Spectator–An Act of Will, a Testimony of Love: Alfonso Cuarón's *Roma*', *Film Quarterly*, 72(4): 54–60.
Hawkins, R. F. (1952), 'In Rome, the People are the Movie Stars', *The New York Times*, 21 September: 112, 240, 283, 284.
Hedling, O. (2015), 'The Trouble with Stars. Vernacular versus Global Stardom in Two Forms of European Popular Culture', in M. Harrod, M. Liz and A. Timoshkina (eds), *The Europeanness of European Cinema: Identity, Meaning, Globalization*, 117–30, London: Bloomsbury.
Hicks, J. (2016), 'Soiuzdetfilm: The Birth of Soviet Children's Film and the Child Actor', in B. Beumers (ed.), *A Companion to Russian Cinema*, 141–61, Oxford: Wiley-Blackwell.
Higbee, W. (2019), '"Beyond Ethnicity" or a Return to Type? *Bande de filles/Girlhood* and the Politics of Blackness in Contemporary French Cinema', in K. Kleppinger and L. Reeck (eds), *Post-Migratory Cultures in Postcolonial France*, 166–82, Liverpool: Liverpool University Press.

Higson, A. (1986), 'Film Acting and Independent Cinema', *Screen*, 27(3–4): 110–32.
Hipkins, D., and R. Pitt (eds) (2014), *New Visions of the Child in Italian Cinema*, Bern: Peter Lang.
Hipkins, D. (2016), *Italy's 'Other Women': Gender and Prostitution in Italian Cinema*, Bern: Peter Lang.
Hipkins, D. (2017), 'Surviving the "Showgirl Effect"?: Tween Girls and Performance in *Le meraviglie/The Wonders* (Alice Rohrwacher 2014) and *Bellas mariposas* (Salvatore Mereu 2012)', in S. Storchi, M. Spunta, and M. Morelli (eds), *Women and the Public Sphere in Modern and Contemporary Italy*, 159–71, Leicester: Troubador.
Hochkofler, M. (1975), 'Il grande inganno', *Bianco e Nero: Special Issue on Vittorio De Sica*, 36(9–12): 209–11.
Hope, W. (2016), 'The Roma in New Millennium Italian Fiction Films: Dissensus, Liminality, Emancipation', *The Italianist*, 36(2): 266–86.
Huyssens, A. (1986), 'Mass Culture as Woman', in *After the Great Divide: Modernism, Mass Culture, Postmodernism*, 44–62, Bloomington: Indiana University Press.
I. A. M. (1948). 'Merito del silenzio e valore di *Sotto il sole di Roma*', *Araldo dello Spettacolo*, 9–12 February: 4.
Iaccio, P. (2006), *Rossellini: dal neorealismo alla diffusione della conoscenza*, Naples: Liguori.
Jacobson, H. (1949), 'De Sica's *Bicycle Thieves* and Italian Humanism', *Hollywood Quarterly*, 4(1): 28–33.
Jandelli, C. (2013), '"Cerchiamo un bambino distinto": La genesi di *Bellissima* nei soggetti di Cesare Zavattini', *Quaderni d'italianistica*, 34(2): 47–64.
Johnson, R., and R. Stam (1995), *Brazilian Cinema*, New York: Columbia University Press.
Johnson, R. (2019), 'The Ideology of Film Festivals: A Psychoanalysis of European a Festivals' Representation of Italian Cinema, 2000–2017'. PhD diss, Leeds University.
Joubert-Laurencin. H., and D. Andrew (2011), *Opening Bazin: Postwar Film Theory and its Afterlife*, Oxford: Oxford University Press.
Kael. P. (1965), *I Lost It at the Movies*, New York: Doubleday.
Kahana, J. (2009), 'Introduction: What Now? Presenting Reenactment', to *Dossier: Reenactment in Contemporary Documentary Film, Video, and Performance*, *Framework*, 50(1–2): 46–50.
Katuszewsk, P., and S. Donath (2020), 'Amateur Choruses: The Professionalization of the Choric Form', *Performance Research*, 25(1): 73–80.
Kear, A. (2005), 'Troublesome Amateurs: Theatre, Ethics and the Labour of Mimesis', *Performance Research*, 10(1): 26–46.
Kenaga, H. (2015), 'Making the "Studio Girl": The Hollywood Studio Club and Industry Regulation of Female Labour', *Cinema Journal*, 55(1): 129–39.
Kennedy, M. (2005), 'Soul Slaves: The Politics and Ethics of the Use of Non-Actors in the Films of Francesco Rosi and Pier Paolo Pasolini', *Body, Space, and Technology*, 5(1), https://www.bstjournal.com/article/id/6672/

Kezich, T. (2006), 'Gli attori italiani dalla preistoria al monopolio', in O. Caldiron (ed.), *Storia del cinema italiano, vol. V (1934–1939)*, 383–403, Venice: Marsilio.

Khan, H. (2009), 'Slumdog Symphony: A Chat with Danny Boyle', *ABC News*, 28 January. https://web.archive.org/web/20121015021437/https://abcnews.go.com/blogs/politics/2009/01/slumdog-symphon/

Khan, C. (2021), 'Sexting, Lies and Unveiled Selfies: The Egyptian Film Exploring the Hidden Lives of Teenage Girls', *The Guardian*, 19 August. https://www.theguardian.com/film/2021/aug/19/sexting-sin-and-social-media-the-egyptian-film-exploring-the-hidden-lives-of-teenage-girls

King, B. (1985), 'Articulating Stardom', *Screen*, 26(5): 27–51.

Kirby, M. (1972), 'On Acting and Not-Acting', *The Drama Review*, 16(1): 3–15.

Kiss, A. L. (2015), 'Reflections on the Creativity of Non-Actors Under Restrictive Direction', *Spectator*, 35(2): 27–35.

Kohlert, F. (2014), 'In the Ghetto: Sociology, the Cagney Gangster, and the "Dead End" Kids in *Angels with Dirty Faces*', *The Journal of Popular Culture*, 47(4): 857–76.

Kracauer, S. (1995), *The Mass Ornament: Weimar Essays*, ed. and trans. T. Levin, Cambridge, MA: Harvard University Press.

Kracauer, S. (2004), 'Remarks on the Actor', in P. Wojcik (ed.), *Movie Acting: The Film Reader*, 19–27, London: Routledge.

Krstic, I. (2016), *Slums on Screen: World Cinema and the Planet of Slums*, Edinburgh: Edinburgh University Press.

Lalonde, G. (1983), 'Agenzia attori', in G. Aristarco (ed.), *Il mito dell'attore: come l'industria della star produce il sex symbol*, 307–10, Rome: Dedalo.

Lancia, E., and R. Poppi (2003a), *Le attrici: dal 1930 ai giorni nostri*, Rome: Gremese.

Lancia, E., and R. Poppi (2003b), *Gli attori: dal 1930 ai giorni nostri, vol II (M-Z)*, Rome: Gremese.

Landrigan, S., and Q. A. Omar (2012), *Shakespeare in Kabul*, London: Haus.

Landy, M. (2004), 'Diverting Clichés: Femininity, Masculinity, Melodrama, and Neorealism in *Open City*', in S. Gottlieb (ed.), *Roberto Rossellini's Rome Open City*, 85–105, Cambridge: Cambridge University Press.

Lanocita, A. (1947), 'Rassegna cinematografica', *Corriere della Sera*, 20 May: 2.

LaPlace, M. (1987), 'Producing and Consuming the Woman's Film: Discursive Struggle in *Now, Voyager*', in C. Gledhill, *Home Is Where the Heart Is: Studies in Melodrama and the Woman's Film*, 138–66, London: BFI.

Lashmar, P. (2014), 'How to Humiliate and Shame: A Reporter's Guide to the Power of the Mugshot', *Social Semiotics*, 24(1): 56–87.

Lavery, B. (2002), 'In Ulster, Reliving Its Day of Infamy', *The New York Times*, 29 September: 25.

Lawrence, M. (2011), 'Hindianizing *Heidi*: Working Children in Abdul Rashid Kardar's *Do Phool*', *Adaptation*, 5(1): 101–18.

Lawrence, M. (2019a), '"United Nations Children" in Hollywood Cinema: Juvenile Actors and Humanitarian Sentiment in the 1940s', in M. Lawrence and R. Tavernor (eds), *Global Humanitarianism and Media Culture*, 15–38, Manchester: Manchester University Press.

Lawrence, M. (2019b), *Sabu*, London: BFI/Palgrave Macmillan.

Leavitt, C. (2018), 'Notes on the End of *Rome, Open City*', *Journal of Italian Cinema and Media Studies*, 6(3): 359–72.
Leavitt, C. (2020), *Italian Neorealism: A Cultural History*, Toronto: University of Toronto Press.
Lebeau, V. (2008), *Childhood and Cinema*, London: Reaktion.
Leeker, M. (2017), 'Performing (the) Digital: Positions of Critique in Digital Cultures', in M. Leeker, I. Schipper, and T. Beyes (eds), *Performing the Digital: Performativity and Performance Studies in Digital Cultures*, 21–59, Bielefeld: Transcript.
Leeker, M., I. Schipper, and T. Beyes (eds) (2017), 'Performativity, Performance Studies and Digital Cultures', in M. Leeker, I. Schipper and T. Beyes (eds), *Performing the Digital: Performativity and Performance Studies in Digital Cultures*, 10–18, Bielefeld: Transcript.
Lento, M. (2017), *La scoperta dell'attore cinematografico in Europa. Attorialità, esperienza filmica e ostentazione durante la seconde époque*, Pisa: ETS.
Leprini, M. (2018), *Le olimpiadi della bellezza. Storia del concorso di Miss Italia 1946–1964*. PhD diss., University of Urbino.
Linthicum, K. (2021), 'His First Movie was Shortlisted for an Oscar. What's Next for Mexico's Overnight Star?', *The Los Angeles Times*, 10 May. https://www.latimes.com/entertainment-arts/movies/story/2021-05-10/im-no-longer-here-movie-juan-daniel-garcia-trevino
Lizzani, C. (1945), 'Roma città aperta', *Film d'oggi*,1(20): 6.
Lizzani, C. (1978), 'Neorealismo come fucina di nuovi attori e scuola per il cinema di Hollywood', *Cinecritica*, 1: 38–41.
Lobalzo Wright, J. (2017), *Crossover Stardom: Popular Male Music Stars in American Cinema*, London: Bloomsbury.
Lollobrigida, G. (1954), 'Gina difende il cinema italiano', *Oggi*, 26 August: 11–13.
Lottini, I. (2013), '"Il delirio del lungo metraggio": Cinema as Mass Phenomenon in Early Twentieth-Century Italian Culture', in L. Bayman and S. Rigoletto (eds), *Popular Italian Cinema*, 147–62, Basingstoke: Palgrave Macmillan.
Lowe, V. (2016), 'Ontological Hesitations and Performing Codes Unknown: Haneke, Kiarostami, Binoche and the "Idea" of the Screen Actor', *Studies in European Cinema*, 13(3): 200–13.
L. U. (1951). 'Per *Due soldi di speranza* ci voleva il sole di Castellammare di Stabia un balcone e una fanciulla bruna che non sognava il cinema. Castellani ha trovato alfine la protagonista del film', *Araldo dello Spettacolo*, 41(27–28): 2.
Lu, J. (2014), 'Walking on the Margins: From Italian Neorealism to Contemporary Chinese Sixth Generation', *Journal of Italian Cinema and Media Studies*, 2(3): 317–33.
Lughi, P. (1989), 'Il neorealismo in sala. Anteprime di gala e teniture di massa', in A. Farassino (ed.), *Neorealismo. Cinema italiano 1945–1949*, 53–60, Turin: EDT.
Lumby, C. (2007), 'Doing It for Themselves? Teenage Girls, Sexuality and Fame', in S. Redmond and S. Holmes (eds), *A Reader in Stardom and Celebrity*, 341–52, London: Sage.
Lury, K. (2010), *The Child in Film: Tears, Fears and Fairy Tales*, London: Bloomsbury.

Maggi, R. (1939), 'Alcuni criteri per la selezione dei cineartisti', *Bianco e Nero*, 3(1): 15–30.

Maggiore, M. (1952), 'Attore non professionista e anonimia del personaggio', *L'Eco del Cinema*, 3(17): 6–7.

Maida, B. (2019), 'L'infanzia in Italia nel secondo dopoguerra', in C. Allasia, B. Maida and F. Prono (eds), *Infanzia e povertà: storie e narrazioni nell'Italia del dopoguerra (1945–1950)*, 29–45, Turin: Edizioni Sinestesie.

Majumdar, N. (2012), 'Importing Neorealism, Exporting Cinema. Indian Cinema and Film Festivals in the 1950s', in R. Sklar and S. Giovacchini (eds), *Global Neorealism: The Transnational History of a Film Style*, 178–93, Jackson: University Press of Mississippi.

Malavade, S., and L. Mishra (2020), '*Slumdog Millionaire* Star Azharuddin Ismail Back in Slums', *Mumbai Mirror*, 25 January. https://mumbaimirror.indiatimes.com/mumbai/cover-story/slumdog-star-back-in-slums/articleshow/73598481.cms

Malerba, L. (2018), *Le lettere di Ottavia*, Milan: Archinto.

Maltby, R. (2003), *Hollywood Cinema*, Oxford: Wiley-Blackwell.

Mancini, M., and Sciacca, F. (1981), *La città-set: La terra trema di Luchino Visconti*, Rome: Theorema.

Mandelli, E., and V. Re (2019), '"Le bellezze italiane sono tutte curve". Identità in conflitto sulle pagine di *Cinema Nuovo* (1952–1958)', in S. Parigi, C. Uva and V. Zagarrio (eds), *Cinema e identità italiana*, 253–68, Rome: Edizioni RomaTrePress.

Mandelli, E., and V. Re (2021), *Le belle donne ci piacciono. E come! Cinema Nuovo, cultura comunista e modelli di mascolinità (1952–1958)*, Parma: Diabasis.

Manzoli, G., and A. Minuz (2017), 'Le forme simboliche: sintassi, semantica e pragmatica dell'interesse culturale', in M. Cucco and G. Manzoli (eds), *Il cinema di stato: finanziamento pubblico ed economia simbolica nel cinema italiano contemporaneo*, 171–23, Bologna: Il Mulino.

Marcantonio, C. (2019), '*Roma*: Silence, Language, and the Ambiguous Power of Affect', *Film Quarterly*, 72(4). https://filmquarterly.org/2019/06/07/roma-silence-language-and-the-ambiguous-power-of-affect/

Marcus, M. (1987), *Italian Film in the Light of Neorealism*, Princeton, NJ: Princeton University Press.

Marcus, M. (1999), 'Visconti's *Bellissima*: The Diva, the Mirror and the Screen', *Italian Culture*, 17(1): 9–17.

Marcus, M. (2008), 'Pina's Pregnancy, Traumatic Realism, and the After-Life of *Open City*', *Italica*, 85(4): 426–38.

Marcus, S. (2019), *The Drama of Celebrity*, Princeton, NJ: Princeton University Press.

Margadonna, E. (1950). 'La legge della vendetta', *Araldo dello Spettacolo*, 18 September: 1–2.

Margulies, I. (2019), *In Person: Reenactment in Postwar and Contemporary Cinema*, Oxford: Oxford University Press.

Marinese, L. (1946), 'Sono necessari gli attori?', *Film d'oggi*, 2(20): 6.

Marlow-Mann, A. (2011), *The New Neapolitan Cinema*, Edinburgh: Edinburgh University Press.

Marlow-Mann, A. (2014), 'Subjectivity and the Ethnographic Gaze in Antonio Capuano's *Vito e gli altri*', in D. Hipkins and R. Pitt (eds), *New Visions of the Child in Italian Cinema*, 267–84, Bern: Peter Lang.

Marmo, L. (2018), *Roma e il cinema del dopoguerra. Neorealismo, melodramma, noir*, Rome: Bulzoni.

Martera, L. (2021). *Harlem: Il film più censurato di sempre*, Milan: La Nave di Teseo.

Marquis, E. (2013), 'Conceptualizing Documentary Performance', *Studies in Documentary Film*, 7(1): 45–60.

Martínez-Expósito, A. (2018), 'Southern Hegemonies and Metaphors of the Global South in *También la lluvia*', in C. Rocha and C. Sandberg (eds), *Contemporary Latin American Cinema. Resisting Neoliberalism?*, 27–42, New York: Palgrave Macmillan.

Martini, S. (1952), 'Vietati due soldi di speranza a Romeo e Giulietta', *Cinema*, 85: 231–3.

Martini, S. (1955), 'Le inchieste di *Cinema Nuovo*. Natale e Luisa', *Cinema Nuovo*, 71: 377–84.

Marucci, S. (2018), 'Cannes 2018. *Ladri di biciclette* ha 70 anni, curiosità su uno dei film più celebrati della storia del cinema', 16 May, https://www.articolo21.org/2018/05/cannes-2018-ladri-di-biciclette-ha-70-anni-curiosita-su-uno-dei-film-piu-celebrati-della-storia-del-cinema

Masecchia, A. (2017a), 'L'attrice e il torero: storia di Lucia, in arte Bosè', *Arabeschi*, 10, Special Issue on *Vaghe stelle. Attrici del/nel cinema italiano*. http://www.arabeschi.it/53-lattrice-e-il-torero-storia-di-lucia-in-arte-bos-/

Masecchia, A. (2017b), 'Maddalena, Clara e le altre: la vita sognata dello schermo', in G. Carluccio, E. Morreale, and M. Pierini (eds), *Intorno al neorealismo. Voci, contesti, linguaggi e culture dell'Italia del dopoguerra*, 191–9, Milan: Scalpendi.

Masi, S. (1987), 'Scuole di recitazione in Italia', in P. De Tassis and M. Sesti (eds), *Bellissimi. Generazioni di attori a confronto*, 43–50, Ancona: Il Lavoro Editoriale.

Masi, S. (2003), 'Destini diversi dell'attore. L'ascesa del divismo femminile', in C. Cosulich (ed.), *Storia del cinema italiano, vol. VII (1945–48)*, 330–43, Venice: Marsilio.

Mason Brown, J. (1950), 'Struggle for Survival', *The Saturday Review*, 7 January: 30–2.

Mattia, E.G. (1955), 'Interpreti e vita reale', *Filmcritica*, 9(44), 34–6.

Mazzei, L. (2008), 'Al cinematografo da sole. Il cinema descritto dalle donne fra 1898 e 1916', in M. Dall'Asta (ed.), *Non solo dive. Pioniere del cinema italiano*, 257–68, Bologna: Cineteca di Bologna.

M. C. (1945), 'Città aperta', *Quarta Parete*, 1(1): 4.

McDonald, P. (2004), 'Why Study Film Acting?', in C. Baron, D. Carson, and F. Tomasulo (eds), *More Than a Method: Trends and Traditions in Contemporary Film Performance*, 23–41, Detroit: Wayne State University Press.

McDonald, P. (2012), 'Spectacular Acting: on the Exhibitionist Dynamics of Film Star Performance', in J. Sternagel, D. Levitt, D. Mersch, and L. Stern (eds), *Acting and Performance in Moving Image Culture: Bodies, Screens, Renderings*, 61–9, Bielefeld: Transcript.

McDonald, P. (2021), 'Doing, Having, and Getting Work: Acting as Creative Labour', *The Italianist*, 41(2): 267–70.
McGurn, B. (1950), '*Bicycle Thief* Star Seeking Laborer's Job', *New York Herald Tribune*, 6 January.
McNally, K. (2021), *The Stardom Film. Creating the Hollywood Fairy Tale*, London: Wallflower.
Melani, P. (1945), 'De Sica e gli "sciuscià"', *Quarta Parete*, 1(4): 1.
Merjian, A. and R. Welch (2020), 'It's a Neorealist World', *Art in America*, 22 September. https://www.artnews.com/art-in-america/features/italian-neorealism-influence-global-cinema-1234571406/
Mestman, M. (2012), 'From Italian Neorealism to New Latin American Cinema: Ruptures and Continuities during the 1960s', in R. Sklar and S. Giovacchini (eds), *Global Neorealism: The Transnational History of a Film Style*, 163–77, Jackson: University Press of Mississippi.
Miccichè, L. (ed.) (1993), *La terra trema di Visconti: analisi di un capolavoro*, Turin: Lindau.
Miccichè, L, (1994), *Sciuscià di Vittorio De Sica: letture, documenti, testimonianze*, Rome: Cineteca Nazionale.
Miccichè, L. (1998), *Visconti e il neorealismo*, Turin: Lindau.
Mida, M. (1943), 'Il Centro Sperimentale al vaglio', *Cinema*, 170, 46–7.
Mida, M. (1946), 'Discorso sull'attore', *Film d'oggi*, 2(34): 3.
Mida, M. (1952), 'Punto fermo su una discussione: attori professionisti e non professionisti', *Ferrania*, 6(2): 18–19.
Miller, J. (2012), 'Cannes Best-Actor Candidate in Prison, Reportedly for Double Murder', *Vanity Fair*, 18 May. https://www.vanityfair.com/hollywood/2012/05/cannes-best-actor-candidate-aniello-arena-jail-double-murder
Minghelli, G. (2013), *Landscape and Memory in Post-Fascist Italian Film*, London: Routledge.
Minghelli, G. (2020), 'Neorealism', in J. Luzzi (ed.), *Italian Cinema from Silent Screen to Digital Image*, 56–85, London: Bloomsbury.
Minuz, Andrea (2017), 'Il cinema italiano e la retorica antidivistica', in P. Armocida and A. Minuz (eds), *L'attore nel cinema italiano contemporaneo: storia, performance, immagine*, 39–49, Venice: Marsilio.
Mitgang, H. (1952), 'On "Two Pennies Worth of Hope"', *The New York Times*, 26 October: X5.
Modleski, T. (1982), *Loving with a Vengeance: Mass-Produced Fantasies for Women*, Hamden: Archon Books.
Morato, S. (1949), 'Assieme a 450 suoi compagni di lavoro l'interprete di *Ladri di biciclette* licenziato in tronco dalla Breda', *L'Unità*, 20 May: 3.
Moravia, A. (1953), 'Il film conformista', *Cinema Nuovo*, 13: 361.
Moravia, A. (1954), 'Il maresciallo De Sica non andò all'appuntamento', *L'Europeo*, 9(1): 37.
Morin, Edgar (1955), 'Notes pour une sociologie du festival de Cannes', *Temps modernes* 10(114–15): 2273–84.
Morin, E. (2005), *The Stars*, trans. R. Howard. Minneapolis: University of Minnesota Press.
Morreale, E. (2011), *Così piangevano. Il cinema melò nell'Italia degli anni Cinquanta*, Rome: Donzelli.

Morreale, E. (2014), 'Bambino', in R. De Gaetano (ed.), *Lessico del cinema italiano*, Vol. 1, 107–71, Milan-Udine: Mimesis.
Morreale, E. (2020), 'Storia e preistoria dell'attore siciliano', *Fata Morgana Web*, 29 November. https://www.fatamorganaweb.it/dal-modello-figurante-alla-fiction-sulla-mafia/
Morreale, E. (2021), 'The Hidden Work of Acting Coaches and Acting Directors', *The Italianist*, 41(2): 264–6.
Morris, W., and A. O. Scott (2020), 'The Best Actors of 2020', 19 December. https://www.nytimes.com/interactive/2020/12/09/magazine/best-actors.html
Mosconi, E. (2002), 'La commedia italiana: consumo e industria culturale', in M. Fanchi and E. Mosconi (eds), *Spettatori. Forme di consumo e pubblici del cinema in Italia 1930-1960*, 62–87, Venice: Marsilio.
M. S. P. (1996), 'La mia scommessa su Victoire', *L'Unità*, 8 September: 3.
'M. T.' (1946), 'Informazioni dal meridione. Quel che s'è fatto e si vuol fare a Napoli', *Cinetempo*, 2(19): 9.
Mur, M. (2015), 'Who Am I? Acting Style in the Art of Anna Magnani', *Atalante*, 19: 43–50.
Muscio, G. (2004), '*Paisà/Paisan*', in G. Bertellini (ed.), *The Cinema of Italy*, 31–40, London: Wallflower.
Nacache, J. (2005), *L'acteur de cinéma*, Paris: Nathan.
Naficy, H. (2012), 'Neorealism Iranian Style', in R. Sklar and S. Giovacchini (eds), *Global Neorealism: The Transnational History of a Film Style*, 226–39, Jackson: University Press of Mississippi.
Nagib, L. (2006), 'Towards a Positive Definition of World Cinema', in S. Denison and S. Lim (eds), *Remapping World Cinema: Identity, Culture and Politics in Film*, 26–33, London: Wallflower.
Nagib, L. (2017), 'Realist Cinema as World Cinema', in R. Stone, P. Cooke, S. Dennison and A. Marlow-Mann (eds), *The Routledge Companion to World Cinema*, 310–22, London: Routledge.
Naremore, J. (1988), *Acting in the Cinema*, Berkeley: University of California Press.
Nediani, A. (1948), 'Attori e tipi', *Cinema*, 3: 85.
Newland, C. (2020), '*Rocks*: The Making of the Must-See British Film of 2020', *Empire*, 17 September. https://www.empireonline.com/movies/features/rocks-the-making-of-the-must-see-british-film-of-2020/
Niang, S. (2012), 'Neorealism and Nationalist African Cinema', in R. Sklar and S. Giovacchini (eds), *Global Neorealism: The Transnational History of a Film Style*, 194–208, Jackson: University Press of Mississippi.
Niang, M.-F. (2019), *Identités françaises: Banlieues, féminités et universalisme*, Leiden: Brill.
Nobili, N. (1945), 'Girls a cena', *Star*, 2(2): 7.
Noto, P. (2011), *Dal bozzetto ai generi: Il cinema italiano dei primi anni Cinquanta*, Turin: Kaplan.
Noto, P. (2017), 'Blasetti e Bellissima', in N. Dusi and L. Di Francesco (eds), *Bellissima tra scrittura e metacinema*, 219–31, Parma: Diabasis.
Noto, P., and F. Pitassio (2010), *Il cinema neorealista*, Bologna: Archetipo.
Nuzzi, P., and O. Iemma (1997), *De Sica e Zavattini: Parliamo tanto di noi*, Rome: Riuniti.

Obensen, T. (2017), 'Cannes: Jonas Carpignano's *A Ciambra* Is First Film From Martin Scorsese's Emerging Directors Fund', 18 May. https://shadowandact.com/cannes-jonas-carpignanos-a-ciambra-is-first-film-from-martin-scorseses-emerging-directors-fund

O'Connor, J. (2008), *The Cultural Significance of the Child Star*, New York: Routledge.

O'Healy, A. (2014), '[S]comparse', *Italian American Review*, 4(1): 65–7.

O'Leary, A. (2008), 'After Brunetta: Italian Cinema Studies in Italy, 2000 to 2007', *Italian Studies*, 63(2): 279–307.

O'Leary, A. (2017), 'What is Italian Cinema?', *California Italian Studies*, 7(1): 1–26.

O'Leary, A., and C. O'Rawe (2011), 'Against Realism: on a "Certain Tendency" in Italian Film Criticism', *Journal of Modern Italian Studies*, 16(1): 107–28.

Open Roads (2019), 'Agostino Ferrente on *Selfie* and Capturing Teenage Life in Naples'. https://www.youtube.com/watch?v=Yp7Ld_NfBYU

O'Rawe, C. (2008), '"I padri e i maestri": Genre, Auteurs, and Absences in Italian Film Studies', *Italian Studies*, 63(2): 173–94.

O'Rawe, C. (2017), 'Anna Magnani: Voice, Body, Accent', in T. Whittaker and S. Wright (eds), *Locating the Voice in Film: Critical Approaches and Global Practices*, 157–72, Oxford: Oxford University Press.

O'Rawe, C. (2018), 'The Non-Professional in the Reception of Italian Cinema Abroad'. https://www.italiancinema.it/the-non-professional-in-the-reception-of-italian-cinema-abroad/

O'Rawe, C. (2019), 'Oscars 2019: *Roma*, Yalitza Aparicio and the Fascinating History of Non-professional Actors', *The Conversation*, 4 February. https://theconversation.com/oscars-2019-roma-yalitza-aparicio-and-the-fascinating-history-of-non-professional-actors-111005

O'Rawe, C. (2020a), 'Raf Vallone. Quando il divo non è inetto', in A. Saponari and F. Zecca (eds), *Oltre l'inetto. Rappresentazioni plurali della mascolinità nel cinema italiano*, 241–54, Milan: Meltemi.

O'Rawe, C. (2020b), 'The Non-Professional Actor in the Reception of Italian Cinema Abroad', *Cinergie*, 18: 73–83.

O'Rawe, C., M. Boccuti, and V. Geri (2023), 'The Non-professional Child Actor in Neorealism: Interview with Alfonso Bovino', *Journal of Italian Cinema and Media*, 11(1): 185–97.

Orsitto, F. (2017), 'Imagining the *Mezzogiorno*: Old and New Paradigms', in F. Burke (ed.), *A Companion to Italian Cinema*, 447–66, Oxford: Wiley-Blackwell.

Ortiz, R. (2018), 'Recuerda, Notes on Alfonso Cuarón's *Roma*', *Mediático*, 24. https://reframe.sussex.ac.uk/mediatico/2018/12/24/special-dossier-on-roma-recuerda-notes-on-alfonso-cuarons-roma/

Pampanini, S. (2004), *Scandalosamente perbene*, Rome: Gremese.

Panattoni, D. (2022), '*Princess*, la recensione: una favola (ir)reale, tra poesia e amarezza', *Movieplayer*, 31 August. https://movieplayer.it/articoli/princess-recensione_27552/

Paolucci, G. (1939), 'Attori ombre e persone', *Bianco e Nero*, 3(11): 62–70.

Papalia, G. (2010), '"Amaro chi ha bisogno": Italy's Racist Episteme and *Il ladro di bambini*', in G. Russo Bullaro (ed.), *From Terrone to Extracomunitario: New*

Manifestations of Racism in Contemporary Italian Cinema, 101–46, Leicester: Troubador.
Parigi, S. (1993), 'Il dualismo linguistico', in L. Miccichè (ed.), *La terra trema di Visconti: analisi di un capolavoro*, 141–64, Turin: Lindau.
Parigi, S. (1994), 'I bambini di De Sica', in L. Miccichè (ed.), *Sciuscià: di Vittorio De Sica: letture, documenti, testimonianze*, 87–95, Rome: Cineteca Nazionale.
Parigi, S. (ed.) (2005), *Paisà: analisi del film*, Venice: Marsilio.
Parigi, S. (2008), 'Zavattini: "Siamo tutti personaggi"', *Studi Novecenteschi*, 35(75): 251–62.
Parigi, S. (2014), *Neorealismo. Il nuovo cinema del dopoguerra*, Venice: Marsilio.
Parigi, S. (2017), 'The Screen in the Mirror: Thematic and Textual Reflexivity in Italian Cinema', in F. Burke (ed.), *A Companion to Italian Cinema*, 512–30. Oxford: Wiley-Blackwell.
Paternò, C. (1996), 'Fischi sul baby-premio', *L'Unità*, 8 September: 3.
Patriarca, S. (2015), 'Fear of Small Numbers: "Brown Babies" in Postwar Italy', *Contemporanea*, 18(4): 537–67.
Patriarca, S. (2022). *Race in Post-Fascist Italy: 'War Children' and the Color of the Nation*, Cambridge: Cambridge University Press.
Pavesi, E. (1950), 'I bambini ci guardano', *Cinema*, 40: 335–37, 353.
Pavesi, D. (2017), 'Non solo la ragazza che James Dean amava. Anna Maria Pierangeli tra Italia e Stati Uniti, tra ingenuità ed esperienza', *Arabeschi*, 10, Special Issue on *Vaghe stelle. Attrici del/nel cinema*. http://www.arabeschi.it/22-non-solo-la-ragazza-che-james-dean-amava-anna-maria-pierangeli-tra-italia-e-stati-uniti-ingenuit--edesperienza/
Pérez de las Heras, N. (2019), 'Zaira Romero y Rosy Rodríguez, una pasión sin límites', *Mujerhoy*, 9 February. https://www.mujerhoy.com/actualidad/201902/09/zaira-romero-rosy-rodriguez-actrices-carmen-lola-premios-goya-rev-20190208163603.html
Pescatore, G. (2001), *La voce e il corpo: L'opera lirica al cinema*, Udine: Campanotto.
Phillips, M. (2015), '*Girlhood* Director Celine Sciamma Talks Paris, Friendship, and Colorful Storytelling', 3 February. https://tribecafilm.com/news/girlhood-director-celine-sciamma-talks-paris-frien
Pierini, M. (2015), 'I non-attori che sanno recitare: pratiche di casting e di coaching nel cinema italiano contemporaneo', *Bianco e Nero*, 581: 12–18.
Pierini, M. (2016-17), 'Inventare una nuova bellezza. Corpo femminile e rotocalchi, tra Liberazione, divismo e neorealismo (1944–1948)', *La Valle dell'Eden*, 30: 33–43.
Pierini, M. (2017), 'Identità femminili, interpreti, soggetti', in G. Carluccio, E. Morreale and M. Pierini (eds), *Intorno al neorealismo. Voci, contesti, linguaggi e culture dell'Italia del dopoguerra*, 148–9, Milan: Scalpendi.
Pietrangeli, A. (1944), 'Bilancio', *Star*, 1(5): 3–4.
Pietrangeli, A. (1946), '*Sciuscià*. Un film "esplosivo" di De Sica', *Star*, 3(17): 3.
Pillon, S. (2018), 'Ciccarolo', *Il ricciocorno schiattoso*, https://ilricciocornoschiattoso.wordpress.com/2018/11/27/ciccarolo/
Pinna, R. (1946), 'Le ragazze aspettano', *Star*, 3(12): 4.
Pintus, P. (1975), 'Che fai, Roberto?', *Bianco e Nero: Special Issue on Vittorio De Sica*, 36(9–12): 158–61.

Pistagnesi, P. (2010), 'Le attrici e i modelli femminili', in E. Laura and A. Baldi (eds), *Storia del cinema italiano, vol. VI: 1940–44*, 247–50, Venice/Rome: Marsilio/Bianco e Nero.

Pistorio, G. (1949), 'Attori professionisti e attori di strada', *Ferrania*, 3(10): 17.

Pisu, S. (2016), 'Nemo propheta in patria. I film neorealisti nel circuito dei festival fra brand internazionale di successo e ambiguità nazionali (1946–1952)', *Studi e Ricerche*, 9: 141–50.

Pitassio, F. (2002), *Ombre silenziose. Teorie dell'attore cinematografico negli anni Venti*, Udine: Campanotto.

Pitassio, F. (2007), 'Due soldi di speranza. Considerazioni intorno al dibattito sull'attore non professionista del Neorealismo', *L'Asino di B*, 11(12): 147–63.

Pitassio, F. (2010), 'La formazione dell'attore e la discussione teorica', *Bianco e Nero*, 566: 43–51.

Pitassio, F. (2015), 'Intorno al neorealismo. I manifesti e il paratesto cinematografico', *L'Avventura*, 1(1): 121–40.

Pitassio, F. (2018), 'Popular Culture, Performance, Persona: Anna Magnani between *Rome, Open City* and *The Rose Tattoo*', *Journal of Italian Cinema and Media Studies*, 6(3): 373–88.

Pitassio, F. (2019), *Neorealist Film Culture, 1945–1954: Rome, Open Cinema*, Amsterdam: Amsterdam University Press.

Pitassio, F., and S. Venturini (2014), 'Building the Institution: Luigi Chiarini and Italian Film Culture in the 1930s', in M. Hagener (ed.), *The Emergence of Film Culture: Knowledge Production, Institution Building, and the Fate of the Avant-Garde in Europe, 1919–1945*, 249–67, London: Berghahn.

Pitt, R. (2012), *Italian Cinema's Missing Children (1992–2005)*, PhD diss., University of Exeter.

Prezzolini, G. (1937), 'L'uomo comune, personaggio del cinema e della radio', *Bianco e Nero*, 1(6): 114–16.

Projansky, S. (2014), *Spectacular Girls: Media Fascination and Celebrity Culture*, New York: New York University Press.

Prono, F. (2019), 'Un caso di studio: *O Key John!* di Ugo Fasano', in C. Allasia, B. Maida and F. Prono (eds), *Infanzia e povertà: storie e narrazioni nell'Italia del dopoguerra (1945–1950)*, 95–104, Turin: Edizioni Sinestesie.

Pucci, L. (2013), 'History, Myth and the Everyday: Luchino Visconti, Renato Guttuso, and the Fishing Communities of the Italian South', *Oxford Art Journal*, 36(3): 417–35.

Pudovkin, V. (1954), *Film Technique and Film Acting*, trans. I. Montagu, London: Vision.

Pullen, K. (2005), *Actresses and Whores. On Stage and in Society*, Cambridge: Cambridge University Press.

Purificato, D. (1942), 'Tipi per un film "nostro"', *Cinema*, 153: 644–5.

'Q' (1950), 'Articolo 10', *Araldo dello Spettacolo*, 13–14 January 1950: 2.

Quinn, M. (1990), 'Celebrity and the Semiotics of Acting', *New Theatre Quarterly*, 6(22): 154–61.

Radano, R. (1995), 'Soul Texts and the Blackness of Folk', *Modernism/Modernity*, 2(1): 71–97.

Ramogida, S. (2015), *Roma città aperta: Vito Annicchiarico il piccolo Marcello racconta il set con Anna Magnani Aldo Fabrizi Roberto Rossellini*, Rome: Gangemi.
Ramos-Martinez, M. (2016), '"Actors Simply Explode". To Act in the Cinema of Straub and Huillet', *Camera Obscura*, 31(12): 96–117.
Randall, R. (2017), *Children on the Threshold in Contemporary Latin American Cinema: Nature, Gender, and Agency*, Lanham, MD: Lexington Books.
Ravesi, G. (2019), 'I'll be Your Mirror: Documentario italiano contemporaneo e cultura social', *Mediascapes Journal*, 12: 121–31. https://rosa.uniroma1.it/rosa03/mediascapes/article/view/15707
Reader, K. (2000), *Robert Bresson*, Manchester: Manchester University Press.
Reich, J. (2004), *Beyond the Latin Lover: Marcello Mastroianni, Masculinity, and Italian Cinema*, Bloomington: Indiana University Press.
Reich, J. (2015), *The Maciste Films of Italian Silent Cinema*, Bloomington: Indiana University Press.
Reimer, M. (2012), 'On Location: The Home and the Street in Recent Films about Street Children', *International Research in Children's Literature*, 5(1): 1–21.
Renga, D. (2020), 'Casting *My Brilliant Friend*'s Authentic Stardom', *Series: International Journal of TV Serial Narratives*, 6(1): 77–90.
Renzi, R. (1948), 'Sullo schermo per una volta', *Cinema*, 8: 240–1.
Renzi, R. (1949), 'Mitologia e contemplazione in Visconti, Ford, ed Eisenstein', *Bianco e Nero*, 10(2): 64–9.
Renzi, R. (1956), 'Elogio della donna vestita', *Cinema Nuovo*, 78: 152.
Rhodes, J. D. (2007), *Stupendous, Miserable City. Pasolini's Rome*, Minnesota: University of Minneapolis Press.
Rhodes, J. D. (2012), 'Watchable Bodies: *Salò*'s Young Non-Actors', *Screen*, 53(4): 453–58.
Rhodes, J. D. (2017), 'Watching Italians Turn Around: Gender, Looking, and Roman/Cinematic Modernity', in F. Burke (ed.), *A Companion to Italian Cinema*, 408–26, Oxford: Wiley-Blackwell.
Ricci, S. (2008), *Cinema and Fascism: Italian Film and Society, 1922–1943*, Berkeley: University of California Press.
Ricciardi, A. (2006), 'The Italian Redemption of Cinema: Neorealism from Bazin to Godard', *Romanic Review*, 97(3–4): 483–500.
Rigoletto, S. (2018), '(Un)dressing Authenticity: Neorealist Stardom and Anna Magnani in the Postwar Era (1945–48)', *Journal of Italian Cinema and Media Studies*, 6(3): 389–403.
Rocca, F. (2020), 'Sono Ale, Ale per sempre' (intervista con Alessandra di Sanzo), *Vanity Fair*, 11 October.
Rondi, G. L. (1956), *Il neorealismo italiano*, Parma: Guanda.
Rondi, G. L. (2003), 'La famiglia Valastro', in C. Cosulich (ed.), *Storia del cinema italiano, vol. VII (1945–1948)*, 592–4, Venice: Marsilio.
Rondi, G. L. (2006), 'Il primo Visconti', in S. Gesù (ed.), *La terra trema: un film di Luchino Visconti*, 281–4, Comiso: Salarchi.
Rosengarten, F. (1998), 'Homo Siculus: Sicilian Essentialism in Verga, Lampedusa, Sciascia', in J. Schneider (ed.), *Italy's 'Southern Question': Orientalism in One Country*, 117–32, Oxford: Berg.

Rosi, F. (1993), 'L'avventura viscontiana di Aci Trezza', ed. V. Zagarrio, in L. Miccichè (ed.), *La terra trema di Visconti: analisi di un capolavoro*, 21–6, Turin: Lindau.
Rosi, F. (2006a), '*La terra trema*, una felice ed esaltante avventura', in S. Gesù (ed.), *La terra trema: un film di Luchino Visconti*, 13–19, Comiso: Salarchi.
Rosi, F. (2006b), 'Diari di lavorazione', in S. Gesù (ed.), *La terra trema: un film di Luchino Visconti*, 57–128, Comiso: Salarchi.
Rossellini, R., and M. Verdone (1952), 'Colloquio sul neorealismo', *Bianco e Nero*, 13(2): 7–16.
Rossellini, R. (2006), *Il mio metodo. Scritti e interviste*, ed. A. Aprà, Venice: Marsilio.
Rosso, U. (1990), 'Addio "Ragazzo fuori" dal set verso la morte', *La Repubblica*, 16 November. https://ricerca.repubblica.it/repubblica/archivio/repubblica/1990/11/16/addio-ragazzo-fuori-dal-set-verso-la.html
Ruberto, L., and K. Wilson (eds), *Italian Neorealism and Global Cinema*, Detroit: Wayne State University Press.
Russo, G. (1955). 'Gli attori levano gli scudi contro i colleghi "presi dalla strada"', *Corriere della Sera*, 8 November.
Sacripanti, U. (1951), 'Schermi e schermaglie', *Araldo dello Spettacolo*, 4 October: 1.
Salazkina, M. (2012), 'Moscow-Rome-Havana: A Film-Theory Road Map', *October*, 139: 97–116.
Salazkina, M. (2014), 'Soviet-Italian Cinematic Exchanges', in M. Hagener (ed.), *The Emergence of Film Culture: Knowledge Production, Institution Building and the Fate of the Avant-Garde in Europe, 1919-1945*, 180–98, London: Berghahn.
Salvioni, G. (1946), 'Carmela scrive a Rossellini', *Star*, 13: 3.
Saponari, A. (2017), 'È nata una stella. La funzione di scouting nelle riviste anni Trenta: il caso *Stelle*', *Arabeschi*, 10, Special Issue on *Vaghe stelle. Attrici del/ nel cinema*, http://www.arabeschi.it/32--nata-una-stella-la-funzione-di-scouting-delle-riviste-anni-trenta-il-caso-stelle/
Saponari, A. (2020), 'Piccole stelle crescono. La rappresentazione degli attori-bambini nelle riviste degli anni '30', *L'Avventura*, 1: 41–60.
Savio, F. (1979a), *Cinecittà anni trenta. Parlano 116 protagonisti del secondo cinema italiano (1930–1943). Vol. 1 (AB-DEF)*, Rome: Bulzoni.
Savio, F. (1979b), *Cinecittà anni trenta. Parlano 116 protagonisti del secondo cinema italiano (1930–1943). Vol. II (DEG-MOR)*, Rome: Bulzoni.
Savio, F. (1979c), *Cinecittà anni trenta. Parlano 116 protagonisti del secondo cinema italiano (1930–1943). Vol. III (NAZ - ZAZ)*, Rome: Bulzoni.
Scandola, A. (2012), 'La verità del non-attore. Appunti sul nuovo cinema italiano', in G. Tinazzi (ed.), *Lo stato delle cose. Cinema e altre derive. Duemila12*, 30–42, Turin: Kaplan.
Scandola, A. (2020), *Il corpo e lo sguardo. L'attore nel cinema della modernità*, Venice: Marsilio.
Schechner, R. (2002), *Performance Studies: an Introduction*, New York: Routledge.

Schneider, A., and V. Hediger (2009), 'Functionaries with Hearts of Gold: TV Comedians as Vernacular Movie Stars in Switzerland', in T. Soila (ed.), *Stellar Encounters: Stardom in Popular European Cinema*, 63–70, New Barnet: John Libbey.
Schonig, J. (2021), 'The Other Side of Digital Cinema: *Tangerine* and Digital Realism', video essay. https://www.youtube.com/watch?v=Dp3fonHZzhs
Schoonover, K. (2009), 'Neorealism at a Distance', in T. Trifonova (ed.), *European Film Theory*, 301–18, New York: Routledge.
Schoonover, K. (2010), 'Divine: Towards an "Imperfect" Stardom', in J. Morrison (ed.), *Hollywood Reborn: Movie Stars of the 1970s*, 158–81, New Brunswick: Rutgers University Press.
Schoonover, K. (2012a), *Brutal Vision: The Neorealist Body in Postwar Italian Cinema*, Minneapolis: University of Minnesota Press.
Schoonover, K. (2012b), 'Wastrels of Time: Slow Cinema's Laboring Body, the Political Spectator, and the Queer', *Framework*, 53(1): 65–78.
Schroeder Rodríguez, P. (2016), *Latin American Cinema: A Comparative History*, Berkeley: University of California Press.
Schwartz, B. D. (1995), *Pasolini Requiem*, London: Vintage.
Schwartz, V. (2007), *It's So French! Hollywood, Paris, and the Making of Cosmopolitan French Film Culture*, Chicago: University of Chicago Press.
Schweninger, L. (2013), *Imagic Moments: Indigenous North American Film*, Athens: University of Georgia Press.
Sciammana, E. (2019), 'Roberto Saviano e *La Paranza Dei Bambini* sul Red Carpet di Berlino: le Foto', *Movieplayer*. 13 February. https://movieplayer.it/news/roberto-saviano-la-paranza-dei-bambini-foto-video_64525/
Sciascia, L. (2003), 'La Sicilia nel cinema', in C. Ambroise (ed.), *Opere 1956–1971*, 1201–22, Milan: Bompiani.
Scott, A. O. (2009), 'Neo-Neo Realism', *The New York Times*, 17 March. https://www.nytimes.com/2009/03/22/magazine/22neorealism-t.html
Scott, A. O. (2018), 'Review: In A Ciambra, a Young Roma Boy Comes of Age', *The New York Times*, 18 January. https://www.nytimes.com/2018/01/18/movies/a-ciambra-review-jonas-carpignano.html
Sedgwick, E. (1985), *Between Men: English Literature and Male Homosocial Desire*, New York: Columbia University Press.
Sellier, G. (2008), *Masculine Singular: French New Wave Cinema*, trans. K. Ross, Durham, NC: Duke University Press.
Serandrei, M. (1948), 'Lettere dalla Sicilia', *Bianco e Nero*, 9(1): 49–50.
Seregni, M. (2019), '"La spontanea mescolanza del comico e del patetico". Cinema, infanzia, e dopoguerra in Luigi Comencini', in C. Allasia, B. Maida and F. Prono (eds), *Infanzia e povertà: storie e narrazioni nell'Italia del dopoguerra (1945–1950)*, 85–94, Turin: Edizioni Sinestesie.
Shankar, A. (2020), 'Primitivism and Race in Ethnographic Film: A Decolonial Re-visioning', in *Oxford Bibliographies*, https://www.oxfordbibliographies.com/view/document/obo-9780199766567/obo-9780199766567-0245.xml
Shields, C. (2017), 'One in a Million', *Film Comment*, November–December. https://www.filmcomment.com/article/one-in-a-million/
Shohat, E., and R. Stam (1994), *Unthinking Eurocentrism: Multiculturalism and the Media*, New York: Routledge.

Siegel, T. (2018), 'Clint Eastwood Reveals Why He Cast Non-Actors in *15:17 to Paris*', *The Hollywood Reporter*, 6 February. https://www.hollywoodreporter.com/news/general-news/how-clint-eastwood-cast-actors-1517-paris-1082442/

Sims, D. (2022), 'What Is Harry Styles *Doing* in *Don't Worry Darling?*', *The Atlantic*, 23 September. https://www.theatlantic.com/culture/archive/2022/09/dont-worry-darling-review-harry-styles-bad-acting/671540/

Sisto, A. (2014), *Film Sound in Italy: Listening to the Screen*, New York: Palgrave Macmillan.

Sisto, A. (2021), 'What Neorealism Sounded Like', paper given at the American Association of Italian Studies annual conference (online), 6 June.

Sklar, R., and S. Giovacchini (2012), 'Introduction: The Geography and History of Global Neorealism', in R. Sklar and S. Giovacchini (eds), *Global Neorealism: The Transnational History of a Film Style*, 3–15, Jackson: University Press of Mississippi.

Small, P. (2009), *Sophia Loren: Moulding the Star*, Bristol: Intellect.

Small, P. (2014), 'The *Maggiorata* or Sweater Girl of the 1950s: Mangano, Lollobrigida, Loren', in P Bondanella (ed.), *The Italian Cinema Book*, 116–22, London: BFI.

Solanas, F., and O. Getino (1970-71), 'Toward a Third Cinema', *Cinéaste*, 4(3): 1–10.

Soldati, M. (2003), *Ventiquattro ore in uno studio cinematografico*, Palermo: Sellerio.

Solleville, M. C. (1952a), 'Deux sous d'espoir payés compant', *Cahiers du Cinéma*, 2(12): 33–7.

Solleville, M. C. (1952b), 'Carmela, actrice néo-réaliste', *Cahiers du Cinéma*, 3(15): 52–8.

Sollima, S. (1945), 'Lea Padovani', *Film d'oggi*, 1(1): 7.

Solmi, A. (1947), 'Il regista a scuola dai borsaioli', *Oggi*, 7 December: 21–2.

Solmi, A. (1953), 'Una signora senza Camelie scortata da giudici e avvocati', *Oggi*, 12 March: 39–40.

Sorlin, P. (1991), *European Cinemas, European Societies, 1939–90*, London: Routledge.

Sotinel, T. (2019), 'Mama Sané, la princesse de Thiaroye qui illumine le film *Atlantique*', *Le Monde*, 2 October. https://www.lemonde.fr/culture/article/2019/10/02/cinema-mama-sane-la-princesse-de-thiaroye-qui-illumine-atlantique_6013873_3246.html

Spinazzola, V. (1985), *Cinema e pubblico: Lo spettacolo filmico in Italia 1945–1965*, Rome: Bulzoni.

Stamp, S. (2000), *Movie-Struck Girls: Women and Motion Picture Culture after the Nickelodeon*, Princeton, NJ: Princeton University Press.

Steimatksy, N. (2008), *Italian Locations: Reinhabiting the Past in Postwar Cinema*, Minneapolis: University of Minnesota Press.

Steimatsky, N. (2017), *The Face on Film*, Oxford: Oxford University Press.

Steinhart, D. (2019), *Runaway Hollywood: Internationalizing Postwar Production and Location Shooting*, Berkeley: University of California Press.

Steno (1989), 'Personaggi inevitabili del film neorealista', in A. Farassino (ed.), *Neorealismo: Cinema Italiano 1945–49*, 130, Turin: EDT.

Sutton, P. (2005), 'The *bambino negato* or Missing Child of Contemporary Italian Cinema', *Screen*, 46(3): 353–60.
Tantillo, A., and T. Carlino (2019), 'Il reato del reale: "Selfie" e la caméra-stylo', *Dialoghi: rivista di studi comparatistici*, 6: 117–28. https://philarchive.org/archive/CASADD-3
Tardy, M. (1975), 'Un enfant raconté', *Bianco e Nero: Special Issue on Vittorio De Sica*, 36(9–12): 168–71.
Taylor, A. (2011), 'Reconceptualizing the "Nature" of Childhood', *Childhood*, 18(4): 420–33.
Taylor, A. (2012), 'Introduction', in A. Taylor (ed.), *Theorizing Film Acting*, 1–16, London: Routledge.
Thomas, S. (2013), '"Marginal Moments of Spectacle": Character Actors, Cult Stardom, and Hollywood Cinema', in K. Egan and S. Thomas (eds), *Cult Film Stardom: Offbeat Attractions and Processes of Cultification*, 37–54, Basingstoke: Palgrave Macmillan.
Thompson, K. (1988), *Breaking the Glass Armor: Neoformalist Film Analysis*, Princeton, NJ: Princeton University Press.
Tognolotti, C. (2020), 'Introduction' in C. Tognolotti (ed.), *Cenerentola, Galatea e Pigmalione. Raccontare il divismo femminile nel cinema tra fiaba e mito*, 7–17, Pisa: ETS.
Tonti, A. (1964), *Odore di cinema*, Florence: Vallecchi.
Torri, B. (1992), 'La più pura espressione del neorealismo', in L. Miccichè (ed.), *De Sica. Autore, regista, attore*, 43–54, Venice: Marsilio.
Toschi, D. (2015), 'Carmela, l'inquietante natura del corpo cinematografico femminile anni Cinquanta', in G. Carluccio, L. Malavasi and F. Villa (eds), *Il cinema di Renato Castellani*, 105–14, Rome: Carocci.
Trasatti, S. (1984), *Renato Castellani*, Florence: La Nuova Italia.
Traverso, A. (2007), 'Migrations of Cinema: Italian Neorealism and Brazilian Cinema', in L. Ruberto and K. Wilson (eds), *Italian Neorealism and Global Cinema*, 165–86, Detroit, MI: Wayne State University Press.
Treveri Gennari, D., C. O'Rawe, D. Hipkins, S. Dibeltulo, and S. Culhane (2020), *Italian Cinema Audiences: Histories and Memories of Cinema-going in Post-war Italy*, London: Bloomsbury.
Tsing, A. (2004), *Friction: An Ethnography of Global Connection*, Princeton, NJ: Princeton University Press.
Turner, G., F. Bonner, and P. D. Marshall (2006), 'Producing Celebrity', in P. D. Marshall (ed.), *The Celebrity Culture Reader*, 770–98, London: Routledge.
TV2000it interview (no date), *Enzo Staiola, il celebre bambino di Ladri di biciclette e il suo incontro con Vittorio De Sica*. https://www.youtube.com/watch?v=XLSeTBnG8ik
Ulivi, S. (2019), 'La storia di Phaim Bhuiyan, romano di Torpignattara', *Corriere della Sera*, 10 May. https://roma.corriere.it/notizie/cronaca/19_maggio_10/storia-phaim-bhuiyan-romano-torpignattara-e81fcdca-7284-11e9-861b-d938f88a2d19.shtml
Upton, C. (2011), 'Real People as Actors - Actors as Real People', *Studies in Theatre and Performance*, 31(2): 209–22.
V. Ca. (1997), 'Lucia Bosè, una diva per caso', *Corriere della Sera*, 21 November: 53.

Varese, C. (1950), 'Il film senza attori', *Bianco e Nero*, 11(10): 12–16.
Varese, C. (1954), 'Questa la donna italiana nel cinema del dopoguerra', *Cinema Nuovo*, 30: 107–9.
Vasse, D. (2018), 'L'acteur amateur dans le cinéma de Jacques Doillon ou l'art du premier venu. Le cas de Gérald Thomassin dans *Le Petit Criminel* (1990) et *Le Premier Venu* (2008)', *Double Jeu*, 15: 121–31.
Venturini, F. (1950), 'Origini del neorealismo', *Bianco e Nero*, 11(2): 31–54.
Verdesca, M. (2016). *Protagonisti per sempre*. DVD, Terminal Video.
Verdesca, M. (2017). *Sciuscià 70*. DVD, Terminal Video.
Verdicchio, P. (2007), "O cuorp' 'e Napule: Naples and the Cinematographic Body of Culture', in L. Ruberto and K. Wilson (eds), *Italian Neorealism and Global Cinema*, 259–89, Detroit, MI: Wayne State University Press.
Verdone, M. (1950), 'Necessità in Italia di un cinema per l'infanzia', *Cinema*, 36: 205–6.
Viano, M. (1993), *A Certain Realism: Making Use of Pasolini's Film Theory and Practice*, Berkeley: University of California Press.
Viazzi, G. (1949), 'Polemichetta primaverile su *La terra trema*', *Cinema*, 15: 469–70.
Viazzi, G. (1951), 'Contro il divismo l'attore realistico', *Il Calendario del Popolo*, 7(80): 851.
Villani, L. (2012), *Le borgate del fascismo. Storia urbana, politica e sociale della periferia romana*, Milan: Ledizioni.
Visconti, L. (1943), 'Il cinema antropomorfico', *Cinema*, 8: 173–4.
Vitella, F. (2015), 'Forbice, album e carta da lettere. "Hollywood" come fan magazine', *Fata Morgana*, 9(7): 51–64.
Vitella, F. (2016), 'Il diario intimo come fonte per la storia del fandom. Ritratto di una Bobby-soxer di provincia', *Bianco e Nero*, 582–3: 153–60.
Vitella, F. (2018), 'Giusti, convertiti, santi. Il discorso divistico al tempo di Pio XII', *Schermi. Storie di culture del cinema e dei media in Italia*, 2(3): 105–19.
Vitella, F. (2020), 'Per un'archeologia del fandom. La Posta dei lettori nelle riviste cinematografiche dell'Italia fascista', in M. Comand and A. Mariani (eds), *Scrapbooks, fan mail e diari delle spettatrici nell'Italia del regime*, 251–77, Venice: Marsilio.
Vitti, A. (2019), 'Il neorealista che amava Hollywood. Attorialità e recitazione nel cinema di Giuseppe De Santis', in V. Zagarrio (ed.), *Mirroring Myths. Miti allo specchio tra cinema americano ed europeo*, 73–96, Rome: RomaTre Press.
Vivarelli, N. (2021), 'Antonio Dikele Distefano on Originating *Zero*, Netflix's Milestone Original About Black Youth in Italy', *Variety*, 19 April. https://variety.com/2021/digital/news/antonio-dikele-distefano-zero-netflix-1234954493/
Wagner, T. (2003), 'Danger: Girl at Work', *The Age*, 10 December. https://www.theage.com.au/entertainment/movies/danger-girl-at-work-20031210-gdwwk9.html
Wagstaff, C. (2000), 'Rossellini and Neo-realism', in D. Forgacs (ed.), *Roberto Rossellini: Magician of the Real*, 36–49, London: BFI.
Wagstaff, C. (2007), *Italian Neorealist Cinema: an Aesthetic Approach*, Toronto: University of Toronto Press.
Walker, T. (2014), '*Captain Phillips* actor Barkhad Abdi Struggles Financially Despite Oscar Nomination', *The Independent*, 5 March. https://www.independ

ent.co.uk/arts-entertainment/films/news/captain-phillips-actor-barkhad-abdi-struggles-despite-oscar-nomination-9171593.html
Waller, M. (1997), 'Decolonizing the Screen: from *Ladri di biciclette* to *Ladri di saponette*', in B. Allen and M. Russo (eds), *Revisioning Italy: National Identity and Global Culture*, 253–74, Minneapolis: University of Minnesota Press.
Walsh, K. (2021), *Women, Method Acting and the Hollywood Film*, New York: Routledge.
Wanzo, R. (2006), 'Beyond a "Just" Syntax: Black Actresses, Hollywood and Complex Personhood', *Women and Performance: a Journal of Feminist Theory*, 16(1): 135–52.
Warner, K, (2017), 'In the Time of Plastic Representation', *Film Quarterly*, 71(2): 32–7.
Warner, K. (2021), 'Blue Skies Again: Streamers and the Impossible Promise of Diversity', *Los Angeles Review of Books*, 24 June. https://lareviewofbooks.org/article/blue-skies-again-streamers-and-the-impossible-promise-of-diversity/
Warshow, R. (2001), '*Paisan* (1948)', in *The Immediate Experience: Movies, Comics, Theatre and Other Aspects of Popular Culture*, 221–29, Cambridge, MA: Harvard University Press.
Watson, W. V. (1999), 'The Cinema of Aurelio Grimaldi and the (De)construction of Sicilian Machismo', *Annali d'Italianistica*, 17: 137–54.
Waugh, P. (1990), '"Acting to Play Oneself": Notes on Performance in Documentary', in C. Zucker (ed.), *Making Visible the Invisible: An Anthology of Original Essays on Film Acting*. 64–91, Metuchen, NJ: Scarecrow.
Wiazemsky, A. (2007), *Jeune fille*, Paris: Gallimard.
Whittaker, T. (2020), *The Spanish Quinqui Film: Delinquency, Sound, Sensation*, Manchester: Manchester University Press.
Williams, L. R. (2012), 'The Tears of Henry Thomas', *Screen*, 53(4): 459–64.
Williams, T. (2006), *Notebooks*, New Haven, CT: Yale University Press.
Willmore, A. (2021), 'Chloé Zhao's America. The Creator of Quiet Indie Dramas is Now the Most Sought-after Director in Hollywood', *New York Magazine*, 16 February. https://www.vulture.com/article/chloe-zhao-nomadland.html
Wojcik, P. R. (2003), 'Typecasting', *Criticism*, 450(2): 223–49.
Wojcik, P. R. (2004), 'Introduction' to *Movie Acting: The Film Reader*, 1–14, London: Routledge.
Wojcik, P. R. (2006), 'The Sound of Film Acting', *Journal of Film and Video*, 58(1): 71–83.
Wong, C. H. (2011), *Film Festivals: Culture, People, and Power on the Global Screen*, New Brunswick, NJ: Rutgers University Press.
Wood, H. (2017), 'The Politics of Hyperbole on *Geordie Shore*: Class, Gender, Youth and Excess', *European Journal of Cultural Studies*, 20(1): 39–55.
Wright Wexman, V. (2004), 'Masculinity in Crisis: Method Acting in Hollywood', in P. Wojcik (ed.), *Movie Acting, the Film Reader*, 127–44, London: Routledge.
Wu Ming 2 and Mohamed, A. (2012), *Timira: romanzo meticcio*, Turin: Einaudi.
Yu, S. Q. (2017), 'Introduction: Performing Stardom: Star Studies in Transformation and Expansion', in S. Q. Yu and G. Austin (eds), *Revisiting Star Studies*, 1–22, Edinburgh: Edinburgh University Press.

Zagarrio, V. (1993), 'Le "quinte" della storia: riflessioni sulla regia', in L. Miccichè (ed.), *La terra trema di Visconti: analisi di un capolavoro*, 117–39, Turin: Lindau.

Zagarrio, V. (1994), 'Tra realtà e studio', in L. Miccichè (ed.), *Sciuscià: di Vittorio De Sica: letture, documenti, testimonianze*, 61–70, Rome: Cineteca Nazionale.

Zagarrio, V. (2000), '*Bellissima*: la recita del neorealismo', in V. Pravadelli (ed.), *Il cinema di Luchino Visconti*, 89–102, Rome: Edizioni di Bianco e Nero.

Zagarrio, V. (2012), 'L'eredità del neorealismo nel New-new Italian Cinema', *Annali d'Italianistica*, 30: 95–111.

Zatterin, U. (1949), 'I giovani scappano da casa per diventare divi dei fumetti', *Oggi*, 17 March: 10–11.

Zatterin, U. (1950), 'Angelo il mulatto biondo ha paura degli uomini bianchi', *Oggi*, 10 August: 111.

Zavattini, C. (1950), 'Il grande inganno. Idea per un film di Zavattini', *L'Unità*, 8 January: 3.

Zavattini, C. (2002), *Opere. Cinema. Diario cinematografico. Neorealismo ecc*, ed. V. Fortichiari and M. Argentieri, Milan: Bompiani.

Zavattini, C. (2006), *Uomo, vieni fuori!: soggetti per il cinema editi e inedita*, ed. O. Caldiron, Rome: Bulzoni.

Zavattini, C. (2021), *Selected Writings*, ed. D. Brancaleone, New York: Bloomsbury.

Zeffirelli, F. (1993), 'Come un toscano insegnò il siciliano per conto di un lombardo', ed. S. Parigi, in L. Miccichè (ed.), *La terra trema di Visconti: analisi di un capolavoro*, 27–31, Turin: Lindau.

Zelitzer, V. (1994), *Pricing the Priceless Child: The Changing Social Value of Children*, Princeton, NJ: Princeton University Press.

Zilioli, M. (2019), 'Dalla carta allo schermo. Il ruolo delle riviste comuniste nella creazione di modelli divistici popolari nel secondo dopoguerra: Miss Vie Nuove e Miss Primavera', *La Valle dell'Eden*, 34: 13–24.

Zinneman, F. (1950), 'On Using Non-Actors in Pictures', *The New York Times*, 8 January: 87.

INDEX

6ix, Abby 191 n.29
15:17 to Paris, The (Eastwood, 2018) 204

Abbasso la miseria!/Down with Misery (Righelli, 1945) 129, 148–9
Abbasso la ricchezza!/Peddlin' in Society (Righelli, 1946) 129, 149–50
Abdi, Barkhad 197
Abuna Messias (Alessandrini, 1939) 34
A Ciambra/The Ciambra (Carpignano, 2016) 163, 183, 188, 191–4
A Chiara (Carpignano, 2021) 188 n.23, 196
Aduviri, Juan Carlos 19
Alessandrini, Goffredo 33–4
Ali, Rubina 183
Al Rafeea, Zain 200–1
Amato, Pio 163, 183, 188, 194
Amelio, Gianni 178, 181–2
Amore in città, L' (Antonioni et al., 1953) 14–15, 101 n.33
Amore tossico/Toxic Love (Caligari, 1983) 178
Amorosa menzogna, L'/Lies of Love (Antonioni, 1949) 93–4
Andrésen, Björn 183–4, 195
Angelo tra la folla/Strange Witness (De Mitri, 1950) 164 nn.84 86
Annicchiarico, Vito 134, 136–7, 148–51, 153–5, 158 n.74, 171 n.96
Antonelli, Alessandro 184–7
Antonioni, Michelangelo 88, 93–4, 98, 100, 103–4, 125
Aparicio, Yalitza 3, 8, 9, 173, 196
Apicella, Tina 155, 156–8, 162, 165

Apparizione/Apparition (De Limur, 1943) 90
Apur Panchali (Ganguly, 2013) 177
Arcidiacono, Antonio 72, 73, 77, 79, 83
Arena, Aniello 192, 195
Aristarco, Guido 11, 43, 131 n.10, 156 n.71
Atlantique/Atlantics (Diop, 2019) 195
Autumn Beat (Dikele Distefano, 2022) 191 n.29

Baby Gang (Piscitelli, 1992) 182
Baker, Sean 4, 173 n.1, 198
Bakray, Bukky 198 n.41
Balázs, Bela 28, 31, 162–3
Bande de filles/Girlhood (Sciamma, 2014) 196–7
Banerjee, Subir 177
Bangla (Bhuiyan, 2019) 189–90
Barbaro, Umberto 28–31, 32, 35 n.14
Barmak, Siddiq 199
Battisti, Carlo 6, 41
Bazin, André 2, 5, 7, 15, 17, 19, 56, 58, 59, 69, 79, 80, 88 n.4, 96, 109, 114, 129, 130, 131, 134, 140, 147, 151–2, 157, 158, 159, 162–3, 206
beauty contests 21, 27, 36, 38, 39–40, 47, 49, 50, 67, 85, 95–101, 102, 103 n.37, 111, 124
Bellissima (Visconti, 1951) 87 n.2, 100 n.31, 103 n.37, 130, 155–8, 159
Benigno, Francesco 179–80
Benyamina, Houda 198
Bhuiyan, Phaim 189–90
Bianco e Nero journal 28–29, 31, 51, 82
Bilancione, Pierino 155, 159–62, 170
Blando, Oscar 47

Blasetti, Alessandro 28, 30, 32, 34, 36, 38 n.24, 155, 156
Blaxploitalian: 100 Years of Blackness in Italian Cinema (Kuwornu, 2016) 188, 191
Bollaín, Icíar 18–19
Bonansea, Miranda 129
Bosè, Lucia 39, 49, 85, 89, 95, 96, 97–100, 102 n.35, 105, 118, 125
Bovino, Alfonso 134, 136 n.22, 145–8, 168–9
Bovo, Brunella 94
Boyle, Danny 183
Bresson, Robert 4, 16–17, 192, 207
Brooklyn (Tessaud, 2014) 198
Brunetta, Gian Piero 26, 29 n.7, 30 n.10, 35, 36, 101, 177–8

Cabbia, Giuliano 171
Campane a Martello/Alarm Bells (Zampa, 1949) 49, 167
Canale, Gianna Maria 96 n.20, 100
Capernaum (Labaki, 2018) 200
Captain Phillips (Greengrass, 2013) 197
Capuano, Antonio 142 n.41, 151, 182
Cardone, Lucia 91, 93 n.13, 95 n.17
Carell, Lianella 56, 63, 64 n.26, 72, 88, 131 n.10
Carmen y Lola/Carmen & Lola (Echeverría, 2018) 198
Carnera, Primo 35
Carpignano, Jonas 163, 183, 188, 191, 196
Casilio, Maria Pia 116 n.58, 123, 124 n.73
Castellani, Renato 7, 21, 25, 42–3, 49 n.40, 50, 51, 78, 85, 103 n.37, 116–20, 122, 123, 125, 140 n.35, 155
Centro Sperimentale di Cinematografia 27, 28, 31, 35, 48, 53, 103, 161, 176
C'eravamo tanto amati/We All Loved Each Other So Much (Scola, 1974) 62
Cesare deve morire/Caesar Must Die (Taviani Brothers, 2012) 184 n.14, 192

Chiarini, Luigi 28, 29, 30 n.9, 31, 35 n.14, 48, 50, 51, 54, 80 n.58, 82, 119
Children 1, 5, 8, 22, 25, 26, 29 n.8, 37 n.18, 56, 62, 110, 111, 112, 114, 124, 127–71, 177
Cielo sulla palude/Heaven over the Marshes (Genina, 1949) 51
Cinema Nuovo journal 44, 82, 86, 91, 92, 97 n.24, 102–4, 106, 161 n.78
Citti, Franco 16, 67
Colore della vita, Il/The Colour of Pain (Benigno, 2020) 180
Comencini, Luigi 61, 177 n.59, 129, 141–5
Competitions 27, 36–40, 87, 90, 95, 100, 129
Corpo celeste/Heavenly Body (Rohrwacher, 2011) 192
Crossover stars 205–6
Cuori senza frontiere/The White Line (Zampa, 1950) 133–4
Cuarón, Alfonso 3, 8–9, 173, 196

Dalle Piane, Carlo 171
Dardenne brothers 5, 16, 192
Davoli, Ninetto 16, 17
De' Giorgi, Elsa 33 n.11
De Laurentiis, Dino 39, 40
De Robertis, Francesco 33, 34, 130, 163
De Santis, Giuseppe 2, 49, 50, 71 n.42, 88, 92, 93, 114 n.55, 118
De Sica, Vittorio 2, 26, 31, 41, 44–6, 54–71, 72, 83, 88, 94 n.16, 103, 106, 124 n.73, 128, 130–1, 136, 138–41, 142 n.42, 149–50, 159–62, 173, 192
Dheepan (Audiard, 2016) 205
Dikele Distefano, Antonio 190, 191 n.29
Diop, Mati 195
Di Sanzo, Alessandra 178–9
Divines (Benyamina, 2016) 198
Djordjevic, Claudia 189
Doillon, Jacques 5–6
Domenica (Labate, 2001) 183 n.11
Doucouré, Maïmouna 198–9

Due soldi di speranza/Two Cents of Hope (Castellani, 1952) 21, 25, 42–3, 50, 78, 85, 116–23, 124, 125, 204

Eastwood, Clint 204
Edogamhe, Coco Rebecca 190
Eisenstein, Sergei 15, 28–30, 31, 45, 57 n.9
È primavera/It's Forever Springtime (Castellani, 1950) 42, 117
exploitation of non-professionals 6, 17, 18, 21, 34, 74–7, 83, 88, 90, 92, 155, 170, 178, 183–4, 195, 198
extras 7, 20, 34, 36, 75–6, 77, 90 n.7, 152, 181, 188

Febbi, Vittoria 167–8
Ferrente, Agostino 184–7
Fiermonte, Enzo 35
film festivals 3, 5, 22, 71, 76, 79, 80, 83, 123, 174, 176, 178, 184, 187, 188, 191–6, 199, 200, 205
Fiore (Giovannesi, 2016) 184 n.14, 192
Fiore, Maria 21, 42–3, 70, 85, 86, 116–23
Fish Tank (Arnold, 2009) 197
Flaherty, Robert 15, 31, 162, 163, 177
Florida Project, The (Baker, 207) 4, 173 n.1
Fotoromanzo 37, 39, 85, 90 n.6, 93–5, 96
Fuocoammare/Fire at Sea (Rosi, 2016) 191–2, 194

Gaggiotti, Miguel 4, 6, 9, 16, 29, 30 n.9, 60, 61 n.18, 62 n.21, 67
García Treviño, Juan Daniel 200
Garrone, Matteo 182, 192
G.I.s 27, 107, 115, 136, 145, 163–4, 167 n.90, 168, 169
Giammona, Agnese and Nella 72, 73 n.45, 75, 76, 77 n.54, 78, 79, 83
Girotti, Massimo 36, 47
Godard, Jean-Luc 7, 16, 17, 97
Golbahari, Marina 199

Gomorra/Gomorrah (Garrone, 2008) 182, 184, 192
Grande inganno, Il/The Great Swindle (Zavattini, unmade) 68–9 (see also *Tu, Maggiorani*)
Greene, Shelleen 163–4, 166–7, 169
Guerra di Mario, La/Mario's War (Capuano, 2005) 182
Gundle, Stephen 19 n.26, 26 n.2, 35, 36, 37, 38, 40, 41, 96 nn.20 21, 102, 106, 139 n.32, 156 n.70, 157

Halilovic, Laura 189
Hartman, Saidiya 22, 170, 179
Hipkins, Danielle 40, 88, 97, 101, 106 n.47, 116, 127 n.2, 168
Huillet, Danièle 16, 204

Iacono, Ciccio 129 n.8, 142 n.42
Ieracitano, Giuseppe 178, 181, 196 n.39
Imbarco a mezzanotte/Stranger on the Prowl (Losey 1952) 25
Interlenghi, Franco 20, 55, 95, 104, 131, 137, 139–41, 171
Io Rom romantica/I, a Romani Romantic (Halilovic, 2014). 189
Ismail, Azharuddin Mohammed 183

Jandreau, Brady 12–13
Jarvis, Katie 197
Jesuthasan, Antonythasan 205
Johnson, Dots 145, 168
Joy of Madness (Makhmalbaf, 2003) 199 n.45

Kitzmiller, John 27, 167 n.90, 168 n.93
Kracauer, Siegfried 23, 88 n.4, 163

Ladri di biciclette/Bicycle Thieves (De Sica, 1948) 1–2, 17, 21, 25, 40, 41, 42, 44, 49, 53–71, 72, 73, 78, 82, 88, 115, 127, 129, 130–2, 133, 134, 139, 153 n.65, 166, 177, 188, 192, 206
Ladro di bambini, Il/The Stolen Children (Amelio, 1992) 178, 181–2

LaSalle, Martin 17 n.22, 207
Lawrence, Michael 137, 140, 148 n.52, 163 n.80, 170, 177
Lazzaro felice/Happy as Lazzaro (Rohrwacher, 2018) 192
Leavitt, Charles 2, 20 n.28, 33, 47 n.36, 67 n.33, 71 n.42, 127 n.2, 149 n.58, 151 n.60, 173
Leymarie, Pierre 16, 17 n.22
Listuzzi, Giorgio 44
Loach, Ken 15
Lolita (Lyne, 1998) 183
Lollobrigida, Gina 20, 21, 36, 39, 49, 85, 93, 95, 96, 98 n.28, 100, 102, 103, 105, 106, 117 n.59, 120, 121, 125, 133, 167
Loren, Sophia 20, 21, 28, 36, 39, 43, 70, 85, 93, 96, 102 n.35, 116 n.58, 120, 121, 122, 124, 125, 199 n.43
Lo Verso, Enrico 178
Luciano Serra, pilota/Luciano Serra, Pilot (Alessandrini, 1938) 33–4
Lury, Karen 8, 62, 110, 128, 131, 132, 133, 147, 152, 156, 162, 163, 170, 183, 198

Maggio, Angelo 132, 164–8, 170
Maggio, Dante 164–5, 167
Maggiorani, Lamberto 21, 49, 53–71, 72, 82, 83, 115, 131, 132
Magnani, Anna 26, 35, 76, 82, 92, 96, 105, 107, 121, 130, 132 n.14, 148–9, 151–8
Makhmalbaf, Hana 199 n.45
Mancini, Liliana 42, 103 n.37, 155
Mangano, Silvana 36, 39, 41, 43, 49, 92–3, 96, 101, 102–3, 118, 122, 125
Manunta, Vittorio 25, 136 n.22, 171
Margulies, Ivone 13–14, 39, 69, 101
Mariano, Roberto 180–1
Marincola, Isabella 114 n.55
Marlow-Mann, Alex 142 n.41, 164 n.83, 182
Martorana, Giovanni 188
Mediterranea (Carpignano, 2015) 188

Meraviglie, Le/The Wonders (Rohrwacher, 2014) 192
Mercato delle face, Il/The Market of Faces (Zurlini, 1952) 20 n.29
Mery per sempre/Forever Mery (Risi, 1989) 178–81
Mignonnes/Cuties (Doucouré, 2020) 198–9
Miracle at St. Anna (Lee, 2008) 169
Miracolo a Milano/Miracle in Milan (De Sica, 1950) 94 n.16, 203
Miracle at St. Anna (Lee, 2008) 169
Miracolo a Milano/Miracle in Milan (De Sica, 1950) 94 n.16, 203
Miranda, Isa 37
Miss Italia (Coletti, 1950) 106
Models of Pickpocket, The (Mangolte, 2003) 16, 207
Moeschke, Edmund 129, 171
Morin, Edgar 41, 163, 193
Morte a Venezia/Death in Venice (Visconti, 1972) 183
Most Beautiful Boy in the World, The (Lindström and Petri, 2021) 183, 195
Mulatto, Il/Angelo (De Robertis, 1950) 130, 163–8
Musolino, Vincenzo 117 n.60, 123
Mustang (Ergüven, 2015) 195

Nacache, Jacqueline 4, 11, 56
neorealism 1–3, 6, 11, 19–20, 21, 26, 27, 28, 32–3, 35, 43, 47, 49, 50–1, 53, 53, 59 n.13, 60 n.15, 64, 66, 67, 69, 76, 80, 82, 83, 85, 96, 101, 103, 115, 117, 125, 127, 131, 134, 137, 138 n.30, 142, 152, 153 n.66, 154 n.68, 155, 156 n.71, 163, 167, 169, 173, 191–2, 200, 201, 204, 206, 207
influence on other cinemas: 174–7
neo-neorealismo/neo-neorealism 173, 177–83
Ngor, Haing S. 13
Noi Donne 91–3, 95 n.17, 122
Noto, Paolo 20, 32, 106, 113, 132, 156

O'Leary, Alan 2, 33 n.12, 173, 175, 203
Orlando, Pietro 184–7
Oro di Napoli, L'/The Gold of Naples (De Sica, 1954) 43, 130, 159–62
Orsini, Inés 171
Osama (Barmak, 2003) 199

Paisà/Paisan (Rossellini, 1946) 21, 72 n.44, 75 n.48, 85, 107–16, 119, 120, 134, 136 n.22, 137, 143, 145–8, 152 n.63, 164, 168–9
Pallotta, Gabriella 44, 46
Pampanini, Silvana 14 n.15, 39, 96, 97 n.25, 100, 102–3
Paranza dei bambini, La/Piranhas (Giovannesi, 2019) 142 n.41, 182, 184, 193, 194
Parigi, Stefania 26, 37, 39, 41, 73, 74, 102 n.35, 109, 116, 127, 138 n.30, 151, 155, 159, 165 n.89, 168 n.93
Pasolini, Pier Paolo 16, 17, 57 n.11, 67, 153 n.66, 204
Pastore, Pietro 36
Pastorelli, Ilenia 196 n.39
Pather Panchali (Ray, 1955) 127, 177
Pedinamento 14, 39, 58, 101
Pende, Nicola 30
Penne nere/Black Feathers (Biancoli, 1952) 132
Peppino e Violetta/The Small Miracle (Cloche and Smart, 1952) 171
Pianese Nunzio, 14 anni a maggio/Sacred Silence (Capuano, 1996) 182
Pickpocket (Bresson, 1959) 16, 17, 207
Pitassio, Francesco 7, 20, 28, 29, 30 n.10, 31, 32, 33 n.13, 35, 39, 43, 45 n.33, 46, 47, 49, 51, 57 n.9, 77 n.53, 94, 117, 151 n.61, 153, 157 n.72
Placido, Michele 178–9, 188
Polvere di Napoli/The Dust of Naples (Capuano, 1998) 161
Ponti, Carlo 39, 40, 142

Princess (De Paolis, 2022) 2–3
Proibito rubare/Hey Boy (Comencini, 1948) 129, 137, 141–5
Pucillo, Samuele 194
Pudovkin, Vsevolod 28, 29, 30, 31

Rafiki (Kahi, 2018) 198
Ragazze di Piazza di Spagna, Le/The Girls of Piazza di Spagna (Emmer, 1952) 39
Ragazzi fuori/Boys on the Outside (Risi, 1990) 178, 180
Raimondi, Sergio 94
Ray, Satyajit 127, 177
Reality (Garrone, 2012) 192, 195
reality TV 180, 206
re-enactment 8, 12–15, 18, 34, 183, 188, 204–5
Righelli, Gennaro 129, 148–50
Rigoglioso, Caterina 14–15
Risi, Marco 178, 179, 180
Riso amaro/Bitter Rice (De Santis, 1949) 49, 93, 101, 114 n.55
Rocks (Gavron, 2019) 198
Rohrwacher, Alice 192
Roma (Cuarón, 2018) 3, 8–9, 173, 196
Roma ore 11/Rome 11:00 (De Santis, 1952) 88
Rosi, Francesco 72–3, 75–6, 78
Rosi, Gianfranco 191
Rossellini, Roberto 1, 2, 18, 21, 25, 26, 32, 33, 54, 72 n.44, 75 n.48, 85, 92, 107–16, 129, 134, 136, 137, 145–8, 151 n.60, 152 n.63, 157, 18 n.9, 171, 203
Rotolo, Swamy 196

Sabu 163 n.80, 177
Sané, Mama 195
Sassoli, Dina 37
Sazio, Carmela 21, 85, 86, 107–16, 117, 118, 119, 120, 124
Scalici, Valentina 178, 181, 182, 196 n.39
Schoonover, Karl 3, 6, 13, 15, 18, 25 n.169, 134, 54, 59, 60, 134, 155, 201, 206

Sciamma, Céline 196–7
Sciecco bianco, Lo/The White Sheik (Fellini, 1952) 94
Sciuscià/Shoeshine (De Sica, 1946) 2, 20, 25, 46, 54, 55, 68, 129, 127, 131, 136 n.24, 137–41, 142 nn.39 42, 143, 152 n.63, 163
[S]comparse/[Dis]appeared (Tibaldi, 2011) 188
Seihon, Koudous 188
Seke, Giuseppe Dave 190
Selfie (Ferrente, 2019) 184–7, 193, 206
Sembène, Ousmane 15, 176
Sentinelle di bronzo/Sentinels of Bronze (Marcellini, 1937), 34, 168 n.92
Serra, Adriana 37 n.21
Seydou, Hamed 191 n.29
Siamo donne: episodio 'Quattro attrici una speranza'/We, the Women: Episode 'Four Actresses, One Hope' (Guarini, 1953) 88–9, 100 n.31, 101
Sidali, Ali Ibrahim 168 n.92
Signora di tutti, La/Everybody's Woman (Öphuls, 1934). 37, 100 n.31
Signora senza camelie, La/The Lady Without Camelias (Antonioni, 1953) 88–9, 98–100, 103, 104
Slumdog Millionaire (Boyle, 2008) 183, 198
Smordoni, Renato 137 n.25, 139–40
Social media 185–7, 206
Sotto il sole di Roma/Under the Roman Sun (Castellani, 1948) 42, 103 n.37, 117, 155
Souad (Amin, 2021) 198
Soviet theory of the non-actor 4, 28–32
Spalla, Erminio 35
Squadrone bianco, Lo/The White Squadron (Genina, 1936) 34
Staiola, Enzo 1, 21, 41, 54–6, 58, 59, 62–4, 66, 70, 129, 130–5, 136, 177, 188, 192, 204, 207
Straub, Jean-Marie 16, 204

Stromboli, terra di Dio/Stromboli (Rossellini, 1950) 18, 92, 203
Styles, Harry 205, 206 n.3
Summertime (Netflix, 2020–22) 190–1
Swain, Dominique 183

También la lluvia/Even the Rain (Bollaín, 2010) 18–19
Tangerine (Baker, 2015) 4, 172 n.1, 198
Temple, Shirley 129, 168
Terra trema, La/The Earth Trembles (Visconti, 1948) 21, 47, 54, 60, 62, 71–84
Tetto, Il/The Roof (De Sica, 1955) 42, 43–6, 56, 86–7
Thivisol, Victoire 5
Touré, Karidja 197
training 5, 6, 7–9, 27, 31, 35, 47, 48–9, 50, 67, 70, 85, 103–4, 107, 113, 117, 132, 155, 157, 161 n.78, 176, 188, 191
Triola, Nando 182 n.9
Tu, Maggiorani (Zavattini, unmade) 56 n.6, 61 n.19, 68–70 (see also *Il grande inganno*)

Umberto D. (De Sica, 1952) 6, 25, 41, 44, 67, 123, 124 n.73

Vallone, Raf 36, 49, 95, 104
Vent'anni/Twenty Years (Castellani, 1949) 155 n.69
Visconti, Luchino 1, 4, 21, 27, 36, 39, 40, 47, 54, 72–84, 87 n.2, 97, 98, 100 n.31, 103, 120, 130, 155–8, 173, 183, 192, 195, 204
Vita, Anna 94–5
Vitale, Mario 18
Vito e gli altri/Vito and the Others (Capuano, 1991) 142 n.41, 182
Vulcano/Volcano (Dieterle, 1950) 132 n.14, 153 n.65

Welles, Orson 80–1, 106 n.4
Wiazemsky, Anne 17

Ya no estoy aquí/*I'm No Longer Here* (Frías de la Parra, 2019) 200
Youssouf, Fathia 198–9

Zavattini, Cesare 9, 14–15, 27, 37, 38, 39–40, 41, 44, 47, 49, 54, 55, 56 n.6, 58, 61 n.19, 64, 67, 68–71, 87, 101, 142 n.42, 159, 176, 179

Zero (Netflix, 2021) 190–1
Zhao, Chloé 12–13
Zurlini, Valerio 20 n.29

www.ingramcontent.com/pod-product-compliance
Lightning Source LLC
Chambersburg PA
CBHW070030010526
44117CB00011B/1765